GET IT

BY: IT

Thru
UffDa

MADE IN AMERICA

This publication provides the Author's opinion in regards to the subject matter contained herein.   UffDa

If Ya don't pay IT forward you will pay IT!

ISBN-13: 978-0692307335 (Absurdum ADD Paradoxico)
ISBN-10: 0692307338

Library of Congress Control Number: 2014919191
Absurdum ADD Paradoxico, McHenry, Illinois

Contents

Forward

Backward

Introduction

HI

How R U?

"I AM" Fine!!!

GET IT

One fine day in May... I was sort of on a mental vacation walking down the street minding to my own business of enjoying the scent of cherry blossoms reflected in the pool at Abraham Lincoln's feet... When out from behind his monument rushed a deployment of troopers sweeping me up inconsiderately along with a nearby contingent of US citizens who appeared to be peacefully demonstrating their right to peacefully demonstrate! I was detained, imprisoned, in terror gated, and held indefinitely, without just cause or counsel. No No No I say how can this be? This is America home of the free! "They" retorted, check out the new decrees... Your First and Fifth Amendment rights negated you will see and as soon as we get round to IT others soon to be... I replied, "Who let this be"? IT was you and IT was me... the only freedom left of rights is obediently obeying you troglodyte!!! Butt I am a citizen of the just US... Butt un-right less law changes are legislated actuation reality... only the chronicle of them is unreal illusory!!! The situation is not my fabrication~~~ IT is damnation history!!!

Demonize me now... just to GET IT out of Da way!

Let's see... Do you??? What's your perspective? When was the last time you exposed or even explored your self truth, let alone had Da Balls that I scribe too IT, for God knows whom to read your hidin agenda livin live truth vibe~~~ If you'll show yourself to your self, I'll show you mine~~~ I think we really need another New Age book! No one has done that lately. That's so five minutes ago... Well let's go for a ride on a course of a different relevant irreverent discourse anyway... GET IT reveals hidden $ecrets to the abundant full life... NOT!!! Well sort of!!! Da book GET IT, started by chance possibility as a few pages of a living memorial gift to my children's children's children~~~ and eventually turning into a note To Our Children's Children's Children as well... After a few more pages I was further drawn into the unity by IT, and my fingers could not keep up with IT! After a while I became obsessed with IT... Then one day I looked down @ the page count and realized I had written a rather lengthy tome. My first and probably also my last. So before they plant me in one I thought I might share IT with others that, like might, have this hole in their soul that I once burned into my self, that many other books pitch concepts to patch, but nothing∞ seems to heal IT. In this put on world I'm askin you to get real! I'm not tryin to out Philosophize Da Doctors with witty Ontologisms, I'm just tryin to make sense of IT all. There is no twelve steps or ten principles or seven habits or flex goals but you do need to reach out to help your self... once you cut the bull$h!t there is only IT and I thought I'd give you a few new angles to consider that work for me~~~ So...Here IT IS... come and GET IT!

IN 1809 William Blake stated "... when the New Age is at leisure to pronounce, all will be set right..." well they been pronouncing ever since and ain't nothing∞ been set right, and @ my age ain't much new!!! But then again what I been takin for granted is what's new for a lot of you!!! Psychologist Carl Jung, a fan of the precept of the age of *aquarius*, wrote in 1940 "... This year reminds me of the enormous earthquake in 26 B.C. that shook down the great temple of Karnak. It was the prelude to the destruction of all temples, because a new time

VII

had begun…" Thinkin, feelin, and believin that your doing right and holy is not the same as actually doin those things as deception of self seems to be an inherent most inhumane quality! We all felt Da tremor~~~ of Da Nazis and they eventually got their A$$e$ properly kicked for falsely appointing themselves God like superiors… Not sure that day of infamy lives on in the hearts of our children? Will the next bunch of superior warmongers find their ultimate solution through similar hunger game exploitations??? Those who benefit from a system never see or perceive, the damage caused, the injured abused, or any kind of a downside, to their miss placed beliefs in a system designed around them… Well the New Age merrymaking eventually got started back on IT's coherent path up in Big Sir and a more humble heck broke loose… Hunter S. Thompson, Jack Kerouac, and the likes of Robinson Jeffers went boho! Henry Miller recounted that a traveler knocked on his door, looking for the "cult of sex and anarchy." Henry's stated objective was, " recording all that was omitted from books..." the vigilante book burning censors didn't much like Henry and I got a feelin they ain't a goona fully appreciate Da UffDa either. Well IT was already being hijacked… The New Age "human potential movement," and Gestalt therapy were raving up the mom and pop headlines… along with the Merry Pranksters, Owsley Stanley, and on Da East coast Timothy Leary, opening up doors of perception that Da New Age never had any conception of! IT was no longer esoteric Heebie Jeebie… Da free IT… was scarin Da $hit out of Da straights that quickly concocted moral lie alibis!!! Imaginary majority opinion supported by a very real ambivalence is the major impediment to finding and living our true heritage! Da counterculture years were wonderful and I miss them truly… but in the last few decades all sorts of people been written, preachin, speech makin, promisen, filmin, and singin, bout the New age of aquarius, Look out for Da Hucksters that may be Pranksters in disguise… If you're looking to update your knowledge of the past take a crack at some of the more comical re-history writers such as, The Cartoon History of the Universe or Mel Brooks version of the History of the World Part 1… they are no more irrelevant irreverently illustrating their take than the rest of the

VIII

Historical shaper <u>fakir</u>'s!!! One of the hardest things to know is the truth of what is going on right now~~~ let alone trying to discern IT's truth later! Information everywhere but little to trust. Anyway… I did not know that I had IT since a wastin IT in my youth, and now I spend most of my time hiding within IT!!! Well I been doin a little info seeking and IT seems that many are actually looking to GET IT but mostly being short sh!tted!!! There is much info out there so @ Da end of GET IT there's <u>a lengthy list of some additional readin</u> you can peruse later to see what you can see… But be aware that there are all sorts of shaper fakir's and fashionable character's pre-forming the reality play~~~ Amazing how reversed our desires and lives are to what we profess to wish and plead we need to live a life worth living~~~ Little gifts of kindness spread out along our way makes love a life worth giving. So merge your internal conflict of multiplicity, settling down to GET IT in unity~~~ not like some maybe "if statement" IT's a GO TO reality~~~ DO IT NOW or else then~~~ You have the opportunity to <u>START HERE</u>!

1%

In the beginning… One dark and rainy night… Once upon a time… To be or nor be? That's the question!

"Oh the heck with having a convention"… What is IT like to be or nor be??? Does IT imply actual physical existence or "be" merely the linguistic copula, which connects subject and predicate? Are you to be one or just another zero? Hey Der… "Let's tell IT the way IT is!" "Ya know"… What do you know? The beauty of IT is that even if you do not GET IT, I do, and in the end IT IS, so even though IT's important that you GET IT, you own your core <u>beliefs</u> and changing them are not prerequisite to my existence in IT nor yours, thus there is no need to simply <u>proselytize</u> in order to meet my quota by convincing new believers in IT, yet I encourage you to GET IT while adding too and riding the positive vibe along~~~ I get really nasty as the world can be a really nasty place but does not really have to be... so if you so conclude that my ultimate reality is just a nasty nihilistic view you are incorrect Oh wise one... I anticipate and generally find joy each and every day in the moment in so many ways, remaining astutely aware impelling loving care, quietly returning to my little cerebrally created idealistically blissful Facsimile Park of Serenity, to live there in contentment yet fully engaged till IT moves me on! But as I assay, Da cerebral surroundings, I reckon not many are GETTING IT... even as they profess too! So rather than remain selfishly in my serenity park, I choose to take my valuable time to explain invaluable truth! There certainly is no need for me to be unjustly jealous with Kant of those that have materially more yet spiritually much much less... as I have all that I need. My cup runneth over~~~ But I keep finding others tainted BS diluting life's wine in my cup! Most of what I run my comment on... and on... and on....... seldom breaches my perception, as I pretty much either, intuit preclude, clash avoid, sense deflect or neural reflect such intentional intrusions yet projecting apposite response. Which is usually construed, by the psyche no logical path Oh's, as an interpolated bit of my pile of negative bullsh!t! So I could have skipped all this, as I am an old transcendent of the unity already and continue to be the change where I can, but when I am no longer being here~~~ my hope is to have wrought a better world then we are currently shaping and that more of US actively participate in the unity for the benefit of all. GET IT is a way forward toward IT.

Writing was never my forte as words get in the way of hopeful helpful actions~~~ which are God's gifts, and are what people generally need to perceive in others exampled acts, in order to affect any change in their own actions or beliefs! I believe we need to dynamically act and think actively rather than reactively!!! IT's not what we say IT's what we do!!! So just consider UffDa your personal idiosyncratic vibe coach, that stops by whenever you need a good laugh or bounce your life off of mine in compare contrast, then maybe we will coherently reorder mindspacetime... Well anyway... through never-

X

ending education my scribing has improved??? So since I can't personally meet each one of you, (Hey Der☺)... in order to get IT's message out I needed to write IT down, as no one would allow me the use of their network soapbox... the fact being that I can only get with or lend a hand to a few each day... and the further fact that we need to attain "the greater good" critical mass sooner rather than later, led me to this distribution of my family's living memorial treasure! So I "Write On"~~~ and anticipate riding IT's positive vibe together with you one day~~~ I might generalize a might too much, so I contritely apologize if you generally feel exclusively not part of some part that I'm rippin apart or you are one of the few that really leads from the heart!!! Before I rip Da ripple in Da mindspacetime fabric let me say just one positive thing... "Ahhuuummmm"!

Do ya know ya can't learn when ya already know IT all! You don't need me to GET IT, I would really like you to GET IT, but what you really need to GET IT is in you! We are all mindful to some degree, as mindfulness is interaction between our attention with our immediate experience and orientation to IT in the present state of being. Being mindful is the fundamental natural state... We create unmindful deterministic fate! By not paying attention to our intentions or maybe too much... because we do not want to admit IT knowingly! Our lives are lived from the moment we're born, sifting in but mostly out, existential fragments that we construct, restrict, restructure, and customize, to what our reality is... not what actually is... but what we SEEM IT to be! Are you checking the pan for a glint of a rare nugget or stumbling through the debris field following your last implosion? Fleeting moments of clarity flowing constraint fully through our deducing valves. Tailoring reality into what we think our lives to be... Deleting many inconvenient thoughts, altering to an invented perception, deceitfully divining a narrative to explicate our lives thus psycho dynamically hallucinating a life not lived!!! Why do we so persist on willfully being unmindful of other minds? An unaware mind colours the pages for us so what our senses receive deceive, becoming only what you believe to be!!! Nothing∞ IS what IT appears to be, as Nothing∞ becomes unity... Like understanding the unity underlying ALL, the brain in IT's diversity is able to comprehend the complexities of a universe of knowledge, but yet not perceive the simplicity of unified mindspacetime. Do you stand for some things or do you steadfastly unify with all of nothing∞~~~ Much meaningful meaningless more or less has been written with and without pun intended while making nothing∞ of something or something of nothing∞, some with great meaning other with less. When we had less we had more! What I write is more about meaning more and less about meaningless, with many a pun entendre!

I am... not the first nor will I be the last, attempting to unify humanity in the belief that throughout the cosmos there is one absolute unquestionable unconditional entity that resonates in everything~~~ be IT dirt, air, water, or blood, and that this entity, many call God, is the same loving entity universally. So listen up if you missed what has been told to all before, before you miss IT again like before! You are... the one... that needs to GET IT! Hey... no need to worry... You will Get IT, as truth always prevails; yet you may not GET IT yet! Often we need to be reawakened from our mistaken awakening or woke once again after we drift back into our wide-awake sleep. Objective truth is!!! As long as IT is relatively relevant in IT's relationship always. IT cannot be both true and false at the same time... or can IT??? What is reasoned true in one system is true to be false in another! Mythic, Consensus, Personal, Parochial, Societal, truth maybe... but the subjectivity implies no proof of IT's ultimate truth. This is why IT can be theorized and inferred by the spooky at a distance physics derived from the mathematics that is IT's self, ultimate universal truth, as symbolized in the fine structure constant... 137! I perceive IT, I experience IT, I believe IT, and I have faith that IT is true, so believing faithfully fortifies my objective knowledge that, my mind receives IT, so I may interact with IT, as well as pass IT on~~~ thus my faith and beliefs are crucial in supporting all my known truths! Not God based on some ancient text but an omniscient God here, now, forever, always vibrating in tune with you! The "Lamb Shift" of tiny zero point oscillations, facilitating the uncertainty principle of Superposition in the quantum vacuum of quantum objects that can be everywhere at once, thus IT's immanence subtly underlies everything uniting all. IT appears this unity entropies and decays to today, although IT maybe everlastingly in evolving states, as we attempt to prospectively reunify the strong, the weak, the electric, with all gravity... this immanent condition that must be acknowledged to be IT's preeminence. I cannot at any zero point in mindspacetime, define, describe, illustrate or express completely, what IT is, as in the eminent union we find IT distinctively singular to each and every??? Just as we find ourselves at a loss doing so with many of the feelings and emotions we attribute to IT, as IT is our ineffability not IT's, that creates this conundrum! I purposefully propose that IT is objective reasoned probable truth that: not only are we able to interact sub-atomically in IT's unity but this is the way IT was meant to be! Scientists, hawking eloquent contentious convoluted circular objections inelegantly contradict IT, even as we live infused in IT's interactive unified mindspacetime~~~ Just as Ptolemy and his henchmen decried that the earth was once flat and the center of all things, today's modelers inter tangle theories like they were epicycles and currently decry the reality of IT while imaging the universe to be flat... or multiplexed... Yet possibility of unified interactivity science cannot deny... try as they may... manipulating statistically the uncertainty that implies p-Brane renormalization, both to disprove our connectivity to IT and yet confirm our unity in IT. Given that the outcomes are model-dependent, may we conceivably model the elegant theory that deduces the possibility of a cause behind the multi-probability random fundamental nature of IT and the intelligent ingenuity of the mathematics of IT! IT appears to come closer to confirmation than negation as they continue smashing discernibly to confine eternity∞ to conformity. This belief that there is unity behind the diversity is one of the oldest scientific theories known. Confirmation of IT is difficult for the reasoned scientists, as they have to give up, control of the know to the unknown and indeterminate, so much is unknown... yet they are the ones who have given us the possibility of knowing the unknown so thus becoming alternatively known!!! This leap in true living belief does not negate or nullify, IT opens new perception conception assessment. Using the same

XIII

parameters that the energetic Quarks, that cannot be seen yet are assumed to be through repeated assessment of the tested modeled theory results, would infer that just as IT remains unseen yet is assumed to BE, through test and trial by those whom interact with IT under the model of their repeated serendipity unity with God. Yet science sees this Bio harmonic resonance with IT as infinite∞ random impossibility thus excluding any synchronicity as a statistical anomaly on their scatter-gram supersymmetric dartboard, as IT harmonically resonates through you, them, and all eternity∞! Dear Popes of Physics: Thank-you for deducing IT's quanta, please take care as you maybe unaware of the possible hidden outcomes that await us in the inherent fundamental randomness of IT's nature that gave us Pandora's present of a singular Big Bang and Da bomb. Random nature does not equal arbitrary physics... May we not need be mistaken forsaken taken Da name Higgs boson particle in vain as this is what con CERN's me Dat many large hardons are colliding already in Dis universe most certainly looking too string themselves along as the Gods of Science! 496 = 496 just as IT did 200 years ago and just as IT is forever unobservable, so too are Da small strings you're cogitating, but not so small as the great unity of IT in all!!! Pretty sure that would involve finding a needle in a haystack the size of Da Solar system~~~ comparin how long six inches is in a manly way!!! Good luck with that! Maybe in one of the other universes or dimensions, I'll get lucky again! Wonderin how much death, illness, and long-term consequences came out of all that wonderful above ground nuke testin back when IT was considered safe to contaminate??? Let's spread a little Lithium 7 around and see how the half-life diminishes our life! Da man that helped designed the Tsar Bomba... the world's biggest bomb, was also awarded a Nobel peace prize... How's that any kind of reasoned possibility??? Oh... and while we're at IT lets keep our minds eye on recombinant DNA play altering Da Eco balance IT provided. Science investigates knowing, while Technology creates stuff. Science isolates, breaks down, and analyzes the parts of the mechanical universe needing yet too fully comprehend the interdependent universal organism of IT! When hypothesizing about particular individual effects, IT's affect on the entire organism affects Da effect! Technology goes where The Money is dubiously pointing... There comes a point at which doubt is no longer reasoned only propositionally possible! Without doubt, self-evidence derived from our insights, perceptions, reasoning, memories, and senses, logically proclaim believed truth clearly! Science is a means of systematically removing doubt thereby discerning truth but has yet to discern all truth, as we know IT! The indeterminate remains unknowable and IT's nature may preclude to occlude IT. IT's simple to tell who cares and who does not... Just take and look around~~~ You may declare, that you don't care, nor does anyone else... well wrongo my friend... some others and I care very truly... and I scribe this as my prayer of care for positive effect in you. Worry affects results but are they the effects you expected? Our expectations affect the experiences effect. Inspect what you expect before you except IT! Begin to overcome worry and repair your care through mindful unbeing a couple of times a day attenuating being mindfully entrained in IT the rest of the way. Have you ever met somebody that truly cares and GET'S IT? Well I have and what a difference they make! I could write volumes on them but I wrote GET IT instead for those that don't! If you think you're already totally in tune with IT? Maybe you do and maybe you need to read on for perceptive intention introspection! I guarantee that there's something in IT for you and for you in IT!

Who and what do you love? Who and what do you hate? Why??? We are much of whom and what we know, love, and hate!!! If God equates your Love what equates your hate? Is your thing berative or not enough stuff, craving the flash of cash? Everything is not some scam or a plan by the man but there is many a plan by man that's sham. Nor can you GET IT by cash and carry. Reject class envy, as what society presumes the structure of class, is cumbersome and backward impeding those that are performing in the caste. Money is just a tally of fallacy class social promotion keeping those with less under you. Just why should being socially conscious and loving mean you're a socialist and only a socialist? Why if your adhering to a covenant of equality within a context of data tracking that points to inequality should that automatically stigmatize you as an antisocial problem, promoting a socialist agenda, when truth is seeking righteous equality and fairness for all? Why are American's, who espouse the home of the free and the land of the brave, so afraid of equality both economic and social? I know the world can often seem unjust and some things are by nature unfair, but should we injudiciously be adding to unfairness and injustice purposefully? Should we buy the lie that fairness is an unreal ideal? Obliviousness seems to be genetically hardwired through evolution into the rich as they appear to be biologically programmed not to notice their advantages! There is enough that there should be no lower class, and as far as the other classes you overlook... because you think your money exclusived your class by inducing a no class act, that's not where IT's at! Something about an eye of a needle type gate and a camel thing, doing with heavenly entry eternity∞, if I got IT right! You can take IT with you, butt your prized possessions possess you here! But I guess if your only living for now and IT, don't matter till later... I just want you to known if your barren NOW, IT bears on your now and future transmittal due of course later... I also thought I should inform you that now affects you always and later is sooner than you think, IT lasts a mighty long time ∞!!! What, do you stand for? How do you go when you know? Lose the hate and want before you're too late... You're constricting and restricting healthful heart!!! Your heart is not just a bionic fluid pump... IT's life force flows through IT!!! First choose to alter your terms, may I suggest dislike or if need be request, then turn the afflictive emotion level down to neutralize this dramatic state that we acquiesce too, as hate and want until released is capturing you in the negative neural paradox that returns to your terms again and again in you "the same as IT ever was∞". This whole New Age Born Again concept of no criticisms, no reprimands, no reproofs nor chastisements, defined as "no negativity" just think positive, deprives IT's reality the truest form of a loving caring purposeful life lessons of kind reformative redress that IT possesses and wills US to conduce. Being re-baptized daily does not remove the sin of yesterday! You are answerable to the unity for your course of actions~~~ Maybe not today butt tomorrow is a comin~~~ Perpetuating negative

XVI

destructive forces by denial of responsible answerable accountability is codependent enablement of eternal∞ negativity! I'm not maxim a minden the log that is a pokin my eye in, but if no one can express righteous judicial judgment how am I gonna know IT's stuck up in there? The world is quit actually an astounding place and finding wonderful good things in IT is surprisingly simple. As a matter of fact IT's in keeping the wonder and simplicity in your life that makes life astoundingly good! I leave you to find that which is simple, as GET IT, is more about the astounding multilayered superimposed layer upon layer of BS that composts our daily lives in complex inhuman waste! So prepare your self in a positive manner prior to sleep or meditations, so you will be prepared to deal firmly and compassionately with negativity during conscious times. What ever happened to the up tempo vibe, the dream of a greater and brighter future aspiration, you know like a Rodgers and Hammerstein musical vision? Many of the middle from the class of boomers lived the Dr. Spock, Leave IT to Beaver, lite childhood life, but our failure to meet and/or exceed the expectations we emotionally attached to that idyllic altruistic existence finds us trying to glue the virtual pieces back in place, while the youth, as they always do, are carving out a new reality that @ the moment appears to be devoid of any principled guideposts or emotional proscribed defined conduit. How do we tone emoting down while reviving the JOY factor? By recognizing the joy surpassing US and being appreciative of joy given as well as received rather than emotively odium hate suppositions! "I'm so glad... I'm so glad... I'm glad, I'm glad, I'm glad..." There is no right or wrong emotion, as emotion is what is truly being feeling, yet the rheostat of expression or suppression of what you feel is either under or outa your control. Often we are wrong or negative, if you're hypersensitive to the negative your reading the wrong book as the yin of the yang is in the eye of the beholder and ones negativity is a matter of relative inattention or lack thereof and needs to be pointed out to them, to restrain them and maybe retrain them! Dis invective is part of my therapy! Most negativity seems to be manmade!!! Learn to apologize more often then you think you need too and reinforce the positive with actions and dynamic meaningful compliments not just empty words or contriteness'... I try to use eu•phe••misms: the substitution of a mild or pleasant expression for one that maybe offensive or unpleasant... Just think what I'm really thinking about negativity~~~ and how often I think twice to disarm retort! LOL though I and you should not dwell long in this thought and neither overly rebuke nor excessively emote thereby allowing negativity to fester, rather identify the perpetrator or cause and subtly display recognition of such negative conundrums to exemplify that you GET IT, then craftily send both the appropriate sine wave and take back the energy that was sapped. So if you have sense enough to sense truly purposeful intended negativity and your intention is to attune your positive, attenuate IT, relate IT, and help to impede those truly negative intentions... you've come to the right space! Waiting infernally seems to increase the negative virility. Eliminating negativity is impossibility but cognitive attenuation with IT moderates detrimental consequential effects allowing positive possibility to increase! If you a tempt IT with the wrong inner attitude watch out what comes bouncing back to stick IT to you, like Da ode children's rhyme "I'm rubber your glue everything you say bounces off me and back to you"!!!

Is being positive without remedying the negative really realizing anything? If your not part of the solution... ya got a problem! Ask not what IT could do for you rather ask what you can do with IT. What is in IT, for you? Well the real question is "What IT is in you"??? Pray continuously yet put on all of IT's armor, including the sword of the spirit! He who winks the eye causes trouble, but he who boldly reproves makes peace (Prov 10:10)! IT is your obligation to discipline, admonish, and redirect those who are ignorant of IT's truth by enlightening and edge you relating all those unacquainted or ignorant of IT's truth, so they may too comprehend and become an progressive part of IT! No preachy, good book, only way ism. There is no one solution for all. Out of the chaos of disquieting conflicting thoughts we need to quiet our selves to begin to seek and find a unified conflict resolution of mind! There are multiplicities solutions that overlap, and in the areas of overlapping, disambiguated solution is

XVIII

attained! Thereby allowing discerning solution from all possibility thus opening the present of new possibilities and solutions in a never ending process of infinite∞ solution loop~~~ Seems Democratic to me, minus the quid pro quo Evil and ergo ego surfing constantly dividing while goodness or Godness struggles to bring together the diversely different in humble unity. Evil negativity hides beneath a cloak of deceit and feigned unawareness. We are all capable of Toxic conduct, but just because we have the capacity does not mean we should elect to project that rather than reflect IT~~~ Oppose evil with the silent strength of Gods love in you, by not fueling evils desire yet positively opposing all negativity nonetheless. Not to be mistaken taken for healthy skepticism of the status quo or open thorough inclusive deliberate of the present state… sometimes the devils advocate is just trying to provoke purposeful remediate (Like me… You got to)! Words of the wise bring healing while only fools reject correction. Those unwilling to conflict their thoughts in the mirror of others are not contributing to the solution of the teams' problems. Conflicting thought is the Democratic process of evolving humane solutions not Da polar imposing of no thought that many tow, but ya know actual loving thought that God exposes! Do you bring light? What the heck do I know? Well… We're about to find out!!! Does my sh!t not stink??? No… I just checked and I smelled nothing∞… or maybe I've built up my impunity of the smell? I have my share of problems, aches and pains, along with doubts mixed in with a measure of negativity! Yet I diminish my pessimism patiently and nurture my reality optimistically! Have I always thought this way? No… I have searched high and low to evolve or devolve while the world revolved and few problems were solved, so I thought I'd GET IT and give IT to you now. Now… I ask "Do you view now, as repetitive uneventful eventuality or through the parallax view of gratitude that comes in experiencing similar events yet again with renewed prospective perception, like awakening this mourning to a new day of possible interrelation exploration or later being thankful for the experiences enjoyed and encountered that day along the way"? Are you intentionally mindful in each moment or strolling about in some purple haze daze? Do you see others as friend or foe, ally or enemy, or maybe a bit more predisposed towards mutual prospective alternatives? Actually exercising your doors of perception rather than keeping them blocked and locked! Dreams, fables, myths, imaginations, or folklore, can be good or evil depending on interpretation of purpose as viewed! When presented with self-deduced fantasy, unconscious learning distortion, or a new reality, are you just perceptive enough to view what others may consider non-normal as another's potential objective perspective, or maybe after a little ingestion digestion you discern they're adding in some perfumed reformative normative Horse dung? Most of our thought derives unconsciously up from the subsystems. Once you learn something, like riding a bike, the process is moved to an unconscious subroutine with little access to the dynamics unless conscious intervening adjustment is retrained into the system through the self-motivated biofeedback loop! Your thoughts are not your own unless you consciously take ownership of conscience! Are you giving today the chance your looking to tomorrow for? We need to agree the ship is sinkin so we can unify behind the repair job! We need to re-envision, reform, resurrect and reinvigorate IT! We been pullin Da load of SH!T uphill both ways and the only way to get rid of Da SH!T is by getting in IT as we amend Da SH!T with IT by resolutely toiling IT back into fertile soul~~~ What is IT? Why now? IT is the vibe you choose to ride and belief you live! I hope IT brightens and enlightens our lives and adds to IT's light! Now~~~

Lots and lots of discerning questions need to be asked before resolution replies find their way inside! Lot's of think they're smart people, ask a plethora of questions but how many listen discernibly too the answers, or Da answerers, nor endeavor to look @ IT thoroughly from all points IT envisions or feel for what the heart is saying. There are multiplicity levels of smarts. Dull-witted like a rock does not mean dim, as sharp as a tack does not mean you have any tact! "Your Wiseman don't know how it feee....eee........els, to be thick as a brick!" Don't be just interesting be interested! Is your knowledge current or are you intentionally living in the past (Tull)? I do... learning from IT not remaining forever thereafter but being in the now again with then, comprehending before,

XX

discerning the present, prospecting the when. Questions seem to find me, I always have a barrel full, seems I'm always seeking... seeking answers!!! Every now and again one comes to me but then I have to get a bigger barrel as with each answer several more questions arise~~~ Maybe you're comfortable in your ignorance? I was... Oh... the bliss of infantile innocence. Safe and secure, I'm sure, but there really is no safety or security except in perception protection! Having only seven or eight words in your vocabulary... f'in this and f'in that, "like" does not lead to any kind of f'in equal ability too f'in reason to think, even if you f'in think so! I may not be as smart as "I think I am" butt I'm smarter than the average bear just by acknowledging IT. Having eaten the fruit from "The Tree of Knowledge", and now knowing right from wrong, I now ask you to partake in the fruit from "The Tree of Life" granting immortality∞ that Gilgamesh denied by ungodly epic lie 4000 years ago then 2000 years later as scribed (1 Cor. 15:53) "Perishable nature must put on imperishable and the mortal shall put on immortality". Oh death where is thy sting??? People have sought the immortality that we were given in the beginning and our spirits maintain through all eternity∞ I do not speak of the eternal∞ peace we dispiritedly seek because of all the crap interposed upon us from every direction. I articulate living a life worthy of eternally∞ living! You see if we live a worthy life we don't have to pray for forgiveness, eternally∞ guessing if IT will absolve US or diminish our eternal∞ life! Mainstream trueΩ religions tell us to suffer our lot or caste in life because this is our punishment in the natural order while promising a better hereafter, rather than to challenge their rules and all rulers whom rule ruthlessly, as we begin living hereafter humanizing in the now! Why do we wait for the hereafter when IT's here now and forever after??? Not perfection... but better than acceptable, better than satisfactory, better than pleasing, better than agreeable, you know "the best" you know! The fulfillment and transformation of the potential possibility in this space, in this time! Nietzsche's, decedent slave morality Christian depiction was on track but his "God is dead" was wrong, as God is life itself... IT's all presuming Religion that is dead and needs last rights for God to live free once more! How can spiritual mankind continue to hide from God in house's built to supposedly worship IT, like naked children caught hiding in this Garden of Eden because they think God will see them as they are! 150 years ago slaves were status quo, women were chattel "third worldish", and workers had no rights... The force of civil disobedient social justice created the freedoms and secured the protections that now ring US. Reforms trickle from the Oligarch, as we squeeze each one out with much blood, sweat, and tears~~~ and these progressive strides are consistently endanger of reform absorb, back to the same as IT ever was∞, as they are yet deficient in effect while considered inconvenient costs that merely cut into profits with frivolous expense to only treat humans humanly! How easy IT is to forget the price that so many paid for US to get to a more humane condition. Just how far will we allow our necks to be stretched as we swing wildly back towards the gallows of inhumane contrition.

By now you've surmised that I can be excessively sarcastic and you are correct. But do not auto conclude substitute deduce my intense emotions as rage regarding our present outrageous problems, or purely summarize that I sarcastically sermonize! I rightly mind the errors of our ways and in due course hope to set a new one! The "problem" lies in our interpretation and implementation of forgiveness, as we're skipping over the steps of recognition, acknowledgement, and acceptance of the offense by offenders who only offer contrived contrition... thus perpetually allowing denial to contagiously continue, as we uncaringly injudiciously jump to merciful pardon, prior to respect being demonstrated or justice given for the transgression committed! Just where is the sorry in this state? Jumping directly to forgiveness without bilateral considerate concession and acceptance that there was an offensive infringement, of another's God sanctified humane rights, produces unending distress for both the offender and the offended while cycling the negative energy throughout the continuum~~~ The default assumption by the wrongdoer should not be that you must forgive them since that's what society has come to expect or because IT's the "Christian" thing to do. Nor should we absolve without admonishment! I recognize the gift received through forgiveness and the elimination of punitive retribution, yet forgiving without a lesson of love being learned or imparted, is only exonerating your ego mind that's flaunting being the better person rather than demonstratively helping the forgiven to be a better person! Transmitting our energy efficiently, neither newly created nor ever destroyed rather transformed, our spirits amalgamating together with IT while our bodies return to the crucible from which IT was derived! There will always be negative along with the positive~~~ yet IT is in your conducting of which, that expresses and perseveres your current alignment~~~ You must both repel the dark energy and compel the light! Most religious thought was conceived during a less enlightened time of fear-based ignorance. The Canaanites, forbearers of three trueΩ religions, who exited back twice in order to finally return with the mono God they now supposedly know, from some writings that were left behind by some questionable post mortem scribers later interpreted by some other self interested scribblers who were themselves subjugated to subjugate others and even expounded dealing out death as a means of converting through the subtext all of the subjects to the suspect subject of the text!!! Early on they, of the Axial Age, first valued acting in a way that changed you compassionately and sought to cure spiritual ills, not dogmatically subscribing to invented tradition religious doctrines or re-doctored prescribed propositions. Ralph Waldo Emerson summed it up well when he said, "The religion of one age is the literary entertainment of the next." There were once magnificent temples of Apollo and Zeus, people prayed to them, made offerings to them. Today few believe that those gods and goddesses were anything but figments of ancient people's imagination. There is much exalting strength, forbearance, and grace, chronicled from this past, yet… Religiosity; is brought to us by man for certain men to be "Da Man" thereby dividing all mankind. If in the end time comes, Da rapture, will IT matter what evil currently lurks within? Will all evil be Absolved Absolutely? Or will IT tail along with your infinity∞ Faith in God once was the living practice of compassion, with empathy~~~ not theology or forever searching for the stairway to Heaven! It is time to reject ignorance and fear and project into this space enlightenment. Lowering expectations through normalization toleration to the least common denominator, by sublimation, to the everybody and everything is OK fine and acceptable in some way diverseness, conceals the derisive regressive truth behind the dark shadow cast by those insisting on us being more than understanding in their exasperating reverting perverseness that recycles regressive inhumanity and ignorance, not enlightened forward living thinking with distinction! These normalizing totalitarians are some of the same people that tell me I should edit my telling of truth that they don't want to hear!!! You cannot control everything or maybe nothing, but you can participate in the now with a plan for your next action. I do not accept the thesis that God is angry and punishing me for wanting to be like God, claiming to be a part of IT, and believing I will live forever in IT! I do not buy the fact that God complains about that and is spiteful. Nor do I believe that the eternity∞ our essence exists in, contains 69 virgins or anything else a self may wish. These false self designed desired Eternities∞ cause our conflicting beliefs in the essence here and now. St. Benedict tried almightily to eliminate free will, he believed "will" was the cause of all sin, rather than expose self-indulgence as the real root of all Evil, never considering one could choose otherwise. This is a bit like halting any and all thought before IT can transpire! Is our will only able to abide IT's will when what we will coincides with IT's or may our will to change IT's will abide in IT's will for us??? Another words... Should we be the change or is the only change controlled by IT? Why are bad behaviors and business rewarded by seemingly proactive backing or economic subsidized reinforcement, while our perception of them is being spun, swirled, twisted and turned~~~ mean time constructive affirmative thoughts and actions go under unappreciated or made to appear reversed in the fun house mirror? Please remind me once more where we once upon a time had worthy role models, or were they always pompous A$$h⊗les disguised as hero's to worship? Now if I get this right, the reformed A$$h⊗le paradigm is: Da bigger fricken A$$ I once was famous for, made money pushin, and expounded eternally∞ into other peoples hearts, the bigger the public illusory forgiveness and the more I'm held up as a wonderful moral model and able to continue my exploit when I start to behave conscientiously humanely while tooting my own horn deploring what the next great thing personality craps out, so they then can one day find themselves in a similar I been saved situation after their done dumpin... Now I know about the parable of killing the fatted calf when the old man saw who was comin up Da primrose path, but what about the poor schmuck bro that selflessly toed Da line Da full time... Seems like somebody who got fat on someone else's calf wrote that! Sorta like Da oligarch, who are still chewin Da fat while I spare change! If I have not had some input as to the path and choices of my life, then God has one strange sense of destiny with a touch of SNL humor. I discard the Neophobia, the fear of change, yet I remain vigilant in my adaptation to the new, after thorough review of the outcomes, not allowing nostalgia nor novelty, overtly affect my reality! The path we are on is a result of previous paths taken, whether ensuing success successively, learnedly mistakenly, or consequentially not taken possibility! Yet future paths will be determined from this zero point forward... Like a river flowing to the sea I find myself flowing to my true path no mater how many sandbars, logjams, mountains, dams, or other obstacles I encounter. Be they self-imposed impediments, barriers erected by others, lessoned like IT synchronicity, or imagined obstructions, I go with the flow sometimes in a round about manor but always returning to be. I complain much about much needed change, but mostly complain about those changes that can and should be changed but never are, or change that should never have been and needs restoration through reclamation but never is. Da man of change that ran on "CHANGE" only changed his positions after he got elected president... Being the change is, and has a responsibility. So the question I submit is: Are we acquiescing to passivity because we are waiting for the perfection to come or should we be acting to persistently progress this imperfect eternity∞ we're living, that needs change now? IT endows us with IT's power so that we can utilize IT here, now, and forever∞. If IT not only allows us to act but deems IT imperative that we do on IT's behalf, then not striving to be IT's agent of change back to the garden, is

XXV

self restraining prophecy! Rewrite that self-fulfilling prophecy so you and all win! What ever your waiting for the kick in the a$$ to have done for you... start doing IT now... If your waiting for some super hero to save the day... well super hero act today. I'm not talking about returning to Pangea and hugging every tree nor just another aspect of pantheism or solipsism. I just know we can do IT much much better within IT's unified consciousness! The ontological view of metaphysics as synonymous with the theory of being should be taken with a good bit of Pantheism, the doctrine that God is the cosmos and the cosmos, God, equating to the unity behind all illusory plurality. Mix in some Spinoza spin, then imagining pantheism as identifying all substance with God and reducing thought and extension to IT's attributes of all substance and spirit, yet realizing we inflect each unique fluctuation, contrasted against the narrow sense of standardized theism. Speaking of tree hugging... if we don't let go of some old growth pine in the West the fires from H e double hockey sticks will soon appear in The Sky near you... A Beetle is blamed, but not unlike the repression of Da 60's by government... policy is truly to blame... Not The Beatles... Oh The Western Pine Beetles... Check IT out... We need to log IT to revitalize IT before IT's not just firewood that we suppress when nature ignites IT's regeneration!!! Millions of acres are already dead and if we don't utilize this resource IT's gonna burn like you ain't seen nothing yet!!! My criticism, of the current world according to UffDa, is like so many others whom saw inequities, ambiguities, and outright distortion reporting, along with inhuman heartless evil, and took action to be the change! Like them I think IT is time we acknowledge the truth composing our self-will and our ability to use IT for change! Government is not the problem, the Oligarch pays too well, too much, to too many, for their Government... considered their prize, we need to take IT back to have IT on our side! If GET IT is interpreted as some kind of manifesto because peace, truth, and love is what I'm intentionally manifesting, then so BE IT!

How do we know anything at all? By intentional attention!!! By sensing!!! By processing!!! Many sense IT calling but few choose to be... Are we hearing,

XXVI

seeing, feeling, smelling, tasting, and thinking IT? This six sense intuiting intention must be perceived to know else the way is forever∞ the unknowing! How are your interpretive skills? Is truth being filtered out or welcomed in? When you involve all senses to immerse your self in nothing∞ you entrain with everything and discern truth objectively rather than inventively! We cannot know what is not so and so I never deny what I know though you may. As Socrates related, right opinion and knowledge are different... we can have true belief and yet not have knowledge, knowledge requires good reasoned true belief, grounded in proof reality. You're permitted to have an opinion but your no longer allowed to know the truth! The easiest thing to be is yourself, while the hardest thing to be is anything else! I have crazily raged against IT, convinced my mind that I was IT, and denied IT. IT has brought me back from insanity and mellowed my intensity, layering a quiet depth on a dispirited mind! Somewhere in this book I hope to have a meeting of minds... yours considering mine and mine expanding yours! You do have a mind! Take off the delimiter and quietly enter the nothing∞... If you're not ready to shift to IT's reality or change your being while allowing others room for change, then reading this will not help you, as you will not perceive the truth pervading IT nor will others sense your will to change your will! When you realize you're at odds with the objective truth, you also will perceive that you have only been fooling yourself relatively and most others have known all along, yet the same may not be said about themselves. What you perceive to be projecting is just one element of what your audience is percepting. Your perceptions of your truth are all there is for you, so you must involve all your senses to reason your true reality. Know your truth and you will know the truth in others. Through learned agreement we consensually determine what our tastes, smells, feelings, sounds, visions, and thoughts mean; our personally perceived Qualia; our subjective truth about our interpretation and interaction with external stimuli. This agreement in thinking does not mean our thinking agrees nor is absolute truth. We are designed to believe others think like you and me. Just because a thought can be thought and is... doesn't make IT true, other than being truly what's thought. We need more than the fact that <u>everyone agrees</u>… Each thought is unique yet may be shared universally. Truth is not this agreement… objective universal truths are reasoned evidential matter of facts, just as truth of the fact of the matter that two parallel lines will never converge! But wait~~~ Then along came <u>Non-Euclidian</u> thought to turn truth into the shaded grey area of relativism conceived in the dim grey matter so IT don't matter as long as the thought is based upon self-consistency. Subsequently in order to <u>Boole</u> us with surreal numbers we were introduced to 0={Ø|Ø}, seemingly creating something out of nothing∞, then used as a representation of nullification by association to the empty set {} without {IT} so that all <u>mystical experience</u> is to be rationed to be imagined rather than so infinitely∞ real? Why do we say "that person has <u>spirit</u>" or find ourselves identifying with and demonstrating a deeper inner "inspiration", if these positive characteristics are not universally comprehended as a part of the empty mist from which insightful experience is derived. Today's absolute fact is tomorrows myth as yesteryears facts are today's! Maybe when we are taught to believe absolute facts today we should inquire with a mind open towards tomorrow's profound revelations! Not that the absolute fact of the matter today doesn't matter, but that the fact may not be the absolute matter of fact tomorrow… OH!!! I think they call this thinking… or are the facts of my postulations only hypothetically possible tomorrow??? I do wonder what will happen next in Da now that will change my worldview… I sure wish I knew then as well as know Da now!!! The new exuded truth eludes the truth of anything without requiring any proof of any thing except itself, so therein actuality reinforcing the proof of IT's truth, as IT is self-consistent relativity! The empty set is not empty… the empty <u>vacuum</u> of space is not empty… <u>empty minds</u> only appear to be empty… and within all <u>emptiness</u> IT is~~~

We conveniently label everything so we can put them inside the box rather than to consciously process the subtle uniqueness of each truth! If you do not dance the appropriate shuffle you will quickly be labeled and dismissed in a hustle. If IT's this IT can't be that and if IT's that IT can't be this! Yet IT IS! No entity is exactly like any other and is constantly in a state of change! If things won't be fashioned to fit the mold we've formed we're slow to adapt as the unbeknownst makes us mighty nervous! Label is a condition we place on our sense filters to ease the workload on our thinking. Lazy thinking begets regrets for that which was neglected along the way! Let's explore "Work Ethic" labeled these days as more hours rather than "actually honestly working smarter". Always amazes me that most bosses are sucked in by people putting in time while appearing unable to make the mental connection to ROI and productivity or maybe they are just expecting more from me and less from them and then rewarding their "work ethic"! Being on call 24/7 just enables some other thoughtless idiot, that did not take care of business during hours, to create a false sense of urgency to take your time to make up for their un-thought work day of chasing their tail or best of all those asserting their priority and/or superiority by expecting you to be @ their beckon call! Work should be ethical not just equated with time spent or dramatic effects, as time is relative and work is not always objective, but oft times staged with subjects in the pecking work group Dis order! If you are a leader, lead by not demeaning by demanding my time after hours, because I ethically did my work today! Oh and one more thing... Being an impediment to others is not a profession unless you're in customer service;~} Oh and if your company was called cheatemnow you can evolve to cheatemlater then cheatemnow&later or CULater Inc. and start rippin off a bunch of the same old customers in brand new ways!!! No crime for being Inc. I suppose I should again be more tolerant of selfish M&Fr's that been busy not thinkin about work, aren't courteous, or not doin their job because they just can... but I'm "not" and my "work ethic" does not include wastin my life time to codependent their care less disregard neglect use IT less mind set, so that everyone should have to work ethic 24/7 to be @ their immediate summons rather than to work ethically which should include ethically allowing others to have their time to take for themselves! I guess I'll have to work on IT??? Are you hoping the Alzheimer's kicks in early to relieve or excuse a life un-thought? Well enough work on that inept ethical thought... but I do think we mislabel things. What do we miss once the label is attached? You live them, you intend them, and defend them. Only

XXIX

you can affect the possibilities they contain and control! Are you super imposing or relating within superposition? The strings of reality we backward recollect may form each experience from the flow of all consciousness and each filament when reviewed positions our perspective of recollection filling the gaps, space, and colouring in the blanks, as we pick up some delusion, include a little illusion, and reduce down bits and bytes of the truth to deduce that slice of life, forming our selective memory and perception of IT! Maybe changing the event itself upon review or not actually creating until after! Within IT all things are possible and opportunities endlessly abound. Act now!!! As each moment is the beginning of the rest of time! Thought is an action and for every action there is a reaction. Though a wise thought is not always followed by a wise reaction! Sometimes something is somehow lost in translation, as in the inferred meaning of nothing∞ to the Judaeo-Christian, as the void between themselves and God versus the Eastern belief of oneness in unity with the cosmos. Either way we all need to traverse the nothing∞ to attain unity with IT. I'm of one mind… well two… maybe three or four??? We have quad core or more neural systems that must reach unified consensus to optimize the inputs and outputs constantly switching amongst our organic multiplexed storage retrieval networks!!! While the East studied neutron star bursts a thousand years ago and explored Da unity a few thousand before that, The West was, then and now, epicyclely caught up by earlier interfering philosophical and religious thoughts about the concept of Nothing∞, as to avoid logical or heretical voids of nonexistent nonbeing. Our universal language of decimal base ten numeric cipher system originates from the Eastern concept of nothing∞, zero acts as space placeholder thus nothing∞ imparts value to the others. Attempting to impart wisdom to you self defined grown-ups is like talking to a brick wall, as seldom is new-fangled life altering tutoring listened to perceptibly or believed absolutely as you filter in or out what you want to hear or know, relative to your current worldview and any lies you live. We need to reach consensus amongst the bits and bytes our neurons ignite, seeking processing time that concurrently is attempting to meld diversity into union with our reality, while in consideration of others and contributing

XXX

distributive processor power to IT! Most of us are transmitting but our receivers seem to be broke! How much receptivity you imbue, emits the possible change in you. You do not need believe everything anyone expounds but concede to use your thought action to receive others perceptions and react prospectively. They may be profound! Utilize your wisdom! Do not follow the rest of the Lemmings or sheep to slaughter just because you chose to fit in the box labeled long ago! Many prefer the comfort and security of the dimly wit box to the brightly enlightened freedom of thought! Whatever group does not see to agree with what I perceive to be, will libelously label me, so what will be will be, but I'm prospecting that individual hearts acknowledging truth will ultimately deduce IT's validity. New thought conflicts with our present apathy and, until written in some book of knowledge, is discarded as conjecture. Well this is "some book" of knowledge; so put apathy aside for the moments you read GET IT and permit potential possibility of intention to exist in you. Where your intentions and attention are focused becomes your empirical experiences and living beliefs. IT depends on who, what, where, when, how and indeed why. In order to move forward we must first rollback our reason to discern origin of our present and rebalance IT's equilibrium, to clear our minds of the false concept rubbish and lifeless belief debris, evolving to see faithful intention universality, focusing inattention and redirecting unintended living! Processes are the pathways to discerned outcomes, which motivate you to persevere along the intricate path of aspiration achievement! Vivid imaged outcomes facilitate your prevailing with actions through the procrastination of participation in the processes to your attainment! Living life should not include redundant returns of ill-conceived contentious reruns, as time marches forward whether you choose to change or not, you can progress your success or regress your regrets! No matter what phase your in you can always move to the next. IT's never to late except to wait till tomorrow in our minds! Release all remains of disgrace or guilt… Let IT go… Find contentment contained in you. Remember… "Much evil is subliminally veiled in the unstable sadness of unloving minds" so safeguard your compassion to impart prudently, as we all hurt inside… some

XXXI

more than others... gifting IT to all while attentively remonstrating reformation of uncompassionate evil seekers! What your searching for is out there but you will only find yours within! Recall that pure loving resonance with the wee small voice within... feel the compassionate warmth IT brings and envision a metamorphose to the living IT's giving... Enjoy IT's wheels goin round and round and then, "I just have to let IT go..."

Have you already had enough of this <u>metaphorical metaphysical metamorphosis</u> well then... tough...deal... learn to deal with IT... I did... I do... I will... Don't get hung up in the wordage IT's your thoughts that count... Some exclamations are stronger than others as are some pauses... even mid sentence or wo...rd!!! There is some rhyme in my reason and occasionally some reason to my rhyme. These spiels are about the real deal and believe me IT is not done dealing with your really being! IT is not always what you think IT should potentially be! Do you think prospective multi-intentionality or are you monotonously playing tic-tac-toe pretending your ad-infinitum∞ potential leads to a draw??? IT IS... and your thinking potentiality should be with IT always∞

Potentiality is an electric term used to describe Capability of being, becoming, or developing, but not yet in existence, an aptitude that may be developed, the work required to transfer a positive electric charge from an infinite∞ distance to a given point and possessing such capacity we all have IT... IT's capacitance permits potential possibility... Intention is a purposeful plan to effect potential change. Each choice we make, given the infinite∞ amount of potential possibilities, determines one series of outcomes from this pool of infinite∞ futures that are all possible... POTENTIAL INTENTION === FREE WILL! Thereby shifting your destiny amongst other outcomes, all real in that now moment of time. Free will is the flexible fabric underlying the unity of the universe that contains all possibility... Good and Not... Wisdom is using this will wisely... This book of IT is only different in that I technically attempt to connect IT all together with effective current scientific theory and I dynamically believe we must confront negative intentional half spun skewed truths and lies with the force of positive intentional truth and Agape love! This is not a rational game of life with everyone ethically thinking of others as they would of themselves. This interactive reality is skewed by ex post facto irrationality as well as inhumane willful Toxicity. Conscience allows no free ride. We all have some version of truth to tell… IT's when you unconscionably turn that truth 180 degrees, paint IT camouflage gray, say you give a $hit and don't, use the verbiage without consideration, feign aid with enmity, deceive just to please, and out right lie, that my toxicity meter goes off the chart, yet I will still follow closely along to hunt you down if you think your revised truth should cloud true vision! Without focused attention or discerning consideration of ordered methodical choices from the array of the possible, conscience choice chooses moral wrong as well as righteous success! Oscillating vibe waves of negative ~ positive which of which we choose to ride and thereby we amplify. What are you consciously doing to insure the success of positive free will conscience? Whether IT be shifting our conscious, unconscious, subconscious thought to positive disciplined interconnected coherent discerned intention and actions, or through positive recognition discernment intervention of the negative energy that's being allowed and accepted, by those who are brainwashed to passivity inactivity pity, thinking they're being Energy Star® compliant! What are you hoarding your Talents for? Positive coherent thought actions create unifying interactions that efficiently resonate positive effects, thereby generating stronger amplitude attitude positive waves through infinity∞. Yet so do negative… and we need to visibly interferingly cancel them! Just as noise canceling headphones counter unwanted noise we can interferingly cancel unknowing as well as the knowing negative vibrational noise. Those that polarize need some mental Superimposition destructive glare reducing pure state interference mind lensing unity! Will this thought only be held theoretically or will the universe actually be changed as we live IT? There will forever be a naysayer, is IT not you? Selfish being cannot selflessly be. You may not like the tack I take but too much tact is fake! You're either a contributing participant or a victim without IT. You can do anything you want as long as you give IT your focus and processing time! Close your eyes and focus on your breath~~~~~~ What did

XXXIII

you sense? Consciousness has been proven to affect matter with coherent thought without deference to both time and space. This is the practical application of IT! IT's strongest verified correlations involve various subjective parameters of the subjects, intention, emotions, attitude, feelings, uncertainty sensing, and information processing, at an unconscious level appears to be involved, making IT difficult to make the objective connection. Consciousness is conditioned by your experience and filtered by your ego, which is then interpreted as your consciousness. What must be done to be truly mindfully conscious is to remove your self from both.

Resistance, another electric term, impedes the potential both in life and in science, which has been know for IT's impedance or is that impudence, until jarring empirical evidence forces science to determine, then conclusively revise the epicycle's in the existing theory yet again and impedes determinedly until the next paradigm shift, just like we resist change in our personal truths. Science conditions us subjectivity all the time by empirical synthetic priori's of pontifical methodological truths. Sort of like other pontiffs! Objectivity is, in reality, only supported by previous perceived subjective concurrence and may be refuted after further investigation or a redefinition and tests of hypotheses, Objective truth is only truly real as long as a pronounced scientific fact, which in fact is not fact but an idea supported by hypotheses until proven otherwise, supports other facts that can thus not be disproved! Exampled in Ice Age theory, which dances around the striations and scouring of the NW side of mountains along with the contents of the moraine drifts by backing incongruent data just as the pre Copernicus Earth Centered universe was held over us by epicycles, thus effectively blocking other possibilities. The new age should be free of the tentacle belief filters imposed by ministers of science, trueΩ religion, politics or money! However; dead ideas, produced by long dead people, conveying unverifiable concepts, who knew relatively little of today's knowledge and new discoveries, are still embed in our thought and decision process, thus filtering and overwhelmingly overriding new prospective perspective perception hypotheses or theories, that will not be funded or investigated because of this!

We believe myth while we deny objective truth; we perpetuate the illusion rather than admit an antediluvian reality! IT, is the real deal… not my fabricated idea of spiritual philosophical ideal… Science has epicycled to the point of decampment. Have you? The unified nothing∞ stands up to Ockham's Razor analysis. In other words, an explanation with fewer assumptions is preferable to one with more, where possible, also known as the principle of economy and of parsimony, nature's propensity to elegant simplicity rather than complexity. But would not the Sun revolving around the Earth, truly be a much simpler proposition? Holographic Resonant sub Planck Zero Point Quantum Entanglement Potentiality Physics really exists and science perceives IT, we are just now trying to concur on IT's meaning. Currently labeled Meta Physics, like Aristotle's book presenting logical proofs along with laws of thought, or the more scientifically deprecating term metaphysics so as to sound ethereal rather than the reasoned IT that is truly beyond as well as inclusive of all physical… IT awaits understanding and acceptance in their ideal idea idling minds because the current scientific paradigm relegates IT to the *reductio ad absurdum*… Is this the whole answer? No, IT is only a nano part of IT. Nano design reflects a complex coherent composition of IT mirrored throughout a meta-multiverse, though any universal multiplicity consists within one and only natural unity! IT somehow saw fit to include Evil, the discordant negativity, and I continue my quest as to why??? If M-Theory is, the model-dependent theory to be reality perceived??? Then in the infinite∞ amount of possible universes~~~ one should consist where IT exists… and thus united through all! Also thus I conceive to believe that under M-Theory some universe should be Evil free within IT and mindspacetime is the means to get there! IT brings the subjectivism closer to a connection with objectivity never quite reaching the Absolute empirically measurable evidence Scientific method reckoning needs! Quantum mechanics theoretical observations are some of the most rigorously examined of all scientific experimentation and have yet to fail any examination. I exhort this as part of the proof of the truth that God elegantly designed our universe with the possibility of possibilities to apply our free will too include self-determination of whether our choices would be of good or of evil…

Resistance varies in strength and form. You must become aware of yours to overcome impedance to IT! ANTI, (**A**nother **N**egative **T**hought **I**ntention), is controlled by you and you must put to rest the repetitive cycle that excuses your being being stuck in the interferential incoherent self-impedingly imposition. As Roseanne_Roseannadanna observed, "Well, Jane, it just goes to show you, it's always something… if it ain't one thing, it's another." Research has proven that you can succeed in countering this negative repetition simply through recognition then self-intervention of this ANTI by substitution of a pre-comprehended positive truth or POSI, a Positive Omniscient Symbiotic Intention! You may have to pass through the valley of depression to reach the zero point of fearing no evil. The evil fear that illusively distorts our perception of perfection. Depression actually changes the way you view the world so take a look at your view and find a different world. IT takes courage!!! Once you make this Quantum Shift there is no turning back, as the veil, created by man-unkind, has been inextricably removed. The Quantum Leap that Einstein was spookily unwilling the possibility Neils Bohr had made… Taking with IT all feeling of separateness, self-suffering, perceived weakness, superficial turmoil, self-induced pain, professed regrets, unnoticeable tensions, and obscure untruths. IT is eternal∞… I will conduce you about the mental-multiverse, only to return to your enlightened intended personal truth that resonates in you and help you to be in touch with the resounding truth of others. Do not fear this true you, as you are much greater than you presumed. So fire up that courage Captain Courageous… As afar as the unified field permits my reality to comprehend, I submit to you only truth is contained here in… there may be errors but not in my intention of truth. (Please send info concerning any discerned errors to:-) I suggest you stop the psycho babble constantly squeaking in your head and asserting your personal domination thereby diminishing others love and usurping their energy by control, so you once more can hear the wee small voice of truth within, this truth is not heard through your ears although IT can be! Your mind and body is a transmitter and receptor of IT. (When I use the term **IT**, I am generally referring to some aspect of God eternal∞; the divine creative source, the source attenuation communication system; the unified field of Pure Abstract Being, Pure Universal Consciousness that unites us all. God... a way to identify IT as the ultimate basis of reality. God as a transcendent absolute perfect being of all possibilities, omniscient in any meta-multiverse or multi-dimensional unity.) I apologize responsibly if your supposition is that, not enough science is postulated accurately here to back IT up. I also ask for forgiveness if you have to struggle with all the science I dare relate to GET IT. I repeatedly attack our unequalled systemic systems of religions, economics, and politician's sleight of hand as IT need be, and in this I only apologize to the un-free me! Unlike an, antichrist, anti-entrepreneurial, or anarchist, my vision is to orderly reorder what we have, to include social conscience reforming to orderly reflect the way IT intended IT to be, through restoration to the concepts of the model IT was based upon! History demonstrates IT will reorder~~~ IT's just a matter of when... and if IT will be orderly! Most reorder is not very orderly though IT can be! I apologize for those that have infiltrated then perverted all of societies systems, as "they" will not! I use terms like "they" or other blanket generalities stereotyping used throughout, mainly as an expressive device because "they" operate behind the scenes under the cover of anonymity, while there are those I can name but whom I cannot risk infernal nuisance SLAP liability to so claim... IT is never always constantly everybody or anything rather equating by defining a superfluous supposition description. Generally generalities are genuinely disingenuous, yet who are "they"... We all seem to say they or them but do we agree upon of whom we speak? They thrive and survive on their ambiguously playing both sides of the fine line diversion. There are too many to name here but I imagine IT has a pretty complete database. I do know when I'm dealing with their ramifications, transacting with them, encountering their rules or self rewarding regulations, subsidizing their compensation, coming into contact with, hearing, seeing, or sensing, one or two or three or more of "them" and I bring heat to their kitchen and shine my light into their darkness! In this book I do portray some of their paradigms, but putting a name to every face of "they and them", needs to come from those close to they and some of them because some of US are "they and them"! We know "they" exist but if we call "them" out we're afraid we might have to answer... This fear keeps US in line and prohibits IT's world from coming about! Please also forgive my absurdly obtuse inane abuse of the Kings English.☺ Never was very keen on Kings anyway... Just like in chess, they consume many resources and contribute little... And away we go...

Our universe consists of a grand Bio harmonic symphony of various overtones of frequency of consciousness! This unified field appears to predispose an inference towards good over evil... coincidentally??? No such thing... IT is synchronic! IT is a communicative benevolent force!!! Boy... are you lucky that IT is, because the amount of BS that is shoveled, masquerading as truth, almost overwhelms IT. Dissolve Dis disharmony!!! In this reality show, the mountaintop moments are truly in the ordinary everyday opportunities that we fully participate in as they transpire as well as those we choose to let expire. Most of life's moments are spent on the side of the mountain working our selves up or down amongst the crags~~~ if you do not like or get good at this simple part of life you will never enjoy the view from the top as you worry about the next valley. Just as there is a surprising mountain top view there is always going to be a unknown valley so prepare yourself for both as the mountain is never as high nor the valley as deep as you imagine. Sadness and happiness, as well as an array of feelings exist, so understand and appreciate their meaning, cause and effects in your life's affect. In my simple youth I thought the elevator only went up when I got higher... Now after many a Nantucket sleigh ride ("Great" Mountain album!) down to the depths I am pretty happy these daze just mitigating the lows while taking immense pleasure from the small peaks that I occasionally come across! You must create and accept a new state of happiness based upon any new reality you might find yourself in! Are you in control of your emotions or they you? IT is about my view of the experience that brings the wondrous joy or depressing sorrow.

Much of life takes place while you were busily planning something else. There is an error in our lingo and our conception of Da Vibe… Everyone speaks and imagines Da Vibe as something dat Da HIGHER Da better~~~ yet Da Vibe is really about Receiving, Transmitting, Blocking and Perceiving a wide range of frequencies~~~ Higher is good but lower is where Da Alpha and Theta live~~~ I get a kick out of those that think they GET IT when they tell me my vibrations are not as HIGH as theirs or my negative Vibe is ruining their High~~~ I guess if IT's all about you… that may be a right perception projection but if you want to ride Da Vibe you need to get over your self and be prepared for both Da~~~Yin~~~and~~~Da~~~Yang~~~ Da up tempo is crescendoin down Da rapids of our lives and in our doing more we're being less! HIGHER~~~WIDER~~~LOWER~~~DEEPER~~~INCLUSIVE~~~DEDUCIVE~~~LOVING

You want reality??? Get up… turn off the TV and Get Real!!! Are you waiting for a wakeup call? Does somebody have your number? Are you living your life or someone else's? What has or is calling you? The calls been placed and nobody answered, so IT's time to wake up the sleeping dead! People say they want or are seeking happiness, which is located in their mind, but most are unknowing of what to do to mind IT and those who think they know seem unwilling to do IT with their mind. Taste a memory, Smell the past, Touch a heart, See Love, Hear the silence, Radiate through the field gratefully! Sense the beautiful love entraining and live a life of possibility rather than restraining. Willfully amplify in phase with the positive love waves that are omnipresent and through composed intentional mindful thought waves aimed interferingly at out of phase discordant negative waves of hate, harmonically cancel that too which is always lurking!

10%

One of those Al's… Yeah… I think… Albert Schweitzer expressed mans aloneness as "being so much a part of the crowd that he is dying of personal loneliness". Yet being alone one does not have to feel lonely although one can feel lonely even amongst a crowd! We are individual identities alone in our shells but united in willful human being. How we express and accept the different bits and layers of our onion like identity builds the concepts by you, of you, for you, in you. Sense the multi-layering composing our concealed complexities; yet allow easy feeling peeling to completely reveal our simple souls. If you already hear the wee small voice of IT's coherent truth within and sense the beautiful love pervading, fortify against domination and usurpment by liars and power thieves. They know the verbiage, they quote the line, and they've rehearsed their response, they're expert expounders and skilled perceivers of your gullibility projector? Their Toxic²... Anti, Negativity, is the devil interferential of coherent resonance with IT. Yet simply do not equate what you do not want to hear or know with negativity, as there are many loving things said and intentioned that are heard or perceived as hurtful or negative! Yet through our choices we enable "D evil" negativity to exist and persist. "IT's not the way that you say IT when you do those things to me, IT's more the way that you mean IT when you tell me what will be." Much of the PC groupthink thoughts need to be disassembled to understand how they conspiringly allow trickle down negativity becoming mans infested destiny. Groupthink is the polar opposite of the collective intelligence; as groupthink thoughts are what we think, others and we should and could be thinking, while the group mind is what is not science fiction rather actually what's being thought and available to those who attenuate IT! Background negative vibes are permeating our minds to the point that we consider the associated pain and depletion to be a normal part of our existence! The PC's stood idling by during Nero's fiddling and Hitler genocides... take a read "It Can't Happen Here" 1935 by Sinclair Lewis; "in America most of us ~~~ not readers alone... but even writers ~~~ are still afraid of any literature which is not a glorification of everything American, a glorification of our faults as well as our virtues," exerted from Sinclair Lewis' 1930 Nobel Prize acceptance speech, the first awarded to any American in literature. His observations seem even more aptly true today! What appears to be grand solution and sold as cure by the, flocking congregational and regime biased assemblies as well as tutorial tedious education totalitarians and office cooler idiots, idiomatically transmutes to another form of fancy fantasy Hootenanny where everyone dances to the same tune that's being played on a scratched 45. Allowing you to accept the false belief delusion that you're not only correct, you are judiciously adding to the positive! When 10% of the German population joins together as the Nazi party did to mutilate millions of their own citizens much like Uganda, Cambodia, and too many elsewhere's, while the idling Political Correct inept not only do not stop them but either join in or are forced to participate, then you begin to understand how being a passive aggressive do naught is actually participating in the problem! The divide between Toxic² and PC is not wide, as those that choose to beat out their negative vibe, whether knowing or unbeknownst have similar outcomes, they need a vibe changing life saving swift intervention or maybe even a little time in mental de-assimilation until they pay attention and if they still insist to persist maybe they need to sacrifice a little public humbling which would involve the people that actually give a sh!t, taking IT to those that profess too as well as those who don't want to bother too. This waiting in Passive Correctness for millennia for them to wake up from the power grabin back stabin does not seem to be workin! "That Used To Be Us," Tells some of the story of "How America Fell Behind in the World It Invented and How We Can Come Back", by Thomas Friedman and Michael Mandelbaum. We need to Get Up, Stand UP! I have stood before gangs, thugs, PC groups, and judges with IT! Not proselytizing but standing up to their vibe with mine and I will do IT for the rest of my life. If we all did IT just think how the world would change… We have the numbers but we lack the will. So what your trying to GET you will!!! Chances are that those who most need IT are not willing to GET IT. We can intentionally help them Get IT! In doing so you are actually positively endeavoring to help them GET IT. This may seem contradictory to what you have been brought passively to believe. This will not be my last view that runs contrarianly along the wrong side of being right! Confucius advocated

XLI

benevolence but not indiscriminate benevolence. Do not repay one grievance with another as this enables a cycle of ill wills. Neither repay with virtue creating false limits avoiding moral hazard. A third attitude of high moral character and calm straightness, not spiteful reactive cycling nor accepted inactive denial, keeping our talents for where they are needed! Nor provoked terrible temper or over-invoked total tolerance but emoting tried true-mindedness. Thomas Schelling gave us "the power to constrain an adversary is the power to bind oneself"! Another words keeping credible your commitment to follow through on an action, you do not want to take, but arranged so that course of action must be followed through with if presented with a given situation. Like the creed on the street only more strongly held in the hearts of the people living there like Ai Weiwei! Chairman Mao banned Confucianism and now China's leadership is re-embracing Confucius because he promoted hard work, order, and adherence to authority. More Authoritarian control under the guise of trueΩ religion! Yet IT is truly amazing that a 90% inferior system is out economizing a 50% superior US system that's under utilizin and stuck infighting stagflation, over regulatin on entrepreneurship and under regulatin those doin the donating, and taxation without representation caus their finin and taxin everything but the rich... and I don't see anyone representing anything but their own self interests! When I was a kid the top US tax rate was over 90% and the rich were doing just fine. Then the Reagan Pagan years began with 33% and now the richest Repub's have lowered unearned income down to 15% for those rich white men only conscienceless Capitalistic gains!!! If they had not gamed the tax system our federal Deficit would be a non-issue! Before the repressive recession 1 of 8 dollars was going to the top "ten percent of the top one percent" meaning 1 family out of 1,000 was receiving 1/8. The top 1% has had a 250% income increase while the rest have lost even their ability to stay even with COLA! The system isn't broken IT's FIXED! This latest jimmy rigging of the financial system has been going on since Reagan and now the rules are written so as to make change darn near impossible! Our Imperial system of exploitation is fixed for the rich and we're trying to repair the system with their same

XLII

system! Just why they call this a Capitalist Democracy and not a Plutocracy is semantics of the absurd! Democracy is not a means of governing... Democracy is a way people choose to act and live! I see very little of civic societal value deriving from those skimming more and more of the cream off the top! Please remind me again why they have the Capital that we must usury borrow in order to partake in the free market where they control the rules and distribution of goods! They borrow our money short and lend US our money long making trillions on the spread. Free market isn't free as it has been bought and paid for by the chumly bailout bedfellows! I compare Wall Streets Free Market entrepreneurs; to the developers who bought the farms next door to my piece of nature, jammed as many houses on the tiniest lots as their consultants and lawyers could get the zoning board to allow, sold them to people who could ill afford them for as much as he could, and then moved on to the next... diminishing every part of my lifestyle along the road to Free Market profitability! As financial and trading institutions grow so does their percentage of profits that are tacked on to everything we must buy with no value added. My local bank, that was eaten up consolidated, went from being in charge of micro local financial reciprocity to playing Russian roulette on Wall Street! Where is the merit in the free market place? My true hope is for all people to reach out too find true mind rather than the oppression, like that which crushed freedom in Tiananmen Square and enabled Wall Street to freely fleece US. But while I wait in hope... China is ethnically cleansing Tibet and the US is enslaving the middle class. While I fervently pray... for US to take action to find a new human value paradigm and reevaluate our relation in helping IT!

Listen up… there are no shortcuts to the nothing∞ so do not short your self and end up... well... you nowhere! You cannot cram for this, as you cannot cram the whole of life in the end of IT. Go to the end of your life and reflect back. What do you see? Do you see Da light or were you afraid to look? I could elegantly stop writing here… as this is IT!!! Yet I will expound further if you did not quite Get IT! Some say I'm full of IT! IT is my intention to humbly be! Please believe, I so love the heaven I find here on earth that I barley comprehend all that is love yet mostly find IT. I sense many are omitting IT and IT seems pleased that I should vibrantly believe I could create something that would possibly enlighten and clear the path of doubt and debris along the way to IT. Please read on with the unconquerable pure unlimited agape love prospective and discerned understanding attempted.

I AM blessed to have survived, what in retrospect were simple challenges presented in my past, which sharpened my soul on the anvil of pain, fear, and anger... allowing me to peacefully enjoy natures embrace, interact within the unity, and rest under IT's protection and the laws God has intrinsically built into IT, thereby experiencing life as IT is meant to be. WHAT is the WHAT, you were meant to be? When you come to nature with the heart of a child IT opens up and never disappoints! Am I sensitive? Maybe too much so. Am I caring? To the point, of empathy! Am I abrasive? Yes I AM hardnosed. Am I trying? Only to help! Many books attempt to tell IT the way IT is! Many teach how to manipulate IT. They make IT hard for you to GET to the way IT is... or to understand the way IT is... Well I do that too, often, occasionally, but only to get you to think about the way IT is! Is there a way to IT? Define IT and you will know the way! Define your questions and the answers will come! Questions defined in positive stated arrangement. There are many rooms in my Father's house and many ways to IT. IT no longer obsessively gets too me because I GET IT and I AM "With IT" not anxiously fighting with IT. IT is the way and the way is IT!!! I'll do IT, when I get round intuIT! IT is a bunch of nothing!!! I know a lot about nothing∞, not the knowing nothing about everything or the knowing everything about nothing but the everything of nothingness∞!!! So I guess that's what I'll write about... Nada... Nothing∞ is my specialty... Maybe IT will become yours! Maybe nothing∞ is the way!!! If I offend you just think nothing∞ of IT!!!

In my research expedition through the nothing∞ I discovered I was not the first, nor the only person to live and write about nothing... As a matter of fact there is a superfluous quantity of questionable quality information out there regarding nothing∞... many express writings that although appear to be about something really amount to nothing... If you want a good overview of nothing∞ may I recommend "The Book of Nothing" by Cambridge Professor: John D. Barrow. If you want to get lost in nothing a good read is Jean-Paul Sartre on the origin of negation! There is much ado about nothing and I only touch on some, but focus on the possible presence of IT in your mind! The only Nihilism here is the fact that I feel all government is corrupt and thus should be overhauled or keel hauled or maybe I'm mistaken. ~~Not~~!!! Something is jamming IT's vibe so IT cannot be asinine *no thing* rather a communicable negative contaminating everything contagiously! This is not some distrusting surveillance from the most corrupt place in the union, rather a depiction of mans love affair with who dominates, who submits, and who exerts Da power on whom! Why must all great Saints live only amongst the dead rather than run Da office? Why do the many scramble for scraps left by the masters? Why except pain as the default condition? Why, why Oh why? Do you have a good antic dote... I need to attain the antidote??? Where oh where, can I get the serum to inoculate my mind from this viral neural mental infection that's jamming the connection with IT? I will find a work around... back Dis truck up and get me some help out here... turn Dis world upside right and leave what's best left alone... Hit Da on ramp caus the main ways gridlocked and there are clearly freer ways!!! Much that I scribe is elementary bitchin and comes across as negative and/or critical but is zilch compared to the many atrocities still prevalent and excepted in this world... my narrative of this negativity is intentional and I throw in a few antic dotes... because we are behaving negatively and acting negatively, thinking negatively, projecting negativity, and basically not only are we not puttin a stop to negativity but by doin nothin with IT we enable negativity to exacerbate reverberate! Yet not being permitted rational response to clarify support of what others may deem negative, or they be given opportunity to even defend a negative position is unreasonable unilateral flaccid PCism, which I encounter often. IT takes less time to PC agree than too clearly see and become negative free! Free thinking self-determination, does not exclusively include only positive thought, freedom is found in disagreement, yet we must discerningly retrain those minds full of negatives that choose to use their free willpower to deviously direct how, when, what, and where, purposeful negativism is being injected and directed ubiquitously persistently. If these A$$h⊗LES are not proof enough that free will exists then I must be an Uncles monkey. Freedom and free will come with the cost of bravery to stand up for IT against those whom stingily detract from IT. Not for you armchair quarterbacks out there! Freedom does not come sitting on the sidelines… IT is a participatory principle! These negative vibes are being created intentionally and are resolutely resonating negatively in our lives. I'm being critical of all Toxic² negativities omni-directionality! Ignoring, indifference and apathy to this negativity is in IT's self, negative action of thought. The power to re-entrain negativity to comprehensive affirmation, is contained in the capability to wisely discern intentionality and then amalgamate your bond with IT coherently, otherwise your allowing the negativity to fester and continue to spread the viral infection you left unattended as if you intended to intentionally. I am told that this negativity is my perception. I no longer pay tribute to this theory. Others living a lie of denial should not be passively allowed to impact upon my positive reasoned coherently deduced truth. Negativity is projected intentionally, even if you don't think so and precursivly endeavor faithfully to advance positively! Society is corrosively eaten away at by those who think negative is the way, those that don't think at all, and those who feign but do not intend good! My intention in addressing negativity is to create positive cognizant reorder! We need to acknowledge these behaviors, actions, and incoherent thoughts, to order and change them, by shifting our perceptions and affecting change through thought! I write my observations of negative relations and my discernment of various institutional oligarchies. I am constantly filtering them as I still occasionally find myself entangled in them. Turning this around in your mind takes time and proactive practice. IT will always be a work in progress! I'm trying to save trees and I probably overstay my welcome as IT is, so I leave out many, at the cost of repetitive redundancy and overwork others out of frustration. TrueΩ religion plays on emotions… this is their tool to turn you into

XLVI

their tool! I incite emotion in the hope of invoking a shift in attitude and altitude as we move to the fulfilled level of conscious unbeing! The rewards for making these shifts are infinite∞ insight as well as soulful universal understanding, intricately interwoven from the macro down to the micro, you must transist to comprehend each point of infinite∞ being that exists in and around you from that wisp of essence to the quintessence of the heavens. Minimize your self to maximize yourself. The radiating influence will melt away the distinctions, distractions, divisions, spaces, boundaries, interdictions you insert between yourself and others whom have done the same. You choose... You can read on and risk exposure or stop and stay with the negatives! Too those of you whom are in positions of power you better believe IT, you better be living IT, and never forget IT, as the responsibility you have chosen creates the reality you make and the eternal∞ path you take is thus Constructed☺ or Destructed...☹ proportionately to how responsibly you institute your authority (Is. 10:1). The two most negative words in the universe are "**I can't**." Together with IT "**We will**"! This is not your average feel good book. So if your goal is just to feel good... put the book down and remain in, rather than retrain, your ignoramus will. IT is good and creation's goodness means nothing else, while you may feel anyway you choose. You have the opportunity to shift and change to, "I CAN! I AM! I WILL!" IT maybe the hardest thing you ever do or the easiest, as IT depends on your will. To shift into attenuated nothing∞ is simple... just let go... nothing∞ (20 minutes twice a day) I have IT. Yet I still seek IT, and will to get more of IT each day. You have IT. Are you willfully seeking IT? I am no expert or Guru, although I AM becoming; I am a simple scribe with the same age-old message, from the ages old dimension being newly defined. With a swig of Granny's Tennessee Truth Tonic~~~

The disruptive technology science may change that I use to expound, but IT will not! I recently wrote a paper for my Astronomy professor, a terrific teacher and a real astronomer (VLA). I pointed out that the book was incorrect and incomplete; this ethnocentric Mesopotamian point of perception expounded on, was preceded 700 years prior by the Chinese Astronomers! They also happened to invent Chinese Purple in 250BC a substance that is proving to have a waveform all IT's own and has super conductive properties that are electrifying our future. He gave me an A, 20 extra points, and asked for a copy of the paper. I'm only reiterating this here to show you what you learn may not be the complete universal truth that is currently available and maybe the experts can use a little help to get past their biased past. But I better polish up my Mandarin as they again precede ahead of US as we once more continue Meso-ethnically expounding incongruent superiority! Why do we allow bad and incomplete info to be passed on like IT's truth, the whole truth, and nothing but the truth, when we know its not? OK... here we go... This is a little side issue... We are either to lazy to change known truths and omissions, such as; the fact that 50 years after Helge Ingstad unearthed the truth that Norsk and possibly others, discovered and settled in North America in 1000 AD, we are still being dis-informed by the Historically Creative Essayists disregarding the actual truth of Columbus' voyage, 500 years after the Norse discovered Vineland of course! Columbus was using their charts to find a shorter route to the spices "Opium" in the East while bringing deadly disease to the natives and returning to Europe with the deadly virus called syphilis (how his men got that?) along with propagating killer Tobacco! At the same time, in 1492, 100,000 Jews were forced to flee Spain rather than be burnt to death or forced into Christianity by the Inquisition along with multitudes of Moslems who were just plain murdered. Our Crusades are their tragedy and our calamities are their Crusades! The current spin doctored life taking calamity involves passage of other still deep waters~~~ Toxically atrophied water leaching chemicals into aquifers then us as we drink and shower whether from tap or bottle, of which the third world doesn't even have the pleasure of at all, as they die of the lack of IT! Our Miss Brockovich could start a jobs revolution just by employing the number lawyers, investigators, cancer specialists, scientists, and other people needed to clean up our H2O! Well the controllers have found a new submission management implement impediment. I am not even free to tap, use, and recycle, the water that flows underneath the land I have title to and am caretaker of. We are the

XLVIII

caretakers of water not the owners. They're pumping the water that belongs to all of us into their coffers, dam IT. Rivers no longer flow to the sea and the IMF and World Bank are drinking from the polluted oligarch trough that water money flows into! Spending thousands of millions here and there rather than spending millions a thousand at a time where needed. We expend yearly 3 times the amount for bottled water than the UN estimates IT would cost to bring safe water to all in the world. Water… Water… everywhere… but none to drink!!! When was the last time you went without water for a while? We are not only taxed up the a$$ but now they privatize to monopolize the ingredients of life and our Genome. Now instituting Lifestyle tax$… will the right to water and air, our basic human rights, be next??? Think carbon credits… Did you know that when you harmonize with water IT's molecules are able to be frozen in cognizant frosty order as Masaru Emoto has demonstrated! We all need to take a step back. Acknowledge what was. Recognize what is. Reach out for true VS relative consensus on what can be. There is a conspiracy of stupidity… reporting the ideology of those in control who have much to lose? Take another deeper look into that faith you profess and see if domination over submissive is the true mission? While your there check the underpinnings of your worldview to see if you see tangible truth, seek factual truth, or just basking in the infantile bliss of remiss unknowing belief ignorance! IT is our responsibility to know truth as comprehensively as our discernable observable insight allows and our fate to live IT even if we don't admit IT. IT's not that we're only using 10 percent of our brains… IT's that our subconscious brains use 90% of our distributed computing power that we're not even privy too, along with Da I don't know jack fact Dat other overwhelming crap contends for the minuscule conscious inattention remaining, we're lucky if 1% of our brain is available for our own conscious genuine thoughts! This is why learning to focus expands Da locus! By the time we think we're thinkin most of the decisions that pop into our consciousness have been formed by popular consensus from Da Sub commander maneuvering you into supposition… While we distractedly imagine

XLIX

we're Da emperors of our own inane! Most do not know their conscious self let alone delve beneath the surface to what quirks in Da depths!

Sorry but I got distracted by the truth… Breath deep… With each breath we can grow in depth… Breath deep IT's free!!! Let's get naked!!! I came into this world naked and I hope to go out the same way. In The Screamin End for the Love we all share!!! The "LOVE study", an actual experiment, directed by Elisabeth Targ of (California Pacific Medical School), documented by Dean Radin & Co. based off earlier studies entitled, DMILS (Direct Mental Interaction with Living Systems), were studies in which Braud and Schlitz verified we syncro brainwaves, as well as Jeanne Achterberg's experimental proof of concept study showing non-local compassion-mediated physiological effects exist that can interact with the brains of others. The results of fMRI; primarily correlated with those trained meditative healers who focused attentive compassion with participants with whom they had previously empathetically bonded (Love)! Our brains appear to be Holonomic, like the particles that make up the universe each containing efficient intelligent information of the whole. The findings of the "LOVE study" demonstrated physical effects of intention and that the physiology of two bodies in IT mirrored each other and became as one. Oh… that kind of naked!!!

Science generally steers clear of love and consciousness… calling IT illusion, disillusion, irrational, ludicrous, and improvable. Just attempting to define love or consciousness creates quandaries of vague personal perspectives. Love is an energy we choose to emote and endlessly receive but not always perceptibly or receptively! Agape love is a conscious expression interactive emotion, so we must retrain ourselves to allow emotions to be sensed and perceived lovingly; as we have been taught they are weaknesses to be suppressed or overtly dramatized acting to make a Be scene using the twisting and turning to screw faulting without care or concern! Bad acting should not be compensated with Academy rewards, so why do we cave in too emote actions we should just ignore to not be! Allowing your consent permits attentive receptive intention. Passion and emotion recognized humanly is realized living, while unreality

L

checked is emoting tedious life sucking odium! Permission commission by the sin of omission!!! Others recognize in us our choice and level of perceptivity, receptivity, motility, and methodology of and to true love! So fakin IT works for a wile on some but really creatin IT affects a smile in anyone... To expect one to understand another's life of love is as if defining infinity∞. Yet to share that love is to glimpse and briefly connect with that infinity∞. Are you busy looking about for the abounding love we need with greed while overlooking others love needs or oblivious to your chance to awaken to love and awake the love in others! Will you be aware when that opportunity, to be or be in love, appears or will you be too self involved or busy with your personal obsess! Take the choice to be the love others are desperately in search of. Make someone's day by letting your being be kind in every encounter. We say we love others yet are constantly acting, showing, telling, and emoting otherwise. We are kinder much of the time to those we kinda know, than those that kinda live, work, and love with us. Take time to remind everyone, including your self, of the love that has been done and reflect upon the love yet to come! Intention to be love and be loved, become love and become loved, know love and know you are loved, thus realizing, recognizing, and unifying IT in your self and all selves. Glorify and enjoy with our being! We all live for something... Let IT be love!!!

Science declares love as, yet to be determined, yet without IT the best medical care cannot keep us alive while dying without IT! We consciously or unconsciously trade even our true selves in order to perceive others are loving and caring for us even though they may not and we are willing to except pain as a substitute rather than the "perceived" empty loneliness of the nothing∞ even though this is where agape can be found... in us, we are all connected! If you expect nothing∞, and accept nothing∞, and ask nothing∞, and are delighted when you receive nothing∞, you will never be deceived or controlled by the pain and disappointment that demanding love incurs. You either live love while growing in and with IT... or you are in the process of dying... You can play the pitiful games to retain a love once known, but once IT is injured or dies IT will never be regained the same and mostly becomes a twisted shadow of underpinnings that are disguised as love! Take mind to be aware and lovingly live, as you may die without ever having truly existed! Be lively and live life. We have been taught to expect a reward when we expend any effort, and interaction with love is a focused giving, yet is only *intentioned agape love* when nothing∞ is expected in return. It is your gift to be given and precipitate freely constantly to all... or blocked by you, thereby receiving and getting only a small part of the love possible, constraining the sea of potential love... constringing your heart... and reverberating only your feeble thoughts. Which do you choose and how, constantly affect your love karma!!! Your faith in and within your self love, allows you to feel IT, sense IT, intention and direct IT, Thus interactive real time participation through your love with others whom Get IT! Cognitive Dis own IT love is unaware without effectual execution. Yet you do not have to believe Love exists to receive and impart IT, as intentioned Love is all embracive and imbued throughout you always∞. The only assurance of love is within... your trust, belief, and faith. Your ability to attenuate, the love you consciously perceive being given or received... Love is not static... IT is dynamic and cannot be stored, saved, or hoarded... Love must transpire in the moment. Love does accumulate but only in the amount you have participated in processing! When you remove the conditions you impose on the love you are giving and burdens you're demanding of others, you are then able to enhance your knowledge of and grow in love and knowledge of self through understanding of others perspectives of the infinite∞ love!

Your heart is actually an interactive energy organic information processor, patterns of energy form information and your heart directly receives and may send signals, outside ourselves, without brain throughput. Your Guts enteric nervous system has almost as many neural connections as your brain. Your heart, your gut, and your brain, are proven to interact with as well as transmit, on different frequencies of oscillating electromagnetic radiation, and bouncing around us are EMF waves from radio waves at the lowest frequencies, to visible light at intermediate frequencies, to gamma rays at the highest frequencies. We are all emitting luminous life forms!!! This will come into play later... "This little light of mine... I'm gonna let IT shine!!!" The best exercise of the heart is to bend down and pick someone up! Spark a heart, ignite some love, irradiate in vibe state! Again I AM writing of my insights, perceptions, experiences, and knowledge, discerned from life and what I have interpreted from reading. I AM reciting not taking credit for any of the scientific study, that I have looked forward through for years, that now makes IT much more clear and I find so very dear. If I have, miss quoted or miss termed or messed up or missed cited IT was unintentional. I hope I have furthered your intentions! Thank you... Wikipedia!!!

IT was the beginning and we were brought into this world in and with IT, exist through IT, and will exit with IT. No beginning!!! No End!!! Just Now and Always!!! You better be prepared to die at anytime because you don't always get prior notification! I would rather die now for a purpose than to die later without one! We can help IT purposefully anywhere everyday when we align with will. I sometimes think I am more afraid of living than dying. I also am more afraid of dying than I am of death! Since there is only Now in the eternity∞ and there is no birth or death, then what do I fear? Oh yeah!!! Dying!!! The uncertainty of how!!! The unreasoned Why??? The fear of what's in store next!!! Well don't fear... Our life shines for inestimable durations oscillating here and there eternally∞... IT's going to be there and happen here! If IT can underpin every sub-Planck atomic particle in every dimension with a Bio harmonic frequency vibration then IT can very well attune forever in you~~~ (John 14). Sign up to be a donor before you do.

Are you an expert or are you learning something new everyday? Do you check your, life's perception filters to make sure they're not clogged? Esoteric as these questions seem. They should be answered each and every day. "The answer my friend is blowin in the wind... the answer is blowin in the wind." We are incessantly making predictions based upon past odds of repetition creating our future by priming cognition with preconception expectation. IT is this expectation that needs intentional intervention to perceive clearly a new reality!

LIII

ERROR~~~ERROR~~~ERROR~~~ Those unwilling to admit IT destine their selves to repetitively nested feedback loops in the internal error of unconscious self-contorted unreality distortion field that inhibits inhabiting your awareness! The conscious brain sitting in the dark interprets the outer world in time delay partial display while the inner mind constructs the interactive light giving us Mind 2.0! A good lesson in sensen is not to overtly trust your preconceived beliefs and practice self-Archeology~~~ Are you adding to the positive vibe or are you living with the dead and sucking energy from the rest. EXCUSES; "I wrote the book" or maybe I didn't? I always said I could BUT! As my Old Polish Mentor, would say, "You can't sh!t the sh!tter!" Yet we all try, then mainly end up fooling ourselves, while others watch in amazement at our lack of discernment of our true self. We do not need to live in Comparativism while thinking about what others think of you? There is a part of the brain labeled RTPJ located above you right ear that does this. This double, triple and even quad of... guess work of your intentional state trying to understand another's intentional state of another's intentional state of yet another's intentions... You would need an UN-interpreter. What we need is to compare in our mind, thoughts and actions desired or imagined vs. thoughts and actions that we actually function and intend in reality, without worry or judgment only discernment.

This is the battlefront of Good vs. Evil, Yin vs. Yang, Being vs. Dieing or just plain right or wrong, which has now been painted in a never-ending shade of gray. I'm right! and everybody else is wrong! I'm right or maybe left? Right or wrong goes much deeper than a record kept in eternity∞ IT is what is right or wrong with and left in you here and now! Who cares whose Right, Left, or Wrong... What I want to know is... who's got Love in their heart and is willing to humbly share what they bring to the party! Just as Thomas Nast fearlessly drew the original Donkey and Elephant to lampoon Da Party Bosses, I too hope to harpoon a few from both parties by eliminating the shady and highlighting the contrast separating, Black from White, the Light from the Darkness, and right from wrong! When you begin to form your thoughts taken from some demagogic hedonistic autocratic delusional party plank or religious disorder then you have stopped thinking... Liberal, Conservative, Centrist, Baptist, Buddhist or Atheist... what you think is what you own and if anybody wants to own your thinking then their thinking is stinking!!! What do you feel and how are you sensed when you enter a party or group in progress? Do you make a grand entrance or try to slip on in? Dominate, hesitate, or assimilate? Is the vibe heavier, lighter, narrower or wider than before your appearance on the scene? Do you reach out to de-stress the instant or insistently convey trauma drama! Do you ask yourself what you can do or how you can be, projecting your desire to lovingly be, available to serve and enhance the present with your presence? During the course of discourse if you come to a point of divergence do you; try to see and explore where the other's view of the point departs from yours, just point out your view to block theirs, agree just to avoid discord, turn on a trance to dream elsewhere, or play on with discourse staying in the fairway? Stay open minded to assimilate the wisdom not the rightness and integrate your spiritual awareness into your life thus, as the result of seeking is to find IT! Be receptive not ejective yet reject what's deceptive. I stay open to the possibility that I am wrong, as this is how I learn. It's truly sad that so seldom any venture in where most fear to tread to have a reasoned discussion of the truths put forth herein and rather keep them constrained ever so deep within! Friends say things like, "You have a deep spirit" or "Your fricken crazy" ... let's presume both are true... and this seems to help allow them to identify with, then demonstrate, their own deeper inner strengths without further commitment. This is a shame as I do appreciate that these characteristics are a part of the mist from which much insightful experience is derived, yet few conduce enough compassion to understand what's inside and show their true self truth, so I may understand where mine may be wrong, thereby helping me to clear the haze of illusion where I am in need of new vision!!! (You can always tell a Norwegian but you can't tell him much... LOL) Not the BS many are trying to pass off as factual actual truth conjured to enhance themselves! Synesthesia... allows some to explore in 4D iMax with Wizard like Technicolor smell O vision. Many do not

LV

even realize they have a modified sensory perception~~~ Other's altering of reality… well… some illusions are brain failures others are self-induced. New truths should be judiciously revealed and logically established rather than distorted, as right has become a variation of wrong, but authentic truth is truth and needs no defense. "Admit what you really can see, IT's right in front of you… IT's never out of your sight."

Science will one day truly prove there is a God! Physics reasons IT as the cause without cause, the source! Holographic Resonant sub Planck Zero Point Quantum Entanglement Potentiality Reality (my term) is IT. The Zero Point Unified Field is the dynamic energy of empty space that exchanges energy and information providing the stability of all matter. Experimentally displayed between the Casimir plates or the equally fantastic conversion of sonoluminescence' of sound waves popping bubbles into a flash's of light that release from the base level oscillations in the empty space of the vacuum. The "Unified Field", fuzzy clouds of potential existence, with no definite location most often more like waves than particles. I am a scientist of sorts. My God withstands the examination of IT. As Ouspensky put IT "A religion contradicting science and a science contradicting religion are equally false". This is open source living interactive belief. No patents, no copyrights, no exclusivity, everyone participates in IT. I am a neophyte in Quantum Physics. I am just the messenger. I'm writing this book to open possibilities in your search for a way to IT and to expose Toxic² behavior to help eliminate those actions. I do not stand in opposition to any person's equal opportunity to improve their material economic condition. I do fervently contest their doing so by taking license to subvert mine! If you are single mindedly searching only for in depth info on, Quantum Physics, Biofeedback, Transcendental Meditation, PSI, Naturopathy, Diet, Exercise or Truth, IT is everywhere so go and entangle yourself in IT! I'm not waiting until they figure IT out (which they may already have… yet continue with disproof), to believe and shift spiritually. I have already waited to long on the periphery of the wrong side of being right!

Most folks on Earth have some belief in God. I AM not trying to make a scientific God. I AM just hoping to help you better understand, communicate, and Get with IT. God is not A religion! If you need some aged text to read in order to believe some distorted view, try our current school textbooks. If you need to listen to someone tell you how to live and behave, the psychotic controllers of truth have many so-called proclaimed facts for you to do. If you just need to be part of a community of fellow graceful faithful, they are all around you and you should be communing with them. If you want to experience Gods omniscient possibilities lose the creed and humbly be gratefully free. Acknowledging God does not acknowledge any "trueΩ" religion. To quote John Locke " Religion… is that wherein men often appear most irrational… and more senseless than beasts themselves". Well I should concede that an inanimate concept, such as religion, is really not the problem… The problem with religions again stem from the people who divisionally differentiate deceivingly and turn IT into hate as well as through those, that suppose to know IT, and then impose "true□" religion on fundamental human rights under the guise of governed controlled love for others!!! Yet IT is impossible to separate love with God out from the current dogmatic regulators as they would be out of work like the rest of us jerks…   Americans believe in God. This is neither a Christian right wing political diatribe nor a call for Atheistic Anarchy left wing revolution (although IT is Revolutionary… just not favored flavor kind biased in nature and Christiania Denmark has IT more right than any of Christianities wings)! IT simply is truth! Because God fearing men and women, whose ideals followed Gods principles, founded this nation then we got lost, and this God based country is clearly documented throughout our, History, Legal system and Legal documents. IT is certainly appropriate to display on the walls of our schools and government buildings and anywhere where freedom rings but on the flip side, the Christian right is wrong, what's left is wrong too and has been for centuries. Separation of church and state is wrongly interpreted as no God… when all of God is what was intended! The separation was meant to protect

God from a careless state and protect US from overbearing religion, not to remove God from our governing but to separate religion from politics! Marginalizing God in the function of government makes for US a devilish place to dwell! Most of our now society is a hijacked bunch of nihilistic crap, and God is the answer, but the question is are you projecting IT or your dumbfounded ego beliefs repentantly drilled down into you not by God but by devilish man controlling others? Our rights... are given by God not issued through religious decree or government grants! We need social order just the fries are cold and stale so lets reorder a new sizzling order! We used to have good public roads that led to good public libraries, good public schools, good public parks, and good health care... Most of this was because we had good people working hard and keeping an eye on things while sharing not shorting IT. Not sure where this taxing toll road rage is leading us to now as everyone shortcuts their true path trying to beat the rest of the crowd to the top? A reformation by US will only take place in our minds! No protesting, No rioting in Da street, and No gun totin unless US devolves to mind control using IT~~~ If that happens you better have both something to tote and a mind too! Let's cut the BS of pulling out the good book to dip into a constituent pool. The right does not have a patent on patriotism as those on the left do most of the heavy lifting resisting when IT comes to our rights listed in the <u>bill</u> of! While Da right chips away through patriot acts! Just what is with this eavesdropping law that says we cannot record in any form the uniformed M&Fr's while performing their duties even though they can record or lie that they have, anything at anytime that pleases their a$$ or persecutes US unduly??? If you want to protest that... we got a nice spot for you just the other side of the Dark Side of the Moon and you can protest there anytime between 1 and 1:01 the fourth Tuesday after any leap year that's odd but not even! I think they just installed a red light camera in my bedroom??? Back to the un-candid jokers debilitating each other and Da country while displaying their geographic ineptitude and foreign policy incapability, as they debate to see who is mentally stable enough to make a run for Prez, they are caught between Der <u>T</u> and Da <u>99 percent</u> who no longer are enjoying justly the scraps from Da money launders tables, that need tossing like Christ did in Da Synagogue, and who want to stake out a place where Da a$$ets are exchanged! Kinda reminds me of the good old days with Billy clubs and Tear gas wafting through Da air~~~ where peaceful protests were being made to demonstrate someone cared!!! Amazing what a few committed people can start!!! Gotta start somewhere... Seems ironically sardonic that they always declare all provocations come from the people, media defined as "anarchists", who are a peacefully marchin for much needed change and describing Da Police as restraint fully intervening and protecting "a$$ets" while really injudiciously a beatin out what they been trained to reenact react, until much later after the fact review shines some sunshine truth on what has been buried by some suits!!! If you don't need or agree with what these people are standin for, just label them as "anarchists" and move along down your self-concern path. When you stand up and complain~~~ Cain labels you Victim even though you are ready willing and Able, and he is out having vanity affairs of denial… leaving only victims of the Oligarchic conscienceless over lorded Demonic Capitalistic fate. I'm pretty sure we know who was jealous of whom and who's countenance fell into Nod when asked if he was his brother's keeper!!! Most of the world believes in God and those that do not are still within the realm of IT. If God offends you, then I suggest you Get IT, as God IS and God's part of our culture and our selves. "I'm a Cultural Infidel… coming from the heart" as Jimmy Buffet poetically croons. We acknowledge the sovereignty of all people to believe all things yet that does not validate the validity of that belief. So stop trying to force your belief in invalidated disbelief on me, disbelief in what I don't know? Can you prove IT? IT is much harder to disprove than the empirical evidence detects that IT exists! If there's no God, to believe in, then how does bringing God into anything disturb your continuing on in your unbelief? If you just live and you die, how can our intended belief to transfigure eternally∞ affect you? Do you not want to live a similar principled life? Please allow God a place in our lives and please stop insisting that I am forcing my beliefs on you because we put "In God We Trust" on our money and other acknowledgements to the place held by

God in the development of this country and universally… Should we put "In US We Trust" on there (by the way where is the value?) or some other useless phrase instead, maybe you have an insistence that you can't believe in that either! I'm pretty sure if you can think something, someone else can find pretext to disbelieve that something! God is God and has been since the DNA RNA helix was blasted into the Cosmos putting the key of life into the door of perception. But beware there is tight security at that door as there is much about ourselves we do not know and much should stay that way… so when you slip the doorman a dime this still only grants you access to the lobby of your mind~~~

Negative third world militaries, Tribal warlords, our own armed politically ignoramus' offensive contractors and Abramoff type lobbyists, along with the controlling cave dwelling mentality of trueΩ religions and Theo-political constructs as well as (20,000+ branches of Christianity alone) fill their coffers by keeping us apart creating the narrative that is echoed parrot-head unlike! Why if what the people we grant our commanding too must repeat and repeat and then repeat over and over and over again until their own echo's confirm their non truth, that is thus inserted through repeated exposure into our belief system! Debilitating our power, interpolating between us, and insisting on our belief in their only true□ God religion while holding themselves up as IT? The holy-roller warrior attitude is mind candy for those that have few prospects and are easily tricked into naive belief that they can be somebody of significance and enter nirvana, without earning, learning, or deserving IT, by controlling leaders manipulatively feeding broken bits of IT! This Meme must be broken our rulers have enough dominion! We do not need to give them our God too. Wake up! People and God are the same universally. Same hopes, dreams, and ambitions, same concerns for shelter, food, and employment, same self-centered ignorance, fears, and selective blindness, different levels of devotion, spirituality, and love, yet relying on the same source. Being in spirit is a derivative of inspiration and we are all occasionally inspired yet you can live in spirIT! IT is annoyed when incoherence with others, whose beliefs are not harmful or detrimental to societal, do not exactly mirror yours appears. Do not impose yours on others nor allow despoliation of theirs over you! You must shift your prejudice to entrain IT. Maybe a little progressive relate ability intercreativity will help everyone to more clearly see IT's light~~~ No one, no how, no way, can change your relationship with God. Only you have that power! There's only one God! There is not a God of those that have and another God of those that have not. There is not a God for the empowered and another for the disenfranchised. There is not a God that encourages war and another peace. There is not one God for the healthy and another creating illness. There is not a wicked God of the East and a Good God of the West! There could be one God that I seek and a different God that you do but there is only one God that either of us can truly find! Your intuIT of God may indeed be true, or IT may be obscured or distorted, but when seen intentionally without deception or invention, The "God" is our God! There are many paths. Please do not be mistaken, many good churches do much good but are in constant control of their message, manmade dogma must go while the faith community should stay and take back the temples. IT is all inclusively a part of IT, but many times held up as all of IT there is, and if you think there is more to IT, your ignorant of IT, and you must go somewhere else to find IT!!! The crypt keepers of the trueΩ "we got all the only answers" religion must be decrypted! The mistake of the so-called unity through a world church (URI) concentrates power and eliminates humanities diverse understanding of and direct connection with God by becoming the mind controlling intermediary Babeling dogma. The spirit in the church demeans the spirit in the Pub yet the spirit in the pub seems to have more in common with IT's spirit than the spirits who moralize spitefully in the church! We need morals; we just need less preachin teachin and more all living less lies! I'm not talking Agnostically nor even Gnostic like because I actively believe that communion and communication with IT and each other together is paramount as well as endemic to source relation... I'm only relaying the facts Jack, that our current form of religion of trueΩ derision division and overt over restraint of our internal external eternal∞ is infested infinity∞ infected infernally! We need to re-gather under those same roofs with renewed truth and return the churches to their purpose not just some social hall that manages after expenses to help few, while adding to societies untrue miscues of no use, only doctored trueΩ religion abuse!!! We are all ministers of God and we need to begin our ministries wherever we may be…

Prayer with care must replace parochial diversion! Prayer is not IT but affirmative prayer is part of IT. IT's curious that one of the first things that when Believer meets Believer they must find out if you are friend or foe by asking what faith or denomination you profess or in the Enlightened New Age what books, sounds, or methods have you tried. Like there's a qualifying round for commonality or spirituality… Do you read the Bible to find words you agree with and comfort your thought or to seek discernment and refine your love? The Bible is used and abused like a drug by the good news dealers that interpret IT to make any point that supports their pillars! The good news is, IT all boils down to the same God and I sense God's unhappiness, with the claim that you must be a member of the trueΩ religion! Keep God, keep the faith, celebrate Gods love in acceptance of positive diverse ways and expressions of attentiveness, lose all deceitful trueΩ religion and Da ministers (hey not mine!!! Yeah yours…), and you will be attuned in faith with God! You and I will sense IT in your soul~~~ If we practice what we know to be true there is no need for an interloping trueΩ religion!!! Let's Get to IT…

Who am I to write this book? Well will get to who I am. But who am I to indeed believe I can write a book on IT… well??? Shazam!!! I have lived a life with a myriad of jobs and professions from logger to sales from chemist to pot discounter, from Da trenches doing cementin to cementin some horse crap deal (watch out for the F&I guy), I have been happily unemployed, but unhappily underemployed most of my time as my skills exceeded their demands, I am a Jack off all trades and Master Baiter of Da negatively intentioned, When they invent a machine that can critique as thoroughly as me I will once again be unemployed! I have lived with more, I live with less, I have lived high end on

Da beach yet only to later be evicted out of Da ghetto to live in Da Street enhancing my creed... I have flunked out, I am a Scholastic and Academic Honors recipient, I have been exposed to an eclectic array of people, I have lived in contemplative isolation, I studied multiple religions (not all claiming to be Da trueΩ) and numerous philosophies in my late teens after being raised in a authoritarian truly faithful family, I have been an atheist, I was rich enough not to need, I was poor enough not to be spoiled, I have been married, I am divorced, I was a drunk, I am sober, I have mixed with different cultures and nationalities, I have been a bigot, I have been a freak, I have been a suit, I have been a power monger, I have given all, I have fought for peace and love, I have prayed for salvation as I was beaten, I wished for compassionate understanding as I blew the candles out on my 21st birthday, I have thought I was superior, I donate blood so IT may course in you, I have made most every mistake you can make, some more than once~~~ I am the perfect me~~~, I have lived out of my car, I have lived in the stars, I love you even if we have never met, I ask for your forgiveness, I live the belief humankind is good and can be resurrected, I have been guided to write this by IT, I have sensed the nothing∞ for 59 years! I have *experienced synchronicity* that was improbable, doubtful, surprising, dubious, incredible, weird, ordinary and according to our world impossible! The plausibility of the probability and the concurrence of circumstance seems to eliminate the possibility of this just being coincidental chance, more likely to be premeditated predefined prospectively perceptive probability! Destiny altering. The force of IT... like in the movie ((side trip) I could not believe my first glimpse of this acetate projection of the hidden force being used to overcome evil, as this force was so like what I was living in the quantum entanglement of IT... Now they're marketing a mind trainer, not sure what wave of IT they are using but might be fun~~~ and newly willed Chronicle) IT gets stronger as you are more open in your discernment of IT and purposefully practice interaction with IT. Yet the dark force is strong. This nano force of vibrating fluctuation intersperses as we determine our free will transformation. As I wrote these sentences I had a synchronic experience, as I was in the midst of altering the

LXIII

"who am I to write this book" section, which I decided not to… but then started to add the, my *experienced synchronicity* sentence and I had several. A Sandhill Crane called out repeatedly (unusual) while two workers on the golf course hit a sprinkler head hole with their cart and their world was briefly disrupted because their attention had been pulled towards mine, not where they were going, while looking at me typing away on my porch (surprising coincidence or synchronicity?). This was subtle but I perceived a slight change in IT and IT is very subtle, like the wee small voice. Knowing the difference between common events and those that have meaning make IT subjective, but using objectivity in a discerning way, I humbly seek IT every day everywhere and with practice my objections become less suggestive while Being in IT becomes more introspective with the subjective. These are my credentials. I am a child of the 60s and we rejected most everything… most things needed to be rejected and still do as the problems and the headlines remain "the same as IT ever was∞" So young or old this book can help you be the change… Think cosmically and act neighborly… Skip the Mega Mart and find the made in USA Mom and Pop shops… Plant a victorious garden and recycle, repurpose, reuse, and then repeat… Cheaper is not always cheaper nor is IT's value or quality equal, nor the enjoyment of transactional participation or the support for our local communal society as satisfying… toil conscientiously now considerate with future intention subsequently… Start today… right now… commit to IT… I ask nothing of you and hope to get IT back in return! I am not a Master, Monk, or Shaman. I do not want any followers. I ask you be a selfless leader by example! I do not want to start a new trueΩ religion. Bring the one your in from the darkness back into the light! I do not want to destroy any faith. Faith can neither be created nor destroyed! I do not want to tell you to change your God. Good luck with that! I only want to help you seek IT. "They call me the seeker… I been searchin low and HIGH… I won't get to get what I'm after… till the day I die!" (The WHO) Follow your heart and do your part. If IT is your own IT then nobody owns IT. This does not mean you can invent your own "trueΩ" religion and have followers, as the many controllers do. IT means that

LXIV

you can be an integral part with IT. IT is called IT only for conversational purpose and inclusion of all. IT deserves descriptions beyond my austere capacity to express IT. Many express and write much more succinctly, clearly, descriptively, logically, methodically, and technically scientifically about our interconnectedness within the unity so kindle your burning desire. IT is really nothing∞ (20 minutes twice a day)! You are IT! "What the world needs now is love sweet love… IT's the only thing that there's just to little of" same as IT ever was∞ All I want is to share IT and be with you in IT! Maybe, like in the Russian Silver Fox taming breeding program, in a few more generations of genetic de-selection of adrenal aggressive toxicity and developing a better breed of finely tuned transcender's we may return humanity to humankind!

Where am I? I mean where was I? Oh back at the ranch… NAKED… Yeah that's where I was… We have our perception of who we are naked. Some of us don't look and others should look a little less. Do you avert looking at a hot body or do you enjoy the beauty that was intended. No, I'm not talking about, Jimmy Carter type "lust in your heart". I'm talking about the whole person. The Physical, Spiritual, Chakra, and the glow from their heart. Naked is great! Your only beautiful as you feel inside! Some of the most beautiful beings in all humankind are not abstractedly attractive physically, yet their inner love and beauty is awe-inspiring! Beauty is the reflection of God through our eyes. IT surrounds us. If all you see is ugliness then your intentioning the glass to be empty. The illumination that will change our world to again allow us to participate in the beauty once more cannot be bought or implemented. We must envision the beauty that is there and develop an attitude of care. IT puts us all on even footing and takes away that socio-economic-class-color-cool-hip-phat-hop BullCRAP, invented by those that have little else to offer. As Carter warned in 76', what is being sold to us as consumerism is consuming our relations, as our mental picture of whom we are is from some commercial where we own some things, we don't really need, or an image of reality that's only real in effects that leave us wanting, so we envision ourselves as lacking IT! While IT unfalteringly displays our humble naked selves and the beauty contained

LXV

therein. We shoulda coulda followed Carters warnings about OPEC and followed his plan to get 20% Solar by 2000 through windfall profits tax. OH that would have cut into Enron's profits!!! Our world would be a much different better place without the oil problems we've faced and have yet too... Like a sign post in a paradoxical parable the Chinese have mounted the solar panels, Reagan removed from the White House roof, in a museum as Carter ironically predicted... We would be fueling with the H in H2O rather than be painted into the corner we're in today. We have paid dearly with petro dollars and still pay for them to continue to play. Da Moneyed players played Carter right out of the game! He got shooed off by the same Repub spin from a 20 headed mule team working with an actor extraordinaire who's second term was stage mother managed and here we are 35yrs older but none the wiser... We need to stop thinking what we've embedded as should, and start doing the good could. Now where was… Oh I remember or I thought I did, but the phones ring tone just played "Let IT Be" but I couldn't, as my boss was askin for the report due last week, on the project they cancelled yesterday, but he doesn't know, because the Information Technology guy left his sandwich on the router and it overheated, the router not the sandwich which was good and hot, so the net was down. BUT! Breath deep… Catch a breath…

Oh I remember now… "Keeping in tune with the straight and narrow"… is hard to do when your constantly being interrupted by the barrage let alone being able to clear your head of the babble going on inside. Let IT be… Pascal once said "All the worlds ill's stem from the fact that a man cannot sit in a room alone" and according to the ancient historian Plutarch, "Know Thyself" was inscribed on the Sun God Apollo's Oracle of Delphi temple in ancient Greece. How much do you know about yourself and just how much do you really want to know? The Illness… I mean the I'ness resulting from the abstracted distracted mind that loses focus every 6 seconds and can't wait more than 250 milliseconds to get an answer back from Google or make an instant judgment, because you now are able to customize your interface with your universe generating an interference pattern amalgamating into what you include, what you elude, how you delude, and what will elude you? The thousands of thoughts we interact with in our mind each day convey our emotional state and our intention relation to our selves and all those we meet along the way! Are you nurturing and propagating Love or averting aberrations??? The toxins you ingest transpose from stomach to brain. The toxins you allow to precipitate through your ears alter your worldview. The toxins you regurgitate through action and words continue the paradigms we're stuck too. Did you bookmark where you were in Life??? You may never get back there!!! Or you just did! Let's see where was I??? Was I??? Was I??? Oh sh!t another text… Studies entailing Texting, confirm that texting rather than talking leads to a lot more lying! Let's see where was I??? Was I??? ………….. Oh yeah I was talking about NAKED! The naked truth, the naked lie, the naked reality, the naked love within each of us…

I don't know when the last time you wrote a book was… So you might as well get used to my ramblings, as my friends and family have! Funny IT mostly comes down to friends and family. Not just the related kind, also the friend kind that become family over time and the family kind that becomes a friend as well as the family kind that you just can't relate to and friends you have stopped relating to. Those idio-centric, phsycophrenic, funny, crazy, demanding, giving, people that love us for what we are and we overlook their … well faults and foible's. Because we love em! Do we really??? And they Love us? Do they really??? Let's again review love… Can you define LOVE? Love is totally unscientific yet IT determines and is involved in every aspect of our lives and world based on how, when, where, what, and who do you love! We spend our lives trying to find and express love, trying to live in love, and many never quite find the perfect love that only exists in their mind. Some are only in love with themselves! We must learn to sense the love we have and explore new expressions of that love to others! We expend great effort in our search for knowledge on a myriad of topics yet how much time do you spend, learning, discerning, and practicing, LOVE? Culture, environment, family, institutions, friends, and foes help to determine and define our understanding, perceptions, and participation in love… I can't quite put my finger on IT. I reckon IT has something to do with God… You can love too much but you cannot have too much love! How did you acquire love? How do you know love exists? How do you project or detect love? Sharing IT does not deplete your never-ending supply of IT and the more you give the more you have… In giving the giver is given. In healing the healer is healed. This self-replenishing flow of love is God! You can give love relentlessly and always have what you started with along with that which is being added to IT! So if you feel or are touched by LOVE and don't believe in God then maybe your feelings are imagined and you are a little touched by thoughts from the matrix… Back to the matter… or does IT? Well do not just dilettante along... let us continue like IT in reality does… I would like to think… I don't think "they" want you to think, I think… what I think… don't much matter, or does IT? By thinking what "they" don't want you to think and loving maybe IT does! Strengthening your intentioning combats others negative inattentions that affect you or attenuates others positive intention love too you and is reciprocal, as IT resonates in both your eternities∞. How is your soul??? Mine is good "Thanks"!!! What is a soul? And how can IT be good? Well let me explain! The soul is found in the Locus of the Focus not the Hocus Pocus (also a great song)!!! The external Locus of control… do you take credit for the good things that happen and blame God for the rest or do you give IT all up to God? Can you contain a soul? Do you entrust your soul to trueΩ religion or to God? Do you sacrifice only materially or give spiritually? Are you focused on what matters. Checking in to see if you're living your life on target. Making room for what sustains, removing irrelevant clutter. Do you seek first IT's Kingdom, and daily reflect Gods belief through you... not what you've construed??? If you answered yes to that last one, your soul is good. The two supposed halves of self, internal to external, form a duality delusion that is in reality functional unified soulful togetherness. Perhaps you inconceivably believe you have no soul… well this premise of the unity, applies to you even if you don't conceive IT! My soul is good, "thanks to Gods being"! How the heck is yours? Life I love you…all is groovy… Are you thankful? Do you sing IT's praises? How do you express your appreciation? The state of pure love is a humble thankful state~~~

20%

I am less than overjoyed for the interactions in the following unremitting in love with self-states... Have you ever met someone that has a problem? I mean a real problem? Like not remembering what time 11:00AM is when your supposed to meet them @ 11:00AM... is this because they really cannot tell time or maybe because your time is worthless and their time is more precious than life! Have you ever met someone that has a problem? I mean a real problem? Like checking every electronic device within twenty miles rather than to have an intimate conversation. Have you ever met someone that has a problem or maybe live with a someone that has a real problem? Like the screaming idiot that equates volume with rational when expressing thoughts or feelings and mistakenly deludes him or herself that the apology that follows or should, could make IT right, forgiven, forgotten, or in any way acceptable. Have you ever met someone that has a problem? I mean a real problem? Like someone who will constantly bitch and complain in your individual company but when in mixed company or trying to make that impression never bitches or complains at all, always testing and abusing your compassion. Have you ever met someone that has a problem? I mean a real problem? Like those who are supposedly your friend to your face and they are backstabbing you when you're out of earshot! Not the talking about others when not present to define, discuss, or refine understanding, in search of answers while being filled with concerned compassion but the stating of things you are afraid to say to their face and are often un-truths... Have you ever met someone that has a problem? I mean a real problem? Like the neighbor with no muffler on his lawnmower, that's badly in need of a tune-up, reverberating @ 7am on Sat or Sun, who when he gets done cranks up Da weedwacker @ jet deafening whining levels, then just when you think peace or death may come, the 157mph blower comes out to blow all the chopped up crap into a cloud that encircles and permeates everything you own!!! Or the converse hasn't touch the yard since the last ice age… Have you ever met someone that has a problem? I mean a real problem? Like a salesperson, taking an extended phone call from some a~~h☹le to lazy to come into the store to actually look at the product your there to buy or just chatting with another rather than doing their J O B. Have you ever met someone that has a problem? I mean a real problem? Like the money snubbing richer than thou, whom sets the look of how much I got not how, economic example of the un-conscientious current version of Capitalist fantasy. Only to find out that the money they were holding over your head was simply money they were in over their heads with and mortgaged to the hilt in, then declaring ignorance as to why when the check came due as to their understanding or responsibility for overextending both financially and egotistically, leaving the bills of their bankrupt immoral self-worth to you and me while being rewarded with thousands because the robo's were signin. Now they want their immoral debts forgiven… I cannot lose what I have not borrowed I say, nor lorded over some poorer Jamoke, not needing to beg for forgiveness of my debt as those who debt to transgress above the rest of US!!! I must forgive their immortal trespass upon IT but I will not too forget IT, and just because you are forgiven does not mean you are exempt when the redemption check comes due? I nor see those that actually have Da real wealth using IT responsibly or applying IT to change negative realities! Their form of Capitalism is the distribution of wealth without conscience by the government, courts, lawmakers and lawyers. Worked pretty good for exploitive white men, when they traded beads for Manhattan but not so much for the Native American. "Free market economy" are just the words we thought meant Fair Merit Conscientious Capitalism was, the dream we defined to be, but our economy is not even close to being free and regulation manipulation is the name of their game and free seems to mean free to finagle rather than fair to enable! You can't even sell peanuts in Da street without going through the bureau of auto crates for a permit, that cost some of your peanuts, then is approved and granted only after you donate some more of your peanuts!

LXX

Equal opportunity requires freedom, if there is not freedom of opportunity, opportunity cannot be equal. If only those in the know with the dough rollicking around in bed with those well FED whores are represented at the table how do we get a leg up out of the mud and mire to get our fair share of swill from the trough? Regulations currently determine Da winners and we have no input into Da non-Nomic game! There are sound reasons why we regulate not chaining exit doors shut, just as there were sound reasons we regulated the risks our hard earned money was exposed to by market makers after 1929! They are repressively regressively legislating US, replacing regulations learned and earned the hard way! With their regulations that do not empower people but give power to their rule through law, by their people, for their people by declaring regulation as stymieing entrepreneurship and enterprise they mostly mean removal of those inconvenient fair humane principles! I think we're the people that were supposed to be free and equal yet all I feel is the power of the heel of Das boot regulatin my choices and chances! I don't much like the fact that there is such great need to regulate... Mostly to keep their heel off our necks! But when the spin-doctors get done explainin the regulatin my neck does not seem to feel any relief!

The self-made billionaire is oxymoronic as, no one who competed fairly and was equitably compensated for their impetus into the return on expended toil, did not abuse and use others that made much less than their inherent self-value was worth. This ruthless competition idealized, as the goal for conscienceless Capitalist self-made Man unkind, is very good for the very few and extremely unequally sad for the rest, yet keeps most competing for the same pot of gold only unjustly over the next rainbow! OUR Capitalism as a system appears designed to reward only a few cannibals with no conscience of having eaten the others! I guess in some societies the eating of others is normative in values and I just need to be a little more TOLERANT... NOT!!! IT is pretty obvious we are searching for a new value system, although appears that some are happier with none! Capitalism is one great tool if united with conscience for IT's purpose. Societies best utilities could be served and attained if we could change and repurpose our no character improvisation defining our current demon erratic Capitalistic cannibal nation!!! This great nation of PEOPLE, not megacorp's, deserves better! Let US invest our treasure in all our people; they have the highest potential return on investment. What we may find is some of the old worked mighty well and that somethin new will have to come from within you! We have a bunch of great philosophical ground work mixed with trial and error democracy and much greater writing than mine: discerning truth, justice, the Constitution, the Bill of Rights, economic, trade, and foreign policies, ect... ect... We just can't seem to sort IT out or do and follow the true path the majority of US believe to be the best for the majority of the people for the people, Mainly because we're being mind manipulated to diversion while the truth is coloured with uncertainty. Just as the framers horse-traded away some of which would have been right and true of a true Free Market Democracy, with limited government rather than government limiting the views that encourages private enterprise to fairly compete with others for economic gain (key terms here~~~ fairly). Their successor's incessantly inserted manipulation of regulations and favored status that has turned a good philosophy into a good way to spin words into profits! IT's all about fairness and there ain't much of IT to see! The trusts were once busted only to return to exploit our laws and lawmakers to lose our trust once more. We are so interest woven with these lustin thieves that bustin them is going to hurt each and every one of US in the too big to fail economizing corporate US. IT's much like your life that you've been drawn into so tightly, that IT seems unfeasible to toss all your tall tales away and reorder your life, in order to have a chance at a fresh new true you. The imminent need to dump so much of the conflicting constricting old you to free you, deeply disturbs the old you so much, that the old you chooses to stay in that busted untrue old you blues. Thus you never have any real chance at your actual potential. Rather than just grin and bearing the pain of letting go, of what really ain't so much in reality, to have what you're really searching for and desiring to be! Now to continue Da rant~~~ Auuumm~~~ The moneyed control both supplies as well as demands because supply is finite, (everyone I guess

LXXII

can't have a Villa in Monaco with a Bugatti Veyron or maybe a Ferrari out front, but why should only Da chosen few while others pick through their garbage for lunch? Is this the way God meant IT to be? Or the way man's twisted thinking twisted free market economic social policy? This accrual is unfairly cruel) and demand is regulated by how much they're willing to pay us or as of late no pay at all; in the we don't need your labor game of accounting principles. This must be why after chasing the almighty dollar around the house of mirrors up one business cycle and down another, I'm losing my home, dat ain't anywhere near Da Mediterranean but tax levied like waterfront which IT isn't, then the money I do make is subject to the regressive tax man, while my car is turning antique with little value! I'm not proposin we should manufacture one kinda car to better mass produce the same old junk, yet how can somebody's having a million dollars to spend on a car be considered socially equitable when others are forced to walk, because we under fund greener mass transportation or because sum succeed in the pursuit of conspicuous consumption while others bear life's tragedies? Nor do I recommend we all live in some ticky-tacky 3-room kibbutz, although that would entail an upgrade for me. Much of what we have been sold as wonderful and good for us has come from the spin cycle of wealth taking, leaving us hung out to dry in the ill wind of image desired economic inequity credit pit disability. America has celebrated long past the fact of IT's Capitalistic unaware decline, as we continue putting on a insincere smiley faced dramatic tragedy, performing as if the fourth act of a three act display of constant consumerism can continue performing in what has become an old empty warehouse! We all want more but more of what??? We seek recognition, friendship, love, appreciation, we want to be considered successful (@ what?), but all most go after is power and money and mostly fail so we settle for some other crap!!! The war on poverty is over and the poor lost again! 1 out of 2 of US have slid into low income or poverty NOW while the top 5% have continued to enrich as of the witting of this (I'm pretty sure this is intentioned)! Slaves to the marketers business plan megaopoly! The idea that needs create, has been supplanted by now demanding needs be created, through

LXXIII

manipulative ideas and Da basic humane needs remain belatedly unmet. Have you ever met someone that has a problem? I mean a real problem? Like those that desire to use the power of intention to conscienceless focus IT only for their own material gain, another cataleptic capital idea! If you think you have been blest or are in IT's grace because you got stuff... Well if you ain't taken care of IT's business IT's got some stuff for you and not the stuff you intended to want! Have you ever met someone that has a problem? I mean a real problem? Like a judge who had three martinis for lunch to wash down his Zanax and threatens you with jail and to pay an exorbitant fine, because your old Lincoln could not pass the IEPA air test and repair was economic impossibility, so the state revoked the license, leading to being cuffed, arrested, and hauled off in the squad after an unmarked scanned my plate!!! My only crime being driving without that IEPA revoked license, as my two young daughters watched as their father and they were hauled to the station too. All because great fines are attached and the Lincoln Towing Service pays tributes regularly! Now I have had other unique opportunities to interact with the system... and always leading to "here comes Da Judge" asserting his power trip of being The Honorable~~~ (Oh sorry side-trip) Da cops want to arrest you then confess you as they're parameters of their training and processing... The DA wants to slam-dunk you for their scoreboard... and the Judge wants to be reappointed or reelected and you're only one vote of which you can't if you're in jail! Put there by strange bedfellows where you will meet some other even stranger bedfellows... Incarceration for profit, Infraction inflation violation, and Outsourcing justice... The crime of unjust punishment (May God bless, protect, and guide all who compassionately serve to protect.) Fund education dollars not incarceration dolers! Have you ever met someone that has a problem? I mean a real problem? Like the cops that dragged me out of a boat and threw me against a wall to get me to resist and then chained me to a picnic table for hours, before arresting me, because they didn't like me voicing my opinion with some attitude, that their safety check, demeanor, and procedures were Bullsh!t (How many forces we got bye the bye?). If I had not stayed within myself all sorts of charges would

LXXIV

have ensued. I should have sued when the charges were summarily dismissed for lack of cause, after threats of raised felony charges from the persecuting States Attorney, implementing aggressive multiple charge upping as their standard M.O., trying to stick some charge to you so that you'll pled too avoid all the others! They also carry complete Supreme Court immunity to cover their exploitive actions and capricious persecutions! Probably should be an answerability quality control process here somewhere... I now wish I had done my civil duty to file false arrest and harassment charges but that was not how I was brought up to be! Police have enough to do if they choose to! Get on those stealin, thevin, hurtin, and dealin hard drug dearths! Don't spend tax money and time bustin recreational softies just because you can selectively choose to enforce a grievous bad law! Ruinin lives, that we're doing just fine prior to your intrusion, because your believin those same crap laws give you the right too! Pretty sure purposely mis doin anything, follows your Karma around trailin like a hound dog in heat! I have tried to shut down a gang of wannabes dealing hard drugs out of a house just up the street for eleven years... I have been told multiple times that undercover operations were ongoing and to be patient... well... after I was informed by a third party, I'd better stay quiet, I found out that the police had returned to these criminals evidence of their criminality, then told them who complained, and further instructed them on how to avoid crossing the fine line of legality the next time... I finally realized why nobody ever gets arrested... Many of these cops are undercover all-*right* and in bed with the cartel, big or small, wherever they pay or preside. I have a repeated proven genuine Toxic Ritalin AiDeD disjoint minded schizoid who is indigent in a vagrantly way and who is communally enabled by all the other Toxic² Zombie ~ enabling him, Da cops are not very interested in him because he has no money and he's a pain to deal with while continuously trying to make me a part of the problem because I passionately relentlessly stand up to threat after threat asking them for a solution to dissolve this toxin! They see this as a neighborhood domestic dispute and categorize IT as such. Done!!! Da Police just handle this repeat offending as another, he said she said now I'll have to fill out another report cause the boss said, incident, but in reality this is the battlefront of good VS evil and I will not be dissuaded! Why do I look around and see indigent repeat offenders consistently pushing the limits and being avoided or even sorta rewarded by police while those with some assets but not rich are treated like desperados getting their a$$e$ fined to the full extent and if you don't plea bargain they raise the charges, even without a case, just to threaten you! Even If you are guilty of no crime (this happened to me)! The negative vibe in a courtroom by all sides is unnerving and intended to be! Manipulation of the objective truth through subjective objection, the dance of lies, the people that live this daily, need to get a new paradigm and check their perception as IT has been frost bitten by repeated exposure to the cold negative side of reality! Repeat offenders are gamin the system while not doin the time for the crime... Truth in Consequences is not the gamed show from my youth. Put these Perp's to work to earn their room and board @ profit to US and the aggrieved! Enough coddling of these hardboiled eggs! Prison should be punitive punishment in a safe environment! Usually by the time you get real time you've shown your true colors. Keep the real criminals separate from each other (No more hangin with Da other gang bangers!) and find them some nice piece work without ability to any more threaten even other inmates or hold class on their next crime! And this fillin of the private prison industrial complex's by backin repressive antiquated drug laws must be somebody's Capital punishment idea for self reward but not a very good system of jurisprudence, almost like clearin the streets to form farm chain gangs when IT was time to harvest Da cotton! Da NSA Homey land insecurity complex! We need a new reality that is not centered only on Da process but is restorative to the balance between a time out for them and our ability to envision a new justice paradigm, allowing us to stay grounded in a new humble reality that actually addresses the problem... Do you really think being a bad a$$ problem makes you as tough as learnin and being the peace player while learnin to be turnin Da other cheek once or twice by takin one for Da betterment of the family? Just how tough are you??? Have you ever met someone that has a problem? I mean a real problem? Like the Jamoke who drives on you're a~~ because you happen to be obeying the speed limit and they are on their way down the highway to he~~ then they pop a U'ie because they passed their exit or can't seem to drive in a straight line unless they're 2 inches off your bumper, even when your doing Da 5 over hustle! These are the same people that seem to have gapers block on every other block because of some mental block. People are confident of their expert multitasking debility, when they can't even walk and chew gum. Some of you already know my car is a great attitude debility adjuster!!! (I should really not take such pleasure in raising their blood pressure! Better check IT~~~ I can and do go slower... I will take some of my precious time to take some of your precious time to host a prolonged driving tour down etiquette lane~~~ I will if driven too offensively defend myself with IT) some call this rage but if Da police won't cage em I'll engage em~~~ with centered focused acuity. And you aggressive Cops that ride my bumper can kiss my... well just kiss my... well just back the frick off as I'm leaving a karma message in your futures in box! Have you ever met someone that has a problem? I mean a real problem? You know... the kind of person that supposedly knows IT @ all... The kind of person that insists they have a clear idea of how other people should lead their lives but none about their own! ("Heee...y that's ME"...) They are unable or unwilling to listen to what you know or have to say, interrupting you constantly, while saying you aren't listening! Many of these same people just start rambling on... Blah... Blah... Blah... while they think of something to say in order to be the one whose speaking, thereby controlling the conversation narcissistically, not allowing coherent bilateral conversation! If you have this problem, listening a little may shift your thoughts off your own know it all condition. Listen to what others ascribe to IT, as they creatively delineate or reminisce on IT's essence and remonstrate IT's being as the consciously indescribable ultimate all-encompassing truth mediator. People do not like, nor acknowledge, even loudly disavowing, that anyone else in Dis unity could possibly be more intelligent or have a firmer grasp of anything than they themselves con cock! Have you ever met someone that has a problem? I mean a real problem? Like those that only

LXXVII

allow you to remain in the box that they put you in, thereby allowing for no change or possibility for growth in either of you. All thought is filtered through the perception of the reflection in the mirror of memory that must be kept clear of the hazy illusion of time. Have you ever met someone that has a problem? I mean a real problem? Like most people you R that person… You just can't see IT because your ego believes you already know all absolute truth. IT can only help those that help themselves. Do you ever remember being self-centered? Maybe take another look-see seeing current reality. You filter out this possibility so there is no discernment. Ego is important as a reflection of love and how brightly our light shines in us. So don't become egoless but repurpose your ego to go with loving finesse. Remove your hardened steel will and rigid perception detection. This is why we all need someone in our lives to reveal to us their truth about us as well as how they perceive our truth and also discernibly assess our truth of them. The quality control feedback loop! Why surround ourselves with a~~kissers! PC neighbors! And the religious passive aggressive faithful! Or the group that thinks but no one does! We do have a need to bond with others like us, so we choose people and things of similarity and we're tuned into cooperation as we perceive our need to be part of the coop but do not let this connective mimicry solidarity stymie your mindful individual reality. What was the last real individual original thought you thought you thought? No one wants to be the first to make a move or choice nor do they want to miss the boat, so most are in the middle of the road waiting to hitch a ride so that when they get there, wherever there may be, they can act like they were the first to make the move or choice! The family that by chance you were born too affects your future; economics, intelligence, health life death welfare, far more than your striving to exceed just because they were moneyed... Now how can this equate to equality? Nestling cozily behind the gate of your community or in the upscale middle of the road dichotomy supposed to protect you and your family from reality exposes the fact that you don't know jack and never will!!! You cannot isolate yourself or your self from what you fear resides there and you cannot begin to redeem the dream if you iso-hate rather than

LXXVIII

interactively participate by aiding and abetting those who live in a less fortunate state, more so, you cannot whack somebody up one side while loving the other side of them from the other side of town! While your hanging out in the middle of the road watch out... for this is where I see a lot of road-kill not paying attention too... Are you ready and willing to prevail of your own? No not alone... for there are many among us to trust but you need to respond in kind when they reach out to you. You are a unique droplet of mist connecting amidst all others to create absolute unity in the sea of life and so are never separate and infinitely∞ a part of IT. Does your connection add toxic² particle pollution or sifting soulful solutions to the unity? Have you ever met someone that has a problem? I mean a real problem? Well we all have problems the problem is in recognition and recondition rather than denial and imposition. Do you define the problems as inevitable thereby defining an allowable excuse to excuse you or is IT your will to find and work to solution? The real sin is in believing that there is nothing that can be done and we are forgiven for our failure to stand for, then... act on solution! Inaction based upon the inevitable excuse is an action itself that allows and supports the problem! Did you ever meet someone that has a solution? I mean a real solution. Well IT is! Are you getting this or do you need to go back and start over? Come on "No way did you get all of what I said so far." And I'm just getting warmed up. This is the remedial course!

Let's see "Where was I..." Oh yeah... In the beginning... what was that creation thing...

Well I'm pretty sure, not absolutely, although pretty sure, there was nothing∞ (which actually must be something) and then there was something (which actually could be the nothing∞)... and I'm pretty sure that whatever made something out of nothing∞ is God... We are all God... God is in all of us... God is in everything... We are a part of everything and everything is a part of us! Last time I tried to make something out of nothing I ended up getting divorced! LOL... I thought I was God but found out I was dyslectic and I was being a doG! Must be part of that perception thing. We being created as part of divine design source are an integral bit of source eternals∞ encoded

LXXIX

collaboration in this co origination. Each moment, is a point of creation, as neither, a beginning or end can be traced to the now. As before there was nothing, time existed, and after the nothing, time will still exist! Hey…(aside) why do we now spend more of our adult time single than married, families estranged with antagonistic relation and litigation! Do you create anti or pro time? Anyway… where was I… Have I answered your burning question yet ??? Well give me time… Speaking of time… Oh Yeah… "TIME… It's a bitch don't give me that do good good bullsh!t"… Is IT about deeds or just the fact that you believe??? The fact is it's about time that we start to understand our own reality in order to use the time that we have in this space. Is that red light really longer when your late, because you did not leave on time for that appointment, or when your getting paid by the hour and the longer you sit there the less you need to do when you get back to the shop! I believe another Al… Yeah… Albert Einstein… He should have observed me trying to get my kids ready for Sunday school as I exceeded the laws of relative relating!!! Well I finally figured out that if you cannot get to God's temple on time with a positive attitude going there is not relative. Where are your children receiving their positive soulful education, or are they? Actually I attempt to enjoy the brief moment stopped @ the red light to contemplate the moment but IT seems I mainly live life where they're green~~~! Well… Let's see… Stuck again… No now riding Old Mr. Time wave in another thought experiment… Al Einstein quantum leaped ahead~~~ changed all of time by bending space. Time is broken down to Planck Time but because IT is difficult to measure the immeasurable so Yocto's are used… is that like a New York minute??? Do you ever find yourself "steppin' in a slide zone… slippin through a time zone?" You know like where things slow down like a movie and allowing you to react to something that is taking place at a much quicker pace or the opposite as in enjoying a bottle of wine with a beautiful person while having great mental contact and the night is gone! Take a step into these coherent thoughts, on time or AM I? Einstein proposed we each have our own time!

LXXX

Our Time Without any sense of time, as in being disconnected from the passage of time and more concerned with place... Watching time as in watching our watch being neither here nor there... Disjointed time, as in spurts and pauses without order... Racing through time, as in unknown relations and fragmented conversations... Weighed down by time, as in the eternity∞ of movements and events surrounding you... Time without a future, as in only this moment, only the present... Backward in time, as in regressing... Time as something that can be captured... Immeasurable time, as in actions trigger other actions with no relationship to when... Time as a location that can be viewed, as in the sky... Time as a commodity, to be invested in or spent... Time as predetermined, as in teleology or uncertain as in theology...Time as a possibility of potential alternatives, preceding, proceeding, and post-ceding from the present...Time as choice, as in hesitating and staying at a point in time, living here and now, or dying to get to the future... Earlier, now or later as in, I could have, I AM, I may be... Time the fourth dimension, creating Spacetime. Time eternal∞ or infinite∞ as in undying...

I am not a believer in regression therapy where you supposedly move back through time to a previous life. I guess this is mainly because I have never clearly sensed nor transcended beyond this particular lifetime timeline. I have experienced vivid memories going back to my birth and often imagine being immersed comprehensively in resonance with history! You know... I thought I was there... You know!!! There are many forgotten and hidden memories that could easily be interwoven in the fabric of mindspacetime that construe you a previous you. Have you traversed this interval to find how you got to this space, then releasing destructive memories of the who that was not as bad as the repeated memory and restoring the who you are now? Use pictures, music, reading, tastes, smells, places, to retrieve and cue up the mindspacetime, allowing all your senses to immerse in that moment~~~ As they trigger a seldom viewed thought ride the backwards timeline in your mind! Protect your PKM Zeta as these thoughts are the doorway to others that we call remembrances! Careful not to construe... well imagining is fun but hard to tell fact from fiction, yet you do know when you choose too or when you make up a story to make something either appear to be a well thought out idea or a retrospect changeable story!!! Now where was I??? Let me remember!!! What's Da story??? Oh yeah... Back at the ranch... Do you have time? Are you a fast reader or a slow digester? Can you do both? That brings me to "Multitasking..." Seems when I meet a multi-tasker, I am getting only a sliver of their attention. They want all of yours, or do they? Yet they are only giving you a small part of theirs! Multi distracters seem to actually be present here and now only now and then. You can do several things simultaneously giving each one a portion of your attention for a portion of time. You can really hold more than one thought in your head at anyone time, as if you could not, your heart would stop when you go to tie your shoe... luckily we have the human jaw upgrade that allowed more space in our heads. But where is the focus? Thought in the Sub Planck time is very quick, as in faster than light fast! 186 thousand miles per second, 670 million miles an hour~~~ Wait I thought that was a law... how come some neutrinos think they're above the law??? Do you have any ability to image the vastness of these numbers transposed over the mindspacetime that constitutes our universe, when light years and scientific notation are required to compute IT??? I multitask but often find myself rewinding the holographic reality tape to the spot where I left off one of the tasks @ to find the focal point where I return to the other. Most cannot adequately do this and spend their lives bouncing up and down the frequencies looking for that lost station of thought as they compete in demo mode in the multitask! Please do not think or feel you are inadequate to any task, as being even a minuscule oscillating energy wave of consciousness in the cosmos, you're capacity fulfills a unique part and a fundamental element, that combine to perfect the universal unity! Is your concerto rhythmically syncing with the cosmic vibe orchestra or are you in discordant concert with the devil! If you think Da devil would comes wearin some kinda costume and has horns you better recognize the real evil cameo disguised as someone or something you love and trust hiding devilishly in plain sight!!! Might even today be hostin some inspiration like camp meetin~~~ I'm guessin that some will call GET IT or UffDa "evil" but I come right out front so you can plainly see I choose not to BE deceived and recommend you too see freely!!! You either harmonize endearingly, receiving in return a proliferation of proceeding echoes of IT's agape love, or dissonantly, picking up disheartening idiotic disjointed bits and pieces of that same love un-attenuated by IT for you. So are you really the great multi-tasker or just basking in the thought? Again… Your choice!!!

Time we got into space or time or time and space or spacetime or maybe mindspacetime. "I got the Sun in the mournin and the moon at night!" Do you have any real current knowledge about our universe or are you stuck on the nine planets of our solar system or is it eight and a plutoid? Well whichever they eventually agree upon, they do seem to agree on one thing, we are here on Earth and everything else is out there… Hard to believe that 95% of what's out there, 22% Dark Matter 73% Dark Energy, is the energy and matter of nothing∞ that has not yet been determined as to what IT is, but inferred by the distortion IT incurs to the observed and does not interact with normal matter in a normal way but is the scaffolding that normal matter is bound by? British physicist Sir Arthur Eddington said "matter is mostly ghostly empty space" 99.9999 percent empty space, to be a little more precise. This dark space vacuum, that ethereally replaces the aether, that was proven to not exist, that in reality is not empty, nor made of nothing, seemingly continuously continues to expand the nothing yet the amount of measured density of dark energy per square meter remains the same! This dark matter may have IT self actually altered and distorted spacetime in the past in remarkable ways! In CERN they're attempting to chip off a particle piece of Higgs space field in search of Da Boson that has already been inferred confirmed~~~ Time, Space, and Matter were all created in the Big Bang Singularity that they currently peg at about 13.7 billion years ago and has been theorized to stand outside of both time and space thus transcending both. So how can IT be ascertained that this was in fact a beginning point? Maybe this ever-expanding universe fits on the head of a pin in some other… Like the billions and billions of stars that exceed in number all the grains of sand here on

LXXXIII

planet Earth! The creation apparently accelerates so IT is assumed to slow backward to a point where IT did not exist? Science knows absolutely nothing∞ about what caused IT or how without IT fine-tuned IT, yet eccentrically I unlike they, do include their deduced perceptions in my theory of IT mostly because IT is all-inclusive and is fundamentally what allows us all to have any thought at all! "They" do use the term cause, because all physics is causal to IT, the Singularity, the cause that has no cause! GOD!!! Aquinas put forward the cosmological argument that all phenomena have an efficient cause; nothing causes itself, and an infinite∞ regress of causes is impossible, therefore there must be a first efficient cause, which is God. This assertion also put forward by Plato, Aristotle, Descartes, and Locke. Many physicists deny the physical law associated with the M-theory of the Everything Big Bang Singularity, as accepting IT is the acceptance of the cause that has no cause and can no further be deductively reduced. GOD! Yet through theoretical invention of a temporal 4th dimension, described as like being unable to go south of the south pole, in boundless tricky time, like some hidden black hole of meaningless... physicists seem to need to toss out God as if IT threatens their reality. (Well I guess giving up any of their capacity to hypothetically scientifically test everything, which quantumly seems to be where they're @, may induce this rhetorical epicycle rational, even as their own theories include un-testable assumptions.) Through this removal of time at the singularity and by using the tightly interwoven laws of nature to define the grand design they theorize but deny their need for a designer of a spontaneous serendipitous miraculous determined structure that is inclusive of the Anthropic Principle, that states: that if any of those fundamental laws of nature were even slightly different even the universe would not exist! Probably just another coincidence... Lucky I guess... Maybe they are right... Maybe the universe is self-created and self-replicating and self-conceived... Maybe that's why they invented the multiverse, so the statistical truth of anthropic probability would not be so hard for the many agnostic physicists to explain improbable constant equations away??? Or maybe the universe is GOD!!! Well maybe??? The

LXXXIV

Penrose possibility of complex probability is so high that my computer does not have the ability to display the factorial!!! They just keep writing those expert books (like this one) LOL, written with expert theories, conceived by experts, confirmed by other experts about the 4% to 5% they see, actually the light spectrum frequencies they receive, decode, and then normatively translate into what they cogitate they are seeing as we really only perceive 1% of the light spectrum with our eyes... (Check out blindsight while we're here) Leaving little room for us non-experts to conceive a heaven clear of misty shroud! A mystic shroud tossed over any theory that includes IT, let alone concludes IT! Why then does this natural physical world appear to be so rationally design??? Why then do we rational people continue to turn toward this unseen for??? Why is there an ordered something rather than a disordered chaotic anything??? Especially given the second law of thermodynamics and the fact that entropy (S = K logW) always increases the chances for disorganization, as IT takes energy to organize or maintain organization and overcome entropy! Certainty of Gods probability is occluded by defacto contentious deniability of the multiplicity of rationed evidential support provided by numerous disciplines precursors that coalesce into a theory, that the metaphysical something rather than nothing brought the physical into existence! Why must I go on asking why when I know~~~ Oh yeah to know IT further~~~ Yeah even as IT was brought together by waves in space, accreting as IT cooled a randomness of so much beauty and careful design that each object was singular unto itself in how IT formed within IT's intention. Unique snowflakes united in the flurry. How cool is that! Your essence is unchanging your self is in a constant state of flux. If you were the artist that planned on creating the ultimate diorama would you replicate mechanically or generate perpetually? This is the fundamental perpetual motion system that self replicates, regenerates, and recycles over and over yet is always changing and increasing. Changing in IT's beauty and increasing the composition of the masterpiece! The downside to this is that in creating individual distinctive beings with freewill, some will will ill will if they so choose not to progress their un-rationed regressive nil will mentality! Science is great and I believe science has made fantastic discoveries both of material value as well as spiritual significance though usually presented as the absolute final experienced truth, which over history has been claimed and reclaimed only to be disclaimed by another absolute final claim to be further examined in Da future. Not a thing disproves my hypo theist claim of mental interaction at the Sub Planck level yet even sciences simple law of Parsimony is deniably unlawful some of the time, but is very useful in disavowing the unknown complex of possibilities that don't fit nicely into the latest greatest paradigm! Often the useful is not in the container but in what IT contains yet without the container IT would not be useful. Can you perceive new conceptions that experience brings? IT is mystical that we can experience anything at all. So why should so called mystical spirit filled experiences be so far fetched as to be un-experiential? All we experience, if regarded so, is a mystical magical moment amongst all others, with much greater range of, feelings, emotions, conditions, sensations as well as depth of meanings and outcomes or conclusions, than we allow association. When we regard them as anything less... that is when IT's conception becomes devalued! So why by classify do we disassociate our conceptual value contextually within the continuous mystical experience of IT? I do not expound that to participate in some mystic IT that you must bypass your normal cognition, deceive any of your senses, or imagine what's not (which your already doing). What I do expound is using your cognition to better sense IT in the mist of the altered state called reality, allowing the sensory input you sift to the back of your unconscious mind to provide renormalization of what we have been told is mythical postulation. We have various ways of distorting our views but consider few that simplify and clarify IT. We only seem to grasp as certain that which we are already certain of! Amazingly as the physicists simplify and clarify, they appear to be painting the same color by number singularity in which The Master Artist has left much hidden in composition for those that seek to find Waldo... Be careful in your seeking that you do not uncover any other devastating secret particles may behold:~: Well as long as we're out here let's go for a little spin around Alpha Centauri... do you

LXXXVI

know where Alpha is? Alpha Centauri is a special stellar system, because of proximity to us as the closest stellar system to the Sun...

Alpha Centauri from Wiki

Visible only from latitudes south of about 25° the star we call Alpha Centauri lies 4.35 light-years from the Sun. It is actually a triple star system. The two brightest components Alpha Centauri A and B form a binary. They orbit each other in 80 years with a mean separation of 23 astronomical units (1 astronomical unit = 1 AU = distance between the Sun and Earth). The third member of the system Alpha Centauri C lies 13,000 AU from A and B, or 400 times the distance between the Sun and Neptune. This is so far that it is not known whether Alpha Centauri C is really bound to A and B, or if it will have left the system in some million years. Alpha Centauri C lies measurably closer to us than the other two: It is only 4.22 light-years away, and it is the nearest individual star to the Sun. Because of this proximity, Alpha Centauri C is also called Proxima (Centauri). Proxima is so faint that astronomers did not discover it until 1915.

If our Sun were scaled down to the size of a period on a printed page then the distance to Alpha Centauri would be about 8 miles away. If the Earth were scaled to the size of a period on a printed page then the Sun would be a little smaller than a tennis ball at a distance 19 ft. On this scale, Alpha Centauri would be about 890 miles away. If the Sun were scaled to a 1-foot radius, then Alpha Centauri would be about 10,300 miles away. There are only 40 stars within 16 light years of the Earth! This alone is a vast amount of space and distance!

"When we stand in the dark and look at a star a hundred light years away, not only have the retarded light waves {forward in time} from the star been traveling for a hundred years to reach our eyes, but the advanced waves {backward in time} generated by absorption processes within our eyes have reached a hundred years into the past, completing the transaction that permitted the star to shine in our direction."

John G Cramer

IT's a pretty big place this space~~~ Again if you have not kept up... The new paradigm, implies a wholly quantum world, classical models of physics and computation are at best approximations to physical reality, and where quantum teleportation is a salient affirmation of the holistic nature of physical reality revealed by even macroscopic quantum processes proposed as intrinsic features in cosmology. The nature of which is reflective of a spiritually discerning mind, Halleluiah! This is all understandable at a seventh grade level so put on you're smarter than a seventh grader hat and Get IT **current.** Alpha Centauri was taught to me as the closest star and I don't want to lose you out in the Cosmos... That's what I named my dog in 1975, meaning (The Universe in its complete order) she was a great Golden Retriever that lived 17 years! Great dog! Oh Yeah... the Cosmos... Spinning around Alpha Centari... I have semi-jokingly referred to going out in my dreams for a spin around Alpha Centari every now and then during the last forty years... I was only semi-joking because people would have added me to their loony list, which you may if you need to, had they thought, I truly thought, I could take an Overview! I am not afraid of their list anymore nor am I afraid to admit I am not always able to leave my body... I do on occasion get out and about through meditation not medication!!! Although a little lubricant can make you ski better... I mean see better... Perhaps you may have envisioned what the view is like as you ride one of the suns photons out of the Milky Way looking back through time at our minuscule solar system, that rotates around every 250 million years, and thinking about how insignificant we must be yet we're purposefully entrained within unity in the universe. Imaging God's greatness expands yours and confirms interconnectedness. Just make sure your not bullsh!tting the bullsh!tter! We will go into Meditation vs. Medication in a while! Another silly consonant that plays across the universe with the ebb and tides of time... Back to Astral travel~~~ Do you need to do some homework here? Anyway... Through use of a yet undiscovered cause...way... probably based on sub-atomic tachyon

LXXXVIII

particles that interact at the Quantum level in any and all multidimensional *Brane* meta-multiverse… Thought… you are able to move outside yourself and into IT! What is IT? I do not have all the answers… or do I? As exampled by RV, not the kind you take on the road or maybe so. Remote Viewing is information present in our intended consciousness. Many astronauts have experienced the overview effect that makes them feel one with the universe, including Edgar Mitchell who has joined with others to initiate the Overview Institute to reflect the changing world! Memory entrains with the timeline that we have come to accept as our only reality based on our experience. For a moment make your intention a time and place in your childhood, do IT now~~~ Look, sense, and feel, be aware of your conscious experience, touch IT… You are consciously processing previously entangled resonant information about your direct experience as a child. You are the Remote Viewer and your entangled experience is the object. Immerse yourself in this observation experience… Adjust the volume… Is it an Imax or a black & white still… Alter the perspective… Are you focused on a macro or a micro view… Modify the field of projection… Is there a scent in the event… Are you omitting or including… Well this internal actuality is where you interpret all of reality, so remember that when your participating in the Now, that you are the controller of the interpretation and that you can adjust both your perception and your response to some point in the range from waste of space negative decay to creating living life positively prospectively! Always have an imaged wonderful recollected reflective beautiful protected favorite memory retreat that can simply be brought to remind anytime you need a break! Each time I ask a question I generate two or more when I discern the last! I will not have ALL the answers until I am no longer here in this body, on a permanent Astral Journey and then only if I have prepared properly and am open to IT… My vision of my future is much larger than anyone else I have ever discussed IT with or read about… We are all too self-limiting!!! Not me… I'm enjoying the ride and learning more each day so I hope I can stay and play for now! IT's never too late to find a new way to a different future yet the sooner the better. If you deem possibility as your done dream how then can you expand progressive unity with IT beyond?

Darn, I keep getting distracted… Oh no that's the way IT is written… Can you follow the plot? Is there a plot! Let's see a… plot… I got a plot of land and I do a lot of plotting… The best laid plans of mice and men… Oh yeah "Speeding through the universe… thinking is the best way to travel" literally!!! Try IT but hold on tight because you have to be able to come back! Back to the NOW! The ever changing now that most of us are bored with… Living continuously Tomorrow Lands dream or perpetuating only your eternal∞ past, stymies your dreamt for today!! Always wishing for a past enhanced remembrance or thinking the future is not today. Wishful thinking does help our succession, yet what IS, is attainment. What have you attained, not obtained, today? Well back to "REALITY"… that's a pretty spooky thing in itself and the reason so many try to escape IT by other means! Our universe continues to expand even though IT should not!!! The weak parsimony of anthropic multiplicity is a discounted possibility because of the extremely high odds of IT's improbability but the multiplicity of harmonic elementary numeric consistencies built into the design objectively collectively and otherwise inexplicably adds up to a physics calculated quantifiable constant cosmic conscious architecture~~~ Either that or somehow we managed to hit the biggest life given lotto in all eternity∞ through prospective predestined synchronicity… If the inflation of the universe diverges on either side of the critical divide and IT either expands faster or slower, then IT does not persist for the billions of years needed to coalesce to accrete create the small fluctuations in the uniform unity that produces complexity in the nothing∞ of the quantum vacuum with zero point motion, then there would be no US here to GET IT! Einstein's biggest blunder, the cosmological constant "lambda", was something, then nothing∞, then something again, or maybe the something is "The Nothing∞"!!! Now… What do you imagine light as? The nature of light as IT turns out, what is thought of as "light," is actually a propagating oscillatory disturbance in the electromagnetic field, i.e., an electromagnetic wave, both a particle and a wave~~~ Did you know we emit light?

Wave–particle duality From Wikipedia

In physics and chemistry, wave–particle duality is the concept that all matter exhibits both wave-like and particle-like properties. A central concept of quantum mechanics, duality addresses the inadequacy of classical concepts like "particle" and "wave" in fully describing the behavior of objects. Various interpretations of quantum mechanics attempt to explain this ostensible paradox.

The idea of duality is rooted in a debate over the nature of light and matter dating back to the 1600s, when Christiaan Huygens and Isaac Newton proposed competing theories of light. Through the work of Albert Einstein, Louis de Broglie and many others, current scientific theory holds that all particles also have a wave nature. This phenomenon has been verified for elementary particles as well as for compound particles like atoms and even molecules. In fact, according to traditional formulations of non-relativistic quantum mechanics, wave–particle duality applies to all objects, even macroscopic ones; we can't detect wave properties of macroscopic objects due to their small wavelengths.

Christiaan Huygens discovered synchronicity in the material world in 1665. He noticed that two pendulum clocks swung in synchronized coupled oscillations, even when he altered the rhythm, the clocks returned to IT. Yet we think of synchronicity as some sort of voodoo 350 years later. In the synchronicity of the Quantum mind we are that limitless, ocean-like awareness that knows each wave as a motion within itself, we are our own essential nature. The knowledge that duality is essentially unity means that the starting point and the end point are one and the same! As a lightwave life form you simultaneously coexistent as an individual wave and as a part of the collective unity. Perpetually cycling between being your elemental individual microcosmic wave and being intrinsically entangled with the undivided unity. The journey is actually what's experienced in the now as we awake in our consciousness provided by the Holographic Resonant sub Planck Zero Point Quantum Entanglement Potentiality Reality Physics which includes Photons that are intrinsically quantum objects and natural long-distance carriers of information. Information can be communicated via quantum entanglement from one place to another by photons and other quantum objects such as electrons, atoms, even molecules, transmitted over incredible distances and transferred instantaneously as in Quantum nonlocality *. Allowing for immediate, faster than light, signaling of our intentions and altering our perception as well as other biological processes information entangled therein... Information from our entangled consciousness is available always... Everything has resonance, coherence, a bond, and an order, that carries the infinite∞ history of IT... Importantly, this quantum entanglement and exchange of information comes out of nothing∞ and returns to nothing∞ in the Unified Zero-point energy Field. IT may be the unified scientific framework for explaining many paranormal and/or anomalous effects such as telepathy, telekinesis and homeopathy thus transforming these paranormal and anomalous effects into the domains of conventional sciences.

Since brain functions involve information, many experiments have shown that is physically real. Sub-atomic and electronics inside the brain play important roles in certain aspects of brain functions such as perception. Information exists both forward in time and backward in time through these resonance waves. We are both a particle and a wave simultaneously, we are receiving and sending and these particle-waves can interfere, with each other either constructively, in phase, or destructively, out of phase, and I propose a reasoned probability, that we can affect which! Your mind created IT and so your mind can change IT! You can teach an old dog, new tricks! The good news is the brain was designed to adapt and assimilate new info. Actually as an old dog you better learn new tricks or lose IT! Frequency amending takes regular practicing and like all skillful abilities you're learning to eliminate errors, so do not be surprised if your mending reverberates the wrong intention~~~ as practice makes improvement in increments based therein upon your desire to develop IT!

Your mind needs to be exercised just as your body does but your body provides the physical health and welfare for the brain, so work both! We are not all pent-athletes or physicists so adapt your abilities to expand them. Experience and environment shape our health. You need to emulate health as well as observe your surroundings... Is your homes environment nontoxic, do you read the labels on those cleaners, R U sifting particulate out of air and water, or is your house corrosive to your health??? Yet please do not obsess or over compensate with constant seditious self-health monitoring, as you are mostly as healthy as you feel and sense, rather than how much you worry and deliberate to debilitate. When viewing your life are you the writer, director or do you need to get a grip? Listen to your body as you would your favorite song. Knowing and enjoying each note and IT's harmonic resonance. Also sensing when IT is out of balance. Your physiology is effected domino like, as one cause creates another making IT intricate to trace IT back to the original cause of a physiological imbalance or illness. Sometimes you start treating a secondary cause, creating a third. People tend to focus on their illness not their resilience! With a little practice you will learn to retune IT! Think healthy coherent thoughts, be thankful for the nourishment you imbibe. Move through life in a healthful state. Your mind and heart are already always monitoring and modifying self, based on input received and perceptions of how successful were the results, so your worry and self doubt, detracts and distracts the health quality monitoring feedback loop already in IT. "Eat... Sleep... and be Merry" Take a moment or two to place yourself in a Non Localization Meditation, focus the resonance of a healthful you placing some care on the details that lie there...

Oh yeah... Space... that gray space between your ears... I find that IT is the true controller of time... and truth... Let me try this again... Oh I don't have to, I did IT right the first time... probably saved us a lot of time there... My mother always said, "If you have enough time to do it right the first time you don't need time to do it again!" This brings up the social truth that, anybody that say's "Let me be honest with you" or "The truth is" probably has not previously been being honest or truthful to you!!! Occasionally corrections to rumors or the gossip going round needs to be injected but generally speaking Truth flows freely from the heart and mind and anyone who has to interrupt that flow to stop and deliberate about what needs to be said or how to explain, is probably making part of IT up or changing IT to suit either himself or his perception of your reception. Truth is… true… Watch for the quick canned response as that maybe deception too. The little voice inside of each of us knows when we are being lied to or BS'd and we either choose to ignore IT, accept IT, or filter our reception and respond with our own reasoned self truth. I'm talking about the truth that lies within us all. The truth before we learned to tell "stories." There is powerful truth that can be exchanged through stories. Much of the power is in the telling, but I am directing you to the truth our ancestors lived. The truth that surrounds us all and we can either choose to live in IT or live without IT. Truth is that truth is. IT need not be defended.

Baggage, I left all those issues at the space terminal! The stuff you haul with and carry around as well as the relationships and the crutches you invent will not allow you to transit through to the positive. This baggage will not be lost by, the baggage handlers! Only you can lose those issues! Problem solution to resolution nah just complainin! Why??? Can't look for solutions, cause you'd have to find a new problem and any suggestions offered are wrong in someway so just keep listenin to the problem because resolution would not lead to a solution!!! You smart a$$ you… We will fight like heck to hold on to our miss-beliefs… We ourselves must admit that the things and paradigms; that have carried us to this point and are the basis of who we are; could be wrong! We live in denial rather than admitting to ourselves, that parts of who we are, is a lie, while thinking IT's to hard or late to change! We blame others, changing only our focal loci, and turn IT back on itself, yell, stomp, bitch, and attack! Do not attempt to change someone's worldview… as they will carry their baggage up Mt. Everest, through the ocean of life and over their dead body! Why should I change??? Why do I have to change??? Do not tell me you know any part of me better than I do while asking me to change… No thanks I will carry this stuff to death after having recycled this baggage over and over on every head-

XCIV

trip I take, then I'll attempt to haul Da crap to the hereafter even if I have to leave everything behind when I get there!!! Drop the baggage and you will feel a load lifted from your soul! Change is and if your lucky someone will ignore your protestations and personal attacks long enough to give you the love you need to adjust your cargo and eject your ego centeredness so as to lighten your load and start to convert your beliefs about both yourself and your subjective truths! On one side of your ocean of change you have open loving entrained relationships, on the other, one sided out of sync associations... do you truly seek to understand, interact, resolve, and sacrifice for others or is IT just a face you occasionally put on so people won't know who you really are? Tear down the titanic wall of change that is ostensibly holding back the ocean of fear that's drowning the possible you. The source must unilaterally attach them to me for heavens sake, as a reminder to be kind, given that I have had a series of one-sided associations... only syncing with themselves... I am too loyal... I am too forgiving... I was allowing them to take advantage of my compassion and suck my energy, while trying to please them, actually expecting something in return! I have lowered my expectations and now I AM not disappointed by these one-sided friendships that leave me standing at the alter of life wondering what I am doing wrong as I now see its not just me! I still open myself up to these associations, except now I expect nothing and am not disappointed or psychologically dependent on them. I recognize them as what they are! That does not let these people off the hook IT just lets me remain strong and positive when they continue to be self-absorbed or fail to hold up their end of the friendship. You attract what your attention is focused upon and intend. If someone, reciprocates, listens intently, offers their time, goes out of their way, and does IT consistently, you are very fortunate and better hold on to that relationship, as this is actually Agape friendship! This is a slippery slope~^~ as others can see in you what you blind your self to, while they also attempt to make changes in you that conform to them. If they continue to suck your energy... Un-friend them... Step away from the negative energy sucking vibe and the fricktatorship! Don't bring me down or warp Da positive vibe~~~ If

XCV

they keep you balanced and add to your and our positive vibe, reflect the love intently. We will all feel and appreciate IT!

Now where was I? Oh Yeah space and time… that space between your ears… IT's about time you used IT! Close your eyes for a second… "Hop aboard the dream weaver train"… how long were you gone from the outer world and how long were you in? This is where the relativity of time comes into play and your perception of IT can be relative… Our brain works on electrical impulses… anywhere from zero to hundreds of cycles per second… to make a long story longer… did you know that you can regulate and interact with these electrical impulses? We each have our own capacity to sense, induct, conduct, transduce, distribute and transmit these electrical impulses… R.E.M. is not just the name of a band… If we're talking bands that were weavin dreams, if I remember correctly, Pete Seeger singin Leadbelly's "Goodnight Irene Goodnight… Goodnight Irene… I'll see you in my dreams…" started the "Weavers" weavin, following in Joe Hills footsteps then covered "You load 16 Tons and what do you get another day older and deeper in debt, St. Peter don't Ya call me caus I cant go… I owe my soul to the company store!" and we started our reevaluation bout Workin for THE MAN (sharecropping from debtors prison), while in "This Land Is Your Land" Woody Guthrie and Pete started a movement with the help of the J edger's FBI who consigned Pete to play folk songs for the kids, after being blacklisted, the FBI thought that was harmless enough! Little did J edger know those kids would soon take to Da streets! J edger emulated Gestapo tackless and could easily have led Da Stasi… he maybe put us all on personality wise during his imposition inquisition!!! Marvin Gay asked, "What's goin on"… Oh distracted… So easily distracted… I really need to get your attention… I mean my attention… or maybe intention… Well anyway let's learn to adjust this attenuation… R.E.M. stands for Rapid Eye Movement part of a sleep cycle that includes the nourishing dreams of non-R.E.M… If you do not get to deep sleep or go through these cycles properly you have a sleep disorder that leads to many other disorders. "I understand you been runnin from the man that goes by the name of the Sandman" Caffeine, Drugs, Alcohol,

Stress, Worry, Sleep schedule deviation, TV, and Fear, are some of these dream disrupters. Unbeing sleep aids are addictive and just disr-uppers! Speaking of disrupters... LSD... Discovered by yet another Al... Yeah... This time Albert Hoffman, he passed today at age 102 4/30/08 as I synchronically was researching the effects that he discovered by accidentally absorbing IT! Licensed by Sandoz Laboratories as a drug with various psychiatric uses, LSD quickly became a therapeutic agent that appeared to show great promise. However, the extra-medicinal "off label" use of the drug in Western society during the 60's led to a political firestorm (you know how afraid the PC can be) that resulted in the banning of the substance even though IT's therapeutic properties remain, and delivered more than what was promised. LSD only brought out, enhanced, amplified, or increased what's already within you... several key components of LSD occur naturally in our brains and was created from a grain of rye. If you were paranoid IT would bring that out and expose the fear within, if you were happy IT would magnify IT and you would explore that happiness. You could control IT but you had to learn and know IT! I am not here to defend Acid, just attempting to elucidate your inclination of perception. Or are you an expert on IT! The sensory and energy pathways that I had never perceived before, along with ability to intensely focus and also the loss thereof and mindspacetime distortion or was IT??? The seemingly new means of knowing made the trip worth the ride but LSD is a little erratic in IT's disruption though... Mushrooms, Peyote, or Organic Mescaline, are much mellower... They disrupted a paradigm that was badly overbearing and that we are still living the flashback of, revealing the urbane veil of deceit by the controllers of the populace! All things have a turn in their time and with moderation... Anyway I was disrupted on my way to an analogy of the disruption of the vibe by one of the "Merry Pranksters", (The Electric Kool-Aid Acid Test written by Tom Wolfe) Neal Cassady kept the vibe by twirling a sledgehammer around and when IT needed to change or he sensed a change he changed the rhythm of the sledgehammer... ... ...

1/12/10 Profuse BAD NEWS FLASH*** Haiti horridly vibrated appallingly!!! And a couple a weeks ago A Swart nagger spermerator was chanting over the airwaves about we need water for California, and today another storm washed over, had he changed the vibe~~~ 3/11/11 now nuclear meltdown after another shake and wake??? There's a time for consensus building and there's a time for action, which lately seems to come with too little too late! Only the BAD NEWS seems to FLASH*** The earth shifted 4 inches and today only those effected remember~~~ How much fallout have we been exposed to and where will disaster strike next??? Will it affect you??? Will you remember... to duck... duck... or will your goose be cooked? Seems to be a really bad idea to build in these places where you know $hit is going to hit and I'm really getting tired of paying for their water view... With Sea levels rising~~~ get the heck away and above IT! Wonder why there is suburban flooding~~~ well~~~ We need to stop draining wetlands, rip out the levies, and let the beavers go back to work. There's enough bad news we need to stop creating more. I wonder what the half-life of stupidity is???

Well back to my flash talking I mean trash flaunting. The new bigotry is economy of the poor and ignorance franchising! Now I digress... as Superior judges open the corporate monetary floodgates to interpose political predatory vibe$$$ (Show me Da money), Corporations can't vote so why should they be able to buy them incestuously? If corporations are to be considered equal to individuals then the three strike law and the loss of other rights by felons should apply as well! Judges being financed for their ideological interests that corruptively eliminate our due process turning free speech into dollars that overrule rather than utils weighed equally! Judges in cahoots with politicos in cahoots with Corporate America have gerrymandered the system and the media reports what they have been told from the circular truth tabloid. Deflated dollars buying inflated commodities! Corporate takeover of Democracy! Oligarchy!!! Media mind manipulation exasperated as talking points that never get to the point! I suppose that if media outlets are beneficiaries of such a ruling that exploits objective truth in favor of their bottom line, they will expose or negate this dollar fueled hate state manipulate. ~~NOT~~!!! Now we were to have toned down the rhetoric so that we did not over stimulate the ignorant hate. What happened to that? Supposedly everyone should be entitled to his or her own equally legitimate opinion. Within this hypothesis even the village idiot's ideas need to be accepted as equally conceived reason. So thus we quietly bury truth amongst all the rabbles babbling, so that in any disagreement we must agree without enmity to disagree, thus we to a very certain point are directed to silently validate any claim no matter what the reality!!! Negative vibes replacing negative vibes, producing fear, whose nature is tricky to tame! We do need to turn some of the animosity into more positivity through acceptance of our agreement in IT. What is your corporate culture and how is IT's soul? Take care in how and where we abode and in whom we abide, as we thump out another surreal survival vibe~~~ In your consciously being aware, focus attention on what's affecting our vibe everywhere. Participating with voluntary relief interactivity provides and meditating prospectively proactively relieves… Lets see where was I before… disturbingly disrupted again… A shift in the force… The good old vibe distorted by new…

All brains are not equal. Some have chemical, biological, environmental, and accidental, interference… so please get medical attention, there is many a remedy… but for the others intentioning and imagining you are different so you can justify ignorant behavior because either you think your thinking is tainted and that we don't understand… or your thinking is tainted, and either way we do get you. Please GET IT together because you're tearing at the heart! And yet for others… If you want to get feel for this~~~ put a thorn in your shoe and walk a mile or two in their shoes and you may come across the log you stuck in to impede your own mind. My observations and insightations will try to focus more in Biofeedback, Meditation, and Spooky Entanglement rather than sleep cycles or psychedelics, they do entangle and overlap, but sleep on your own time because IT is primordial rejuvenation and trippin… well… will save that for some other book! If your mentally tired you can have your brain action potential reset their sodium & potassium ratios when the brain is in a Theta state

(Ride on… I mean Read on). The sodium & potassium levels are involved in an osmosis, which is the chemical process that transports chemicals into and out of your brain cells. After an extended period in the Beta (Awake) state the ratio between potassium and sodium is out of balance. This is the main cause of what is known as mental fatigue. Stimulus and our responses produce the chemicals that cloud our choices. A banana and brief period in Theta (about 5 - 15min) can restore the ratio to normal¿ resulting in mental refreshment. Find your pause button and use IT! If you're havin sleep issues get a sleepy Dr. to give you a Polysomnogram. So there's some lotsa homework… but take a nap first~~~ research R.E.M. and non R.E.M. on your own… follow and allow your own dreams… prospective processing and thinking forward~~~ practice by pretending intention as your mind cannot differentiate this envisioned thought reality from actuality… Tripping is no longer recommended, as you must watch out for the brown acid and smoking bananas really never was as spacey a turn on as eating them is!!! Like most of the drug myths~~~ Do you think that I could form a postulate or even reasonably fabricate, the suppositions I puzzlingly expound, had LSD, fried my brain, as in the propaganda you choose, true propaganda is perpetrated on those that defend a system even as that very system victimizes them… maybe Da acid has fried my mind and I don't mind or have one? But I'm done being a victim… Remember Albert Hoffman lived clearly to 102, will you?

I pose another question to you as well as a presupposition… How many mornings do you have in your life and how many of them did you want to sleep in? Lets explore the Holographic Resonant sub Planck Zero Point Quantum Entanglement Potentiality Reality of "Ba Da… Monday Monday" mourning! If everyone makes a giant groaning sound at the same time each Monday, or any mourning for that matter, and have this negative output from many brains into quantum reality what do you figure we are all potentially picking up and entangling first thing each day into all our unified reality? If TGIF is what you shoot for… well anytime is fine time to inject a little gratitude into the fact that now is a gift you will never have again! You can live the endless summer if you

C

perceive IT. Stop for a few minutes along this road to the way the day is going and check your level of fluidity for 20 minutes to ensure your happiness mechanism is working properly. Are you waiting for happiness to come, I will be happier if, when, because… Happiness does not come from getting what you're wanting, IT comes from wanting what you have! Once your basic needs and wants are met, chasing the, if I hada coulda shoulda or would I GET IT, keeps you waiting eternally∞ for happiness, satisfaction and fulfillment! Choosing to be grateful gives you the opportunity to experience the joy here in the now! Today was I here!!! Or just here… Why do polls show people are much happier with their professional public life than they are with their spirit less private life! Narcissism in Da me is multiplying astronomically, as those who believe mostly in Da me, supercedes Da we imperative hollowly!!! Today choose to be all those things you're thinking you're missing. Grateful prayer presents a present now that you will not ever have again. What do we miss when we're chasing the next flight out while rushing by what and whom tarry along the way to our destiny! Get on the slow down boat to nowhere and you will be amazed when you graze amongst lush substance while flowing soothingly down the river of life to your destination. Just a little mood for thought; Be ready for when you discard this shell of a body, at the end of this phase, as we move into a new kind of humanity. There are only transitions~~~ no death~~~ "and in the gray of the mourning my mind becomes confused between the dead and the sleeping and the road that I must choose"… Carpe Mortem! Seize death to live life. Confront what you fear of the inevitable, recognizing that a sense of priority, interest, and endeavor now will take you through then. Hard to ever get back those moments lived at minimum velocity as well as those that stream by at light speed! They are wonderful to have in your quiver of life… What's in your quiver? Back at the ranch… where'd I leave the ranch??? Oh yeah space and time between your ears… Your brain has waves~~~ these waves are at the forefront of Psychological and psychiatric research as well as dementia and Alzheimer's deterrence. The entrained entanglement of minds helps deter the amyloid fibulae nerve tangles. The

CI

information that follows may save your brain... least of all you may begin to understand what you're not using!

We spend exorbitant effort altering the environment surrounding us, in physique anxious awareness, on body maintenance and appearances, yet spending little time on the mind! Learning and discerning these wave functions and implementing their use is the future of brain styling and conditioning as well as proactive brain therapy! I just can't wait until they shove a chip up my butt so that when I lose my mind they can find my body! Be careful here folk's, get medical help immediately if you are finding yourself unusually depressed or riding extreme highs then lows, do not fear any stigma as this is your life. Make sure the treatment is not worse than the dilemma or just substancetution rather than solution. The Biochemistry changes in your physiology may be caused by your perceptions yet it is difficult to alter the chemical changes induced, leading to an imbalance, as you produced them you may reduce them, but doing so is multifaceted so include a good Physician. Many physical disorders go undiagnosed and the brain is a physical identity yet many are treating mind dysfunction as a brain disorder! Too many people go un-diagnosed, too many self-medicate, too many are miss diagnosed, while too many abuse use. The earlier the recognition the better the prognosis. Natural processes are seldom offered as solutions, rather they treat the symptoms, so beware of the☹ Psycho's in eulogy who are the new Candy man street dealers trading in legal drugs, the institutionalized instructor's recommending young mind sculpting, or formerciatrists that are promoting untested, unreliable methods, and A typical drugs, to enslave millions of us to the experiment! There are excellent options to put you back on track yet discernment here is a wavy line. A million children are now considered Bi-Polar, which formerly was known as "Manic Depression... searchin my soul". If you medicate for depression and you have Bi your feeding the monster. I must be Bi-Polar as one of the main symptoms is "Grandiose thoughts" and find IT difficult to stay in the positive at times. I am not any kind of an expert, so go find a good one as seeking help is half the solution. Just look out when choosing where to begin! If it quacks like a duck you better walk… Acknowledging or telling another is burden removing. Our friend Al Einstein would be given drugs today, as he was slow to learn the rote, thought grand thoughts and was rebellious in nature enabling him to block out the deterring status quo and nay Sayers. He was a fiddle player, understanding IT's resonance through IT as well as a seeker of God, which drove his search for the theory of everything. Al's brain was found to be different~~~ I use exercise, Binaural[1] sounds, along with meditative intention, to overcome depression! Audio with embedded binaural beats alters the electrochemical environment of the brain. This allows mind-consciousness to have different experiences. When the brain is entrained to lower frequencies and awareness is maintained, a unique state of consciousness emerges. This state is often referred to as hypnogogia or mind awake/body asleep. Slightly higher-frequency entrainment can lead to hyper suggestive states of consciousness. Still higher-frequency EEG states are associated with alert and focused mental activity needed for the optimal performance of many tasks. Perceived reality changes depending on the state of consciousness of the perceiver. Some states of consciousness provide limited views of reality, while others provide an expanded awareness of reality. For the most part, states of consciousness change in response to the ever-changing internal environment and surrounding stimulation. Not everyone is able to self-tune mental entrainment, so if ill seek help, seek IT carefully! Depression is a medical disease, try talk therapy before acceding to medication, talk by the way is often not covered by insurance but drugs are! If you've spent your life tripped out, some of these drugs may help you get back to where you once belonged but mostly IT's up to you to find your way back to IT. Psych I artists think there may actually be a few people left that still have brains that function normally but that the rest of us have some physiological brain defect, according to their standards. I'm pretty sure some of these defects are inherent and are there as individual opportunities to work within on shaping character, personality, and spirit. Building inner strength! Much illness institutes from either choosing to break Da program and lower the standards or express a malfunction of one or more sensory or genetic subsystems… We have the ability to initiate a workaround in many cases!!! Do not overtly ponder gloomily or burden your self with dejection as you may only have a mild temporary dysthymia. If you think IT's broken get help. The brain is a genetic overspecialization organ developed to a high degree to interpret our environment and evolving beyond our capacity to translate or control the information input! Every day stress turns into distress in a world that is over stimulating, isolating, frustrating, and satisfaction denying. How do you… handle everyday stress??? Stress in IT's basic form is the motivator of living… that can also incapacitate life!!! You ride stress to success or are driven by stress to distress! Social groups are being formed neuron-biologically in reaction to stress as neurons integrate antagonistic signals that control choice of social or solitary. Laughter is the best medicine as you can not hold on to stress while you use your sense of humor... or would that mean we have even another sense? NPR-1 maybe the genetic behavior gene transacting with RGM inter/motor neuron, determining whether you are an inward looking introvert or outward searching extrovert but more likely we are seeing ambiversion. This could mean help may be on the way for the Autistic. Autism is more than likely a mix of genetic switches thrown disruptively bio-socially epigenetically. Some research into this is leading towards a series of interactions triggering the DNA switches that are believed to be genetic predisposition. The anti immunization Dr. that was financially attached to the outcomes of the studies that proved to be bad data without any investigation should have to live an ill health state for recompense that left so many exposed without immunity. Give some of your attention to prayerful intention to solve this internal social emotional disorder… Back on the trail of stress… Mind science is leaping and bound to make great strides that will mend many brains, just please remember there is a difference between brain and mind and not all doctors are creative equally. I do not contend that thinking is a cure all alternative to any proven medical intervention for healing. IT is a pretty good preemptive preventative, as well as a mighty force to be conjunctively holistically imbued along with the best modern medicine has to offer! Just be astutely aware you may end up taking a drug to relieve yourself of anxiety and stress that your self is actually creating as only you yourself can change, not reiterate the state of mind that induced the frame of mind. Resulting in these chemical imbalances. The drugs are supposed to be temporary! Giving you a peaceful time to discern a restorative mind. Laughter is truly the best medicine. Laugh a little… Laugh a lot… Laughter stimulates you both mentally and physically so exercise your laughter often! Anxiety and stress are tools in the quiver of the mind not to be left stuck closed in the ever-draining shorted power position but turned on and off as needed to conserve IT's energy for future use. Like all tools there is a learning curve in wise use and you must stay up with the practical practices in their use! You know, I learned how to use a hammer once… but now seem to bend a nail or two when I go to whack IT.

30%

Antimatter… positrons… The P in PET scans. Anti-matter is being used for wonderful images of our blood flow in brain research… The machines themselves are a form of chemically based computer entangled interactive design. Biological evolved engineered solutions demonstrate, that the senses are a chemical simulation of physical reality. Learning, filtering, adaptation, communication, information input/output, and memory are physical signals in the form of energy, physical dynamics, which quantum holography prescribes, enabling optimal efficient processing cognition by allowing reengineering up, sideways, down… or down, sideways, up whichever order the pieces fit. Although now sometimes the pieces are being reassembled experiMentally to anti medicate preemptively based on MRI's, fMRI, and PET scans, some good some not so. The Neopulse® and Neostar® wand pulses interference into your brain (Transference Magnetic S) treating depression and pain and alter RTPJ your moral judgment center. The latest and greatest is MEG whole brain imaging using SQUID superconducting quantum interference device~~~ which appears to be a little more holistic. Because while they're looking at a slice of where your neuron lightning or blood is flowing they think their knowing is knowing your knowing, but the brain ITself is multidimensional and full of independent subsystems, of which some are derisively demented yet having input to a variety of complex independent systems composing the whole that work best when Der waves are in sync, making their mapping an elucidated guess at best! Trying to best guess your syndrome based on studies, surreptitiously funded and ghost author planted by the pharmaceutical companies, is unholy! Look for something a tad more biofidelic! They like to use the term "may" connected up with an unknown probability factor to lead you to believe all sorts of weaseling things. Drug literature has become propaganda. Sugar pills are as effective as many anti-depressants dispersed! Not in all cases but is IT yours? Those who believe the pills work have much higher statistically proven results than those who don't. Included in all of these studies is a little test, called the Placebo Effect... That means the treatment or medication must have a discernibly higher statistical success rate than doing nothing∞ or putting a little mystical sugar in IT! This is not only in your mind... as your brain can both manufacture chemicals to help change your physiology and modify your psychology!!! ~~~Now~~~ You find Brain Messer's at your local strip mall ready to speculate what "one pill makes you larger and one pill makes you small... the ones that mother gives you don't do anything at all". Selling us hopes and dreams. Selling you what you wish or what you wish you could do or be! Coming soon to a store near you... How do I stop the madness??? Well start off by not being so mad~~~ Might just want to question the efficacy of Genetic mind sculpting!!! Looking for happiness??? Do you really know what comprises your happiness or what you think makes you joyful? How can they know when you don't? The assumption is your brain is ill! This speculative symptomatic systematic syndrome serendipity is a crime and equates to lobotomies from our past! Keep conflicting info from getting to Da bottom of IT! Keep modifying Da context of IT so IT cannot be defined? We just wanted and still want an easy way out of the hard reality surrounding us and created by us rather than to use compassion or therapy to work with these

CVI

minds that have been wounded or traumatized in some way by one or more experiences! We entropy to our easy! Lobotomies took care of some problems but we're flattening personalities to the point of zombieism and considered to infringe upon persons civil liberties so they switched to psychotropics, which only infringe on the people that have to deal with all these drugged people! Our prisons replaced our mental institutions and with no truth in sentencing and seeing how the warehouse is full, we're moving our inventory to a street near you... The old news is... many have mental issues but are just being processed through not progressed too recover from what is often a biological chemical disorder and with biofeedback many could be social conformed reformed! Then the recidivism and the slidin could truly be up to them and when default mode is once again the marginally biologically chemically imbalanced insane then the scapegoat quote "he or she is not responsible for his or her actions" because they have a brain defect no longer will cut Da crap! Most people would chose to seek enjoyment security if given the choice but the insto reward gotta gratify now system overrides the prefrontal reasonable social accountable! Many times we need to develop new skills not new pills. IT is the only thing that comes close to a miracle cure... Any medical course of treatment should have repeatable peer reviewed quantifiable results determined in multiple controlled blind randomized clinical scientific studies and without anomalous negative side effects that under mind IT's therapeutic value. The statistical tracking of those predestined to continue backtracking based on biologic brain activation patterns is here today we're just not enacting IT. In intervening years convicts may be able to choose between a little time~~~ reshaping their unsocial prefrontal through sublime mind interactive imaging or living the continuum of crime, then more time, if their minds are of the kind unopen to modification modulation, like da clockwork orange unminding criminals into citizens reversion! All are not capable nor desiring to become useful law abiding citizens and this is why we build prisons, not to house those with a broken unconsidered risk to instantly reward mentality! The way we are being and the way we're modeling our children they better make lots of space because "I got to have mine now"... We are not all created equally (great words but with little truth) nor have our neural connections followed the same conduits to intuit and current law acknowledges this somewhat... only the define line does not zig or zag with the individual~~~ the law draws the line in the sand between adult and child @ 17 or imbecile too wise man based on how he took what test that day. The new good news is we can choose to enter into a neural biofeedback loop with ourselves and reorder some of what impedes others and us!!!

Preschoolers who experience multiple traumatic events are more likely to have attention problems and much more likely to be overly emotionally reactive and/or to show signs of depression and anxiety, than children who had not had such experiences. These children are not hyperactive, but hyper-vigilant because they are looking for dangers or threats. Hyper-vigilance can look like hyperactivity or inattentiveness in school because these children are paying attention to "distractions" like the teacher's face or another child's movements, not their schoolwork. They are in protection mode! Children suffering trauma symptoms actually have higher than normal levels of neurotransmitters that are raised even further by stimulants: like Ritalin and Adderall, the brain cognitive enhancers of choice that high-functioning, overcommitted people take to become "higher" functioning and more overcommitted. Sleep becomes a secondary inaccessible reprehensible waste of now! Beginning a detritus spiral of sleep deprivation and neural short circuit misfire flickering~;~'~. We all experience some traumatic events and emotions that become stuck to us and we in them. The mind may become stuck in the time that becomes your paradigm. This life of the past keeps you from fully living the now. Sticking your self to any injured past is a lonely and repetitive time... Do you rise and fall with the news, like a riptide? Do you emphatically ride the Dow or Tao, Colbert or Da Bears with your fortunes as theirs? Are you symtomizing medical ads "ask your doctor if _____ is right for you" or personalizing work related hearsay "he said she said" like the chaos intended? Do you consider Springer, Stern, or Maury for real??? What wave~~~ are you riding? Do you think in words, pictures, concepts, feelings, sounds, smells, or any combination thereof? Brainwave electrical wave cycles have names, and there is going to be a test, so as I now get a little technical, please read carefully. The test is open book so do not worry... or disrupt your brain waves~~~ take a deep breath...

Brainwaves from Wiki for those of you that haven't been hyper clicking~~~

Brainwaves are commonly detected by (EEG). Electroencephalography is the measurement of electrical activity produced by the brain as recorded from electrodes placed on the scalp. Just as the activity in a computer can be perceived on multiple different levels, from the activity of individual transistors to the function of applications, so can the electrical activity of the brain be described on relatively small to relatively large scales. At one end are action potentials (An action potential is a "spike" of positive and negative ionic discharge that travels along the membrane of a cell. Action potentials are an essential feature of animal life, rapidly carrying information within and between tissues. They also occur in plants. Action potentials can be created by many types of cells and are used most extensively by the nervous system for communication between neurons and for transmitting information from neurons to other body tissues such as muscles and glands. A single axon (An axon or nerve fiber, is a long, slender projection of a nerve cell, or neuron, that conducts electrical impulses away from the neuron's cell body or soma) or currents within a single dendrite (Dendrites (from Greek dendron, "tree") are the branched projections of a neuron that act to conduct the electrical stimulation received from other neural cells to the cell body, or soma, of the neuron from which the dendrites project. Electrical stimulation is transmitted onto dendrites by upstream neurons via synapses, which are located at various points throughout the dendritic arbor. Dendrites play a critical role in integrating these synaptic inputs and in determining the extent to which action potentials are produced by the neuron.), and at the other end is the activity measured by the scalp EEG.

The data measured by the scalp EEG are used for clinical, research purposes as well as providing you the ability to receive feedback of your mind state. A technique similar to the EEG is intra-cranial EEG (icEEG), also referred to as subdural EEG (sdEEG) and electrocorticography (ECoG). These terms refer to the recording of activity from the surface of the brain (rather than the scalp). Because of the filtering characteristics of the skull and scalp, icEEG activity has a much higher spatial resolution than surface EEG. Or magnetoencephalography (MEG)

The waves are currently broken into five segments of Brain Wave Frequencies:

DELTA (less than 4 Hz)

THETA (4-8 Hz)

ALPHA (8-12 Hz)

BETA (13-30Hz)

GAMMA greater than 30(Hz)

The lowest frequencies are delta. These are less than 4 Hz and occur in deep sleep and in some abnormal processes also during experiences of "empathy state". Delta waves are involved with our ability to integrate and let go. It reflects unconscious mind. It is the dominant rhythm in infants up to one year of age and it is present in stages 3 and 4 of sleep. It tends to be the highest in amplitude and the slowest waves. We increase Delta waves in order to decrease our awareness of the physical world. We also access information in our unconscious mind through Delta. Peak performers decrease Delta waves when high focus and peak performance are required. However, most individuals diagnosed with Attention Deficit Hyperactivity Disorder are children, they naturally increase rather than decrease Delta activity when trying to focus. The inappropriate Delta response often severely restricts the ability to focus and maintain attention. It is as if the brain is locked into a perpetual drowsy state.

Side trip~~~((Sorta like me without coffee in Da mournin :~{ Didn't take me long to interrupt! Well just for a moment while we get our brains around IT~~~) Our brains entrain (sync the waves) and sometimes our minds get stuck either in a different cycle or unable to sync at all! Lots of disorders account for this including faulty sleep. This syncing neural entrainment is natural and allows higher cognitive interactive response. So even though IT may seem like nothing∞ the space in which this partakes is

neurofeedback linked to entrain the brain and you can expand the amplitude through frequent neural frequency training. Holding on to nothing∞ is quite slippery at first as how do you know if you're holding IT? Relax~~~ that's all IT takes to reach this state~~~ I said IT comes naturally. But we do a lot of drifting and distracting and you know~~~ just like me ☺ probably better... why you're not in tune with IT already!!! Well surfs up let's go ride some waves...))

Back to Delta~~~

Delta:

Distribution: generally broad or diffused may be bilateral, widespread

Subjective feeling states: deep, dreamless sleep, non-REM sleep, trance, unconscious

Associated tasks & behaviors: lethargic, not moving, not attentive

Physiological correlates: not moving, low-level of arousal

Effects of training: can induce drowsiness, trance, deeply relaxed states

Theta 4-8 Hz (cycles per second)

The next brainwave is theta. Theta activity has a frequency of 3.5 to 7.5 Hz and is classed as "slow" activity. It is seen in connection with creativity, intuition, daydreaming, and fantasizing and is a repository for memories, emotions, and sensations. Theta waves are strong during internal focus, meditation, prayer, and spiritual awareness. It reflects the state between wakefulness and sleep. Relates to subconscious. It is abnormal in awake adults but is perfectly normal in children up to 13 years old. It is also normal during sleep. Theta is believed to reflect activity from the limbic system and hippocampal regions. Theta is observed in anxiety, behavioral activation and behavioral inhibition.

When the theta rhythm appears to function normally it mediates and/or promotes adaptive, complex behaviors such as learning and memory. Under unusual emotional circumstances, such as stress or disease states, there may be an imbalance of three major transmitter systems, which results in aberrant behavior.

Distribution: usually regional, may involve many lobes, can be lateralized or diffuse;

Subjective feeling states: intuitive, creative, recall, fantasy, imagery, creative, dreamlike, switching thoughts, drowsy; "oneness", "knowing"
Associated tasks & behaviors: creative, intuitive; but may also be distracted, unfocused

Physiological correlates: healing, integration of mind/body
Effects of Training: if enhanced, can induce drifting, trance-like state. If suppressed, can improve concentration, ability to focus attention

Alpha 8-12 Hz (cycles per second)
Alpha waves are those between 7.5 and 13(Hz). Alpha waves will peak around 10Hz. Good healthy alpha production promotes mental resourcefulness, aids in the ability to mentally coordinate, and enhances overall sense of relaxation and fatigue. In this state you can move quickly and efficiently to accomplish whatever task is at hand. When Alpha predominates most people feel at ease and calm. Alpha appears to bridge the conscious to the subconscious. It is the major rhythm seen in normal relaxed adults - it is present during most of life especially beyond the thirteenth year when it dominates the resting tracing. Alpha rhythms are reported to be derived from the white matter of the brain. The white matter can be considered the part of the brain that connects all parts with each other. Alpha is a common state for the brain and occurs whenever a

person is alert (it is a marker for alertness and sleep), but not actively processing information. They are strongest over the occipital (back of the head) cortex and also over frontal cortex.

Alpha has been linked to extroversion (introverts show less), creativity (creative subjects show alpha when listening and coming to a solution for creative problems), and mental work. When your alpha is with in normal ranges we tend to also experience good moods, see the world more truly, and have a sense of calmness. Alpha is one of the brain's most important frequency to learn and use information taught in the classroom and on the job.

Alpha-Theta training can create an increase in sensation, abstract thinking and self-control. You can increase alpha by closing your eyes or deep breathing or decrease alpha by thinking or calculating.

Distribution: regional, usually involves entire lobe; strong occipital w/eyes closed

Subjective feeling states: relaxed, not agitated, but not drowsy; tranquil, conscious

Associated tasks & behaviors: meditation, no action

Physiological correlates: relaxed, healing

Effects of Training: can produce relaxation

Sub band low alpha: 8-10: inner-awareness of self, mind/body integration, balance

Sub band high alpha: 10-12: centering, healing, mind/body connection

Beta above 12 Hz (cycles per second)

Beta activity is 'fast' activity. It has a frequency of 14 and greater Hz. It reflects desynchronized active brain tissue. It is usually seen on both sides in symmetrical distribution and is most evident frontally. It may be absent or reduced in areas of cortical damage. It is generally regarded as a normal rhythm and is the dominant rhythm in those who are alert or anxious or who have their eyes open. It is the state that most of brain is in when we have our eyes open and are listening and thinking during analytical problem solving, judgment, decision making, processing information about the world around us.

The beta band has a relatively large range, and has been divided into low, midrange and high.

Low Beta (12-15 Hz), formerly "SMR":

Distribution: localized by side and by lobe (frontal, occipital, etc)

Subjective feeling states: relaxed yet focused, integrated

Associated tasks & behaviors: low SMR can reflect "ADD", lack of focused attention

Physiological correlates: is inhibited by motion; restraining body may increase SMR

Effects of Training: increasing SMR can produce relaxed focus, improved attentive abilities,

Midrange Beta (15-18 Hz)

Distribution: localized, over various areas. May be focused on one electrode.

Subjective feeling states: thinking, aware of self & surroundings

Associated tasks & behaviors: mental activity

Physiological correlates: alert, active, but not agitated

Effects of Training: can increase mental ability, focus, alertness, IQ

High Beta (above 18 Hz):

Distribution: localized, may be very focused.

Subjective feeling states: alertness, agitation

Associated tasks & behaviors: mental activity, e.g. math, planning, etc.

Physiological correlates: general activation of mind & body functions.

Effects of Training: can induce alertness, but may also produce agitation, etc.

<u>Gamma</u> above 36 Hz (cycles per second)

Gamma is measured between 36 – 44 (Hz) and is the only frequency group found in every part of the brain. When the brain needs to simultaneously process information from different areas, its hypothesized that the 40Hz activity consolidates the required areas for simultaneous processing. A good memory is associated with well-regulated and efficient 40Hz activity, whereas a 40Hz deficiency creates learning disabilities.

<u>Gamma</u> (40 Hz):

Distribution: very localized

Subjective feeling states: thinking; integrated thoughts

Associated tasks & behaviors: high-level information processing, "binding"

Physiological correlates: associated with information-rich task processing

Effects of Training: not known

End of Wiki Ref: Back to trying to follow Da forever wavy UffDa~~~

This is just some of the info on the brainwaves~~ I do not agree with all the stated effects or uses and there is much much more but it is a start and I am not one of the current authorities on neuralfeedback so seek more and IT will be yours.

Their publicized progression to mind meld interaction, includes <u>DARPA</u> robotic arms manipulated through thought and also <u>BrainGate</u> mental interaction by paralyzed participants with computers as well as a little understood Low-Energy <u>Neurofeedback</u> System (LENS) that may be the miracle we need to GET IT. The unpublic mind contravention remains unpublicized??? Much is still to be learned and being learned each day, new research is being conducted on multiple applications and uses including the dreaded <u>mind control</u>! From my observations most people are not in control of their own minds so maybe that research has already been successfully implemented!!! For this discussion I focus on Alpha and Theta to intuIT IT to you… Not the Alpha ness we're always trying to excerpt and exhort over others?!*… With practice and acceptance you may then one day synchronize to the high Gamma bursts of insight~~~ We are having a discussion??? Because I hope your thoughts are interacting with mine as you read this! Anyway… Bear with all my Wikipedia excerpts as; some may know what other don't and others know what others know don't, I like the Wiki open construct I do not always agree with all Wiki'ans but you may submit your differences for disambiguation, WIKI works well for most further descriptive information and defining more adeptly what you may already think you know! (I'm feelin a high Gamma burst so watch out for the matter) If you hyperlinked out through them all this is probably one of the Wikiist wordiest books this world has ever beamed!!! Just like Marconi's waves~~~ this book is now bouncing around Da Universe~~~ as IT has been wirelessly transmitted, transmuting some of you~~~

Another different form of Wiki… Leaks the truth while being accused of endangering Americans because of making known the truth that our government is actually surreptitiously lying, endangering, and hiding truth from US! If you bring up their troubles you will be stigmatized as gender issued or some other issue people can quickly label as defective to explain away why someone would do something like expose Da truth!!! Like Da Deep Throat dat leaked Da Pentagon papers, equating him to a porno Deep Throat, when he leaked unwashed truth about Vietnam, thereby awakening even conservative understanding of how US in the fog of war is run or the NASA report by the Brookings Institute that recommends; that for fear of social disorder NASA should consider not telling the American people if evidence of extraterrestrial intelligence is discovered! And just when did communicable disease become top secret, as in how much we the people should be allowed to know about the bird flu epidemic? If they need some social disorder to fear… how about when the people figure out they been being A TAXED like dey being social without Da amenity benefits of a social society while Da elite live on easy street and ain't to awful socio-economic crisscross sociable. "I'm alright Jack keep your hands off a my stash!" Now there must be some kind a trouble with me but "I ain't lookin for no trouble now" yet I'm sure they'll find some for me!!! But… I'm pretty sure I'm coming out with all my everything crap I got in GET IT so what do I have to fear… well they got plenty of inventive to pick from~~~

The WIKI Leaks documents and communiqué's reveal enough to embarrass slick Willy's wife again… because of more hiding of Da truth and them consequences that in part contributed too Da Tunisians starting the Arab spring with Mubarak's overthrow! "YEAH!" maybe??? Yet more people are dying at the hands of armed thugs who are still in over control mode! The citizens continue to seek freedom from obtrusive suppressive governing! How much is suppressed from US? We can help just by giving IT our attention… Evil does not like light shined IT's way… Remind me again… how that is a bad thing??? Well the dynamics of the Middle East is rooted in the Babel of religious rhetoric dipped in oil to make IT easier for US to swallow. The Arab kingdoms Dis serve the Palestinians as their token wedge between their money, authority, military power, and their subjects! Peace is not in their interest… There are Dis Placed populations of many nations including Jews encircling the globe, yet Da UN protects only Palestinians in perpetuity and of those chosen few DPP's are part of the miniscule (1%) indigenous population of post 1948 Palestine. Like all things in the Middle East the facts are covered with a shroud then entombed!!! How far back can you go backward to remediate Dis Placement, as mostly Muslimism expansionism displaced many North Africans along with a huge chunk of the native Middle Easterner's, like Kurds and the Kalash, then add in those most permanently relocated through annihilation like the Armenians through genocide! More inhumanity insanity in the name of trueΩ religion!!! Anyway… Will this spring uprising turn into a summer of love or a Moslem winter... like ours later ended in Da Chitown Demoncratic convention of Da baton swinging terrorist pigs and Kent State? Both later blue ribboned as fine examples of police riots! How many have died previously because of US lies!!! Seems there are more and more unhappy campers around Da world of

CXVII

every mindless state of all kinds of <u>uneconomic systems</u> that are being unkindly treated, misrepresented, or just mindlessly screwed... Protest Dis Protest Dat Protest Da Protest... One story is released publicly, another privately, then another surreptitiously, another slyly, and yet another filed, then the truth is orally exchanged covertly never to be recorded so that IT's truth one day never comes into the Sunshine of a <u>Freedom Of Information</u> request! Only available on a <u>need to know</u> basis and your not knowing is their needed! No one knows the width, depth, or breadth of our <u>clandestine companies</u> and spooky elite, nor who's purposes they're there to endow! The Worlds Dictators have hired Madison Avenue to spin their images of deception! Demonizing Da Snow den, labeling chicken for not coming home to be roasted by un-constituted court. 21st century patriot now communing in Siberia!!! Some <u>leeks</u> are better than others, some even fight Cancer. If our government chose a straighter stronger course, they like the Toxics[2], would not need to fear the truth!!! Even Leaks get corrupted when dictatorial supercedes editorial, so now as luck would have IT we have <u>OpenLeaks</u>... Just can't stop IT's truth from leaking out!!! Keep protesting~~~ but start changing the spot that you exist in to reflect the world you want to be in!!! Well back to brain cleansing... I mean lensing... No... now that I think of IT my brain could use a good washing to GET IT back to where IT once belonged~~~ Not quite like in 50 year old <u>Cuckoo's Nest</u>...

<u>Alpha Wave</u> From Wikipedia

Alpha waves are electromagnetic oscillations in the frequency range of 8–12 Hz arising from synchronous and coherent (in phase / constructive) electrical activity of thalamic pacemaker cells in the human brain. They are also called Berger's wave in memory of the founder of EEG. (Blazier 1970) Alpha waves are one type and predominantly found to originate from the optical lobe during periods of relaxation, with eyes closed while still awake. Conversely alpha waves are attenuated with open eyes as well as by drowsiness and sleep. They are thought to represent the activity of the visual cortex in an idle state.

An alpha-like normal variant called mu (Ụ) is sometimes seen over the motor cortex

(central scalp) and attenuates with movement, or even with the intention to move.

For Example: Our brain uses 13Hz (high alpha or low beta) for "active" intelligence. Often we find individuals who exhibit learning disabilities and attention problems having a deficiency of 13Hz activity in certain brain regions that affects the ability to easily perform sequencing tasks and math calculations.

Did you Get IT through all that??? LOL! It needed to be done, read, and digested to give you a reference point as well as a believability factor to my thought. Now we are going to be able to play around with the possibilities this allows for~~~ which are infinite∞… I by no means am any kind of an expert in anything… except maybe meditatin and drinkin! And I don't drink as much anymore because spread out over forevermore I just drink less… although in moderate amounts beer and wine enhance bone density, promote heart health, reduces stress, and may ward off Dementia but good sleep may escape you, which alcoholics never get because they just pass out brain dead for a while… OH!!! Da blackout blank spaces _____ Now Where was I??? Hey all you irresponsible drunk mnfr's… you know who and what you are… stop degrading my reputation and including me in the laws you cause because you choose to be an Ignorant Sick Drunk mnfr and blame IT instead of your Toxic behavior, not Da liquor… Well "Excuse me…" again and again and again~~~ no drinkin is just another one of your excuses to hide your true actions under the breath of deception well excuse me as I'm not drunk I'm just drinkin… and IT is my responsibility to be responsible! Take care of your problems… Stay off the road… Eat right… Provide your body and mind with IT's needs and then Enjoy because there is little enjoyment in the slow death spiral, ill's, and all of life's spills that result from thinkin drinkin will bring enjoyment to a broken mind… If you can't moderate and you know you can't, or you been told you can't by more than a few, that you can't even have a few. then you got to stop

CXIX

cold! Hey den how did I get to this meditate too much state~~~ How, you may ask, can one "meditate too much"? Well you stop interacting with everyday reality and may start Psychosis, which is another form of avoidance! There is anecdotal data that meditation can cause some people to experience psychotic episodes, particularly in those with a history of psychological illness, or those who participate in long meditation seminars with little prior meditation experience. ("Well that explains a few things for me~~~ Thanks for telling me now!!!☺") Although cutting ones self off from the world occasionally, cleanses the mind of the constant intrusion and removes the debris from your perception filters. You need to live in the world, not existing conceptually in a dream! I have eternity∞ to contemplate but only moments to live! My cousin, the one I started this senses mental journey with, chose medication, anti this and anti that and just kept on drinkin earasin thinkin. He anteed up his life. He has had six DUI's and an equal amount of rehab stints and now his innards are shot and his outlook is dim. At the waterhole of life you have the drinkers dilemma... Animals face thirst or possible death from predators where they need to drink, while people face predatory death from their thirst for what they think they need to drink. So I do perceive that most of you have little knowledge of or understanding of some of the most important information a person can assimilate as even those that have had opportunity to, get lost! He is part of the reason I am writing this. When part of you is lost you search for IT. I'm trying to Get IT through coherently using common terms for common people to a common thought...

Big Brother and the Dow Holding Company want to keep you stupid! So hang in there and on because you are about to raise your IQ, Moral Standards, People Interaction, Compassion, and Love of LIFE amongst an array of other things... All Good! unless **you**... CHOOSE evil ☹. Is there evil? A fallen Angel? You may call him Lucifer (He's in need of much restraint)? Is there a Prince of Darkness or Beelzebub? Is darkness the absence of light or is lightness the absence of dark? The negative!!! Where the H..E... double hockey sticks was I?

Oh Yeah... the light brain waves in space... that space between your ears...
Read this techno bulletin and we can continue...

<u>Mirror Neuron</u> Defined Wiki

A mirror neuron is a pre-motor neuron, which fires both when an animal acts
and when the animal observes the same action performed by another (especially
conspecific (same species)) animal. Thus, the neuron "mirrors" the behavior of
another animal, as though the observer were itself acting. These neurons have
been directly observed in primates, and are believed to exist in humans and in
some birds. In humans, brain activity consistent with mirror neurons has been
found in the pre-motor cortex and the inferior parietal cortex. Some scientists
consider mirror neurons one of the most important findings of neuroscience in
the last decade.

The Doctor is in with <u>E-gor</u>... **Dr. Cadaverino, Dr. Paul Bearer, <u>Dr.
Sardonicus</u>, <u>Dr. Demento</u>, <u>Dr. Jive</u>, and <u>DR. ATOMIC</u>** who are??? For those
of you who do not know who I'm referencing, try this thing called... Google... I
know... everybody knows... Google!!! But how many of you actually know
how to use IT? <u>http://www.learnwebskills.com/search/google.html</u>
<u>http://www.googleguide.com/</u> May save you some more time and trouble...
Aey! Da <u>Panda ranking</u> inconvenient <u>Al-Gore-ithm</u> and elimination of some
<u>LISTSERV</u>'s is aggravating my old <u>aggregating</u>! Better check your results and
look beyond the first page for your truth as some of the first should be last and
some on page 2, 3, or 4 are more of actually what your looking for not what
Google thinks you'd like to see... Anyway I'm not exactly sure when I stepped
out... I'm back in... I guess I'm back but whether I'm in or out is yet to be
determined...

Did you get the part about the neuron "mirrors," the behavior of another animal,
as though the observer were itself acting!!! Could this lead to <u>compassion</u>?
Why would our thoughts interact to include the behavior of an animal other than
ourselves? Why then do many behave <u>altruistically</u> only when they think they
are being observed (your being is always observed) or when they risk being

CXXI

caught cheating in their scheming and may be exposed (we do know)? One great question is what do you do when you think no one is watching??? I'm pretty sure I cannot answer these questions… Except for my own self that is!!! I certainly see permutations of possible ramifications and implications from the cerebral intra-inter-communication. Our motor systems have output as well as input beyond biomimicry and the negative may shine as surely as the positive so be sure to check what you're reflecting. As children we want to do what's right… we share… we care… volunteer to help… and we are willing to go out of our way to do IT and enjoy IT!!! We're trusting, honest, and choose not to cheat… then we become self aware and the opposite negative responses are then un-cultured into our views!!! "Through the eyes of a child you will see~~~" The eye is a direct connection and reflection by nerve to our mind and open door way to the soul. The view for some is not quite as clear looking in as IT is when perceiving out yet for others IT's inverted perception is harder to recon than the light lensing leaded stained glass our souls enfold as IT is a swinging door in as well as a window out!!! The minds eye is a multidimensional linkage of spiritual interrelation to all souls! So keep a sharp eye out for what kind of minds you may chance upon. I hope your stopping along the way to smell the possibilities… this is about coherent thought by the by…

Again if you are in search of the Holy Grail to your mind, IT is here! You must apply that mind and search in your own for IT! Monty Python spoofed the English with crass but another English show, Dr. Who, was a head with class… The Dr. and his usually lovely companion slid through time and space inside the Tardis (**T**ime **a**nd **R**elative **D**imension(s) **in** **S**pace), a Blue English Police Box, which can blend in with its surroundings through the ship's chameleon circuit, when you went inside you entered another dimension as it was much larger on the inside than it appeared on the out. Of course we had The Twilight Zone, Outer Limits, ECT…ECT… The Dr. was politely done with an English twist and an eye on time and space. Oh Yeah Time and Space…

-

A little historical perspective… I was born in 1950s Chicago… I'm an Old Fart… in our scoring system, but a neophyte in the relative mind of space with time. The significant part of my age is the generation gap and mindset swing of those who grew up with Elvis swivelin his hound dog and those who grew up with the Beatles playin around in Dorothy's Strawberry fields forever takin us on a little magical mystery tour through life and my chasm with today's music of Qomar thump… Qomar, of Star Trek fame, didn't have a true understanding of the real meaning of music, and that IT didn't only revolve around algorithms, binary syntax and quadratic equations but around emotions, artistry and soul. I do understand the need of each generation to express and distinguish themselves yet this thump junk is not just generation separation... this thump Da thump is negative in expression and deceivingly altering the vibe along with being just another invasion of all our sonic space! What ever became of Da in strum mental, R&B, Jazz riffs, Shankar 108 beat theka Sitar or Emerson's 64th note, Da Scat Ska from Da Marley Rasta island man, or Jive of Cab Calloway??? Like Beethoven's 128th breath beat~~~   You know... something that actually took talent to create! Or do I just got to dis my ho and grab my crotch to rap a wry man? Again synchronically, as I write these sentences, a seven year old comes on WGN noon news and blows me away~~~ with her own piano composition. Anyway… I was born in Chicago, yet never lived there. I was baptized Lutheran but never went there. My family lived… well out past where the suburbia wave broke, on the other-side of nowhere. Northern Illinois was about 200,000 people then however given time people discover your better place to live and devolve into where they came from!!! Today we have about 1,000,000… about 800,000 more than we need ☹ they have paved and built and paved and built all the way out and are now reaching into cheese land. Yeah Urban Sprawl is the oblivious Capital way to go... Put the jobs in Da city and keep the employee's driving back and forth to the homes they can barely afford so they're to tired, exhausted, and angry with road rage to focus on the facts while their kids grow up without parents! While everyone's health is degraded by an accumulation of pollution along with mental and physical tolls of the

CXXIII

commute! Tear down a park put up a parking lot"…there was another song Old Pete liked to sing about "little boxes" but these are by no means little… Then you have the stink of dirty deceitful award winning politics Illinois is know for, which is really endemic everywhere, yet seems to be more parochial the more local you go… exampled by government condemns by eminent domain to claim to take over your property for pennies on a dollar and then develop it them selves or turn your property over to one of their contributing developers. Could it happen? You bet this doe$! This trendy acquisition by village officials to line their pockets with new development money, TIF's and the donations they conspire to inspire. The eminent domain laws are being abused all over the country and local politicians are becoming millionaires. While we're here I find I need to mention the wonderfully thought out "**S**pecial **A**ssessment **D**istrict" SAD… that allow new owners the opportunity to sadly pay for the infrastructure that the developer should be required too and that you generally think homes include or at the least IT be told to you bout the fact that "we're cheatin and how" is their company motto!!! Isn't that "SPECIAL"!!! Oh Da corrupt where do I start??? Well after our Congress takes the crack me up crackdown way, to put a stop order on their insider trading stock acting ways, in this so called free but unfair market, maybe we can find some truth in libeling!!! These reincarnates of Tweed's Tammany family have spread their thieves about our wigwam redefining even the term of truth. We all know money talks and that's why politicians can't hear US! Buy some shares and go to a shareholder meeting to be heard like National Peoples Action!

Out here in Suburgatory we got our broken windshields, with sand and gravel on Da road and in the air but none of that rubble comes from the gravel pits… just ask em!!! Approving a Pritzker money mine, just feet away from a grade school my Dad helped to build! The Moody Blues had a line on our times forty plus years ago that goes… "How is IT we are here on this path we walk… Men's mighty mine machines digging in the ground… Stealing rare minerals where they can be found… Concrete caves with iron doors bury IT again… while a starving frightened world fills the sea with grain…~~~…~~~" We chop

CXXIV

off mountaintops strip mining and have filled the oceans with plastic particulate... How big is your personal serving size garbage pile??? Seems we had less when I was little and IT lasted longer for reuse, then later repurposed a lot more... Profound... Precognition... just maybe the Moody's foresaw reality for what IT is!!! Well if you can avoid the tax man hangin around at every turn and time your life to avoid Da rush while ignoring sound emanating from all directions you just might be able to remember the idyllic life or bump into old friends as you once mistakenly took both for granted. I am a N.I.M.B.Y. as they sell and market what declines my lifestyle because more houses brings more stores and supposedly creates more revenue but mostly just raises tax$ for infrastructures we did not need before! I really would like to hear something new but just between me and you, I'm a gettin old and IT could use some help from you!

I spent the first five years of my life in an apartment in the top of a carriage house on my Aunt and Uncles 50 acre estate... We were renter$... This was where I first became attached to nature... We moved into a Swiss like redwood house by a river when I was five. I started school and began my education living amongst what turned out to be killers and HillBilly rednecks!!! The term HillBilly comes from Irish discrimination... my neighbors were not Irish just remedial mental midgets. Not that I do not have a fond appreciation for good old country boys! I am one! Not the cronyism kind~~~ but the well-socialized men who live in rural US!!! HillBilly rednecks list intelligence and compassion way down the list after beer, fighting, cheating, and BS. Literally... my next door neighbor became a serial killer... this neighborhood made NYC look like Sesame Street... most of Da boyz and I from Da neighborhood became friends, after we fought to keep the pecking order straight. Some of them evolved up to HillWilliams. I was lucky to survive out of this to Good ole boy status. But I can tell you one thing... once I grew to manhood there was no BullCRAP of any kinda harm that would be allowed to happen to anyone in my neighborhood. We pulled our share of pranks and stunts but Da boyz I hung with were brought up to be good hearted! Everyone is a protected part of the family and I still

CXXV

stand up dangerously strong against all that choose to bring any crap into my hood, yet not with hurt as my intention only protection as my contention! Providing protection unless harm is intended, as all are welcomed as honored guests unless proving the privilege was mistakenly placed thus provoking revoking favored person status. Just why do you think you can treat some place else like IT's not your own? Pullin some bad crap elsewhere like Momma's not able to see you over the neighbor's fence! How can you do anything in this world like your momma's not a watchin? Doin her heart like IT don't matter! How is IT different? How is IT the same? What you doin different to watch over your hood? This is how IT's done. If we all did... well if just more of us did... well if we did IT well... What a world this would be!!!

Brrrmmm... My Dad bought a nice MirroCraft rowboat and 5hp Johnson motor when I was ten... then I became a river rat... Oh the natural beauty and actual freedom this brought me. Trips to <u>Chicago</u> on the weekends to meet up with the rest of the family at Grandma and Grampa's. Wonderful summers with magical vacations whether in the car interfacing with each other and singing songs! Together!!! Or reading the Burma Shave signs and counting the miles to Wall Drug... Are we there yet??? Living each moment we could outdoors with our family, friends, or being alone exploring the nature of nature. Unconcerned about the next moment or what happened last. No check off list of to do's or time to remediate the past. We all had chores and responsibilities that were mostly set-aside for a few months each summer allowing for the good life to be lived. Recharging the mind and body while just enjoying what was happening day by day hour by hour... minutes divided by seconds that flowed with the ebb and tide as we conspired to live doing whatever would float our boat in the Now!

I became a 4 Sport athlete and thought I was a <u>Head</u>, I skied, both water and snow, along with Hockey in – zero weather... outside---° Skitched a bit, Baseball... and a different kind of <u>kick the can</u> down the road!!! I say 4 Sport; Football, never let your kid play (injuries); Wrestling, toughest individual activity not WWF; Golf where I ran into a~~h⊗les worse than Hillbilly

Rednecks and they were Country, a different country... "The" local Country Club... The First Tee enables and IT is great that they make more than enough of our money to give some to charity, as great cover for the evil ego flaunting more dominating the nineteenth! Teasing by taste of the lifestyle of the rich and infamous with the green, does not grant you access to the club house nor afforded to be granted social membership in the excluding club, as they choose whom they groom to perpetuate their invested interests. Just as their all ways "gifted" children of the club, have more in common with the important exportation of fat cat expectations that adds to the scores of spoiled billionaire children of the club around the globe, than there are the rest... who work to live on pennies a day. Every now and then someone climbs the ladder out of a fairway bunker to succeed too exampled status, but disparity is the only way this game can remain to be played, as there are only so many holes and most of them are already filled by A$$e$ playing with your A$$et$! The parents in this club focus on mutual self-benefit and are the so-called shakers and movers, who are all connected... to what I don't know? If everyone at the country club makes really good money, it can't be that hard because they're mostly idiots... These people like to point to the great donate they think they make, but if they were not making so much off me I too would have enough to make my own contributions. Though the numbers show that those with less give more so maybe if we all had more we'd give less! The "IN" crowd kept you out there... they thought and acted like they were connected! Mainly to the concept! They were connected but not entangled... well some of them were entangled... with someone else's spouse... That's not the kind of entanglement I'm expounding on! The social promotion divide of who's got, who's allowed, and who's not in the ra ra ha ha stratus seeker ego tripping childish world personified in this PC group exclusion by the status gate keepers, from cheerleading to chair managing, from Da Club to even who's allowed to drink in your Pub!!! Did you know your just not good enough!!! This is anecdotally inferred in "The Electric Kool-Aid Acid Test" "Either you are on the bus or off the bus." Do you throw somebody under Da bus to save your own a$$ or maybe choose to impersonally exploit others because your under the false assumption that there is no cost to you??? People have assimilated the assumption that any old apology can get their "buts" (but this but that) out of most anything as we're designed to empathize. Butt "I'm sorry"~~~ intended actions speak much louder than non-sensed words!!! Well this is too true of the want to be Rockefellers and their children. Who were born on third base, overweening their vain assumption that when they scored they actually had hit a home run, in the game that started in the ninth with all the runs on the board already chalked up too their score! While their parent's wine and dine, the owners, umpires, and the commissioner, on an expected ROI basis!

Aristotle wrote, "Nature abhors a vacuum," and so did he. His complete rejection of vacuums and voids and his subsequent influence on centuries of learning prevented the adoption of the concept of zero in the Western world until around the 13th century, when Italian Bankers found it to be extraordinarily useful in financial transactions. Thus we have zero in Da bank today! Speaking of the Rockefellers… If Da pundits are looking to derivatively reason or seek a receipt listing Da lack of supply of Demands by my brethren who Occupy Wall Street… Well IT's… Da empty suits, Da major stockholders and Da Bankers… Who made the laws, played the laws, broke the laws and US! Callin these scheming speculators... investment bankers is like calling credit card companies... payday loan sharks... Wait... they are usury!!! More than 40% GNP is made of fairy dust!!! Just paying petty fines to get back on the wealth track with their profit over people business unicycle to despoil US with more of their selfish unprincipled business practices. Upon further review all rich A$ $h⊗les need Invest-a-Gate forensic financial audits to determine where their fortunes derived from to see where they stole them from and who they screwed as well as whom should get reparations and what crimes were committed! Now that what their forbearers did, to acquire their wealth, is illegal... how am I supposed to get mine? What IT's about is not so much about how much you got but how you got how much you got; and who or what, was backed, provided for, or supported along the way, and how much and what you're doing with IT today. If you think there's no more law bending robber baron's, check out the 60 Minutes episode on Country Wide and Citi Bank to open your mind on the continuing immoral impunity immunity! Ya can't make stuff like this up even if you deny~~~ Speaking of denial... I suppose asking for the money that was moved to the general fund from the Social Security fund be returned makes me some kind of Socialist nut! These guys trash a trillion in our ASSET$ and are bailed out by US and Da bill that is immune to any court review, while Bin laden's terror attacks amount to about 200 billion... so we spend a trillion distractedly going after him and nothing just nothin on indicten... and can you remind me again where these A$$ET thieves are servin time??? Even though after Enron, Duh Bush just like his father X CIA director H Duh Bush (wonder if they're connected like through the Carlyle group to Binladins, Unocal, Halliburton, Enron) signed another sweeping corporate ethics reform bill into law, stating never again!!! While almost simultaneously IT was swept under another rug??? This bailout was the best executed intelligence OP our government has pulled off ever! A real financial coup d'etat... Hope they don't plant no more Bush's under which we'll reform! I don't remember betting my retirement on some 3 Card Monty Ponzi scheme yet the results are the same! Seems that the laws ain't worth the ink let alone the paper they produce reams of in DC! Before the OWS used Da 99% I was a usin a more moderate range but the thoughts still the same! How can 5% control 95%? Have you ever stopped to realize how much money these A$$h⊗les actually have!!! We would each need to work longer than the world has existed to earn what they collect annual interest on... Please remind me again how this is democratic republic capitalism??? The carrot they been a holdin out in front of me is rottin and I want a taste of something new! Just because I was late to their game and missed the starting gun I should need accept getting laid off, just as I am about to pass GO or have too mortgage all my property to pay rent for landing in their monopoly!!! I am not a commune type though my social group @ college may have been considered one... I do not believe in true socialism, as the individual incentive to be... is less... although there is a social contract that binds US all to

CXXIX

be more. Capitalism is great in theory, but like most great principles man perverts, so clearly we need leveling intervention to be compulsory (regulation), because the unsocial rich seem to need to be reined in as their controlling use of societies Capital often keeps others at a loss, and by continuously reiterating consequential ethical fair play regulations, only then will the heavily imposing controlling self-interest groups, riding the we can cause we can tilt-a-whirl economic policies. Then and only then will they "GET IT" because their forced to comply with Da social economic contract! Then and only then will we eliminate the, Dis incentives, convoluted Subsides, Special Interests, Income disparity, target Tariffs, Off-shoring, Black money funds bribes and illicit actions both here at home and abroad. Each and every time we begin to rein in, check or begin to rebalance, these usury abusers they whine and decry like the toilet seat caught their junk between the seat and Da bowel, as they went to crap on US once more! Seems much of the money today rides the infinitesimal dismal fine line defining legal from illegal just to make a dime! Oh and what happens to all that fine money that they fine doe's fine companies dat are not providin such fine products or services??? It's fine that I didn't get mine but did you ever get yours??? IT's only with conscienceless Capitalism can we price a life and except Da cost! Will the company you work for profit by collectin on your death by bettin the downside with some dead peasants life insurance that does not benefit anyone but them? Da lower your ethics Da bigger your bonus! A Trillion dollars sits offshore waiting for the next Bush like tax holiday. A Trillion dollars sits in corporate treasuries waiting for the economy to pick itself up from the sidelines. Trillion dollar wars for freedom and subsidized economic aid to despots! Trillions of dollars in unfunded pension liability is waiting in all our futures and Trillions have already been dispersed to Da banks that then took our homes and all we have left is an IOU. Let's throw in a Trillion electing whomever their selecting to run the Muni's, Counties, and States and a quagmire of other local government overlord's that are upside-down about more than Trillion! A trillion owed on student loans! Funny how a Trillion here... A Trillion there... adds up to Real money when you live within your budget! And

Jobs... well I heard he died... another ego-tripper marketing US a new reality distortion field of self-absorbed and deceitful nature... Almost Gates like by design but badging counter culturally intuitively tapping slightly into the unity but we were just part of his bottom line   Wonder who was the smart a$$ that spent $100M on project slippage and scope creep of Newton... Sorta The Donald like in past recessions! And I thought Pullman had the lock on rent controls! Probably very much exampling the power of inten$ion... IT's not just about Da money, although sharing "our default state," is unlearned through ego power mistaken. IT is about the way people and process are manipulated and castrated forever under Dis guise of wonderful new policies and best practice super imposed! Current Productivity has increased on the backs of the workers while the added profits support lifestyles of the rich and famou$!!! Cutthroat is a trout that you catch and release not the way humans should be caught up in the anti social business cycle! When this business cycle cycles the economy back to the up, which IT will, will we have learned that what matters is the people and their contributions to, through, and from IT, or will we continue the cycle of short term Cutthroat at any cost depletion of our human resources?

Me thinks Mr. Pun D IT... IT's not funny Dat what we Da man d of Da Wall Street man and Da Polly tick kings is to stop playing kick Da can down Da road and hold accountable the corporations that our labor enables to continue the immoral traditional rite of serf etude with minimal wage! Where is Da support Da general welfare part of Dis selfish non-correcting baleful failure Market state? We are citizen's not just consumers, We have inalienable rights too more than leftovers, We are the stakeholders not boarders, We deserve respect but this is suspect circumspect!

Interesting how little interest the out of possession party shows in progressing to recover economically in any way, shape, or form, that might acknowledge or make the other party look successful! Hey I know TEA partiers... Let's hold the countries budget hostage and shut down the government until we get ours... and I thought hostage taking was only for terrorists!!! I know lets infiltrate and usurp Da movement of Da people!!! Six banks control sixty percent of the assets and their unspoken noncompetitive agreements speak volumes on business as usual!!! A few of them are feigning to make reparations for their greed but mostly hide behind some charitable foundation or cause (like sellin French fries behind Ronald), supporting with some spare change, while continuing the rape and pillage of our class stratification economy and fatting their bottom line! Just as primate chimps cannot control their greedy impulses to work towards mutual needs, the greedy chumps in charge have not outgrown their primitive need to express their selfish greed and mimicking the apes they ape, Da chumps do not GET IT even when we point IT out! A very few may have earned their a$$et$, but how can someone's toil be worth 10X's or 1000sX's what another's labor brings and how can we live on less real comparable dollars than we did in Da past? This assumption that a great investment banker is worth multiple times what a great nurse or excellent teacher is, because the banker works so smart and hard and that the money earned is a perfect indicator of a person's value to society is untruly twisted! If what these A$$h⊗les are competent (questionable) doing were not currently drastically overvalued, would they really just be able to move too, other employment that should be more highly valued, and do an equitable conscientious job worthy of million$! Come on my fellow lazy jealous bastards, buckle down and get rich... we have nothing but opportunity, just elevate ourselves, fight for that crumb that slipped off their banquet table!!! Many make the free market Capitalistic argument justification, that eases their conscience and allows them to overtly accumulate by manipulation without fair market restraints, rather they support and help to impose their slanted restraints on their so-called free market, that only hinders those who don't know the game while rewarding those who can afford to bend the rules and tie up the judicial system, continually calling for interpretations and rulings, that they also manipulate! Didn't they get Citi's Plutonomy memo??? We still have one person one vote and there are 99% of US so why Da he!! can't we GET IT done? What was the "free" part of that market thing in the bizarre bazaar??? Greenspan was bought out by the, deregulation collective, that insisted Congress relieve them of the supposedly erroneous uncompetitive restrictive burden of the 1933 Glass-Steagall compartmental banking controls on speculation that were signed into law after the last big crash to protect US from them! Repub's decry that regulation stymies corporatism... I mean capitalism... Oh yeah I do... While I admit there are a few too imposing, most were composed to protect US from their overt control, like the denial of the ponzi derivative problem, facilitated by no doc 125% refi plan, exacerbated by the too big to fail, enabled by Gieghtner... who like his friends failed his way to success, this was facilitated through the Fed "who knew" when notified, by the FBI, in 2004 of epidemic mortgage fraud then transferring the white collar crime agents to look for unfound terrorists while the real obvious financial terrorists were milking our countries equity blind, that cost a generation maybe more$$$ IT's wages! If you're to big to fail you are just too big... and should be trust busted just as they have busted ours! Rape the people of their asset$, Rape the people of their asset$ then repeat when they get too much, seems to be their modes operandi... When I get done divining this truth I feel we need to scrub everything with some of the old magic soap of Dr. Bronner and start over fresh and clean! This nations debt will soon exceed the GDP! For those that don't know, understand, or even care... In 1984, Paul Zane Pilzer testified before the Congress "that, if left unchecked, the S&L "problem" would become a $200 billion disaster by 1988". Congress did not listen to Pilzer... "Imagine that"... Pilzer who then began advising Reagan's administration helped expose the crisis in a book entitled "Other People's Money". Just as in 1998, the Chairwomen of the CFTC (Brooksley Born) warned US and informed Congress that the nontransparent Black Box OTC hedge fund trillion dollar bets were putting Democracy at risk and for her conscientious concern was called on the carpet by the secretive jokers of the Presidents Working Group and the comedic Congress to be hostilely rebuked in a TV lynching, as she asked for intervention while Greenspan expounded that fraud should not be regulated...Well... Isn't that special!!! Interest that is... One part of Da machine promotin quittin smokin whist the other part is a subsidizin growin tobbaccy or one part marketing

CXXXIII

mortgages whilst Da other repos our homes!!! While those in the private financial sector are required by government to meet the expected fiduciary standard of the Prudent-man rule, the uncivil servant's imprudently mismanage most public funds almost unintelligibly! The fix was in... Da 1933 Bank rulebook was out... The deck was stacked... We got a Modernization deregulation Act... Banks balance sheets didn't... Deregulation of Da checks tripped the balance... No or low Doc's... The funny-money-men guarding our economic life, allowed the systemic risk to fester for 10 more years until the bet was lost as the laugh their way to Da bank because US will never again let them fail. Had we... Capitalism would have proven to work and US would be stronger now! Rather the chorus was croaking whocangettherichestquickest!!! The firewall that protected the risk our savings were exposed to was blown open like a failed safe! Like offshore banking, offshore headquartering, offshore drilling, outsourced industry, fracturing Da Earth or any of a multitude of areas government oversight regulation is tasked with overseeing, the regulators are being discriminately regulated by those they are too judiciously oversee and the whistleblowers are being fired! How can the Repub's be running on Free Market Deregulation after this last fiasco confirmed we need vigilant oversight of every nickel they're still betting everyday that does not build our equity but exploits IT! Many of these people need to be justly regulated right into jail!!! Again... US went to committee and after further review... Nothing... and not Da good nothing∞ Every time we have any National Emergency, we are unprepared, unknowing, finger pointing, and institute institutional house cleaning while we reinvent the wheel! If Da new plan seems like something that should have been done in the old plan just wait till you see the next plan then repeat! The politicians seem to be incapable of even agreeing on what the problems are, let alone ever finding solutions. Just think if US is that disorganized when tested what is happening the rest of the time? When asked a straightforward question about plans, cuts, or solutions, they quickly twist back to their view of the problems never actually answering the question or explaining what they will actually do to fix IT! If these crack jacked private equity thieving business moguls and un-riddled ADD venture Capitalists try to fix US like they economized downsized our free economy, first in Da short term we'll all be askin "do you want fries with that" and then after some more short-term shortin, slave tradin will become a respected profession again! In this leveraged buy out of all America, we need to take names and kick some A$$, not assent to the change that never changes, just as "they" are data base red flaggin US for future criminal like investigation, because those of US that stand up for what they do believe better be prepared to be shot down, What about me??? Free US from marginalization labeling and groupings like; social misfits, the disenfranchised, communists red subverter, red or blue states??? (Why would Republican states be grouped in RED??? I wonder???), anarchist, Anti-dis-establishment-of-totalitarianism, Antitheist, Antichrist, or perhaps any Anti dis too Ante dat!!! These nametags stir the fear in Grandmas political pudding! Today even the President of US is media remarked as unpatriotic!!! If I were the President of these United States, you could chuck my poll numbers and my approval rating would be minus 1% as I would be doing what we need, not what we want. Most people won't do what's good for themselves how do you expect them to do what's best for the rest of US yet we're always polling their opinions even though most are not their own! In case you were wandering~~~ I am a card caring member of nothing∞, unless independent unity within IT, is lie enabling classified by sum as more than the one! I guess I can soon expect unexpected unacceptable guests lookin into my quest for redress of their mess!!! Well… see what you can see~~~ as I got nothing∞ to hide behind and only IT's word wrapped around me as persevering protection!!! Unless they put me in sum freedom degrading Tricky Dick Bag of federal FI<->B persecution!!! My only crime is "being" me~~~

Dis party line Voting because of opposing opposes US against unified resolution! Narrow margin victories based on the swing in our state of hate are loudly interpreted and taken as mandates, when really IT's about 50/50 but the winners say the he!! With US losers! When they charade under a TEA Party label the Repub's latch and hold our government hostage by openly funding,

CXXXV

supporting, encouraging, and chasin after the campaign train to climb aboard but when our Soul train attempts to start IT's emancipation engine like the Students for a Democratic Society or something much more rational yet aptly named Occupy Wall Street or the wider arrayed Occupy Movement and try to similarly protest for more spare change~~~ then the backers, leaders, or anyone remotely connected to IT are demonized, ostracized, labeled as pinko red fan addicts and grouped linked in to any faction that will cause a negative media reaction because the PC's thinking is always "selfish" less correcting our course to Der inheritable right$ not what's Righteous for all of US! Over the first 70 years after Da crash "with regulation" the market averaged an 11% return, in the past 11 years the "unregulated" return has been ZERO as the market yoyos out of control from 13,000 to 5,600 to 13,000!!! Bettin some made sum during this time, but Da 401K was set back 200% based on the 11% return that should have had. Over the course of the next 5 years till retirement even if the return returns to 11%, which IT won't, Da 401K will have been reduced 450% of what IT could and should have been, based on compounding the value at the average 11% per year, that these "deregulated" regular bastards stole for themselves!!! I know there was no guarantee nor was I entitled, but I was told if I worked hard, fully funded Da 401, and built equity in my home... all would be fine. Well I wish I had bought gold, shorted the market, and rented... instead of investing in this country and giving the financial wizzers my hard earned dollars! Let's take inventory for a moment... House... lost half should have gained half there is 200%... Real Estate Taxes went up on it 200%... 401K~~~ well maybe I better just have a beer instead... Oh yeah drinkin went up 100%... while those committing fraud are being optimally option rewarded for shortsighted shorting, as in this last debacle, liar loans were taken off their books at the end of every quarter, gains today that decline our tomorrows, and bets against the American dream. Shorting oil futures to manipulate US in presidential election, while sucking windfalls of cash we pay at the pump! For the first time in the history of this great country our children will have less than we! How can an economic and political system promote the short-term mega bonuses to those whom are defrauding people's lives and dreams with no independent review of the policies and agencies involved? How can the solution involve more of the same rewards for making foreclosures profitable to these same predatory lenders? Credit default swaps swapped our good credit for their defaults! Billionaires had to act like they were only millionaires for a while!!! The true cost of this financial debacle in, pain, suffering, divorce, hunger, even deaths, along with the ongoing toll on families, our children, and Society as a whole, will never be fully comprehended nor atoned for, much like the Gulf wars and the Gulf leak, this third financial Gulf, between I got mine and screw U, is toxic^2 and depleting!!! When you ask yourself if having yours is Da way, when you look around at others and Da view of our future, do you truly like what you see and are you happy to be? Maybe you know someone who had to move into his or her car or go without food him or herself to feed their children. IT's been a cold cold winter in the hearts of these perpetrators of poverty. Brooksley was forced out in 1999 and now predicts a series of downturns if those Gambling fanatics aren't reined in. There are seven bloated bureaucracies that are the overseers in bed with this off the books financial bedlam... No one found responsible!!! No one indicted... Just like no WMD... and No answerable oversight on a cleanup plan for anything!!! Was there something gained after 10 years of war,,, beside for Da Military-industrial Complex's bottom line? The 2010 financial reform bill was compromised window dressing designed to make us believe they have all found new righteous Wall Street religion while those in charge continue to slobber from the same trough of good old boy oligarch-economics-cool-aid! I knew Barney was a dinosaur, I just didn't know he was also a Congressmen! When they reformed credit cards we just had less and we're charged more! Keynesian government intervening on our behalf with equitably fair regulation in support of utility economics, appears to have been killed dead by Conglomerate's desire to return to Adam Smith's laissez-faire adherent do nothing "don't interfere" proponent Milton Freidman's promoting the Heydk view of the maximum profit deregulation e con man!!! Basically don't interfere with our big business while we interfere with governing IT!!! The too big to fail

CXXXVII

are bigger than ever and the term "financial services" is a cover for profiteering pirates. The old "what's good for Wall Street is good for America" is a bunch of bull! They have thrown a T.A.R.P. over the problem, eliminating transparency and awarding blue ribbons, instead of making credit available to small and midsized entrepreneurs and those underwater because of predatory lending! The greedy people and the predatory lenders that walked away leaving behind blight in our hood, continue hauntingly in our lives with their irresponsibility as they get money from the government to cover expenses but do not keep up the properties, utilities, or assessments and then when the new repo millionaires fire sale these places, first our values decline even more and the second they're sold, for the rock bottom value your home is now worth, the Assessor says "that's not an arm's length transaction" and thus takes no action to reduce your assessed value, that skyrocketed when the ex-neighbor overpaid, which was calculated on the way up at the proper arms length! I have seen the theft, listened to the insider deals being made, and dealt with the many mega egos fueled with wealth stolen without indictment! None of which ever became public but that there was much public knowledge of! There is many an unreason why these deals are cut in Da backroom... Because if people were privy to what was goin down they would be appalled more than they already are. The pall of Da smoke filled room has been ventilated so you don't catch the scent of the wealth distribution brokers utilizing clandestine plumbers to flush that privy down regularly! Well I worked in Dat Der backroom and did not speak unless spoken to but listened intently! This is much like the Rothschild's empire or Da Mafia, which supposedly became disorganized crime, while Da other mother's are into world banking! Now their sons and daughters are doctors and lawyers but still banking Grandpa's dirty money! We're all supposed to have Chicago Amnesia... Robber Bare in money passed down from generation to generation to the detriment of their futures and ours is ill-con-ironic economics as being born to money is almost more life debilitating as life without. They consider redistribution of their stolen inheritance a socialistic plot... Remind me once more why some dumba$$ Wall$treeter or any other kinda dumba$$ inheritance endowed frikup, should make more cash than the guy cleaning up his crap in Da latrine? Aren't Da worker BE's providing the royal jelly??? Well we need a plot to take back what has been stolen under the guise of Free Market Capitalism that enriched mainly those connected in the know, unlike a conscience fair market of equal enrichment of all through merit. Try to pull Da $h!t now that they did to acquire their buck$ then! Get yours then change the rules of the game to insure your future wealth! I started this rant out talking about one kind of Golf and got detoured and mired in other Gulfs but maybe they're related through attitude and intentions...

Well before we finish our hot dog and start the back nine~~~ I need to take a few practice swings at some other ball busters... Special Interests::: We all have our own self interests which when grouped into a group acts in those areas that are "SPECIAL" to them and this special status is imposed over the rest of US that may not feel quite so special about their "SPECIALNESS". If IT isn't represented specially in DC then IT is going to be put on the back burner in the boiler room haul$ of Congress!!! Hiring practices::: If you been takin up space in a position that has a remotely similar job description that you can cut and paste into your resume you then have at least some kind of chance to get past the not so super computer scans for keywords. If not when was the last time you were able to get inside past reception to talk to a humanoid about your desperate desire or demonstrate skill sets? ForgetaboutIT... you either got a connected network or you ain't a goona work!!! But you may be able to TEMP at half of what Da works worth while we devaluate, I mean evaluate, your value to the company... another words see how many of the unquestionable discriminative issues you be bringin to Da table... along with appraisin which a$$ kissers like you for a praisin them and which ones don't! Oh and while we're temporarily here Dat Temp badge is like havin to wear Da star of David because your other so welcoming employees you intruded me too that first day and then scooted off and left me in der culpable hands, well they just love the thought of helping me compete for their job, raise, or next promo let alone show me the best way to do their job!!! And benefit$ isn't that a quaint idea... But if I can bull$h!t enough of you long enough and not step on a hidden agenda landmine I may be graced with a chance to take up some new space for a few more years before the copos check my documents to verify my longevity in Da climb up Da latter as they rightsize caus they can't figure out what's Da matter… Well back to Da game… I did learn a great deal about elitism and elitist's by carrying their baggage, spotting their balls (they're small you know), and fetching their drinks and later sharing their drugs… As a matter of fact this is where I was later introduced to drugs, Da recreational kind that is! These folk's got the best-dammed Doctors and drugs, money can buy! Doctor shopping is a hobby with them. Yet I guess if these drug store truckers stay off of the harder street drugs, is this a bad thing? But then why suppress and arrest those whom are hooking down what they buy on the streets because they cannot afford designer doctors and have no insurance to fund the pharmaceutical companies outrageous market manipulated profits? Anyway to make a long story longer… I had a playoff for the fifth of five playing positions on the golf team as a freshman and won! I never was allowed to play even once in any competition! I was not one of the chosen! Never was given another look or help from the coach! I was lucky to be disconnected! Early! As I thought this, Socio-Politico-Economico better than everybody else, was where I wanted to be! Lucky again that the beam directed me away from this negative consuming culture and proved to me once again that nepotism reins! Golf is actually a great game… A hard working grind if you can call golf work. A few Pros even occasionally act professional and avoid the moral traps, alcoholic hazards, restaurant penalties, and hotel hovels that take their toll on the road Tour… that ascribes to most pro sports yet we hold them high as idols to ascend too! Golf is just mostly played at Country EXCLUSIVE Clubs by a bunch of unsocial climbers or those who would like too, who have a false sense of entitlement while taking mulligan's along the cart path to perdition!!! The "members" of this club do a grand game a great disservice. Many "members of the club" get high and drunk so they can stand each other and hope no one saw them use their foot wedge or self pad their handicap, which is mostly their unlicensed altitude attitude, as they lip out on

CXL

the low side not the pro side of the cup! I wonder if these country clubs were free to join if the unsocio-climbers would just move over to tennis or horses or boating? Oh that's right… they have! Sometimes raising the fact that they raise a few bucks for charity, as did another Al… not so Nobel after realizing his dynamite money was tainted with death. If you think I'm talking without knowing, then digest the fact; that I was on the inside of the creation of Taylor Made™ in 78', by one of the same A$$h⊗les from Da club, who grew up stealing from IT and to whom they have dedicated great memorials! Well when the metal faces flattened and heads were flyin off~ because he just said superglue em and ship em… get em out Da door… I think QC might have gone missing!!! Not sure who got what from whom in golf's ancient ruling authority to allow dis deflection but this fore sure altered the game forever, and then they have had to alter Da courses so the average hack can spend even more money to regale at hitting the ball even farther off the fairway and still lower his handicap!!! Their finally reining the profiteer's in… After two years of Golf Team futility I switched to Tennis and made lemonade out of sour Mashie. I had toked with the affluent, got "Burnt Weenie Sandwich" by the Mothers of Invention, and went down to the "Crossroads" with Cream... I was cookin now... Little did I know then that Tennis is just another clique and I don't! I went on to become pretty good with my Wilson T2000, so that's how we get to 4 Sport athlete… They only want a one maybe two sportier athlete today because you must specialty train year round to be comparatively more competitive! Now how is this relevant? Oh yeah we're on historical info… Perspective on my perspective… we ought to change the name of HIGH School… dumbfounding how Da players and Da cheerleaders are so much more highly honored and miss sought after than the honor student seeking higher knowledge!!! We ain't born chasin Da Socio-Politico-Economico~~~ so nature of IT must be nurtured out of us by society, and Socio-Politico-Economico screw IT, nurtured in, reflecting that same crap game! I quit football my senior year because I was missing the party… although our team being 1 and 32 might have had some influence… IT wasn't the losing I could not handle, as this was great preparation for life, IT was the not learning or striving to do anything to right the stinking ship! Coaching was based on that same freaking thing that society seems to promote… A~~ kissing and brownnosing… I became tough here! Both physically and mentally as I learned that my body could put up with much while retaining my independent thought. Although I also caught an attitude that I carry part of to this day along with some of the pain.

Wouldn't IT be wonderful if when you walked in to talk to someone at your child's school about an issue that concerns all, that you would be received with open arms and open minds… well I'm just sayin IT would be… but just ain't so… Socio-Politico-Economico has infiltrated every aspect of schools from sports, clubs, music, and rah rah poms, too board meetings and especially administerin and voting… this will not be eradicated easily! If you encourage the image you generally perpetuate the, demean those who ain't scene! There is no answerability by unionized teachers, mediocre administration (please just send money) or from school boards elected by evangelical Christian coalition subterfuge… while the leftists over stayed their college education and have taken over our universities… and this is what's programming generations to come! Instant infotainment gratification grade inflation education! Everybody that tries gets an A, of course everybody plays and gets a trophy, they high-five missed free throws, and do a little celebration dance anytime they hike the ball!!! IT's supposedly all about character counting but no one has any examples to look too when admins and instructors just lip Da words and Attitude has a smiley face. What ever happened to the bell curve, striving for excellence, and the most competitive being acknowledged rather than beginning a false sense of entitlement that lasts a lifetime in a world that only rewards the smartest, best, fastest, and hardest working or why the connected? So don't be attemptin to question most teacher's self-distinguished educated contention that they maybe ain't always a knowin what's a best or plausibly offering alternatives, because we should better be a payin more gratitude for their ignoble inattention to any stipulation of perceived situation reconsideration caus we're just parents not teachers you see! How dare you question the half a$$ed education they paid good money for and even got a stamp, a sticker, and even a certificate sayin so! Einstein said, "You cannot solve problems with the thinking that created those problems." The most intelligent are influenced and induced toward the average by the social expected accepted! We slip gamblin under the social cost radar by CPA's playin with the credit debit columns, so the Poly's can squawk that the money is going to education, while their only sleight of handin the cash to some other pet project! D tracked in time again… Smart… phones, cars, houses, or toasters are information interactive but do not make us any smarter… Well actually making you use your thinking cap less and Da touch, mouse, or Joy stick, to find the info once accessed neurobiologically~~~ Now only better able to fashion our environ… The master controller by design, no not IT… I think his name was Steve, controlled our image of him and IT is Yet TBD what his legacy will be in the flow~~~ so function conscientiously while using the tools he imparted... the i may stand for integrated i spy! As a matter of actuality… having devices do your thinking will probably enable your stupor as you immerse your senses in self entertainment not entrainment while producing too many devicely distracted from Devine reality of personal relational interaction. Did you see this app (500,000 and I stopped counting)??? Have you received a text or sent a tweet in the last two seconds??? My stratus status is I Phone 9.9 and you got Tera that bites… Can you find your way to the corner let alone Florida without IT??? Chips and the tools they're in are very very useful, so I was early to Da curve, and even earlier to recognize they suck real time right out of you~~~ and So after I learned to program in multiple languages, ladder logic, and CNC, project manage and Administration, TCP/IP and Da net, swapin in and out boards, drives, modems and wives, I quickly left this road through perdition to this new world without a map or Father's Bill and residual Job's spinning life wasting hourglass or pizza of death, taking the lessons learned and a chip load of tools to return back to coherence in Da unity with IT~~~ Now I'm leaving you a warning message, internet addiction disorder (IAD) is real and I'm moving back to natures cave where I can sit quietly and think about once being around people who held discourse and personal elucidation above being able to access all knowledge but having little, while acting disjointedly rather than kickin back and smokin one to get inside a thought~~~ I think… I think I am… Therefore I am… I think…

40%

We need to add a third **D** to <u>ADD</u>, **Added Distractive Disingenuous Divicing** existence, allows shirking more personal responsibility **ADDD**'ing to your excuses for why you should be excused from thoughtful actions, because you were interactively distracted in your terra formed devised world. What I perceive when attempting to interact with an **ADDD**'er is that I'm a distraction from their constant device interaction! Devices are tools… Maintain them and your skills to use them but store them when living in real <u>time</u>~~~ The Dinosaur in me misses those days when the phone was attached to a cord and could not follow me out into reality. Back from D tracks to Al's problem with problem thinking creating and continuing problems… Our schools are now <u>awarded additional funding</u> as teachers coerce parents to put their child into the world of drugs so they conform. Admin's are falsely signing up students to the school lunch program, including their own children, so that more funds can be tapped, and if you audit more than 1% of the applications your a criminal and can face punishment! We should call it PREP for more school if you're lucky… and **your worth le$$** if you're not school… <u>Teaching to test</u> does not serve our children, nor aid in the measure of what needs to be and has been imparted, but does improve their ability to regurgitate. Critical objective thinking may be measured somewhat but critical subjective thinking, the study of creativity, emotional socialization, collaboration, as well as other fuzzy ideas and the values that deserve to be conveyed, currently do not measure up to the test! Retaining and grading the teachers based on this test mess prevents them from passing on their gifts and is only a guess of their ability to prepare all the diverse minds to meet that particular measurement. <u>Tenure</u> must go as we must have some measure of the me "Be made', reinstate discipline through <u>judicial</u>

reform and yes… punishment… that is not punitive~~~ removing Da sadists while stopping Da whining uncivil debilitate carrions allowing order to restore civility in our schools, ensure the three R's are rote, one year of national service for all or boot camp for those that find themselves unable or unwilling to serve. For the teachers a combination of, peer review, student/parent feedback, subject matter skills assessment, and meeting some but not all criteria employed by the business world in best practices and quality control, as some of these practices are yet redundant and punitive and are only there to assert control. Everyday is a test that prepares for tomorrow! Stop marking students down for disagreeing with you and up because they do! "We don't need no education.~..~.~..~~~.. We don't need no thought control .~.. No dark sarcasm in the classroom .~.. Teacher… leave them kids alone! .~..~.~..~~~.. all in all your just another brick in the wall."

"By the way which one of you is called Pink" Well onward and hopefully upward… Went to my first DEAD concert in 1970~~~~~~~~~~~~~~ Woodstock had happened, I had been to and seen, San Francisco in 1967, missed Monterey, and wondered what the heck all that was about? After the Dead concert I knew… I became a friend of Timothy Leary~~~~~~~~ Owsley's Monterey purple~~~~~~~~~ Eight-way sunshine~~~~~ Blotter~~~~~~~~~~~ the Native American Peyote Church~~~~~~~~ pre-Neolithic mushroom Gatherers~~~~~~~~~ Sumerian poppy growers~~~~~~~~~ Middle Eastern Keif users~~~~~~~~~ I chose to Ride the Tiger… "IT's like a tear in the hands of a western man…Tell you about salt, carbon and water…But a tear to a Oriental man…He'll tell you about sadness and sorrow or the love of a man and a woman!!!" (Jefferson Starship formerly know as Jefferson Airplane) Those who sit in judgment of this have no clue what they are judging, missing, or not perceiving as they have not been there themselves and are only reflecting preconceived prejudices formulated through heresy! I mean hearsay or do I? Some of the same drugs that enhanced my love with IT in the now can, I'm sorry to say, escalate the level of instability in the mentally unstable, yet there are many other legal triggers that initiate mental

CXLV

disorder and are not so easily discerned or blamed. (Major side trip rough road ahead~~~)

IT's not the trigger on the gun or the rhetoric of the selfish to inflame pundit, that murders nor any weapon of choice, media, or pen, but the whack job abusing IT. You cannot legislate nor regulate triggers for some that are nontoxic to most. Although we are already being arrested for our own safety! Civil discourse is of course a source of distorts through retort or even court torts and as such veers off course from civility! Yet if you feel your disagreement goes unheeded and is given the short shrift of "we must agree to disagree" while an actual valid issue is wrongly ignored, what's a person to do to express and elevate the matter of fact, when in fact control of all thought outlets are thought to be controlled? And while we're here… I am a pacifist that believes in conceal carry as the criminals will always have weapons and they need some righteous counterbalancing, just as our government needs US to be armed (second amendment) in order to retain our balance whether the threat is from, left, right, overseas or internally… having weapons in the hands of most of the common law abiding citizenry secures our safety, freedom and liberty! Seeing as we're not all going to put the club back on the ground where we found it outside the cave… On a similar note, do we stop initiating war because war causes Post Traumatic Syndrome Disorder? No!!! New batch returning daily… Do we jail those who drink wine with dinner because drunks are responsible for most of the mental disorder, just like the legal drugs? No!!! There is this thing called responsibility aided by self-moderation!!! But yet you better LOCK YOUR MEDICINE CABINET just as our folks locked their liquor up (Didn't stop us but slowed us down!) for your drugs are being hooked down by others recreationally~~~ (Seen IT road ahead)

Almost all are aware of the boorish behavior their drug of choice releases in them and just care less about IT! Conversely… Shall we jail those who fail to take their drugs as they soon reversely deteriorate to an unstable state because they care less about caring? The drug blame game is like perceiving a Dali painting through the eyes of a blind person. Salvador Dali when asked if he was on drugs because of his creation of provocative art responded " I am the drug… take me!" We all have light and dark within. I have never encountered the innumerable wild negative effects, which those who never have indulged expound regarding the dangers soft drugs have. I guess I must have chosen to care rather than use the use as an excuse for not caring!!! Now… Crank, Meth, Junk, Crack, and Da new "Bath Salts (MDPV)", are known habitual addictor's that have some really negative behavioral interactions and end points so if you need to blame societies ill's on drugs please be a little more specific and stop jailing a lot of good people based on your prejudice of the unknown. Monkey mung may be the junkie's next drug of choice but they're not getting there from only blowin a joint or two… Some people just slide into they're addictive persona and find that not habituating takes work and self control which they did not have to begin with! The numbers of problems and dollars these junkies cost society because we're jailin, not interrupting the source, and not healin Da broken humanity is staggering and shoulda coulda woulda be contained and constrained if we concentrated our manpower on solutions and rehabilitation not incarceration… where they still get and do drugs! The makers of ephedrine and Da pseudo were in bed with Da meth cooks and all these crooks were allowed to operate while Da users lives were thrown out to Da trash because congress overrode DEA recommendations for the last 3 decades and directed them to allow the ceuticals to continue profit cookin and use the DEA's assets on incarceratin Da street users and allowin Da carnage to continue… funding political contributions was their option of choice! If I want to do an occasional twisty I should not have to risk joining these people in prison!!! Children grow up in crack houses. We're surrounded by desperate thieves who need Da fix and these people, on the edge of society bring a really negative edge to all interaction, whether IT be the unified vibe or just walkin the hood, surround US! Who's foolin whom with the lives destroyed and Da damage done??? Oh… I'm an addict!!! That's my excuse … IT's not me… IT's the drug that's addicting me… How could I possibly have any responsibility??? This junk is their excuse to screw everyone, thinking themselves as victim regardless of their own culpability! Do you see the true cost and the price we are paying for this street pharmacy game of dopes allowed by other dopes to keep doing dope??? There were two Bill Grahams that came along to alter the social fabric of America's youth. One crusaded, preachin as if God, to manipulate political stratocracy under the guise of evangelism and direction of media mogul, William Randolph Hearst, while the other escaped concentration camps to open doors of perception, like that of Huxley, by promoting musical venues of vibrational connection to IT. I'll leave the question of who was whom up to you! But yet another case of info spin management to put those who dared to care on the wrong side of being right!!! I do not promote Drug Abuse. I did use some, but mostly partook. "Remember what the door mouse said… Feed your head… Feed your head!!!" Lewis Carroll was rumored to partake a bit! Part of IT was harmful then and most of IT is dangerous now! The Linguists, History rewriters and the Demento Popes have removed all recognizable references to any drug that may have been used in Holy Sacrament from times of antiquity and instituted Taboos on innumerable matters yet proclaiming absolution when accompanied by remuneration! Just keep the nature of IT natural.

I did graduate HIGH school, just barley… I had worked my way down to a D average, it actually took work to get down to a D average spending most of my time in supervised study hall or in school suspension and still managing to stay in school, I had it down! The inmates controlled that institution and still do because of the easing of expectations and discipline along with the authority to! I experienced this shift to forward back a$$ thinking! I raised my IQ even HIGHER and lost all interest in the garbage they were expounding on and attempting to brainwash me with. Yet IT amazes me how the truth stuck amongst the muck. Seems the truth is retentively pleasantly present and the op ed melts away in decay!!! IT was getting crowded out in that Space and time of Kant! I became a student of the, "I AM" UffDa in Unity Universality… This has both pluses and minuses, as you pause your collegiate development… which certainly @ that point in my lifeline had more plusses to pausing and fewer minuses to a mind then expanding too other worldly reason~~~ You thus retain your soul... I'm pretty sure IT was a good trade-off! "To everything... Turn... Turn... Turn..."

Went off to college anyway, as the WAR was lying in wait and I was not dying with hate that the CIA was instiGATEing, took the classes that my parents thought I should, attended them once or twice and partied with the boyz from NYC that were sent to the farmland of Wes...Consin to keep them out of trouble! They just brought it with them! The best parties and some of the plotters were on the Governor's farm during the student War protest upheaval in Madison and post UWW Mathematics building explosion! Madison was a hot bed for change and the revolution was on!!! "All we are saying... Is give peace a chance." Not quit sure when we moved from student grants, reasonably fair tuition, and professors that taught... to un-reconcilable high interest student loan shakedowns that Da banks are borrowing @ 1%, a$tro tuition increases so less attend, rent a prof's who write books students must specifically buy that cost even more a$tro's!!! This is how we're treating our smartest and brightest with their futures... the two thirds that ain't a goona get no extra schoolin will never know even the opportunity that was never present but I guess somebody's got to be enslaved for this capitalistic Ponzi scheme to function rightly! Just remember that when Da middle class kids get pissed Sh!t happens... The down side to all this ending the 60's psychedelic's and opening the 70's with the HEROIN (Brought to us by **Beyer**®). 'Alexander the Greats' army traveled on opium, more marching and fighting on less food while feeling less pain. Considering that Alexander was a student of Aristotle you might deduce that he may have been introduced to morals or maybe learned some ethics, yet he became identified, in the East, as the two-horned one, and was a sexual predator megalomaniac. Toxic☹ like, Alexander conquered much but he was not so great. His desires brought death and torture to many people, including his own! Leaving behind an invented historical legacy in his demonic destruction of civilized societies and all consuming conquering exploits inspired by self-obsession, while looking for the shortcut to the orients opium amongst other herbs, spices and other peoples treasures! Almost seems like his tutor was @

some Pentagon think-less tank… rather than @ Da Acropolis learning rationality… Anyway… drugs and booze started this country and they're still runnin them! The rebellion began early old George Washington a Freemason… was the biggest producer of Rye Whiskey in the States! It was easier to ship the grain as alcohol than as grain! Alcohol is really the opiate of the people and the Morphine used to treat alcoholism was called GOM God's Own Medicine… **Beyer®** introduced heroin, in 1898! This is when the first laws were introduced against illegal drugs. Like today's laws the first illegal drug laws were introduced as discriminatory laws against, what were considered lower class citizens, not to effect the truly American habit which was fed by the physicians and the pharmaceutical's! Pharmaceutical companies project science but their business is marketing, the traveling medicine show. Only in the United States and New Zealand can they market direct to you. They spend the most of all lobbies in Washington along with The Bankers. The Constitution guarantees the right to ingest any chemical that you wish! The term "illegal possession" allows the FDA, doctors, and the pharmaceutical companies to take over the legal drug trade!!! Which opened up the illegal trade to "Da MOB" and Now "Da GANGS supplied by Da Cartel's!"☹ Congress is reviewing, in Da mean time more people are a dying from combining prescribin mixin than in all car accidents… will see if the lobbies buy another pass or we get some more legislated trash. Where is the FDA oversight, when was the last time the FDA sent somebody to jail for drug manufacture corruption, in the era of self patrolling just who is protecting US from what we imbibe from the marketplace? Maybe this is one of the reasons they want smaller less intrusive government!!! Why should those that have lost the bread winner of the family to drugs or just plain old injury and death, or been snake bit by medical issues and bills to brokenness, or maybe just been cursed with parents that just either don't GET IT nor give two $hits about anything… why should these poor souls be penalized for their financial eternity∞ just because the Capitalists backed law makers without conscience that made the laws to disenfranchise the weak and voiceless? Where is their Democratic Fair Market Capitalism? Legislated gridlock by the NO engenders

CL

MY WAY not the HIGHER WAY! Exampled by the way we like to always say and still sometimes believe… that we are the greatest country on earth… which we may have once been, but there are now a multitude of other countries that certainly should and could lay claim to that title… including tiny island countries, such as miraculous "Mauritius", that provides IT's citizens with much that US does not have. Including free college and health care along with a higher rate of home ownership. The Mauritius people have picked themselves up by the bootstraps, Mauritius has no great natural riches, so they invest in themselves!!! Unlike our all consuming, wasteful, carnivore, pagan feast at Da trough where Da biggest pigs take up the most room and hog resources… Not only are the Mauritius people better off and happier… they accomplished most of this in the last 50 years… and they have done so despite the fact the US has illegally possessed one of IT's islands and pays Great Britain for the lease and use!!! Why do we continue to follow a bunch of crooks whom cook Da books and tell us we're better off than we are, along with Defacto that we had best appreciate their patriarchal willy nilly generosity and behave like the patriots we've had framed on the wall of our minds, when we are only tossed back the scraps from the fruits of our labor rather than a unifying equitable vested piece of the ownership that reflects the true value and strength of our participation in oneness? I know… I just deserve a little more because I work… try… I mean lie to myself harder!!! Word on Da Bull Sh!t Unemployment Street is, that if you been unemployed more than 6 months you no longer qualify for consideration… You must not be a stellar performer and deserve to be streamlined into the circular file! I thought that we just might attempt to transition to this employment 2.0 where there are jobs awaitin without workers to do em, but the Capitalists just willfully pulled the plug on labor and now they expect you to have retrained yourself to fit their needs…

Truth is a fine edge that leaders interminably seem to be sharpening and reshaping! History is the truth methodically retuned to fit Der script??? I am not a crook Nixon started the DEA. Nixon was a real piece of work! He maintained a secret enemies list that included such names as Joe Namath… Barbra

CLI

Streisand… Robert McNamara… Bill Cosby… John Lennon… Paul Newman… Dick Cavet… and a whole lot of others he did not like!!! Sicking the FBI wags on them, auditing them and those around them by the IRS, or any other illegal act he could think of to make their lives miserable… The FBI is there to defend our liberty, yet seems inclined to suppress freedom while creating derision diversion division! Biometric data accumulation, cameras scanning everywhere, unfettered wire tapping, political sabotage... should this be part of the SOP that the secretary hands you when you take office? How many presidential secrets corrupt the democratic republic and how many are kept from the president? His threatening the FM stations via the FCC helped to unify the antiwar movement. The lying SOB brought us Operation "Golden Flow" that was instituted in Nam… You could not return from Vietnam unless you could pass the urine test for junk! It was all right if you were there and shot the enemy, as you shot yourself! But you had better stop shooting yourself when it was time to come home or you became the enemy! Isn't this a great country??? As I write this I am watching the testimonials of IVAW Iraq Veterans Against the War... Watch IT sometime... Unlike US, they were there and saw what we sent and them to do! Again our young men are tested, as whether the Gulf Vets can pass the assimilation test back into society or incurred PTSD memory failure, which is a normal reaction to the abnormal immoral war, which will recur as an excuse to cause more death and mayhem over time back here at home than 911 and by bringing Da Chaos here that was lived there. Sadly thousands of these Vets have already committed suicide. The victim mindset of PTSD results from holding on to the stress baggage to which you were imposed and exposed the image that you continue polishing over and over that burns the event onto your permanent mental hard drive! Saying your confronting your fears does not mean you are… IT just means you think you are while maybe avoiding solution once more. Sorry to tell ya but avoidance is what we all do, there are just degrees and greater perceived conscious-quenches for avoidance. Some of this avoidance is really covering up the fact we're avoiding something else! Walk through to the other side and see what you think you been avoiding but constantly reliving~~~ then forget to remember so you can remember what you once were!!! Not sure if one out of two is having some form of PSTD is man u fractured or if maybe there is some benefit attached. There are no longer clear lines of demarcation of who's on one side and whose on another, making the good vs. evil triumph a mixed up hodgepodge of killing and wounding the good with the bad. As in all my general realizations I'm sure there're many truly mentally injured, so get help as needed, but I'm also pretty sure that maybe one out of two from that disordered group are still Warmongering that takes yet an even higher toll than what occurs on the frontlines. The other long-term social disorders and attitudes reverberate like the pills they're given to get back to the fight and/or sent home to fight the night as prisoners of their dilemma! I do not figure, this way of thought is going to make me many friends but truth seldom does. My heart goes out to you but the idea of joining up to go to war as a means of making a living has been passed down too long. We should train everyone in defense to be prepared, mostly for what we find down the street, but seldom should we find need to offensively defend all over Da world. We can't even protect our own citizens, so what we doing actin like were protecting someone else's, when we're really just shielding corporate interests that are mostly pilfering others birthrights! Help citizens everywhere to be free but let them do their own heavy lifting or else were just Ignoramus Invaders! We need to stop stacking weapons up on all sides to prop up whomever, just because dealin arms is another way of life that must repose. Keep your weapon in your pants at ease and come to attention. I've seen the anger and hate that makes for a good grunt so if you view me as another bleeding heart wimp go ahead my heart bleeds for you, I support and defend our freedom daily and would gladly give my life for our families future freedom but never give IT up cheaply for others diversion!

I'm fighting my own syndrome, "P.U.M.A." Post Up My A$$ syndrome left in me by Da Oligarch over 60 years of Das $hit! Either the DEA is runnin the drugs, the CIA or the NSA because the flow is so great that it has to be monitored and controlled because if it were not, these same shipments could

CLIII

contain anything!(x$*#) Allowing terrorists plenty of leeway to ship in whatever they need! Or maybe they can and do!!! This must be why I do not feel very safe with all these security agencies creatin insecurity!!! Nobody on duty because of cuts but everybody eternally∞ kept on some un-leveling alert~~~ Since the days of Da Al... Alexander, the poppy has been used to sooth the pain of war that is run by the Old with the lives of the young. What ever happened to the leaders proclaiming "follow me men" as they strode into battle? 58,272 dead in Nam with 300,000 plus WIA and over 25,000 killed or wounded in action in the Gulf not counting those whom returned to fight the addiction and PSTD affliction they then spread, the forever-continuous war. How much is enough? The hate they carry and intend must be removed and we must shift our perception to why we go to war so that anyone must die to begin with. How is it that most Generals seem to have attended the General George McClellan School of war miss management like Custer??? Gen. McClellan was purposefully running Lincoln and his army into the ground so he could use his own failures against Lincoln in the next Presidential election run against him!!! Sound familiar??? Unlike Unconditional Surrender Grant, the determined drunken average get r done man, who finely overcame the Southern gentleman aristocracy... although the southern gentry conspired to keep slaves in peonage for another hundred years... The first CIA CEO Bush in 1989 should have invested a few bucks to Capitalize an Afghan stability... then he stopped too good generals and instructed them to turn right instead of left returning back to where they come from... what inhumane waste... Little Bush takes on Sadam a second time leaving our Colin hung out to dry in Da UN wind and then we drive into Babylon like we won... Hey I'll stand on a carrier declaring triumph while we take and think we dissolved the 4th largest standing army and send them home without any way to earn a wage to try and feed their families... Yeah that's how you win a war!!! 10 years later we're kicked out losers... Remind me again what we gained at what cost and what made this different than Vietnam??? Now we'll just use drone predator's that have a 33% error kill rate on civilians as they hover over Iraq, the Stan's, and now here above your home,

CLIV

virtually controlled by Lost Wages Nevada conscripted video control Chreecher's, who's penal adrenal glands were moronically pre-stimulated by battlefield frights like Call of Duty Modern War unFare Three simulations and small penised grandiose well rewarded recruiters! If they were stationed in Phoenix their location name could match the immoral assassination program run in Nam! Like Da virus running loose in Da system Dey play… Whack a mole and be home in time for dinner with the family! Then some of the offensively offended Stanies families step up to replace them and The Game cycles downward to the next level! War is not a game! But we keep checking the score anyway… mass scale war should be relegated to antiquity! I just can't wait till they scale these drones down to the size of a bug that hovers wherever they please with ease to permanently remove any right of privacy! I am not a wimp dreaming ideally in some unreal perfect world… I believe we need to occasionally project our power and treasure in the direction of negativity but discernable selectivity seems to be @ issue. I cannot believe that some Assl-l☺le sitting in a trailer in NE Illinois saw this whole gulf of fiasco's be painted for US then unfold and always figured there was info I had to be missing because outcomes were obvious before actions were dubious! Does management have think tanks and brain trusts and just ignore them because of the power in their own heads? I am also conflicted in how and when to honor the troops as, unlike most in Nam, these people chose to go even as most do not really comprehend what they're choosing! Although Da Rich Uncle US enticed exten$ively! (Conflicting road signs please check back)

I'm conflicted that those returning from war, I did not like and I helped finance, are now held up as role models and hero's to the next generation, and are considered a "special" group to be subsidized every which way, as they jump ahead of me waiting in the unemployment line! I'm conflicted because I do respect the fact that they faced the enemy without proper (Bush) backing, many being killed or injured unnecessarily while their minds were war ravaged and families torn apart but then again we all make regrettable choices. I'm conflicted because saying anything against them is not PC permitted even if

CLV

their choice supported more manufactured conflict sold as patriotic necessity. Some blamed the troops and treated them sadly returning from Nam but most of those Vet's had no choice unless evaded or later holding a foot shooting party! All Vet's deserve respect for what appears to generally have been an able effort and honorable representation of what our armed force are capable of, yet may I assume we did not see most of the screw-ups and mistakes made. All these service people chose to codependent enable US to fight wars we did not need too, while earning greenback$ paid by many who did not want too~~~ This is another one of those things where we're all supposed to get behind and cheer, because old bastards are programmed to defend against any illusive unseen or imagined enemy, with our full force and our funding their wrath, behind a guise of national security patriotism, rather than projecting strength and wisdom which we are capable of but which there is no interest gained. Remember in Kindergarten... I'm pretty sure that those unable to settle disputes prudently and calmly were given a timeout!!! I am conflicted because of the conflict yet to unfold @ home when healing some more broken bones, mutilated bodies, and mutated minds! Some syndromes are real others are imagined, some are imposing while others are imposed, some are contagious while others are self constraining, some just are and my heart and prayers go out to welcome you back from your tour of duty in disunity. May IT find you well! Anyway... I hope they don't JSOC IT to me one day... I know many of you are mind-bent that we are protecting freedom and democracy, but what we're mainly up too is spending trillions to protect corporate overseas interests, a$$et$, and a$$e$! The only A'rses on the line are our future, and some of them will become armed leaders who know war, how to study war, and how to make war while others will come apart one day causing more societal deferred havoc! Broken: Relations, Marriages, Career's, Parenting, etc... just like after Nam and Da first Gulf... Do you think we maybe have wasted more than the few thousand innocent lives that were taken on 911??? How do two wrongs equal Da Right? What makes our killing more righteous than theirs??? Can't ask the dead about what they thought about war nor would most of them think the cost was worthy of IT? Playing the rewards against the randomized survival odds in a heartrending Terror Roulette death match or the much greater possibility of debilitating injury rather than fatality because of finer faster medical attention seems like a wanting choice in retrospection. For all those that are permanently scared on all sides I pray for you and our future… Please do not insidiously insist that I'm less than loyal or unpatriotic because I stand against death and mayhem under the of freedom! IT takes much more to stand up against PC untruth than consenting to an outdated warrior mentality as some kind of patriotic reality! More bad karma creation against US!!! <u>P.U.M.A.</u> This lie of the all volunteer army through "economic conscription"… needs a job depiction, default manpower acquisition of Da poor unemployed, by Ca$hin into Da inescapable "Join Da Army" paid patriotic warrior vibe~~~ because some Illegal has taken less to take away my entry level job opportunity and thus lower all wages through over supply and under demand. Calling this Voluntary altruism requires quantifiable description because IT's just fiction… I might volunteer if they cut me a big bonus check and overlook the fact that I'm almost 60, but can still put up a pretty good fight and would defend Da America I love to death, even if IT's now mostly with words!!! That's why I'm defending IT here! I praise the merit of all that serve yet separate off the value of the policies that puts them in harms way to begin with. Well… Drugs are now used to fund overt abuse and covert ops as well as given to the fly guys and "special" opp's. <u>Bankers that are invested in thugs</u> finance Da drugs! <u>Poppies are still the currency used in war</u>! <u>Dorothy was warned of this danger in the field</u>. I'm pretty sure the transition into the land of OZ from <u>black and white to color</u> was not just a technology analogy but also another analogy for the <u>veil of perception</u> being removed from Dorothy's consciousness. Removing her fear and anxiety. Opening up imagination and creation of solution. And I'm imagining that the rainbow stood in for the Holographic Resonant sub Planck Zero Point Quantum Entanglement Potentiality Reality. Unlike Dorothy IT did not end "Happily ever after" for <u>Judy Garland</u>…

The Big H started to literally suck the life-blood out of a lot of good people... I was fortunate not to be one! Many a good friend no longer is here with me... the insurrectionists of SE Asia have been funding their revolutions on the backs of our children through Heroin for decades and are now abducting the poppy farmers daughters if they don't grow and pay up!!! "If I had a rocket launcher!" How could all these drugs get into our country without assistance from our government? The people at the top never get busted!!! Conspiracy? Covert Coincidence??? We started a mystical psychedelic experience that now is a spastic flash mob Rave⊗. No longer searching for cohesive enlightenment but rather a distractive disconnecting buzz. The Big H was the beginning of the end for many!!! "Are you experienced or have you ever been experienced..." We lost two James' and a Janice in a year! Reminiscent of the conspiratorial loss of two Kennedy's and a King... From deep in the corrupt heart of Lyndon, Covert Elections No Troops Tonkin Gulf Resolution, Johnson to good ole re lie fables Tricky Dicky, who traitorously undercut the Paris peace talks prior to the election offering a better deal to Saigon when he finished dividing America... down through torture George born-again divisively pointless WMD Bu$h, who was barley elected or was he? Musta gone to Da Daley steal an election school of mismanagement!!! How can anyone with a brain bigger than, than, than, well just about any size... not see them for who they truly were? Then again... even though I am anti war I gave Bush's the benefit of the doubt and supported the Gulf wars until one Bush weaseled out and the other weasel lied to US about WMD! Or maybe I'm the mistaken village idiot!!! Who authorized these misleading free-spending demon erratic war of attrition brinksmanship mongers? What drugs were they on??? Remember this is all TRUTH and nothing but... So God help me! And these are the people the people supposedly chose??? What Drugs were they on??? Let's see... Now they have legal "not for human consumption" Bath Salts that are twisting minds with their imbibing along with Meth (Shake and Bake) and untold prescribed vibe benders... adding to the life suckers list and equally lifeblood sucking! "I've seen the needle and the damage done, there's a little part of this in everyone" (Neil Young) I'm pretty sure this is an illness and not a crime!!! Unless you're voting for A$$e$ under Der influence!!! Are you judging me yet!!!! Well go ahead we all do! Judging prospectively is intrinsic introspect. I would not change this life changing experience for anything in this world… will see in the next? Not many of us made it into middle age unscathed… The veil was removed… Speaking of the veil what is IT… Read a little Carlos Castaneda's, Laozi, Eckhart Tolle, Deepak Chopra, Thomas Troward or What the Bleep… A path is a path, they all lead to nowhere… but does the path have heart, is it a path of love, and in the process of following that path are you engaged with IT? Side trip time…

The veil is the tightly woven matrix of lies, deceptions, and illusion that surrounds us and we surround ourselves with… organized planned pretexting, connived misrepresentations, historical whitewashing, along with all the excuses, fronts, and spin doctoring that we perpetuate… The veil invades our conscience mind, programs our thought, deceives us, excuses our behavior, protects us from reality, keeps us in the box, its almost invisible and once the veil is removed you cannot put IT back into Pandora's where all that is left is hope… This may have been the fruit of knowledge from a long told story! Maybe Ignorance is truly bliss, yet ignorance is no excuse! We can get back to some of this later… we need to get back on the road… "We're on the road to nowhere…" Oh Yeah Historical Perspective… I must have missed my turn… Can you pass along life's long road without checking your internal GPS, God's Prayer System, and still reach your destiny?

Well needless to say the College Dean sent me a couple of warnings, that I almost read, I didn't even know who he was and I'm sure he did not know who I was… except my parents had paid good money and he wanted to keep the money coming$$$ So after an electric year of learning about the inner workings of my mind and psychoanalysis Freud could only dream of… (Did I mention he was a crack head fixated on his countertransference anus) Just another A$$h⊗le know IT ~~not~~! I became one with the unified mind! Again on the wrong side of being right! I bet there're some analysts that would get a kick out of crawling around inside of my head!!! They'd probably recommend removal of the tool…

CLIX

Now… An unemployed 19 year old with long hair, a so-called bad attitude with good intention and no prospects yet prospectively… I was attuning inner attainment and happy!!! Remember happy!!! I was lucky… I managed to save a couple of bucks working at the State of IL. Lock & Dam, till I was told to buy a ticket to the Repub fund-raiser but didn't, observing the social commotion and personal peculiarities, that ran the gambit from fun in the sun to stress to impress, was my guess, as a sundry of people went through the locks on the sunny days. Interesting how people act when confined in a box. I watched the river flow that summer until my cousin, the now Alcoholic, invited me to go with him to Florida for the winter… I had about $350 so I was flush and it was getting cold… So off we went… I cannot even begin to tell you what Lauderdale was like back then!!!!!!!!!!!!!!! Ironically we were guarding lives on the beach by day and risking ours in the bars and streets at night. First thing we did was see Jethro Tull "Flying so High"… The concerts were constant and we got a kick out of watching the rich and powerful sending their kids to the concerts with their chauffeur out "Alligator Alley" to the "Sportatorium", over to "Pirates World", or down to Jackie Gleason Theater, while the chauffeur's waited for them in the parking lot, the kids would be buying drugs as soon as they were out of sight… I am not an advocate of any of this as I keep my own kids and yours as far away from drugs as I can… But IT was what IT was and so easily available (even more so now… boy that war on drugs sure is a workin)! As your mental development changes for a variable while or takes a bump, when you start any substance, from sugar to cocaine, to Cola, to Souped-up energy drinks that are mostly high fructose corn syrup and caffeine… teen minds have not yet developed and some never will… This is pretty obvious! Excessive sugar consumption has been linked to excessive aggressive behavior and Antisocialism! Ouch!!! I Do Not! I repeat… I Do Not…advocate abuse of drugs! Yet do you have any idea how many do both legally and illegally partake of drugs recreationally, leisurely, or frivolously… We would have to lock away half the country… Oh yeah… they're trying!!! Except for those who can pay enough! This appears to be the appropriate place to place my drug use versus

CLX

drug abuse statement. Do not use... Do not abuse... Do not make a lifetime mistake... If you do the outcomes are your making... You could easily harm or kill someone else or yourself as caution is distorted... You change paths and consequences... There is no way back to innocence while ill heath affects may become permanent... Escape sounds great but what are you escaping from or to??? You cannot escape... You may not be able to escape the drugs black hole hold over you... I am lucky... I mean really lucky... my love and being loved saved me from the stupor and keeps me in the clear... Yet I still enjoy a beer... or two... now and then, but yet another drug! So I'm not completely clear~~~ Drugs are frequently the first choice of altering or numbing our conscience, so memories fade and we can forget, that which causes our distress. Temporarily causing a euphoric state, empty of the distress but the emptiness remains and the euphoria does not last, eventually leading to the compulsive use of the drug without the benefit of the distress relief! When and if we return~~~ the distress has not diminished but our ability to deal with IT has. Forgetting actually helps to relieve, and having the ability to reflectively selectively discharge life's debris using the delete feature, your memory possesses, allows focus of the locus while cleaning the slate of the negative state to resonate with today and remember what was clearly dearly. Just remember not to forget the lessons learned and love discerned that came along with the irrelevant your thoughtfully forgetting! I have spent years trying to get back to where I once belonged. Back to where I can remove the veil, ride the endorphin high, and be in Holographic Resonant sub Planck Zero Point Quantum Entanglement Potentiality Reality without drugs or other enhancements, back to where we once came from naturally! Too all loved ones~~~ Please do not do drugs!!! Even the soft ones ain't so soft no more nor drink obsessively convulsively too stuporedity!!! I did not GET IT through drugs and drinking degrading Da means of thinking within IT's inner sanctity, I already had IT~~~ and even though I knew IT somewhat~~~ Dis incoherence demolished my inspirit with IT... My mind was forever altered and I was lucky to have only temporally lost IT... Most were still looking around on the ground for theirs after the concert and I was in the infinitesimal percentile of those extremely fortunate few not to have killed my self myself or especially someone else, that would have left me consequentially departing to the dark matter without enlightenment, out of sync and possibly eternally∞ impeding my way, without the love I shared since... The love that is Divinely essential existential in furthering unity with IT, because I senselessly selfishly self over medicated me! This was not all just blind luck you see, we are again not all created equal, as our genetic predisposition position combined with life's multitude of different impositions to come together to form our chances of addiction probabilities and mental instabilities. But I thank my lucky genome that IT was prepared for what I threw at IT and the fact that I amended IT with meditation not more medication! The biologic impact of Da drugs molecular structure is like plugging into your internal reward system function with a commercial 220amp four-prong toaster that's designed to fit a specific receptor and burns IT to toast most efficiently! There are better means to GET IT and a good part of me was lost while my being was tossed during disingenuous discordance with IT, spending precious pending years stitching incomprehensible disharmonic puzzled pieces back together, in my eternally∞ elusive re-elucidation in the all inclusive unity with IT... back together again~~~ I was young and wore a thick implausible shell of invincibility that did exist~~~ only I did not know how I was depleting and diminishing IT, as my parents and ancestors had laid down lifetimes of love along the pathway to IT only for me to lay in waste:!: Concluding MY way the only and you old folks don't GET IT new way! (Sorta like I do in Dis Book! But this mourning 11/17/11 I asked IT with all sincerity... if I should delete 5 years of writing the 100,000 words here too risk fully open the personal access direct think link because of my very real fears of misuse abuse of IT~~~ but that is already occurring~~~ the question was should I just hit delete then continue to example IT's other opportunities present or continuum on~~~ Providence again stirred as IT stilled the wee small voice within thus allowing me to see IT was good to go increase IT and reassured my faith in my quest to GET IT) I had misspent part of IT's talents in my youth seeking unmitigated immediate self-satisfaction cus

I was unstoppably acting out my insecurities with the who I was, and the who I was too become! There is no selfish or new way age… There IS only the good old IT from eternities∞ all wave~~~

The lies we are telling and the zero tolerance that is dissuading our police from chasing down the real criminals… Is a crime in itself! They call Marijuana the gateway drug! Alcohol is really the gateway drug or is it cigarettes? Oh and while I'm on Da subject… Those A$$H⊗les, that sat before Congress, lying through their yellow teeth about the un-evidenced smokin… can you tell me where they're doing immortal time for inhumane crimes??? Or where da reparation CA$H went, that was paid by US smokers from Der immoral profits, then moved to Da general government spendin fund$$$. Yet as always the number one hard drug, "booze", does more damage than all the rest combined, booze is available at most any supermarket, just down the isle from the pharmacy and the cigarette counter! Prohibition showed us that outlawing only makes the outlawed more desirable and raises the rate of adulteration of the substance prohibited, putting those indulging in what becomes increased consumption at higher risk of illness and death as well as encouraging the law abiding to throw in with the outlaws with contempt for the law!!! Make smiling illegal and people would be laughing in the streets, ban being jovial and merry pranksters would be everywhere!!! When did we authorize the Federal government to poison us??? They poisoned alcohol during prohibition just as they poisoned pot with paraquat… for eight years they did not care that we were smoking pot they had poisoned! Unlike medical marijuana that heals many ills, the prohibitive war on drugs selectively imprisons and kills! This is the plant that gave us the key to the interlock device of receptors that opened mind research to forgetting and this research may eventually provide re-keying of amyloid proteins of the dreaded Alzheimer's! Oh and don't let me forget High Fructose Corn Syrup… (WHAT?) We need to inhibit the alcoholics and the addicts not ban the substance and make criminals out of the conscientious consumers. We allow what is convenient and outlaw what cannot be controlled. Half the country has smoked pot… So if a third of our jailed population is there

CLXIII

because of pot you better turn yourself in to be a good citizen... Well I guess since Marijuana is the gateway to the Dealer. Pot smokers only go to the dealer because there is no place else to get Marijuana and the dealer has a lot of other $hit that's really nasty! I guess for our own good then... poisoning IT might be just a government service for their good citizens... I know... lying about IT didn't work so let's truly poison IT, lets make those that partake of IT sick or better yet kill them! Now dosing of the Marijuana can be a much more dangerous thing!!! If we could buy it under controlled circumstances while eliminating the criminal element and reducing the national debt, the really bad drugs would be less accessible... The police could go to work on real crime... Then we could start to tell the actual truth... so that when a kid smokes a joint and it's not the big deal he's been sold about! He or she doesn't go back to the Dealer and try the next thing that is actually bad! Really BAD!!! I did most everything you could do because of this lie!!! I was one of the lucky few survivors! Bad drug policies and legal drugs have killed more than Vietnam and maybe, all the wars combined!!! I know many more people that died of drug overdoses than in WAR! The street war drug thugs make our city streets look like the My Lai massacre! The war on drugs should be turned against the gangs and stop the war with our youth and mentally impaired! They should be treated not mistreated!!! Just because Reagan found his drunk dad on the front porch when he was 11 does not justify the indignity of POT being one of the main targets in Dutch's War on drugs when really the real Demon Alcohol... is the one people should be educated on... This from the guy who tore out Carters solar panels and borrowed 300 billion from social security to pay the interest on the national debt he inflated that never was paid back (Reaganomics) talk about High Times... boy could this guy take a cue and read a cue card! When someone's high on just pot, they are usually very docile, passive and wary when they drive or move through the world but put a car in the hands of an a~~h⊗le on a drinkin binge and look out caus Mr. Death is comin and the world has to deal with me!!! You tell me which is more dangerous to you and me! Yet go to any corner and you can buy a bottle!!! The wars on the wrong product guys...

CLXIV

The wars on the wrong people guys... The crack, meth, heroin, and liquor dealers are doin the damage!!!

"Kid's...What's the matter with Kid's today" NOTHING!!! It's the freaken parents. This song line from "Bye Bye Birdie" was in one of the many musicals my father acted in... Kids need to play:~) not scheduled events. Kids need to experience the imaginative wonders of nature. They need a safe place to play! The media plays off our fear, so that even though crime is down, fear is up! It is safer than you think. Play allows children to experience and recognize their strengths and faults. Play entrains fantasy. IT's life's interactive reality training ground. Not just some structured play date. Just PLAY! Urban children have a greater sense of community than their insulated suburban counterparts. Kids are learning early to mistreat each other from us! As in the past the kids are not the problem until they are poorly formed or attended to, by self-involved parents!!! They need to be shown manners and boundaries with consistency. All three lacking in dis society! No means No you know! Just give them your attention and they will follow your example not your kibitzer advice! You are not their friend! You are not their stage Mother! Quit hovering you're smothering... You're raisin a kid not reliving your childhood! You are not their big brother or sister! You need to give a seedling a little room to grow! How do you expect them to become tough, smart, and strong if you do all the defending, thinking, and heavy lifting for them? You need a license to have a dog but you can have all the kids you want without any requirements at all...This is why we are our brothers keeper. I know parents that are becoming handicapped by alcohol and drugs, because they were able to convince some paper pusher that their child has a learning disability, facilitated by them, that funds their drinking and drugging ability! All those kids with ME parents need us to be their family... All those parents that are living the ME... well you will have to live your destiny in eternity∞ not that you can license birth but there should be some kind of a slap up side the head when inopportune breeding is about to occur! Seven billion and counting... Oh now Eight... now... how many is enough! Pull out before you spawn <u>Overpopulation</u> you Mcbreeder... the trueΩ religion and people that are against population limitation should have to raise these kids, feed them, provide healthcare for them, educate them, and employ them rather than just adding to their collective number$ that now continually appear on TV to guilt me about how their suffering is transuded as my responsibility! Is IT just me… or does this just seem like a well thought out population plan by those who can't out think US, to overwhelm US, by outnumbering US!!! I got sympathy but my empathy seems like IT's getting played! It's a shame we promote go get'em son and keep your legs crossed girls… You might as well accept this as it is, for the girls need to keep their legs crossed because boys not only will go get'em without being encouraged, they're primal instinct is to be the Bonobo's we are! We could and should work on this paradigm much more, yet survival and perpetuation of the species is in the genus! We can get into a long dissertation about it being a double standard and how men are just as responsible… But most of the men I have met and known are not very responsible in this area and never will be, so how can this ever be passed on to a young buck in Rut! "IT's nature's way… IT's natures way…" There is a Fidelity other than the quality of sound coming out your component stereo… Problem is this low Fidelity has a genetic component (RS3 334) that is set to "move along" not Da stationary monogamy… We're all horn dogs! . As Debbie who lost an Eddy to her good friend Cleopatra says, "You can't lose a man that doesn't want to leave". Men… just because you could taste a different piece of gr-ass on the other side of the fence, doesn't mean you should! This indiscriminate social promotion of penal homo erectus propagate, directed towards female subjugate, continues too discriminate based on traditional abusive biased male dominate potentate, thus continuing one of life's big mistakes! The reason you have no reason is you never matured your prefrontal lobe impulse beyond getting to home base instinct. Allow your sub routine to put you pee pee on hold while you answer the call from your heart! You have responsibilities and if you choose to be irresponsible the consequences are yours for eternity∞ Do you want to wake up in the next eon or maybe as soon as

CLXVI

tomorrow haunted continuously by some bad choice you laid along the way to today?

Let's see… Where was I? Jethro Tull…"Flying so High" Ian Anderson can take your mind on a tour of the bio-verse with his flute… They rewrote musical notation for him… He sang a song called the Teacher and in it he sings "Go out and have yourself some fun… no sense in sitting there, hating everyone". Music is made of the vibrations of IT and lubricates the soul! IT should be given as nourishment and instruction to children as IT fortifies, enhances, structures, and raises the IQ and entangles you in IT. Jimi Hendrix rewrote music forever!!! The vibration reaches deep into our being and pulses through all the multidimensional universe… A Bio harmonic resonance… They hit that note… I have seen Tull five times and taken my daughters too, they have vibed with the Moody Blues and full symphony orchestra twice, Kansas, Charlie Daniels, and others but at the time I know they wanted to see the Back Street Boys:., The music industry is cheating our youth of the creativity and inspiration available through music and continues this manure… I mean maneuver… I mean manipulation… I'm not sure which but some things amiss! I am thankful that the Internet is taking the power away from the sound distributors by allowing the freedom of inspiration to be heard. Buy them a guitar and be a real hero not just some facsimile like game that emulates, yet is fun. Of course this is both good and bad, so spend the time with them so they can find the difference. That's the part of being a parent. TIME! One day I'll bump into Jimi and I hope he'll play a couple of cosmic riffs for me!

My kids are starting to GET IT and have thanked me! Many kids are starting to GET IT as I see them listing to the old Rock, asking about IT, and beginning to create their own new positive vibe. I do not remember going out and picking up my parents music but I new IT and IT was great once I reopened to IT and love much of IT now! IT is positive vibe. I also learned to enjoy Gospel, Jazz, Folk, Bluegrass, Blues, and the old Hymns, and most vibrational expression, as I once had classical piano lessons and IT is technically related and resonates with love. Tones are a distinct division of frequency vibration. Except for the Thump-

Thump Hoppity Hooper junk, which is mostly hatred in both words and volume and is all-invasive of IT, thus creating antipathy. Paul McCartney was once asked about the Beatles influence over a generation and his response was, "what if we were evil?" Well much of what is being stuffed into our youth's ears, eyes, and minds is evil. My generation found inspiration, and love of creation in music! Which is very hard to find in the wasteland of sound and video I discern today. Psychedelic love music from flower children transfigured to Death inspiring Rap'n from the Gang of wantabee's distorting cohesive thought! I'm not just in favor of living like Mr. Goody two shoes, I do wonder though where in the heck positive reality went??? Well... I should have taken my girl's to see the Back Street Boys. "Regrets... I have a few" but not many..."The Moody Blues"... where oh where can I start to explain what they are about and what they have meant in my life~~~~~~~~~~~~~ Later with that... we need to get back to the ranch... I was lucky that my Aunt and Uncle had a convention at Doral outside Miami to come to that spring of 72' or I would be dead, in jail, or playing vibrations with Jimmy Buffett... well the chances of playing with Jimmy are slim to none and slim left town! The other two options had a high statistical probability! I almost met Jimi H on that road but I do vibe with Jimmy B! Getting back to the ranch in Illinois was lucky and IT took a while to sort things out once I returned... I got a decent job with a couple of friends and their dad... I was learning sales, sort of... I was not a salesman then nor will I ever be, although I have sold a lot of things and been sold a lot, including many lines of sh!t! I was learning and always made my many delivery stops, which converted to steady work... It was during this time that I heard about this thing called Bio-feedback and Alpha waves~~~ this was cutting edge in 72' and we had all heard about the Maharishi and Transcendental Meditation, so since everyone else was trying to kill themselves by seeing how high they could get I decided it was time to follow a more natural high to counterbalance the damage we were doing to our selves and maybe find a better way to that HIGH plain!!! The Tibetan plain is a high plain to live on! How was I supposed to know I would get IT right? Lucky Huh... I went with my cousin and we paid $100 to buy an Alpha rhythm feedback monitor~~~ this was a lot of money back then to spend on nothing∞ (20 minutes twice a day)! We were a bit skeptical… and IT took practice and patience, which is in short supply when your 19… We could get to Alpha and stay there after a while… IT was a lot like nothing∞ (20 minutes twice a day) mindfully… little did I know IT was connected to everything∞ So we were still pretty skeptical about this nothingness∞! The nothingness∞ turned out to be less about chasing thoughts from your mind and more about being open to what flows through IT. Thoughts are natural elements of meditation and you may learn to guide them, ride them, or let IT be. About this time we also paid $45 (now $2,500) each to become followers of Transcendental Meditation, brought to us by Maharishi Mahesh Yogi, and started our chanting of the mantra~~~ just as Oprah and O's whole company does NOW, along with a host of multitudes of others to long to be A listed, have connected to Da chant~~~ Well stick your cult label on IT and stay in your cube or GET IT with Da Auumm!!! This is another long story, well I got time, how bout you? Time is ~~not~~ money… Time is a much more precious commodity… and how, where, and with whom you spend IT is the sum total of your life! I am a time dawdler, I have traded most of what other people hasten after, such as; a great deal of the many convenience comforts, most whimsical entertainments, Da popularity contest, and even economic security… In exchange for nothing∞ I have received living life in IT every moment~~~ getting inside of the moment to slow IT down and enjoy the beauty of IT! Most think I'm just lazy or slothful but when the days are done being counted… I will have truly lived IT more then most~~~ and in the end you can take IT with you!!! Oh… and one more thing… of course ☺… Unlike money, once you spend your time there is no way to GET IT replenished. Let's get back to the rant… There I go again… I mean chant… Aaahuuumm~~~ TM was taking the country by storm~~~ and because organized trueΩ religion was crap along with Da facto our inner selves knew drugs were going to kill us as well as not being a reliable true path, to enlightenment~~~ just a temporary way of getting HIGHER that soon turned lower!!! IT was time for change! I left my church and all religion behind and thought I would never return to either, as they were both irrelevant. My cousin and I went to learn to chant… We were told not to share our mantra with anyone else so what was the first thing we did after our training? We shared our mantra with each other and by golly they were the same… I still use IT to this day… And I will share IT with you… As sharing is a part of Love! My mantra is~~~ "I m"… repeated over and over IT becomes who you are and allows the mindful Nothing∞ (20 min twice a day) to creep in… later I recognized that IT also was an affirmation of self and by coincidence or maybe not, I'm pretty sure God is called the Great "I Am"! Well this went along pretty good for a while… all the effects and outcomes take awhile to manifest themselves both proprioceptorily and neurophysiologically… but your perception mechanism is weak so you do not sense all of the subtle changes you've experienced incrementally or the positive shift in your being! Karma… a continual process of becoming. Thus, Karma is, **action** (a verb), energy, a manifestation and the evolving entity of the individual. Extraordinary that we could focus at all, living as we did, let alone stay with nothing∞ (20 min twice a day) as long as we did… I had only begun the spiritual journey that some never begin let alone achieve, the empathetic connection to, the Holographic Resonant sub Planck Zero Point Quantum Entanglement Potentiality Reality. The ability to mentally move anywhere in any time, using your conscious, unconscious and subconscious brain, to entrain the nothing∞ (20 minutes twice a day). Doesn't sound like IT's worth the effort but the synchronicity and the Karma alone make the endeavor pleasurable. There are a multitude of benefits beyond the untold future value of IT in the continuum! Once dismissed as hippie mysticism, the Hindu practice of mind entrainment that Maharishi taught, called transcendental meditation, gradually has gained medical and spiritual respectability.

Ironic or synchronic that Maharishi began studying meditation after completing a degree in physics in 1942! The Dalai Lama also has physics training and leans towards science if the reality of religion needs change. He is as well accepting and sympathetic of all religions as part of the greater one! The Dalai Lama interviewed on 3/20/08 regarding the recent uprising in Tibet, when asked; "some images of the recent casualties have been graphic and disturbing. Have you seen them? What was your reaction? We heard you wept!" The Dalai Lama replied: "Yes, I cried once. One advantage of belonging to the Tibetan Buddhist culture is that at the intellectual level there is a lot of turmoil, a lot of anxiety and worries, but at the deeper, emotional level there is calm. Every night in my Buddhist practice I give and take. I take in Chinese suspicion. I give back trust and compassion. I take their negative feeling and give them positive feeling. I do that every day. This practice helps tremendously in keeping the emotional level stable and steady. So during the last few days, despite a lot of worries and anxiety, there is no disturbance in my sleep. [Laughs]" So what you give renews what you take goes with you. What are you giving and taking from this world? Coincidentally or not, I was sad to learn that again while writing this, on 2/5/08 Maharishi Mahesh Yogi passed away, alert, in yoga posture. On the same day the Beatles' "Across the Universe", was beamed across the Universe to celebrate the 40th anniversary of the song, the 45th anniversary of the Deep Space Network (DSN), and the 50th anniversary of NASA. The song's distinctive chorus 'Jai Guru Deva, Om...' are the Sanskrit words Maharishi once taught the Beatles. Now let's see, where the heck was I? Oh yeah writing... a book about... nothing∞... No... A book about how to Get mindful nothing∞ (20 min twice a day)... Yeah that's right.... Oh yeah... Historical perspective or was that Historical perceptions? WHATEVER... No... No... I despise that word, No... "No"... that word is overused abused too. "You know" "Like" "You know what I'm talkin bout" *What ever* happened to descriptive adjectives, that actually illustrated or expressed what was in point of fact being clearly explained or thought about an idea or occurrence within some reasoned framework, that many people can only seem to elucidate by relying on our imagination matching their experience, because they only know about sixteen words and I can only guess to understand what their trying to explain "You know what I mean~". I can imagine what you mean but if you actually tell me what you mean the meaning will be much clearer and may accurately depict

CLXXI

what your trying to explain or mean! Although I have to admit that this makes me work harder to get inside their mind to co-experience the actual event as well as sensing where their story diverges from the true! And we wonder why people don't GET IT even when we say IT and explain IT… you know… well I think this is what I mean… Does IT match the picture in the game of memory in your mind??? Maybe I used the wrong adjective or adversely conversely conversationally just too dammed many of them ☺… only you know!!! Well anyway…don't touch that dial... we have taken over control of… well nothing∞…

 My folks had bought a small farm 30 miles NE of La Crosse Wes….Consin… this is truly God's country! The people were warm, friendly, and lived a simple country existence… do not expect to get much done during hunting season or the opening of the fishing season or for that matter you better be prepared to wait in any season because life is timed on a different watch there… This is a good thing… This is where I became a good ole country bumpkin well the bum part anyway! Today Industrial Engineered Corporate Monocultures have displaced the farms and farmers who once proudly raised our food; which now is bio-distorted, processed into chemical form, then put on the mega-store shelf carrying a picturesque label with some homey lingo so we think we're buying food off the old farm or an order of hot lies like from Da Fast Food Nation and Food Inc.! While Black OP investigators make sure no one is growing and keeping seeds to plant because they're patented… Some country …Hey God!!!

Well I quickly hooked up with the step son of my Polish mentor and off to UWLX in La Crosse… An enchanting town, laid at the confluence of five rivers, tucked under the 600 ft. Grand Dad's bluff, on the bank of the river just north of where Mark Twain daydreamed… La Crosse had 234 bars; the Old Style brewery should have just run a line down the street to conserve energy… this town rocked… I was again lacking in attendance but my intention was improving… This time I was spending my own dime except for the use of the farm, which ended abruptly with the first good snow, as those coulees have treacherous roads that run up and down through them! On my own dime I chose the courses… I took Psychology, Philosophy, Political Science, the three P's U know… Just a tad different from the 3R's… This gave me a foothold in the 3P's… The Professors… (That's an interesting term)… had no clue or any answers to my inquisitive questioning nature! Though I soaked up a good history of where the 3P's had brought us to that point in the zero pointless forest. But they appear to favor wisdom over mankind! In the pointless forest nothing∞ exists until IT is consciously observed! Outcomes predetermined simply by observation. This is the indeterminate of quantum physics. Einstein said, "It is the theory that determines what we can observe." We are the determining factor as to whether or not there is a point in this forest. Einstein was failed by one of his Physics professors for basically being insubordinate "Same as IT ever was∞". They are still trying to figure out what he was thinking about and they did not understand me in the ether. Einstein used thought experiments to test his theories. The point is to see the unproven as a possibility rather than seeking only in the kaput corrupt paradigms presented.

Let's see where is this headed… Oh yeah back to Florida… How the heck is that… well… you have Spring Break Ya know… and the skiing was getting poor… oh I mean school was out for ten days… should not have stayed three weeks… Stopped at Disney World again as I had been at the opening in 71' on my first trip through… Disneyland in 67'… and by now we were living in the "Magic Kingdom"… Nixon was killing our boys and breaking into hotels… and we were living on the beach because we could not afford one $$$. Gas lines were long in some parts of the country… Why only selectively in some parts? And the truckers controlled every entrance and exit on the interstate! (sidetrip) Not sure why they did not do that again with this NAFTA/Mexico/Truck thing…Oh Yeah the Unions are crap now! What's the big deal with Free Trade Agreements if all your signing is a contract to Fair Exchange does the agreement just layout how and who's screwin whom in the future supplanting whom and how they were getting screwed before? The Haymarketer's that died, so we could have, an eight-hour workday, healthcare, vacation, and a living wage are rolling in their graves as we allow the Tyrannical Tycoons to pack our country with cheap illegal labor and outsource overseas many of the jobs that actually pay a living wage. Subsidizing the rich lifestyle and feeding our hunger for cheap take out, is the prerogative of the Plutocracy deliberately ignoring porous borders that dilute our unity and the value of our citizenship. The Fox cannot guard the hen house, Public service unions have direct access to the nozzle on the trough, where in the private sector the flow is balanced by co-opted profit when open understanding of equilibrium is maintained and each side participates within mutual interests. Back to defining... this time though the difference between private defined worker contributed pensions & healthcare versus unfunded defined only the public contributing to government gold standard benefits. Equality in healthcare and old age... what can I say... Soylent Green here we come!!! The middle class is sinking into the working-class, whom have no work, are now the workless poor. Now (2007) when the trucker's protested diesel prices only a few hundred showed up. Though while waiting, still again (2011), to find a way to GET IT published, coincidentally or ~~not,~~ revolutions hit the Middle East and my home for revolutionary learning Madison Wis. As the union went to a TEA party disguised as teachers using the social media net to fight for their cushy contracts that make IT hard for the working poor to negotiate the bargain they're being billed for while feeling no gain for their pains, or to relate to not getting some work rules to go with the tenure guaranteed salaries and pensions that give little and only take collectively! Even after conciliatorily negotiations the powers that be, be bent on bustin ball$ because they're contorting the power pendulum vacilating in their direction at the moment and we all know absolute power corrodes absolutely!!! The jokers who put us in this position, are working for or are now collecting pensions from, both the private and public sectors and are standing nowhere near where the other shoe is dropping! Yet I'm pretty sure if you are any group of people really gettin badly screwed somehow, you will not need be granted nor ask for permission, to protest or walk-off any job to demonstrate your thought!!! Da OWS conflagration protesting financial overindulgence is almost as nonplussed muddled as the protests of the Viet War seemed to the

Jean & Joe six packs of the time, yet time will demonstrate the human capacity to demonstrate their free will right to fight for what's right! Not sure of OWS intended purpose is selfless or noble for they do not always stay within bounds of the stated peaceful equality objectives nor adhere to non violent occupation only, as they should know the only change will come from within Da walls of Da street and we need to ethically work our way into every street corner where we live! This early 99% Spring in Chi town with the Kennedy Peace Summit bringing the Laureates and the Deli Lama in April then I be celebrating SYTTENDE MAI with a little Aquavit and maybe parade around some just as Da ~~G8~~ (was moved from our camp to decamp) and NATO summit "please come to Chicago"...The Peace summit might be better held when NATO gets here, I got my old Bears helmet out and dusted off my aged peace sign... Let's switch and bait the dates to permit peaceful protest only when the free falls in the forest and no one is present to hear IT! Please do not perceive believe that I'm jumpin on the OWS caboose once IT is rolling stock down the twisted tracks left by the tycoons as I been identifying, observin, scrutinizin, and remarkin about these undistinguished recourse hogging capitalizing carnivore A$$H⊗les most of my life and most of what I sarcastically outline here was scratched down in my $550 a month studio apt. back of Da hood, in Florida in 2008, dusted off and resurrected in 2012. Seems today even a few millionaires are jumpin aboard the high-speed rail too bottom line social fiscal strength! My procrastination cost me some possible prognostication~~~ But most of the words and thoughts were digitalized and awaiting IT's time here!

Those promoting righteous indignation while citing Da good book by verses that ease, has never been right in spending our children's; lives, capital, international goodwill, and enacting bad karma that sticks to all our souls, by defending, supporting and enabling Israel to continue confronting the pharaohs under the guise of peace in the Middle East... while under disguise we fuel our auto consumerism or pretend to defend our preemptive democracy by antisocial reengineering cultural infidelity conflict. We have a Dark Ages Feudal government in an Enlightened Digital Age!!! If this is government by consent

CLXXV

of the governed I'd like to have a few minutes alone with those that consented to this wreck of a process!!! The systemic mess is so kaput that as soon as you even try to hold a reasoned discussion about modifying the present system you're already caught up in the log jam and by the time anyone tries to change the system from within your already playing on their field in their fixed game and haven't yet realized you're Da rube! Our Democracy is systemically dysfunctional we all need to reunify in the unity so our percentage of the pie is not reduced to the infinitesimal dismal. There will be a "New World"... whether or not IT will have "Order" remains to be dreamed~~~ Or maybe if we had a Wiki form of Congress where we all had virtual input that reached the peoples consent consensus... No that makes too much sen$e for US... Yet until we rip this system from end to end to enlighten process progress, the sleight of Da black hand will continue systematically playing the systemically distressing system game that once you start to play your already losing! How do you change our deranged Democracy without revolution in Da street??? Well by having a virtual meeting of the minds~~~ We need to take Democratic action to put Da capital OF Da People back to work FOR Da People BY consensus to be Da people... Anyway... I was dreaming for a minute and fell off the third rail. Now back on track~~~

Well... during my first journey to Florida I had lost my Virginity and my mind... not sure that's a bad tradeoff! Now because we had tripped the life fantastic in Disney's Magic Kingdom for an extra week I was out of school once more (had not been attending much anyway as the skiing was excellent) and again without prospect yet always prospecting... happy once more... A little more burnt around the edges! The Farm was the perfect place to party during the age of "Free Love" and party we did... The Farm also was a great place to meditate as it was in the middle of nowhere next to the center of nowhere! Streaking was in and rock'n roll reined, beautiful people having a beautiful time...the cows didn't give much milk that spring! I wish I could stop right there and live for eternity∞ I do virtually visit often! Reflect upon eternity∞, IT may just be a tad longer than you imagine, but IT is relative! Mine includes The Farm…

At the end of the school year I reverted back to the ranch… Oh Yeah the ranch in Illinois… I revisited Wes….Consin often and lived there again for a time… Not sure how my folk's put up with my trips~~~ yet again I was lucky… and they were always caring! You know "you can never go home" … that's true and not true… some of those people back home, are sitting on the same stool now as they were when I left for college the first time! The part that I sensed IT was about was, when you leave… you change and so does the home… home is a spiritual place and you need to be at home wherever you are!!! Home is where your heart is… The party is 24/7, everything is ever changing and this change is true anytime you are not present in any situation… IT will change… yet remain "the same as IT ever was∞" I guess you better get used to IT! People criticize me consistently for not accepting and buying into the way things are, particularly nepotism, elitism, institutionalism, PC, groupthink, and most of the other ism's, by saying that is the way they'll always be. Traditional ritual! I like some colloquial traditions and even a few rituals. Well some traditions and rituals are inconsequential patterns, others provincial customs, some important resolution, others elementary discernment. Like drinking green beer on St. Paddies Day☺! Those that are unimposing purposeful of grace and promote civilized ethical cultural love we should celebrate! Then there are those traditions and rituals that are used to, enslave, entrap, threaten, overpower, reject, discriminate, and distribute hate by perpetuate! Relics of a Dark Age, like covenant baby prick choppin here and there, or mutilation of young girls clitorises in parts of Africa. Could anybody tell me what is wrong with them in their natural state? Might you not carry an attitude about IT afterward? Not sure how prick and clit choppin became legal but probably involved someone that had theirs done already!!! These habitual traditions and anemic rituals are presuppositions that need righteous reconstitution! There are too many others to illustrate so I did not display a full color illustrated picture here! Customs make the bizarre customary and Memes (better look it up), which like genes are passed from generation to generation and have no defined size yet communicate cultural information from ages past, need to be knowledgeably recognized for what they are and the cultural information they impart must be permutated removing the subtle underlying lies contained within their cultural infidelities. Again I find myself on the wrong side of being right or correctly judicious of PC irrelevancies! Old needs to move out of the way of new after discerning review. The people of this world are not discerning let alone reviewing. Reagan is a regressive problem in my memory, as he raised tax's on the 99%, cut tax's on the 1%, and hugely grew the deficit, while making US think that in the long term the short term profits would somehow trickle down and now both spouses work and still don't make a living! Most of you either choose to ignore IT or have no long-term memory and the short term is well... short of insight, but must be mighty profitable as the average length of time a share is held is down to 22 second$. Hard to work a long-range strategy in between trades where your server better be closely hardwired to theirs to make too much cents to quickly in a world of no value based nonsense. These monkeys are filchin the manna out of our bananas before they ripen on the tree... most Chimps have better memories when so rewarded. Well believe me when I tell you, if you suppose your going to get by on ism or privileged connection in the eternity∞ suppose IT don't!

50%

Have you heard of a discipline called Change Management? Well IT allows you to work with change by recognizing the stages involved in change and process implementation. We are being managed as well as manipulated through good and bad change and we must stay alert as to which is which and be outcome aware. Now you have more homework... Change... some say I never will... I hope this is not true... as I feel a sense of change... We are all subject to, subject of, and influenced by, change blindness! You must give others the room to grow and the benefit of no doubt, to allow them to change in your own mind and in your own mind the benefit of no doubt and the room to grow to allow the change in you. I have changed over time, not always with the times, and do not change for the sake of change! Have you ever met someone that has a problem? I mean a real problem? Like coming into your world... insisting on making changes... being with the PC no think group! And then moving on to disrupt someone else's world and you are left with their expert changes... Were they ever really committed to the here and now or were they just trying to prove something to themselves and impress others on the way through? Then I am stuck with their changes... So if I seem a little reluctant to change, it's probably because... well... they changed my dammed religion ever since "The Crucifixion"... and will continue long after I'm gone! Change is good if there's a reasonable rational reason or even unreasoned if IT positively alters today's discontinuous society. George Bernard Shaw observed, reasonable men try to adapt to the world, unreasonable men try to adapt the world to them. I am an unreasonable man in that I want to change the world that you and I as well as our children, and descendants, live in! I have been blest with a subtle inner strength to reduce the negative paradigms and intuitive intelligence to evade detractive teachings that entangle the masses. Quit recycling your compost pile of a mind on mine as IT has enough trash to filter already! Bring me your newfound truth. Ernest urgency enhances the chances of important change management while false failing stress only disconcertingly changes the important "just because"! You can keep a sense of urgency without social discontinuity and changing everything constantly to the point of zero, not remembering where or what you had to begin with or what life once was! Insisting this is a new improved product! What IT offers is not new. IT is as older than time and IT remembers. Remember??? Well I'm starting to... but now I forget... What's the difference... between what we retain and what we think we do not? Can you trigger your past? What do you remember? Is IT real or conjecture? Slide through time in your mind and piece IT together bit-by-bit... any bit... expand IT... bit by bit... IT's chronological both forwards and back! IT will elicit your future… IT can change our World… Just keep IT positive!!!

In the flow of time… today in my space it's MLKJ day… Does the substance of your character reflect that IT is free at last… free at last? Now I don't want to piss off a lot of people… well if IT makes them think maybe I do… like Petey Greene "The Talking Machine" said "Don't come weak to me" but… I am pretty sure that Martin Luther King Jr. would be marchin again if he could see the dissention sown by leaders that say they have followed in his footsteps… and the excuses used to hide behind lack of personal responsibility! This can be said about an awful lot of peaceful people that man puts on a pedestal and then forgets what they stood for! Rather than create unity, they give lip service to the end goal while actually endeavoring to pick apart each progressive step in the process to that end goal, as being insufficient or somehow flawed while continuing to put on the disguise of unify. Actually keeping us diverted with their slight of word practiced distraction so we overlook their switcharoo waffle making. Sorta sounds like politico preachers!!! The only way to peace, is for those who would fight to find IT give up the ways of war by division and diversion some leaders demonstrate! In the past, the Negro people have been horribly mistreated, enslaved, and murdered just because their pigment made it easy to differentiate discriminately. I cannot comprehend the atrocities of what perverted white men deemed as their privilege to inflict on any person in such racist unjust ignoramus inexcusable domination nor can I begin to tell your story of degradation but we can begin to right our future liberation! IT is not in my power too nor do I feel a need to be forgiven, for things in which I had no participation and openly abhor. Hard to fathom there's a pill that alleviates both high blood pressure and bigotry now! Raising questions concerning just who should be medicated yet I sense there are many of every bias! Some of what was done was truly twisted and I will one day encounter these sick bigots, as they are being retuned in IT, when I get to the other side of this life I will expect to see an accounting by IT! As you can pay forward now or when your destiny comes due later! Vengeance is mine sayeth the Lord, so I will await! These bastards owe me too as their actions still reverberate in my today and probably all our children's futures unless we can all grow up together!!! As a people we have all come a mighty long ways, but now seem to self impose self regress impasses, that we clutch like a crutch, that only impair our own growth and preclude our future harmonic unity in IT. Why do we give more power to another word beginning with an "N" than actually recognizing what was behind the creation and declension of IT. Insisting on a label or the social promotion of stratification and tokenism affirmative action does not create positive interaction. I have yet to find that a human being can be described or defined by words or gain autonomy through nepotism! Why step back from coming down on Da terrorists in Da hood because some of their agenda is privilege reparation. Continued acceptance of enabled ignorance and will to accede to lower normative expectations, destroys opportunities to rise beyond the past... To like today where there was the most positive African historical dance reenactment by a wonderful group of local kids @ Da Tarpon Springs Library! IT only lasted 7 minutes! I was one of a few Caucasians (don't like the differentiation of this label either) in attendance. I was crying because of the power and the positive coherent love projected! Then on TV that night I got Spike Lee pissin an moanin on whitee... rather than together again in perfect harmony of ebony and ivory... and I am returned to repetitive subtle whining negative... How do we get this thing back together??? "Which side are you on boy... which side are you on???" Even though I'd actually prefer being revered to as "Crazy Norwegian", that would not show my humility~~~! We must make the mental transition to being a global human being part of the humane race first, and whatever wherever our ethnic base camp is based second... There can be no side to pigment so why do we need months to celebrate or recognize our heritage that should be endemically a part of us, passing down generational spirituality everyday? Is this because we are trying to artificially recreate what was missed by neglect of a fraternal responsible normal state? Integrated balanced life practices shall overcome condescending hate when we choose to band together again in IT's fellowship, as for a very short time we were all just

Hippy Soulmates… Brothers and Sisters… I was watching an old " Soul Train" episode, the other day, and wonder when the vibe left the tracks the "Freedom Riders" laid 50 years ago? No matter if you're jammin with the family on the porch or speaking up at the PTA, DIScoursin outside the bodega or cheering in the stands during the game, there are social excepted parameters that apply to consideration of the situation of others… this we must honor and convey. People in attendance are usually there supporting theirs so realize you're all there together but you may not all be in agreement and probably only out for your best outcome or even sometimes fronting for someone else's narrow-minded agenda. Are you just a pawn in the game or are you encouraging all brothers and sisters to reach their unlimited potential? Through Rock n Roll, Jazz, and Da Blues we all were as one, until then??? Da rap of You be White… I be Black… Who's who strife… rather than let's just "Let It Be" & "Come together right now…" and be IT together! The past is destroying our future. What is missed when we live inside any label? I know that all Caucasians (label) do not feel as open as I now am and strive to be. I have been touched by IT and I do not accept racial bigotry anytime. What does it mean to be a different shade? How can this label define who we are?

((**side jive**) I am still bigoted in the fact that, if the content of character is negative, is lowering social norms, or covertly antagonistic, I will send Dat vibe reverberating intentionally back mindless of shade. I do this with all shady characters!!! When people choose to be known as or form a community and use that community as a cover for: obstruction, destruction, speculation, sponsorship, and investment, whilst subverting IT… I do not care what tradition, condition, ritual or belief that underpins Da lie, as Da truth lies somewhere else! Dis makes critisizen A$$H☺les akin to hypercritic defamation yet Da fame is IT's; so please pass along a bit of IT's forgiveness for they know not what they wrought and seldom thought that those who GET IT would or could unify!!! Like Da good old hipster's I once jived with~~~) One of my main intentions is to take back Da streets so Grandma and Da rest of Da family can once more safely live in peace and freely stroll about the world abounding US, without steppin in some horse dip tat sign crap!!!

Most people alive today were not when the crimes against a noble race took place and yes there are new crimes of hate but there seems to be a unrepetitive need to continue like that reality is somehow ours in the continuum, like we're still fightin a struggle that was over long ago that only irritates and reiterates the regurgitates negative reverberate! (By the way why some of you still flyin Dat derisive Confederate flag??? Dis here is Da US!) Hey I got crap my ancestors got screwed with but I've moved on to the screwin I'm takin now! Maybe I could do a parody show on black-ish called white-ish, I wonder how that would go over??? Or maybe we could schedule white history month!!! I acknowledge bias remains in me but IT is not ethnocentric yet too many think IT's eccentricity! The struggle still exists... IT's just not race biased, except when the bangers race by in some jacked car a shootin and a claimin police abuse or Da brother-sisterhood racing to the polls answerin Da precinct captains call that they goona lose sum social subsidy or his precinct position... with no interest too what's best! Social subsidy subsidized the male right out of Da family... I have equally been maltreated by theses Fricker's implicit bias... and I'm pretty sure IT had nothin to do with me being Norwegian~~~ but that fact probably didn't help my reaction to their illegal intervention interaction☺! We need to be brothers and sisters again to Interrupter in the Crossfire of violence, dealin, bangin, and the hoodwinking... Being proud of who we are and where we come from not pompous or retro degrading... IT's not the shade of skin that makes us different or is IT? Studies are showing that direct correlations between melatonin and our behavior are related??? More Sh!t to overcome, to be free at last~~~

If you're from some muddled eastern brother hood, whether Muslim or not, you best remember that brotherhood includes everybody under the one Gods roof, and nobodies got no excuse even if some old flawed rule book like cherry a pickin #5 that perpetuates hate under Da skies of Whoa-hobbi-schism. If we acted like we see you act, a screamin in Da square, and if we burned your flags like you do ours, or hung your leaders in effigy just like you do ours, then shouted ignorant crap into a TV camera your grandmother was a watchin while threatening death and retribution every time two or more are gathered under the spire, how do you think as a Muslim people you should react? Should we begin to persecute the Muslims here just as you continue to persecute Christians there? Where do you get off playing this religion as I see IT women subjugation game? We all need to tend to the weeds in our own backyard before we pick at our neighbors fruit. Expectation of bigotry is no different than expectation in general. If you expect IT you are intentioning IT. What's with Sunday mourning being the most segregated time in this Christian space! I know there are toxic^2 A\$\$h⊗les of every flavor and there is a real bad discriminatory predisposition by all, that I hope IT can overhaul with a little help! Amazing how people like to be different and then use those differences to proclaim their being indiscriminately discriminated against! There are even redeeming qualities in toxic^2 city, just prevent the toxicity transfer flow to your soul. Enough said on that... Please use my reviewed *Golden Rule!!! " He ain't heavy... He's my brother..." Where is this going to lead us??? IT's the love in our hearts that either diminishes or strengthens our uniqueness in the unity. We all have something different and IT's very slight differences in the vacuum of the nothing∞ is what enables IT to exist at all~~~ So realize that uniqueness for the wonder IT brings~~~ differences allowed the unified harmonic universe to coalesce, differences are what brought the unified quantum zero point possibilities to gather together to form us. Let our variety of humanity coalesce to bond us together with IT eternally∞! We all have to overcome something~~~ that we mostly lay down ourselves to stumble across~~~ whether, genetic (Yes over time we affect our genetics and expose our predispositions), environmental, chemical, biological or mental ambiguity! How does one state; expressive derisory opinions, with true love, on what seems to be perpetual perceptional prejudicial consternation of a situation, that plays a vital part in the Bio harmonic frequency vibe of our lives? Amen...

Let's see where the heck was I? Oh Yeah! Change! No! Historical perspective...that's it! My folk's were unbelievably patient with this spiritual journey and without them I would just be going through the motions of life not knowing you could have purpose!!! Oh yeah! Did I tell you about purpose!!! Will get back to that later... we need to move forward or sideways or up maybe diagonally... just not back or down... well maybe intermittently! Did you ever notice it's pretty hard to take a move back in life! Even if you incoherently thought you did, the imperceptible change ripples Holographicly throughout the multidimensional universe for millennia... Little changes made today are the life changes of tomorrow and the world changing future! Our unconscious is always learning, but making intuitive life changes is like learning to see or walk for the first time~~~ the ability is innate, yet we must practice, practice, practice... to interpret the new sensory input in order to assimilate IT into our unknowing! Life is IT... Life as we know IT is the only real thing... Reality... Here... Now... What is! IT!!! Everything else may be a figment of our imagination... Or is IT? Well I believe reality is what I perceive to be NOW... No... NOW... No... NOW... Oh well its hard to stay in the NOW! I try to live in IT! That's even harder! You must ask the consciousness question in many ways now and now again to begin to realize how, when, where, why, whom else is, and if you were truly conscious or drifting through another daydream! Oh Yeah... The Magic Kingdom... Ya gotta be judge'n me big time by now... We all go through some phase of this in our lives only some live life to the HIGHest and I certainly did during this time... Lots of good memories... or are they hallucinations??? Or are they flashbacks??? Where are those dammed flashbacks they promised me? Oh they're just the vivid video like memory neurons I musingly reconnect inside my mind that the de-informationists were terminally using to insert fear of flashing back into IT like IT was a bad thing!!! Please do not do all I did, as there're many forks in the road and a few twists which if your not watching ardently may lead to treacherous chasms or **dead**... ends!!! IT was risky business but how many of us know when we are taking the

CLXXXV

most important risk of our lives? Back to this time thing again... "I close my eyes... only for a moment and the moments gone~~~ IT slips away..." IT ripples too~~~ through our sub-conscious and we live in IT during consciousness... In the Majestic Kingdom... the Kingdom of God! Time is eternal∞ You got plenty of IT... take a little to relax a little...

"Don't worry be happy"! What a great coherent thought! Happiness!!! Yeah... Happiness!!! If only you will let yourself? Well turn off the worry circuit... The incoherent thoughts generated here are not real so tell yourself this and tell yourself that worry is just fear thoughts that need to be realized then modified. Everyone seeks happiness yet IT can only come from feelings within. Why do we always seek IT externally and look for others to provide IT or approve IT. Don't let "the wheels in your mind drive you crazy". Some propounding that are not resounding articulate that you don't GET IT but they do, and you better listen up... but they do not GET IT nor either or either continue to seek IT as they expound unsound just the same! So watch out for Disdain Game!!! Maybe if your force is strong you can assist them back to the plain but be mighty careful as a lot of these fame plane crash, taking you down in flames with them!!! Try Faithfully forbearing knowing others benevolently with evil detector deflector shields arrayed... Well anyway... I am not going to bore you with the next ten years of drinkin' and partyin' and being pretty much ignorantly happy... I was lucky to hold on to the thought of IT... Self-indulgences and disappointment, in the disintegration of the revolution and re-division of racial evolution encouraged pessimism, so everyone used the party as an escape from reality... The now... IT was only about the now because few of us thought we were going to make the then... IT could have easily escaped me as I erased my mind daily! IT was electric! Do you realize you replace every atom in your body yearly! I am proof you can either re-grow, regenerate, or move your thought to another section of your brain that is underutilized! Maybe this thought is kept out in the cloud and I only retained my wide mind connection to IT! Is thought kept on a mainframe and we are just servers? Are there many minds or are we all a united part of the one mind? Anyway or anyhow, or is IT anything, or is IT everything?

Back at the ranch… again… 1976… I think… seems like only yesterday or so… I think… I met a wonderful girl… well yeah… I moved off the ranch… lived together for 4 years… Worked in various construction trades… "If I had a Hammer…" Handy to know how to swing one, bend some pipe or pull a few wires! Well we got married in the church I was born to… and still a member of… If they don't excommunicate me for this!!! How can I be a member of a church you may ask??? Go ahead ask!!! Well almost all churches are part of IT but most don't GET IT and like mine still have a community of believers that enjoy communing with each other and are trying to GET IT yet most don't! Again could that possibly include or delude me??? Maybe… Butt me thinks perhaps judgment has some strange effects! Ironically, synchronically, or maybe even demonically the word community was removed from the name of my church, as have many recognizable attributes including the all-together now feeling. What's with that??? Good old change! Well back to them changing things for good old norms sake and losing the good part but changing… Anyhow…Anyway… Now at my own ranch, major fixer-upper, six years later we started a family! WOW Kids! Kids!!! Kids are IT… They are the future and your past! They live in the now and help you to believe in a future! Kids get you off self and into reality! Kids I have two of the best… of course… we all dream that our kids are greatest! I have been truly blest, by paying ahead on their future and mine… A little tune helped me to raise my kids right… the prophetic tune called "Cats in the Cradle"… Written by Harry Chapin sung by a Cat named Stevens, whose later metaphysical metamorphism to Muslimism was critically defamed! Well paradoxically I'm allergic to cats. The paradox is antipathy of my reaction to a naturally occurring substance! I have been overcoming this too through exposure! Listen up.:. The life line in the song goes like this "And the cats in the cradle and the silver spoon, Little boy blue and the man in the moon, When you comin home, Dad, I don't know when, But we'll get together then, You know we'll have a good time then." I made sure I was

HOME… together we celebrated living~~~ as I protectively directed our affirmative interactive instructional intentional fantasy like lives all parents with children should partake through participate, and I was present for the guided tough Agape love fest while including lessons in real life time! Oh how lucky I was, to be made aware of and premeditatedly enabled, to enjoy this greatest of gifts before IT was unintended regretted history. "He'd grown up just like me, My boy was just like me.........." Check out the rest of the lyrics… There is more great thought, feelings, symphonic resonant synchronicity, and insight expressed in lyrics and music than most books. More homework… Kid's they are truly great! Kids IT's where I finally figured out to spend my time… I always wanted and figured I could change the world… That fallacy eventually passed and I figured out if your lucky you can save yourself and then if you stay on the beam maybe, just maybe, you can touch one or two kids that need direction at a point in their lives when they seem unwilling to accept IT. If we were all successful in this, eventually IT would supersede! They are really payin' attention! And they Get IT! Kids ain't nothin' wrong with them; anything that grows needs a little love, attention, space, and light to grow! You know! Not hovered over insistently with your helicopter halo of protection that suffocates living and development of their own selves. Oh yeah… Boring… No… Kids are never boring… though they say they are bored quit often. They are never boring… No… I'm boring you! Sorry!!! I'll try harder!!! It's hard to keep my attention on intention… when I'm dreaming about Kids! Well a year later we had another… got back to my church attendance but tried dancing around the dogma and demagoguery… Ut…Oh… religion… again… take cover!!! Here goes nothing∞… Thank God I pray… Well during this time I helped to regenerate a flagging interest in our church as it aged both in membership and in doctrine, by using my hammer to do some remodeling. I wish I could remodel our doctrine and hierarchy as easily, but Luther's hammer doesn't seem to work any more and the hierarchy is superiorly digressive automaton like! My objective is to unveil their hypnotic command and control of the flow and IT will be demystified of demagoguery… Except I'm seeing the

CLXXXVIII

unacquainted disconnect of the many whom have known no other way, revert sheepishly to follow some dogmatic charismatic that intermediately intercedes by helping them cosmetically be better feel good people and opens up another new social network. They eulogize as being the only option broker, separating trilaterally by trinity our selves from IT and others souls indecorously. Dispatching us to wait ambiguously alone in the mega-anonymity of another true☐ religion rather than opening heavens universal unity right here on earth both now and forever∞. This new generation of the born again wise men and enigmatic re-legion creators does accomplish much good, by adding considerably to the positive flow and cracking open the door to your soul searching, yet still they're preachin and teachin too much doctored doctrine denial of the singular soul of IT unified within all of us and us soulfully directly united to each other and IT. Not sure what the trilateral myth portrays or represents that's requisite to anyone's relationship with God except some benefits for the interceder. Do you want to achieve meaningless repute and senseless fortune or to remain nameless while your deeds and cents help those less fortunate? If we spent more time doin and less time meetin and prayin about IT we could be makin change for IT! The community needs to gather to increase the amplitude of the common and we do need to put the community back in our church's to work in faiths name verses dictatorial doctrine dichotomy philosophy! So live forever communing in faith and let soul-controlling trueΩ religions die!!! I digress… I guess…

During this trial revival I helped my father revive the missing men's group that is still going! Taught High School Sunday school and helped with the Youth Groups… I would sit for an hour and debate with a wonderful meaning old biddy (kinda like Church Lady) the meaning of life and Christ in front of five to seven High school kids… I figured these kids deserved a little more pragmatism mixed into their restricted religious conviction… I was careful to stay inbounds and age appropriate~~~ They were an impressive bunch of good smart teens so IT was an interesting debate that at the very least made them think! As synchronicity would have IT~~~ Da now X Taylor Made® CEO showed up in my men's class… as he had returned home from LA LA land divorced and dying of cancer… now practicing some new found religion searching for IT! He was welcomed with open arms, but I was the only one still there, as there are others, that know some of his secrets but I do not think he knew I knew! Hey do you want to know a secret??? Do you promise not to tell??? I just Love secrets!!! ~~NOT~~ I find a need to rectify illusions… IT becomes habit forming~~~ I have a fair understanding of the bible thanks to Guttenberg and the many hellfire sermons listened to on hard benches unlike the flowing meadows where Christ spoke his gentle words. New interpretations and augmentations are reversing some of the muddling and heating done yesterday to make a cooler view today then the Thee's and Thou's of King James and the sermonizer's frightening verbiage yet is just gentler in rephrasing and still frighteningly restraining. I think the rewriters must have been smoking some herbage! Nevertheless… Guttenberg probably was more responsible for opening up understanding than any one other person through the realization, of open distribution, of the book of knowledge and other great writings previously read by the controlling few. May E-books do the same! Martin Luther, a Catholic monk, and Nicolaus Copernicus a scientist, came along synchronically with William Tyndale, to use Gutte's press to open up the all conniving trueΩ religion of that time and nevertheless endless controlling. On All Hollows Eve 1517, ironically or comically now called Halloween, Luther nailed his discerned truth through the heart of Rome, the first and still global megacorp! Part political machine, part business, part landlord, mostly about money and power, Rome pretty much controlled your existence and soul. They thought they were what the universe was centered on, and they, and way to many people still do! It was a mystical spirit riddled place filled with unspiritual hedonistical people. The Vatican was covering up child sexual abuse as late as 2009 in Ireland… Sound familiar? The Roman Popes levied tithes collected in court and sold forgiveness, called indulgences… How can you follow and enable this cult that indulges in sexual child abuse then waits till the dead mnfr's can't be called to

CXC

answer? Red Hats are reforming Da church to keep from parishing, making being a mnfr saintly with benevolen$e... Maybe if we were less self indulgent and transgressed with offense less often then just maybe we would not need to rely upon forgiveness from somewhere above in order to return to the good grace place that you choose to leave by doing evil knowingly to begin with, praying that you will be forgiven for you know not what you do! Hiding behind some presumed ability to alter the perpetuity of your transgressed stupidity because the son of God died to make IT so, is the biggest scam ever run by man!!! Are you sure you want to assure your way of life here as well as your eternity∞ based upon 2000 years of self indulgence or any of the old time religions that mainly benefit themselves at someone else's cost? We're all God's children~~~ so when you choose to go against God beware that IT is aware of your choosing and this thought discord forever alters your resonant harmonic eternity∞ with IT. IT's not so much IT will not forgive as the fact that there are no take backs~~~ IT considers your intention to err as to whether, accidental, inadvertent, unintentional, or purposeful and if you have a true desire of repentance in your heart to atone or just faking IT up!!! So if your looking to change your eternity∞ Ya better start makin choice changes here and now rather than dwell under the misconceived notion you will be forgiven later by some magical mystery tome! Maybe if we lived our lives considering the consequences of our actions, we're so busy repenting of, we could drive our lives looking out the windshield not the rearview mirror! Only you can forgive yourself! So do you think the actions your taking align with IT? Maybe try an app to more easily keep track of your poor choices for Confession that perhaps connects direct to PayPal for your next spiritless indulgence??? Speaking of known unknowing...Two millennia earlier Aristarchus, an Ionian, postulated what Copernicus later had quietly researched, then documented, and withheld the accompanying knowledge he kept to himself till death because Rome wanted to kill all of the cosmic tinkers. Luther lay bare the gift that God has always given freely, salvation! A branch of my family comes from a neighboring burg in Germany and I too submit, almost 500 years later, the

CXCI

premise that trueΩ religions usurp the power of IT! He believed he was in heaven through a direct relationship with God. So do I! And as he said, and I too say, "here I stand I can do no other, Amen!" I am not apologetic. This is what I believe! I have sent in my check for forgiveness! IT's in the mail... I hope it was enough! Forgiving; withheld release of resentment revenge punitive punishment transforming forbearance perception without excusing, releases a new you. Forgiveness is yours to give within. Blame is yours forever∞ without! I do not agree with Luther's Christian anti-Semitism, nor his disbelief in his responsibility for evil perpetrated on the serfs during the reformation, May God forgive his ignorance and mine and while we're at IT yours. Maybe one day someone else will write about UffDa being consciously anti-A$$H⊗leistic and blame me for mind altering control of the populace. But I do not believe that in bringing positive power to bear where there is negative will I need to disavow my attempt to enlighten you of that possibility. The modification wave that emanates from GET IT~~~ has been discernibly considered to enable an unambiguous yet somewhat irregular pathway through shining bright conducing contrast on the grayscale smog in life. Hoping to bring new life light just as The Bibles printing enlightened blind faith! (Not Clapton's band) Let's hope I got IT clear~~~ The Good Book as read today, has been messed with through ages of self-serve-attitude and opinion reconstruction. IT is yet one of the foremost books to follow if you are able to understand IT metaphorically, paradoxically, and discernibly in Aramaic, Greek, or Hebrew while including the Dead Sea Scrolls, the Gnostic Gospels, as well as the Apocraphies??? These and 500 other books associated with the bible are holy writings that were not considered to be part of the Bible by Popes of Rome or the corruption of doctrine by the Universal Church established by the Emperor Constantine in the Fourth Century AD. I wonder what else they may have not liked or maybe censored! Maybe IT was the lesson plan for connecting directly with God rather than them!!! If IT's time has not yet come, maybe future generations will connect together my thesis entangled today... Liberate yourself and your relationship to IT... release your self from enslavement of selfish... embody what is true... All truth and

CXCII

nothing∞ but universal Agape truth. So helping God! I do... try... Like the Ionian's may we not need to wait two millennia for the next profound person smart and brave enough to connect the dots from our minds throughout every multiverse.~:~. If you feel that Get IT is wrong in some way or new knowledge of IT deduces in some other day remember too stay open to the source and go with IT's know, to be the change! OK... off we go... into the wild blue yonder... climbing high into the sun~~~

Gore (What Da What... "Supreme Court gored us all" Al)... How'd we land here??? I thought you were piloting... Anywho... Al Gore came along and invented the Internet... LOL... so I could open IT up, a little more than before... The Internet was actually brought together in 1973 by United States Department of Defense Advanced Research Projects Agency known as ARPAnet and the synchronicity with IT may be problematic??? The unconscious mind cannot determinate discretionally between, the creative virtual manipulation in real time of our emotions and altered states we experience in this supplementary universe, and reality whatever that has become. Optic fibbers and trance-in-ducers cannot help relinquish the fear in you that limits our personal bandwidth. Will our future depend upon how much bandwidth we're allowed and why are we currently failing in the world, as a percentage of broadband penetration? The big players are positioning to keep us off the net neutrality field! Congress slipped up on Da SOPA as usual only vaguely knowing what their voting on~~~ as Plutocrats like how bills sound on the media cover page, but like always... the billionaires lobbyists hide the devil in the details and some people still read Da fine print if IT's not censored!!! The pile of words hiding the bill for most bills is indecipherable! Are we all alone or alone with all on the net? The government controls the on/off switch, so do not be surprised when IT is shut off on some convenient revolutionary like day! Socially interactive VR worlds and work groups proactively forming bonds wherever you are, so search about. People and organizations are being paid to disseminate deceptive disinformation using false fronts and backed by a multitude of self-interest groups as well as our government, the UNations, G8, and the E...U! These unions of ambitious manipulative unanimity are keeping questionability in the mix, with a plethora of the false, mixed with the true, just there to confuse rather than infuse! Even when fact-checking multiple sources... many times tracks back to the same, veiled source! McLuhan declared literary literacy irrelevant and heralded in new multimedia as a seamless web in the global village. Well so far I perceive this audiovisual sensory barbarianism overload as the tribal equivalent of The Lord of the Flies! The kids are using the net to anonymously degrade each other and themselves through multimedia multiplayer death games, chat roulette, and of course u too Boob, Faceless tweaking tittering dither and Bully-shi!!ing! This multi communication environ is enabling effortless communication of the negative without thought, to the detriment of social reciprocity... Texting, Email, and IM'ing are all useful cyber tools, yet keeping us playing tag in the constant contact game reducing communication to bits and bytes of broken incoherent attenuation comprehension, you know... the digests condensed version based off the cliff notes~~~ eliminating deep transmission of greater concepts or singular linear thoughts that involve insightful consideration. They allow a wider range of speakdom and co modality while carrying the cost of personal intellectual connectivity and perplexing our insightful truth. Cyber-video-phones and conferencing make for better everyday give and take but no touchy feely really me...

Back to the historic perspective... Side tracked once more... IT's almost like my journey of faith!!! Well I had been in Real Estate for a few years, actually born to IT, as my mother was both an Appraiser and a Broker as I became, and one day the market went south... Imagine that!!! I couldn't get much broker!!! The 20% in 81, the 12% in 88, or the 5% in 08 was a stagflation like cyclonic thing, yet sometimes more like a tornadic dichotomy. We like to attribute success or failure in diseconomy, attaching responsibility to the President and he has little real control over the economy, but does form the Supreme Court, which affects us more! I got a dollar so I'm goona buy me a bully pulpit! Who is behind the money that is superciliously supporting negativity and surreptitiously devaluing my rights and freedoms!!! These amazingly rummy dummy new wanna be in charger'$, promise the impossible immeasurable as they bounce all over the board passing Go @ every turn while trying to avoid elimination in Da race to commandeer the chief political dog spot, while appearing apparently clueless as to the authority of the office or the constitution! Let me get this right in my mind... You fill out a slip of paper in Iowa then a few people vote in New Hampshire and after some hissy fit cat fighting, fast double talkin, they pledge and promise just about anything the people want to hear about sh!t that don't change nothin... then we get to SC home of Da military option and Newt raises his head that should be neutered. Good Newt Bad Newt Which Newt What Da Newt is next when we are then stuck with who did not get eliminated, or caught lying, or cheatin on their spouse, or stealin from some fund, or some combination thereof while they accuse and abuse others for doing the same, you then have passed some kinda test to primarily be one of two to run our country, if you don't trip over your wang dang doodle??? But if you do... just say you're born again and all will be forgiven forgotten! What a great country!!! Well in one state the media anointed Da winner he wasn't, while winner take all delegates disenfranchises the majority. Wonder if there could be some way we could interactively participate... Oh yeah we got this Internet social communication thing... Wonder if we could use IT??? If you're Ron Paul you gotta be scratchin your head a wonderin why... with Dis inept Republican fratricide competition, cheer leaded by failin Palin blowin negative wind… why ain't I a winnin? Or maybe I won but Maine won't count! Well Paul's got some unique foreign policy positions that don't include war and a few extra special interests he's seems token too, but Da butt heads downplay his popular support and my best guess is ignorance mixed with fear stirred by Rightwing financiers for their own self-interests have cultivated the unsound byte that the media spins on him!!! Ron Paul is giving free lessons in liberty to the rest of them though! It would be nice to truly feel free again! Harvard must have a pretty good copy machine to keep producing all these Harvard Law and Business types, that come from quote "humble origins", and are slippery as greased pigs

CXCV

with lipstick ringing around Da dollar! They could fix things but the fix is in and fixing our prospects is not instructive! The Econ profs keep coming up with new styles of management, the latest greatest being, value based leadership. My question is, of value to whom??? Can somebody tell me why… if you need to trade your soul just to run for office, as you trade for funds to run, why anybody that wasn't on some kinda trip would want a job where if you do IT you're targeted for replacement, your life and beliefs are lied about, and everything you ever said is broken down to be replayed out of context??? Is there some rational I'm missing or is desire for self-abuse a prerequisite to enable the power grip trip? Many good people start off with good intentions and high ideals, but the infernal habitual self interested system sucks those principles right out, as in order to accomplish anything politicos must systemically quid pro quo what's in it for me bro and why should I play with you at all??? We were promised CHANGE and the only change we got was greater polarization gridlock X|X|X the better to separate the classes that support your reelection contention! Where is Da Unity~~~ Where is Da Love? What un-fulfill unable promises will the next prez saddle US up with? Little miss Frigidaire is lying in state awaiting her coronation! Or was that Brother Jeb's turn? "THEY" do not want to make this process functional... "THEY" want to be the only players in the game that can manipulate Da rules! Maybe the only way to run is to not run and expose all your foibles, so they can't pick apart the carcass... Then be anointed by the divine at Da convention! There is a "THEY" and our inability to nail them down is what keeps "THEY" elusive exclusive! IT's you that votes, or maybe not, for the local yokal that's screwin us all the way from top on down whose being selected for us by the local party players whom really only do what they do because they are being rewarded with some political favored power... No altruism to be found anywhere near here!!! Only the words that fit your fancy!!! Like what's in IT for me? None of this crap has anything to do with who will be the next Prez if, the economy takes a dump, or we have a simulated gas impact, or some real or unreal controlled maybe uncontrolled mayhem comes from Europe, Iran, Da Stans, or Da Mouse That Roared comes to town to bring US down cause we then lose to Da fear mongers and elect the one we want to hear! As they say in Chi town... Vote and vote often!!! Then take a shower to get rid of that abused used feeling...

Back tracked to Da real state~~~ In economic thinking cycles, Inflation, a tax on income, results from throwing our children's future welfare down the hole we dug. I had to get a real job... I was not exactly cut out for this, considering my job training, academic record and resume... I was a skilled thinker with few of the qualifications desired by the Jack-in-the-box world for a Jack-of-all-trades kind of guy! I qualified with the highest score to serve on the county tax board of review, but the Repub's did not want me appraising the real Real Estate value truth nor was there much service involved. 3 years later I was divorced ☹. Mostly about money! Unsung victims awaiting Reagan's trickle down:., We had turned on each other after awhile... We can get too intimate in familiarity, not allowing the other a secluded place to be, while knowing where every button is to push. I still love her deeply to this day! A bilateral agreement destroyed by a unilateral withdrawal! I thought the way IT went was, whomever brought together by God let no man put asunder... I was married in a church and divorced in a court of law... that was interesting... An A$$h⊗le judge, will call Arnold, offered me "thirty days in the hole" over my repeatedly asking if he had listened to a voicemail tape recording (he had not) where I had called repeatedly to tell my Ex I loved her. Well this got me a restraining order anyway!!! You know you can restrain a lot of things but restrained love is mind bending~~~ I do not dwell there! No-fault divorce??? Allows you to be forced to be divorced from all your stuff and your kids, through a faulty legal loop that revolves without opportunity to resolve! Not that both parties aren't at fault~~~ IT is just that punishing one without recourse, by taking every resource, makes for a bad future course~~~ when the fault is in making the breaking deceptively faultless thereby creating a faulty perception of faultless marriage relationships that continue broken into the forever future!!! I'm sure some of you know how hard it is to walk back into your house of worship, friendships, and family; while, during, and after going through that! At most of, if not at all of the activities, with my children from then on, I was the only man most of the time or one of the few men! What's with that??? Men… put down the remote… and your control… Ladies either you are blocking us out, doing too much, or contending like you are. Well back to the story… I mean my historical perspective part of the story… Oh this is the story… Well that's somethin' anyway… about nothing∞ everyday… I hope God is readin'… Oh no he's writin'… Oh no IT's not works its faith… Oh Yeah… I remember! Thank God!!!

Faith and Belief… there are times in your life when yours is tested! What you were taught to believe has lost your faith. The faith you were brought up in has been lost to your beliefs. Yet you somehow still have Faith and want to Believe. Your faith is real and your living some form of that faith through belief without communion with IT. We need to start practicing that community of faith again I believe, in our everyday existence. Well IT's a good thing mine was strong as IT was tested often and thoroughly! Not quite Lot like! But enough!!! What is there to believe in and how can you have faith that your belief is true??? Believe in yourself… Believe in your self… Have Faith in yourself… Have faith in your self!!! This is the first step on the path to enlightenment!!! And maybe the last!!! Because what else can you believe in since you are the one doing the thinking… Or are you??? Back to my mainframe server analogy… You need to believe in yourself, in order to trust and be with your self, in order to sense being selfless, in order to entangle in the nothing∞ (20 minutes twice a day) with all selves! OK Already… Pages of pages of circular profession of IT believin, and bitchin… When do I GET IT???

Well if you've made IT to here and still think someone is going to tap you on the shoulder and hand IT to you I guess I should have saved us both a bunch of time and money by just creating another law of intention deception rather than emptying your self through nothing∞ 20 min twice a day. A lot of people feel empty! Well that's not what I'm talking about. I am talking about empting what you keep at the forefront of your intellect to subside, allowing your attention to slip through the layers of consciousness. while retaining your awareness, just removing your self and finding your being! Listen to your heart as the blood passes through your ears! Listen to your breath as IT passes in through your nose bringing in the good fresh air and exhaling out your mouth the dispirited! Feel your muscles relax~~~ starting at your toes remove all the groans and ending with your mind and only your mind!!! Your unconscious mind keeps bodily functions running as your lungs keep breathing in the positive and out the negative and your heartbeat lowers your pressures!!! Fill your self with IT, while empting yourself of indulgence. Touch the source let IT touch you... Oh yeah we were talking about Belief and ... Faith... Well you can believe something but Faith is the belief put into practice! We can practice our beliefs within the universal community by accepting IT as the cause of IT all. We're halfway through GET IT but each of us are in a different place in the journey but united in the Agape love of IT. For those of you that GET IT, or are beginning too, or just hope too, let's move on like we're going too~~~ GET IT!

Well back at the ranch... Oh did I mention that I came home again at the age of 38 to a loving... caring... family... that's the great thing about good families! I'm pretty sure we're all family... So why do we treat each other like we do? Let us be a great big good family again!

Home again, and I thought "You Can't Go Home Again" Thomas Wolfe... This time I was there to help take care of the ranch as my parents grew older and I was able to tap into their souls as I had become wiser... Wise enough to see how wise they were... and stupid I been!!! I made a choice at this time that affected the future of many including myself... I decided to go to school again and workout... How' pray tell does that affect others future? Your reading this aren't you!!! LOL!!! You walked right into that one... No but... Ya Know people use "No but" way to often... even when agreeing with you they start with "No" and then continue to say exactly what you said *butt* maybe worded just differently enough to distract you from the fact that this is what you originally said, so that they are right, thought by them first, and you already started out wrong and they just took hold of the discourse! *No but*... No butts about IT... Back to my choice... School and working out was a choice over

CXCIX

going back to find my stool at the bar and drinkin' my life away... Well I did not exactly give up on God's gift to man. I went on a medicinal prescription of drink rather than a way of life... or more likely death??? Well anyway... 10 years later you have a hardheaded Norwegian, who could have been getting paid for overtime rather than overly paying to be over educated, with 47 years of "real" life experience, that had the misty veil removed 30 years ago, inducted into the National Honor Society, in front of his kids, (that's the best part), Now you have a hardheaded Norwegian that is then laid off by Motor I don't O ya and too old to start entry into the downsizing! Oh No!!! Not that!!! Well look out now! Now an "Alpha Sigma Lambda" how the heck did that happen! What about his damaged brain... damn him he survived!!! Didn't they check his credentials? Couldn't we overlook him again! Are you sure he deserves to be here... in the now... with the know??? The most influential information I perceive was discerned from riding the vibe not learned from edacious scrolls and that you're now entangled in IT! I do know one thing for sure; along with all that readin, ritin, and rithmatic, I did some teachin! And practiced the arts of meditation and biofeedback, that I had put in my toolbox long ago! IT turns out the longer you use IT the stronger your flow, your cortical thickens and intention increases with age! Research has even determined that your grey matter may increase in correlation to the number of people you're interacting and caring for on Facebook... Not just how many you can get to click your invite! Must be that entanglement thing~~~ Look out!!! Here we come spinnin out of the universe!!! Thought, IT is a remarkable thing... IT makes kings and beggars, just coherent thought can make the world better!!! Lets explore a couple of those ... those... those... Oh yeah ... Thoughts!!!!

"I think... I think I am ... therefore I am... I think..." not... an original thought by the Moody Blues, yet I didn't know that then! This phrase of philosophy is attributed to Descartes who gave us our antediluvian scientific view in that consciousness was produced in our brain, isolated in our head, and IT wasn't matter. This I found deeply profound and IT still is, not the antediluvian bit but the thought that consciousness may be evolutionary and thus yet evolving not

CC

just a mechanical byproduct. Descartes could not, in his day, imagine interaction in the grey area may be with matter, because IT interacts through the infinitesimal tiny that is purposely elusive!!! Biolution by consciously modifying and thereby cultivating our baser instincts is still a work in progress... Did Da man in Da cave say, "hey, I think I'm going to do a little painting, that should change all of mankind's future in a figurative sort a way"? Not likely... And what makes them think IT was a man rather than the woman, who is usually in charge of Da interior decorating? IT was a conscious decision to open a new view but the revolutionary evolutionary step taken was barley denoted! How many original thoughts come by these days anyway... Interaction with our subconscious prehistoric programming punch card subroutines allows deletion of old crapware and defrag mental mitigation of legacy genes, as your knowing self produces enhanced physical and mental health! Science attributes all to the Big Bang... Well then... As a separate entity then, when and how did consciousness come about??? When will IT end??? We will get to the Moody's... well now's as good a time as any... they were the Beatles of the thinking class... Although John Lennon could hold class on different thinking... the Moody Blues started their melodic journey about the same time, minus the super egos, so they remain on the 45+ year road relevant to this day... Just saw them 3/27/08 from the 11th row, still amazing~~~ their music is one coherent thought package delivered on A & B sides of vinyl... Remember vinyl... yeah that big disc you used to put the needle on to experience Beethoven, Glen Miller, and Sinatra... or maybe Santana? He prides himself on "getting inside the note, the sound you are born with! If you have an open heart you can articulate life. If you have a closed heart you can only do one thing." Devadip Carlos Santana ("Devadip" - meaning "The lamp, light and eye of God.") and Mahavishnu John McLaughlin (Mahavishnu is the collective of all souls in all of the universes) complimented each other's style in 1973 while studying under Sri Chinmoy. They composed an album together entitled "Love Devotion Surrender." These two lead guitarists intertwined binaural[1] beats backed by a resonance that's fused Latin to Jazz and was electric Nirvana

CCI

(not the band)! More recently on the album Supernatural Carlos sings "Make somebody happy... make somebody stronger." Well anyway IT was analog and there was no signal loss unless your friend decided to self-cue... You experienced the full spectrum of depth and colour of every note and tone! When the Moody's sang "Speeding through the universe... thinking is the best way to travel..." and then the Mellotron kicked in you were~~~~~~   Oh by the way the mellotron was the first multi voice tape synthesizer and Mike Pinder, the Moody's keyboard player, was the guy that turned the Beatles on to IT so they could use IT on "Strawberry Fields... Nothing is real" and that changed the Beatles sound! When the Moody's brought IT to this country the Mellotron did not quite get along with our voltage and got a little quirky sometimes~~~ they also brought us vinyl stereo through Decca... anyway... You have some more homework to do and this is a fairly long enjoyable assignment... So go out and experience the Moody's preferably in the order they wrote and produced. I can be a taskmaster... I will not ask anyone to do something I have not done, enjoyed, or be willing to try! Let's see Oh Yeah... The Moody Blues... "Lovely to see you again my friend... walk along with me to the next bend..."

Back at the ranch... Yeah my folks finally sold the ranch and I didn't have a basement to live in just like back in the 70s anymore so... You know what it's like cleaning up after 40 years of ranchin'... well it took a while... so you better get started now! Talk about baggage! We tend to do and repeat those things that we know how to do well and our minds have become expert at! This is rote thinking and does little to generate or stimulate new thoughts and actions! You reason that by performing well at those things you do well that you are well but you are creating a mental rut that you travel well. By traveling around some of the side roads and seldom used backcountry trails to explore the new, delve into the once known and reexamine the knew, we ski different paths upon the same slope yet maintaining our neural network placidity! Treadmills in the gym and the treadmill of life both keep you moving yet neither do they expand fresh skills that develop or rejuvenate the seldom used either. The rote subroutines are fine most of the time, and quite instinctively mind handy, until one or sum of your brains subsystems delusively reports askewitively, mucking up your acuity, resulting in malfunctioning ambiguity and ridge edged neural incapacity. Try new things or old things new ways or anything anyway… Like black-light Ping Pong or any old thing you ever wished to try before you say goodbye! Do the bucket list and start a new… one… live the list of things you dream of, always adding more! IT's about being aware, aware of and accessing some of what has become automated instinctive, to understand IT, then optimally amending input to output of what has become, negative auto-reactive hardwired neural throughput kaput!!!

I told you earlier that I was a good old country boy… not by everyone's standards, but that's who I am! The country rock music we had with the New Riders of the Purple Sage, Poco, CCR, Mason Profit, IT's A Beautiful Day, Quicksilver Messenger Service and many others is beginning to be emulated 40 years later by some in the commercial country merging newly accepted into the main county lane… Seems my thinkin is always lookin ahead of Da curve while I slog along wondering why we're stuck in Da jam! The NE Illinois country, I was born to, is now one big mess of over development… so what was a poor boy to do except get lucky and get back even farther to his roots! I found a crappy little place on a crappy filled little lake on a crappy golfer course… is there such a thing? Daily looking over the lake… enjoying the natural state of a State nature area! Walla… what had once been a Hunt Club in my back yard was now my home! Tiny as my trailer is… Nature is huge… What I discern though is that, living in a trailer in my area, is a socio-economic crime! And should be avoided at all cost… including your soul!!! If you haven't already traded IT in on that new car, digital device, or an unmanageable mortgage… there is peace in the Fox Valley… "You got to walk♫ that lonesome valley♫ You got to walk IT by yourself♫"… The mountain top experience is wonderful and mystical but you must learn to return in small ways, through the hills and sometimes the valleys to tarry beside the mountain streams by sensing the subtle beauty and enlightenment found along the way to IT. When you have little you have little to lose. When you have nothing∞ you cannot lose IT and so you can choose choices others fear making because someone might be taking some of what they don't want to give. To seek favor includes the fear of losing IT and fearing disfavored disgrace. Where was I??? Oh yeah... Florida... No not yet... well almost... at least in this winter... still livin on the land I was raised on to this day... Although I been a lot of places in my life and experienced a lot of things~~~ when Mr. North wind begins to blow there is a call in the air to follow IT South. On Dec. 1, 07' I took off "In Search off the Lost Riff" on a Jimmy B Holiday and am writing this, with a view of the lighted cross tower of a Greek Cathedral, in Tarpon Springs Florida at the south end of the Nature Coast... Now... I need to take time to define and describe "the wonders of nature rolling in the rushes down by the riverside" this is from the Grateful Dead... more homework... I am multitasking as we speak... oh I mean writing... I am writing and you are talking to yourself so how is that defined? Anyway... the Dead would like this as I'm ripping their music... not my choice of process terms, that's what my pe..uter calls copyin! And writing about them at the same time... you can perform multiple tasks simultaneously, just one of the tasks need to be a less important one than the other, focusing back and forth or to and fro while you prioritize rather than doing several things inattentively poorly while realizing where your current focus is, not just your perfect image of how great you are at doing none of the tasks precisely! We choose what we do and we choose what we remember... Remember... Oh Yeah I think I remember... will get into remembering in a while, right now we're remembering my Historical Perspective! Yeah that's it! Sorta... Kinda... What is your perception of your connection to the comprehension of nature? Have you ever rolled in the rushes down by the riverside? I have and I got the hives... LOL... But took a chance on the roll again. Do you remember each time an element that once brought joy began to be considered inconvenient or a negative hassle such as snow, wind, and rain or flirting, consideration, and serenity? Do you hear the trees singing in the breeze? Have you ever "who wa who who who'd" back to a Mourning Dove? Do you feel all of nature as God's creation and sense the interconnection as well? How do we prove this? How do

CCIV

we perceive this? Ever thank animals like the pig, fruit fly, or horseshoe crab for your health and wellbeing, as we owe them much for today's medical advancements. Ever see a flock of birds turn on a dime or a school of fish flash as one, as if they are all in touch! Ever become one with the flight of a dragonfly, you following IT or IT syncing with you? Ever sense the tingling before, during or after an event that gave you an uncanny warning or synchronized coincidence? Ever have your pet send you a message? They can touch our minds a lot better than we can read theirs, they have less to fill theirs! Ever have a lucid dream? Ever have a wide-awake daydream? We have stopped trying to sense IT, although, IT's not about trying, IT's about not... Trying... Consciously... let IT go! Be present... Be aware... un be... Then learn to subtly refocus... We have stopped believing! In ourselves, In others, In IT! We have been programmed to think we are crazy if we feel or sense this otherworldness (SuperNatural) is possible... yet most of us do and believe IT regularly... whether sub-consciously or consciously... even those who don't believe are entangled to the source. What exactly do you want to call that? Ever try to will a squirrel not to run under your car? Ever notice that feeling of being watched, IT touches our mind? A form of ESP precognition... Atoms, people, and actuality behave differently when observed. Even when its done remotely, under scientific controls, without them supposedly knowing. Are we all whack jobs or maybe we just been told it's safer in society not to acknowledge IT! Just as we have learned to block IT, We can, and I do, entrain IT! We are composed of atoms... Not the inanimate lifeless atoms of Aristotle but the perpetually active energetic soulful atoms we are finding elusive to observe. We are in continuous communication and mentally "communicate" to each other faster-than-light as well as forward and backward-in-time, this is where lying haunts you and trashes your vibe, while fine tuning, projects the empathetic connection! Tuning into nature is where I spend way too much time! As I grow older that is where I find peace, feel love, and IT caresses my soul! I am selfish for hiding in nature because IT keeps me from the tasks set before me! "Where have all the flowers gone...Long time passing...Where have all the flowers gone? Long time ago...

Where have all the flowers gone? Girls have picked them every one… when will we ever learn… when will they eeev~~~veeer Learn?"

Nature Definitions of **nature** on the Web: **Wiki**

na·ture

Pronunciation: \'nā-chər\

1 a: the inherent character or basic constitution of a person or thing: essence b: disposition, temperament

2 a: a creative and controlling force in the universe b: an inner force or the sum of such forces in an individual

3: a kind or class usually distinguished by fundamental or essential characteristics

4: the physical constitution or drives of an organism; especially: an excretory organ or function —used in phrases like "the call of nature"

5: a spontaneous attitude (as of generosity)

6: the external world in its entirety

7 a: humankind's original or natural condition b: a simplified mode of life resembling this condition

8: the genetically controlled qualities of an organism

9: natural scenery

- $\frac{35}{17}$ the essential qualities or characteristics by which something is recognized; "it is the nature of fire to burn"; "the true nature of jealousy"

- $\frac{35}{17}$ a causal agent creating and controlling things in the universe; "the laws of nature"; "nature has seen to it that men are stronger than women"

- $\frac{35}{17}$ the natural physical world including plants and animals and landscapes etc.; "they tried to preserve nature as they found it"

- $\frac{35}{17}$ the complex of emotional and intellectual attributes that determine a person's characteristic actions and reactions; "it is his nature to help others"

- $\frac{35}{17}$ a particular type of thing; "problems of this type are very difficult to solve"; "he's interested in trains and things of that nature"; "matters of a personal   nature"

³⁵⁄₁₇ Nature, in the broadest sense, is equivalent to the natural world, physical universe, material world or material universe. "Nature" refers to the phenomena of the physical world, and also to life in general. ...

"*Nature*" is a short book by Ralph Waldo Emerson published anonymously in 1836. It is in this essay that the foundation of transcendentalism is put forth, a belief system that espouses a non-traditional appreciation of nature.

Nature is innate behavior (behavior not learned or influenced by the environment), character or essence, especially of a human.

Is nature what you thought it was? Maybe more! If this is nature why are we startled by the term supernatural? Would that not be just a superior level of the above definition? Or does the spooky entanglement of nature have to include ghosts and goblins? What can be said about nature vs. nurture? Well we better define nurture!

Nurture: (nûr'chər) pronunciation

1. Something that nourishes; sustenance. To nourish; feed.

2. The act of bringing up. To educate; To help grow or develop or train..

3. Biology. The sum of environmental influences and conditions acting on an organism.

[Middle English, from Old French, from Late Latin nūtrītūra, act of suckling, from Latin nūtrītus, past participle of nūtrīre, to suckle.]

SYNONYMS nurture, cultivate, foster, nurse. These verbs mean to promote and sustain the growth and development of: nurturing hopes; cultivating tolerance; foster friendly relations; nursed the fledgling business.

Nature and nurture -- you can't have one without the other. They do not add. They combine in a wide variety of complicated ways." In fact, sometimes it is even hard to tell which is which. Consider an organism whose gametes (sex cells) have been altered by exposure to radiation: to that organism the effects are environmental (i.e., nurture) but to the offspring that is produced from those gametes, they are genetic (nature). >Christopher Green, January 28, 2002<. The Nature vs. Nurture debate has been going on for an extreme amount of time, the main problem with a question like this is that any one person at any one time can, of course, do both…

Subtle interaction that plays across the Universe with the ebb and tides of time… God built into his creation everything IT needed, to be nurtured and provided for and so IT was. I am not quite sure I got this dog eat dog nature or nurture food chain thing down yet, but this is probably one of the reasons why, our raptor instinct, gets in the way of humane evolution. Nature is morally messy; life, death, predator, prey. If you are raised as an animal you will be an animal… Running around out of time while losing the humane race and looking for a reason that's got no rhyme… Here's a concept for Ya… Human beings acting humanly… Humans emoting humanly… I know IT's not rational, IT's not practical, IT is possible! Unlike gethumanoid, people would actually GET IT! The free Radical that I am, I believe there is a chance we could all act humanely toward our fellow humans if we were humane to ourselves!!! Human beings being raised humanely… How do you expect to go out into humanity if your not feeling human? The so-called human condition archetype human experience that Carl Jung labeled "acausal", is inhumane. Humanity deserves a radical makeover of human being! Analyze humans through the eyes of Bonobo's (the Hipper primate) rather than Chimps (the Warring ape) and you have a whole new human perspective! In Darwin vs. Creation nobody includes the possibility that the *environmental entanglement of the species consciousness* might be factors in entraining its evolutionary path and that this might be advantageous from an evolutionary perspective. Not even "Evo Devo" switch throw, accounts for conscious intention gene selection! Just as men… and ～～women～～ did not stop the new and improved mental revolution the day they moved Da fire pit into the house as they continued to work on expanding and developing, exploring and probing, examining then exposing new thought and conscious awareness that created overlapping neural systems and altered our minds along Da evolutionary timeline scale, resulting in a thought competing organism that is either deleting some redundant seldom used sensitivity and devolving to separate our minds or continuing to a unified exercise of sensory perception to connect IT all! Sciences origins of life theory, electric discharges through a primordial Earth's evaporative atmosphere producing an combo amino acid protein, may be partially correct, but the left handed ones appear to be otherworldly while, new life forms and Hobbits like me that don't conform, are being discovered then obscured to dismiss, yet this don't change the fact that they exist! (Timeline of human evolution) While genetic copying errors create DNA mutations that indiscriminately scatter the direction evolutionary paths takes! Transducing with nurture your babies' genome by induction of love through the epigenome nurtures their nature while reinforcing their positive memes and switching good genes on or bad genes off. The epigenome directs the genome and is malleable as well as susceptible to contamination from environmental factors, diet, and even input through our senses. So even if you are predisposed genetically to a specific trait, which may have been acquired through an ancestor's interaction with their environment or a random gene carbon copy DNA mistake mutate, you as well can have direct input into how or if that trait is expressed in you. We hear so much about genetics and Da Genome but what we don't hear is that the genes, environment, nurturing, stress, and even good old desire combine together to express the things we're predisposed of! What we what to hear is that the geneticists have miraculously saved us from ourselves... Know now that you're unknowingly passing predestined epigenetic futures down. Scientific theory cannot account for a yet to be determined intervention, that skipped ahead out of sync with time needed to transpire for the step by step evolution anticipated by Darwin. We have about the same amount of genes as a nematode worm and less than many plants so how we're choosing to express those genes has more to do with who you are than only the genes themselves. Evolution implies some sort of forward or positive progress while what is truly occurring is really a form of adaptive change that is not necessarily progressive nor positive but reactive to the current environmental interactive war of predatory attrition! Which may involve my previous reference to devolving... in some ways~~~ Civilization is proving to be much more advanced, than the theory precludes, in long lost ancient times. Some things are just too advanced to fit the paradigm. Currently being answered by the Catastrophic theory and De Novo Mutation based on a couple of skulls that probably are not what the Anthropologists present them to be or a number of permutations that allowed us to grow our opposable thumb while throwing some switches defectively to mutate our DNA in order to reduce our jaw muscle and permit space for our brain. Switches throwing switches... Timing is everything... IT's embryonic and space and time is flexible and probability indefinite... If we truly were only the result of the strong over the weak then where and how do we account for humans that are predisposed to helping those less fortunate, our willingness to sacrifice our lives for others, or our humane humility? I'm advancing my inner sight with a mind towards the future, yet my flight or fight response inherent in my genes is switched towards fight for what's right~~~ so you better consider taking the next flight out of my mind range if you think you can fright me. Not anger but direct considered appraised action in response to direct devaluing Da mindless deeds! Devaluing my children, their children, and my own rightful place to positively evolve to further mindspacetime. This is especially inclusive of Da need for change in corporation… I'm not angry so much as anguished… because I play within the confines of their rules and still lose badly because they continually move the goalposts, play with Da deregulation manual, take their inflated balls and move the game offshore where the chump fishing is better! Der switch the bait tactics are making me lure shy and now I refuse to bite, but will try to let the other fish know to stay away from allure today to have more life tomorrow as the bottom feeders throwing their switches have played off their gullibility to make them toothlessly tolerant! No longer struggling to succeed in the evolutionary war to pass on to future generations inherent rights! Deregulation only profited Da Deregulated and Da deregulators!!! Did you get yours?

60%

What orchestrates the synchronic symphony playing intense vibrations on superstrings of infinity∞ reverberating both backwards and forward in time all the time? This rhythmical pulse of doing beats and restful pauses streams the lively tempo from source to receiver to source! Science is stating that we may never completely understand the micro mini "spooky action" because of IT's elusive observable nature. Another synchronicity in my travels through the research of this spooky book is the discovery that they're already tele-transporting virtual particles on Tenerife in the Canary Islands… where my parents wintered on occasion and my father would teach the little ones "Do Ra Me" at Da La plaza in the afternoon after spending the mourning rereading the same page over… and over… and over… spooking my mothers curiosity as to why he read so slowly~~~ only later he told me, the European girls bathed in the photons "topless"!!! Now that would make my quanta leap~~~ We either attune to IT's rhythm and dance within ethereal orchestral ecstasy or deny the beat and live the sleep of mind deafening dispirit. The proof of IT lies in this logical contradiction. Scientific Realism minus pessimistic meta-induction equals ontological monism thought reductionism. Though the logical positivists would certainly or probably critique my language and succinctness! Living in Flatland proliferates apprehension comprehensively and perceiving other dimensional proportions magnifies the enormity of the unknown for you to known. *Brane's* of the extra dimensions enhance the chance of interconnected iBrains. The epicycles are building… The exclusion of inclusion of Get IT clueism adds controlled quantum signal induced chemistry that was then unknown and is the heart of life's evolution. How will we evolve and how will our new story reflect alternatively altering historically? Not the history of the re-writers but the history of mankind's interaction with IT! Often Myth, when it is brand new is called truth. Mystics through out time have prophesized that we are all interconnected in mysterious ways. Buckminster Fuller, stated that "If you want to understand the human condition you must understand the universe. If you want to understand the universe you must go within to understand the self. We should be using this raptor instinct to love and appreciate nature and each other, as IT is our deepest connection, but is mainly used to flee or for aggression! We have been taught to suppress this instinct as a way of taming the raptor… Wake the yawing slumber of inane soul to imbibe eternal∞ wisdom. Well I guess by now you've concluded that I'm pretty far out there, maybe even gone… well I am… I didn't go far… "I went to the doctor and the doctor said… no more monkeys jumpin on the bed!"

Seemingly often, mental disorder accompanies great genius, superior creativity, or artistic inspiration, but what is added to and admired by society apparently overrides our desire to proactively incarcerate the ingenious or rich. Mental health has taken a turn down Outpatient Street near you and I to "Deal" with IT! Its now time in this space to go on a diatribe about Meditation vs. Medication… touched on earlier, its only a silly consonant but seems like a constant!!! Every other insured person is on some kind of medication that gets entangled in his or her physiology. There has been a 400% increase in Anti Depression psychotic drug taking since 1988 and only two thirds had seen Dr. Late ly! Does the problem lie within the subject or the substance? A lot of IT has to do with the subject's substance!

DISCLAIMER: For those that are truly compassionate, comprehensive, and diligent while working in the Medical field I apologize ahead of time! Herculean miraculous leaps and bounds of scientific methodology and mechanism are graciously gifted thanks to many selfless individuals. Of course this is about everybody else not you... of course! You perform a difficult service and work under conditions, created by government embedded insurers administering healthy care supplies sparingly and a broken system that causes a lot of undue stress and burnout. If this is you I apologize... Health Care has become an industry no longer a system of human care. The insurance industry has already delivered health care rationing. Will the miraculous advances be enjoyed and employed by all, as good health is really the only essential! You have my empathy, yet I remain emphatic in my disturbance, in perversion of a healthy system to another unethical Capitalistic institution that receives the most and gives the least. Doctored up by government intervention with some good intention yet lobotomized by lobbies that make us losers and determine the detriment of profitability in healthful living! Change is only brought about from within...Let me know if I can help... The California Nurses Association is getting IT, as they represent the front lines where time for compassion is placed. As healing also comes from real compassion and should be approached with passion needing empathy to break down the antiphony of selves between us! Please don't BS the BS'r if you only assume "its not about me"...

Everywhere I turn I see self-medication and little self-meditation!!! I reiterate again and again seek help but know what you're seeking!!! There has been a rush by multitudes of people to "Run to the shelter of Mothers little helper" and IT ain't workin even for Rush... what a Fluke! Take away our purpose, our meaning, or our identity and we will become ill! If there's somethin wrong with me, I meditate... The machines that were to make our lives livable took away our jobs, incomes, and functionality, making US redundant empty space holders... Thank God space is not empty and illness is mostly in the mind... as I identify with the Creator self, whom creates good and sometimes bad internal ordered chemical composition rebalancing; I get with a good Integrative Holistic Naturopathic healer, hard to find a true☐ healer (you may be one)! On occasion I get some antibiotic to combat infection. Otherwise I find the illness within and listen to my body when in need of rest, nutrition, or a little work and exercise... Besides Da vibe~~~ Nutrition and exercise are key to coherent thought and good health. The humane body, that is fueled properly, is an amazing living macrobiotic self-repairing self-healing organic biomechanical machine! Drink water... Cut the caloric and stop the salting, do the fruit and yogurt thing. Retrain your taste buds to taste what's great for you! You may try a little fish oil for various lubrication or CoQ10, Goto Kola, for lively lucidity and energetic plasticity of mitochondria, eat real food in small amounts through out your day and gobble up vegetables don't become one... you know the routine lots of salad limiting the dressing... keep moving... those legs were meant for truckin... throw in some of the C's; Cinnamon, Cumin, and Curry, and Turmeric to prevent old timers. Oh and did I mention to drink some more WATER! I do refer you to the numerous other proficient sources for a healthful life! There is a classic disconnection on the interconnection between healthy bodies and healthy bank accounts thinking one induces the other. IT does take time and thought to eat right, this helps to explain why residents of so many other nations, including many poorer countries, live longer and healthier lives than we do! The time we plan and prepare enhances the time we eat and enjoy! Now the theory has been proposed that people associate the level of care to the price they pay. The psudo implications of this are inestimable. Also the well to do seem to overindulge in most everything and even though they get better care they don't seem to care to well too be listen and follow another's healthy advice! The main piece of your healthy wellness is in your mind and many are boggled! Some of the best proof of IT comes from healing sympathetic response. Those that take placeboes, are prayed positively for, or even cared about more than others, heal better, faster, and have sustained recovery. They have made great strides in many areas of the Health Fields and I am fortunate to have good health! Some of the strides have led us astray and medical care has become far too much about pay to play! Medication is still being practiced by people getting paid to medicate! This is why they are called the "MEDICAL Profession" most of the practitioners are professional medicater's ... I guess that's their profession! I profess most don't have a clue about the oath* Old Hip implied! The oath itself appears to be more strongly influenced by followers of Pythagoras than Hippocrates. Pythagoras, of your so much fun geometry class, who also brought us the knowledge of the relationship between the length of a vibrating string and the tone IT created. Anyway Old Pyth's tip of Hip was pretty astute of these old hypocrites!!! And they have made some modern changes that do some ethical adjusting? **Contrary to popular belief, the Hippocratic Oath[3] is not required by most modern medical schools.** Doctors have become providers and Patients must have some. This whole process needs to be put under a macro-microscope! Did you ever try to get one too say another or God forbid themselves have ever made a mistake??? The code of silence is deafening! They lobby to get US to release our rights of malpractice redress, as we must be mistaken about them makin any mistakes and the value our peers place on those mistakes, that we're mistaken about, are not worth the cost to insure or ensure correct! Before prescribing try emoting what you're quoting to compassionate your skills as they relate. People are getting so whacked out on legal medication they cannot think clearly enough for meditation!!! Judging how these people act on their pharmaceuticals, their Drs. of choice prescribes, maybe it's a good thing they are doing drugs because they are barely tolerable to be around on these psychotropic drugs! They take the pill, then they can tolerate being an a~~h⊗le to you because, every things cool man, I got no problem, I got no pain, I got none of those pesky feelings you claim! The fear of not having "Mother's little helper" or what they would have to face in the mirror each day keeps them locked into a matrix of delusion! What do you see in the mirror? Listen... Mother... May I... make a suggestion!!! If you are not sick do not make yourself ill by will deluding pill and... note to self: Do not get sick!!! Do not get sick!!! This is where IT gets ugly!!! I have buried two parents!!! One too soon and the other not soon enough... Dad focused on people even though he was always involved in some task... Dad died of an aneurysm in his brain caused by a fall in the bathroom while the doctors played with his level of Warfarin, a rat poison that bleeds the rat to death... Warfarin supposedly keeps you from getting blood clots that can maybe kill you or maybe not! Now we are getting pig intestine medicine from China that does the same thing a different way. There are a number of foods and supplements that are known to thin the blood. These include foods with high amounts of aspirin like substances called salicylates, omega-3 fatty acids, foods with natural antibiotic properties and vitamin E supplements. Dad was never told to avoid these nor was he told how they might affect the level of thinning in his blood or that he could use these natural nutrients to adjust the thickness of his blood! Researchers have confirmed that drinking even moderate amounts of alcohol can affect blood coagulation, acting as a "blood thinner", which can have both positive and negative health effects. So he had to stop his moderate drinking because he needed to be on Rat Poison? While you still have time figure out what to prioritize, in terms of tasks or people, so that when you look back through your life you will clearly see which you made more room for and which made a difference. And this is where IT gets uglier!!! My mom was in a car accident and cracked a few ribs and re-broke her leg that had been butchered in the 50's and replaced in the 90's... we have made progress, however we are moving backwards as well, as bedside manor and care are ...where Dr.s? I don't know! Like a thing of the past! Yeah gone and forgotten! Just like my parents! NO they're not gone or forgotten!!! Their presence is here they're just not present here now and all those they touched will never forget them!!! Oh Yeah back to my Mom... Well she was complaining about her stomach hurting and I pushed and prodded "The Professionals" to the point of being obnoxious... or maybe I was being an a~~h⊗le... Yeah an A~~H⊗LE! You better know how to be one because many of the doctors today live there! They mean well except they got "No time left for you... on my way to better things." Anyway other real concerned doctors discovered mom had Cancer... the other "Professionals" had missed, even though she and we knew there was a major problem... She was a real trooper from the "Depression Era"... Do you have any idea what that means! No you don't!!! Unless you lived it!!! I don't and I've studied it and talked to many who lived through it... You lived through it not in it... and I still have no clue! Well her father died in 31' and she and her sister were farmed out to relatives, literally on the farm! Do a little more homework here as we need to know where we been to get where we're goin! Taking her to the doctor, reminded me of cleaning the house before the cleaning lady came, IT was a social event as well as being a service. This coincides with the social desirability phenomenon; that patients often desire to know how to respond correctly to the prescribed treatment. We also desire success in our choice of going to the good doctor that can cure and heal us as well as say howdy to out on the course or at church. Doctors are highly educated and go through rigorous training yet are not necessarily the scientists we anoint them to be or always the healers we think we're going to see. Good days bad days Wednesdays... Patient "Doc when I drink coffee my eye hurts..." Doctor "Take the spoon out of the cup when you drink..." Well In her mind you did not question the system, she put her faith in the system, out of decorum she limited my questioning of the system and it turned out that missed Cancer required an ileostomy and gallbladder removal latter, which was to be to late! It eventually found her lymph nodes! We got her back home for a year and IT was a pretty good one! Though prescribed a neuronal intercept medication to slow her decline I'm not sure that this medication did not just selectively advance the decline of some thoughts more than others seeming to extend the suffering decline? She then had an episode of some sort where my daughter found her on the floor in the closet and she went in never to return... Now I do not blame all this on the Doctors, who apparently skipped the course on investigator bias, because they now not only have to recognize their fallacy of false causes they must stage-manage Systems Utilization Reviewers as your only worth not much time and

CCXVII

little resource of course without recourse and they along with the IN "Patient Advocate" started moving her out the obverse door as she scarily got her broken soul in through the emergency door, before ever being thoroughly diagnosed, profanely overriding her prognosis by osmosis. When a Cardiologist changes mom's prescription in a doorway as she's being discharged; to a nursing home (never to return) where she will see a Doctor once a week and not that Cardiologist ever again, without knowing the result of that adjustment, based on a conversation with me; I figure he's not much of a Doctor and has "No time left for you... on my way to better things"! The insurance that my Dad worked all his life for was out the window while Medicare and insurance rules... Absolutely Rules!!! And they ain't good rules and they ain't enforcen their own! Their broke, their being ripped off constantly, they have poor coverage of needed procedures and cover the superfluous, while the Center of Medicare and Medicaid Services is supposed to notify the accreditation group for hospitals, typically the Joint Commission, of all complaints received concerning hospitals. But according to an October 2011 report by the Office of the Inspector General, CMS rarely does so. CMS regional offices notified accreditor's of only 28 of the 88 sampled complaints against hospitals," according to the report. That's less than one third. The lack of reporting, "compromises Medicare's quality oversight system," says the Office of the Inspector General.

Hey... take a happy pill... and chill... Nah... that's only temporary... we'll learn how some are being happy temporally... Soon... For now we rank 34th in the world in infant mortality and 38th in overall medical care yet spend the most dollars per person. Declining healthcare costing more than ever... When healthy immigrants come here their health begins an inverse adverse degrade. Depression and hypertension rises to our confounded level. Little clue here... if your loved one goes into the hospital or nursing home (We got a good Christian one (still scary)) you better have another loved one on 24/7 because the actual caregivers, and my hat is off to them, they are overworked and underpaid mostly compassionate and friendly under fire... Time spent in intimate associations and close family ties are healthful, while social isolation kills and ills. Happiness is relational... YEAY!!! HAPPINESS... Science has determined that people we relate with, up to a friend of a friend of a friend, have an effect on our weight and maybe many other conditions, including our state of happiness. Another words you are likely to be fat or happy if your friends are fat or happy, thin if they're thin, and so on... Happiness is viral so spread IT, not your waistline! Do not reject or deject friends, because they have what you may consider a flaw that you may accede to, as what someone else's state of fate is probably troubling to them as well. Just be aware of others contagions that also spread virus like and start preemptive inoculation! Maybe inform them of your concern for both of you... I used to go to visit my mom, and she would be depressed and disheartened whilst when I left I would be depressed and disheartened, but for a brief time my happiness would become hers as I returned some of the happiness she had given me! Yet IT took time to lose my funk and recharge my batteries but if I was not with IT I could easily have gotten sucked interminably into the depressed heart disorder rather than to be able to return again and again to restore some of love and happiness my mother had invested me with!!! I also made a conscious effort to encourage and compliment all who were in the homes proximity... but this is my normal mental connection projection, so this did not take additional effort, I just want you to do the same... especially support and praise those who toil daily there with care as they will then have more of IT to pass on. IT is part of a forward payment of love and care that may then be waiting to be redeemed if we find ourselves disheartened in some home.

We seem to be adaptable to circumstances, situations and conditions we think are out of our control yet worry and obsess impossibly when things do not change fast enough that we think should or could. Don't believe everything you think! Think about what you believe you perceive to be, as there sometimes incurs a loss of sense in Da control tower and our own self-projected inventive expectations we have of ourselves and especially others that are non-existent and never meant to be! Rather spend some of this bothersome worry on validating, acknowledging, conceding, what others may be obsessingly expecting and you may find your relational happiness quotient enhanced. We fixate on stuff when it is new and the dazzle quickly becomes same old same old hassle. What's the difference between my stuff and your junk??? IT's mine!!! Will your stuff, that is really junk, visit you, grieve you, or love you??? Most people seem nice until you get close enough to know them. But IT is in the necessary defining of boundaries that bonds are made. Ask yourself "In this conflict do I fight fairly?" Is your discourse constructive or hurtful? Overbearing and uncaring or hopeful and soulful! Are viewpoints shared or are you in need of repair? Do you attempt to partake in unifying solution or jump into self absolution thus avoiding conflict leaving no resolution? Falling in love is easy but unbeing in love is work. Illness cannot be cured without love. If all physical needs have been met and no love made available emotional disrepair ensues. If this occurs, as a baby, the love circuit is blocked never to be turned on. Whiles we're here… lets explain how we began our perception conception!!! The birds and the bee's… no… SEX!!! No will skip conceptually ahead to the fetus floating in a warm sea of love listening to the muted sound around. Environment is already shaping epigenome, synapse, and health. Parents please start to socialize with your fetus, as your child is already interactive! What we fail to impart to our babies and pre-kinder can never be re-inducted later no matter how much time or treasure we expend in trying to reduce stupidity!!! You are the first and best teacher as babies have more synapses than at any other time in their lives waiting to be trimmed and shaped into who they are to become! They need you live… not some facsimile baby entertainer like the Blues Rays or 3D TV though some music does nice things. They entrain their social learning and verbal skills, develop eating and sleeping habits, that last a lifetime and this is where you learned to put your focus of perception. Then we grow up and get stuck in this story… The more you participate in the give and take of love the more resilient you become and the more adaptable your happiness. Most people have a happiness set point that no matter what happens in their lives they eventually return to IT. It's not about how hard or how many times you've been knocked down IT's about how you got back up! Illness, unemployment, divorce, or death, are amongst the numerable life molding incidents that can leave us shattered and wondering who we are? Now what??? What's next??? IT's not the actual events that occur IT's how we think they did. Uncertainty can become possibility. There's no great secret to happiness… IT's a choice. We need to live in the mindfulness not just learn about IT! Self-help is like kids at a playground, they are going to bring home a lot of dirt, a few burses, and maybe a few germs yet something good seems to have taken place. What I mean by this is don't believe everything you see or read… unless of course you GET IT… LOL. There're as many books, tapes, videos, web sites, and practitioners as there are trueΩ religions. Some good some not so and some are introductions to one of the over 5000 cults proclaiming whatever they think you'll think and believe… So be careful which you pick and practice! The older we get the happier we are and appear to be, as life seems to come into focus without the burden of futures weight. There is no time to dwell on the negative because time is fleeting and the oldsters are staying in the now by looking at today and good reflections in their mind. This does not mean you can wink wink nod nod away the bad you just do not dwell on the negativity. Swiftly reflect the negative taking care to let the negative know you're positively there. Seniors support each other. If we support each other, thereby lifting each other up, we can intervene in the toxic[2] negativism that is making us all ill! There's no way we can do everything or maybe anything alone but we can all do something maybe anything together. Live a life of danger… creativity… caring…maybe even bliss… Move out of the expected accepted and into the expanded existential. IT's connections… and we're all connected in the unified field… Engage!!! Let's see… where was I… Oh yeah sick and tired of being sick and tired… There's the bad tired of imprudent constriction contorting to please others dream needs and there's the good tired derived of knowing and passionately acting upon your hearts intention and aspiring to IT. Just one more thought… I have been in more than my share of health treatment institutions and isolation is endemic. Only high quality time and caring shared association at the frontlines will healthfully overcome ill isolation. The megacorp bottom line does not include expenditures for intended healing social time nor is the esthetic design easy on the mind.

So where was I … Oh yeah a diatribe… about a consonant… No a constant… Yeah that's IT… Meditation vs. Medication… First its like a little science lab experiment designed at lunch with the Pharmaceutical salesman and then you are used as their guinea pig, because a few studies didn't kill anybody or cause them any of the symptoms that are really a turnoff when they run the commercials or cuts into their profits because of liability! The deniability now lasts longer than the celebrity sales pitch cred ability! They are repackaging and repurposing approved drugs for unapproved "off label" uses. Find the doctor that has thrown the sales rep out of his office. Do they really believe if they say it fast enough people will overlook them? Well they do and we do… overlook them!!! Suicidal behavior is a known side effect of certain antidepressants and even a single allure Allergy drug! The continual advertising of medications for illness's, of which I have no clue, puts us in an anxiety mode as we listen to what the symptoms are and mentally check if we are having them! Many of these symptoms are everyday occurrences in healthy normal people, there are still a few!!! We are told to go and seek out a medicine dispenser! Then when we start on one we need another to counter that one and then we need another to counter that one and pretty soon we forgot which one started the mess we're in… Then we start to forget which one to take when… Then we forget who we are! I hope there's a better way to move through to completion of this journey because my plan calls for, a bottle of VO, a very cold winter night, and sleep on the ice. All under the stars with the Unity that is there to accept my quintessential essence, leaving mortality behind!!! Only if I'm lucky and avoid the system! Funny how easy death, on your terms, looks in the mirror of the dying in the System… Dr. compassionate Life Kavorkian had IT right and those tight asses that put him in jail… may they rot in a nursing home… Sorry that's a little harsh… no that will be easy compared to what they got comin!!! Other countries are life years ahead on dignified death with dignitas~~~ The Dr. is In… well who do we have here? Doctor Strange Love… "deterrence is the art

CCXXII

of placing in the mind of the enemy the fear to attack…" yeah I been told I'm pretty strange! I also have been told I have a lot of LOVE!!! Let's get a handle on this compassion thing and use IT to produce positive outcomes! We need to deter these greedy bastards that are running everything and get some results that are not slanted only in the direction of the almighty dollar… by using the almighty dollar to put fear in their pockets!!! This is true in all areas of Corporate America… or was that Global Pangea? How is this compassionate??? Well the sympathetic consciousness of others' distress together with my desire to alleviate IT. By irrevocably coaxing these money grubbing A$$H☹les into feeling the only course they have is in helping to row the boat under a corrected direction that is better for ALL~~~ You know, with discernable true passionate compassion not just some more lip service marketing. Maybe a little different take on what you thought compassion was but being a weak kneed weenie does not help others suffering! Why do we pay for all the research at our universities that somehow becomes their products and then pay them again when we check out at the store? I'm not deriding the God given birthright to improve your lot in life through effort. What I'm referring to is how you get there and what ripples through your karma and mine as a result! Stomp them where you can and let them know "I'm sick of it and I won't take it anymore"! As Arlo Guthrey put it, if we all just started singing "You can get anything you want at Alice's restaurant" we might start a revolution… you know the one… like the War… we never finished… you remember… back in the 60's and 70's… Oh yeah… I forgot… No one remembers what went on in the 60's and 70's… We never quite finished the revolution and we atrophied back into being our parents! Is it because of the stupor we were in then or the one we're in now??? Rise before you die and join this silent salient eternally∞ interactive revolution of unified reconstitution. Take IT to work in you and spread IT around for others to see. Information gathering and processing is the anti-atrophy… in order to keep the brain agile IT needs to stay flexible, not rigid! When we compensate or adjust our bodies or brains when they are injured or damaged to the easiest solution by default, we are losing perspective and perception of what is maybe best for us rather than easiest! Losing a step or only getting back part of what is injured or damaged may only be because we do what's easy and we're willing to settle for less! Studies show the more you struggle and use your body and mind the more that comes back. The more you work the brain coherently the more IT synchronizes and heals itself. Are you working yourself till death or have you just been puttin time in til retirement? What are you retiring to? When my daughter was 3 or 4, she asked her Pop Pop, what his job was and he said "I'm retired" and her response was "I tired too!" Don't even think about being tired or retired as now they are issuing credit cards hooked directly into your 401K. Maybe you won't want back what you have lost in brain function??? But if you still do… start retraining, trying, living, shifting to the new after methodical consideration of what to keep and what to lose… continue the use of what you have while striving to Get IT! IT's also preemptive against much loss! IT's the process of paying attention and engagement in life leaving behind the mundane and status quo. Compelling systematic improvement, through interest development and thought processes, that you move your mind and body through. No pseudo personality development to hide our behinds from what we make believe that others need to perceive in me! Leaving your comfort zone and repetitive behaviors behind! Recognize positive behaviors and embed them rather than repeatedly encoding critical negative self-talk. Your mind remembers the bad and the good equally… Axion to neural transmitter to synapse… if you have pain your neurons will remember the pain and make synapse connections in the neural network that remembers this pain and they will continue to connect until they are disconnected by, unbeing, less frequently used or forgotten… the selectivity of learned memories are both positive and negative and you can have input into which they will be!!! These neuron level connections, receptive field and synaptic plasticity, are what memories are made of, through the Hippocampus. Use IT or lose IT! The good new news is if you lost IT you can bring IT back via revitalization using rehabilitation thus rejuvenating a restorative regeneration of neural connection. Synapse entangled together fire together making them all stronger. If we are motivated to selectively change the connections by stimulating neurons initiating a positive feedback loop through behavior modification, diet, physical activity and we protect our mylin, we then may modify the way we live inside and outside ourselves... however, like when I am writing this book, the changes I make are just temporary until I save them so do not give up until the changes you undertake to make are neuron-synchronically saved! The physical universe has been in a state of atrophy since its inception on the contrary knowledge continues to expand... Knowledge and processing of information is the anti-entropy, disorder to order. Why if we have all this ability and knowledge do we allow the rules of the game to be dictated to the players... What is this Pro sports? No they got a Union... I do not like what unions did to actually getting the work done but we better start forming some kind of union or we gonna be working for the man 24/7 and still not makin a living! Union of the oneness! We drifted into a different tirade altogether... Well that'll happen... I hope you don't reason that I live my life goin from one tirade to another! Well I do meditate now and then~~~

My life is actually quite blessed and getting better everyday. I just see room for improvement and believe I know the way to change, through IT! There is plenty to bitch about and very few doin bout, so maybe my bitch bout... I mean write to talk-a-bout IT... someone may sense the tree falling in the zero point forest even though no one is there to hear IT! And IT will shake them out of their medicated stupor haze.~!? This medication fascination is blurring the future of America to the point that Lenin and Marx predicted! Enhancement of short term IQ and feel good too by making us short term dopes duping dopamine. We need to start living and loving again!!! We're all in our own world and IT gets crazy in there... How can we wean ourselves off of this Insta-Fix mentality? Why are we not willing to put the work into our selves that we endeavor ourselves in at work and with our family's? We want to be recognized for our hard work and effort. Recognition is one of the best ways to compensate someone that does anything for you! Starting with a simple "Thank You". Do someone a favor... ask them to do one for you. We do not seem predisposed to acknowledge others help or even accept IT when offered. We do not recognize ourselves, put the work into ourselves that is necessary to provide a positive outcome, or acknowledge our own success! IT is just easier to defer to the fact that there must be something wrong with us, and if we can get the Dr. to agree, we can solve IT with a pill and get back to running about in the spinning cage called life!!! Do not get me wrong, as my hope is, I am on the right side! Again if you are out of balance, somehow physically, that is affecting you mentally or physically please... please... get some kind of help, the right medication, diet change, or lifestyle change to bring you back to center. Except please... please... if you feel or experience, stress, anxiety, sadness, or pain do not instantly go for the medication!!! That's Life... In most cases mental medication should be temporary reconstitution solution. Once you begin IT is hard to find your way back as normal or happy become an elusive recollection. Choose a different consonant and go for the meditation!!! If the disease is physical, research, research, research... then ask, ask, ask... then confirm and repeat. This is the Golden age of medical technology and the dark age of medical application! R u Retired or just plain tired? How bouts a quick meditation visualization revitalization... picture a large body of water... close your eyes now~~~~

Let's see what is next on the wheel of fortune! Lets spin IT and take a chance... Why do we like to take chances? What is with the endorphins generated that makes taking a chance such a rush? By any chance have you started to gain any insight since you began this journey to the center of your mind? "Risk" is a game of World conquest and domination. Fun, but the risks you must take to change and grow as a person, in this experiment called life, need not be a gamble. We all have risk aversion quotients, but do any of us really know what's at risk?

Let's start with Gambling... what is the definition?

GAMBLING... A tax on stupidity... I mean...

GAMBLE Defined Wiki

1.a. To bet on an uncertain outcome, as of a contest.

1b. To play a game of chance for stakes.

2. To take a risk in the hope of gaining an advantage or a benefit.

3. To engage in reckless or hazardous behavior:

Many risk-return choices are sometimes referred to colloquially as "gambling." We gamble with our lives... Are we holdin aces and eights? We gamble with others lives... Holding futures in our hands each day! We gamble with our futures... Leaving too much to chance! We gamble with our elected officials... Impacting both locally and globally! Gambling, like any behavior, which involves variation in brain chemistry and waves, can become psychologically addictive and harmful behavior in some people. Reinforcement schedules may also make gamblers persist in gambling even after repeated losses. The gamblers fallacy that the previous random outcome affects the probability of a next random event costs millions each day. Almost everything has a risk factor of some sort and much is spent on Risk Analysis and Risk Management...This is what we need to personally incorporate into our thought and get better at IT so we are no longer gambling randomly with our minds and souls! I'm not sure the thrill of finding out you have an addiction, or the rush of discovering you once had a life worth living, is worth the gamble! Calculate the possibilities... events do not have to be random nor do outcomes need be considered coincidental as focused positive thought and action proceed synchronic outcomes and often advance affirmative probability potential! Turning random into envisioned!!! You also may find random negativity does not always seem to be reinforced congruously but eventuality the probability that random coincidence will!!! Spend some time in the valley of peace and get your rush from the wonderful life you are creating and the astonishing synchronicity that flows from your vision! Believe IT or not what you envision and what you imagine becomes your reality!!! You believe your reality to be THE REALITY... Is IT??? Imagination, leads to inspiration, leads to visualization, leads to intention, leads to creation, leads to application! As I have told my children many, many times, "Happy... Happy talk keep talking hap... you have to have a dream, if you don't have a dream, how you gonna have a dream come

CCXXVII

true"!!! What is your Dream? What is your vision? What is the reality you would like to create? Does IT include a helpful enthusiasm of usefulness? These things need to be defined! So take a little time off from reading and spend a little time lookin for the meaning! Once you have a plan check back to see if you are working on IT or is IT desiring change... All good plans have a flexibility factor built in for change, based on the outcomes up to that point along with redefinition of future goals, to facilitate growth. The meaning of life changes with the seasons of life!!! Joseph Campbell reflected, "People say that what we're all seeking is meaning for life. I don't think that's what we're really seeking. I think that what we're seeking is an experience of being alive". You need to manage the risk in your life and when you understand and evaluate the level of risk you take in order to reach the dream you make then IT is no longer a gamble and the rush you get is part of the thrill you feel as you successfully navigate the dream you are now seeing through to fruition! The only high left to gamble about is your answer when someone asks you if they look fat in this or that! Well that brings us to the risk of telling others what we perceive to be truth, a half-truth, a white lie, or an omission! How do you stay in the objective truth when telling IT hurts one or another? Do you say "yeah" "no" "maybe so" that it flatters your shape or it doesn't you fat slob... (Even if IT is your spouse) or go about explaining that "what I think isn't nearly as important as what you think about IT" this answer applies eternally∞ internally!!! But opens up the possibility of having to continue a conversation you maybe dodging that you both carry around with you in the background of the forefront of your lives!!! Which of the above options do you choose? Does IT depend on who's IT is and what the situation is? Really doesn't matter if your Da boss or worker, brother or sister, mom or dad, priest or sinner, ect... ect... ect... What people think themselves is the most important item in human interaction~~~ This is a gamble as you are risking the other's wrath, indignation, friendship, and Love! Situational ethics is a slippery slope^~^~^ you better keep your edges sharp! Speaking of sharp edges... Why do people with sharp edges always make us a little edgy, or push us close to our edge? This is not all bad, as we need to leave our comfort zone once in a while to find out where our limitations are... Answer this with patience and love and turn an edge back on itself! Remind me again if you could... what the qualities and qualifications are required to be a dignitary??? You know those who indignantly do not have to wait in line or make you wait for their motorcade... or those that add some title or honor to their god given name...You know... those that are a cut above or best... Is there a dignity descriptor in some funky waggle that qualifies some to this distending standing or how do I become anointed? Let me try to recollect how often we've indignantly rebelled against royalty preclusion imposition despotism? Yet political dynasties connected to the moneyed pedigreed lineage and those acting the part indignantly portray themselves as the blessed, above and beyond the rest! Not only are many of these people wasting my time their spending my dime!!! Do me a big dignified favor and stay home in your Mc-mansion. Hey... you wanna bet a billion that I too could be president if I could first collect on the bet from the bankrollers thereby eliminating any risk or gamble! They should have to wear uniforms with their corporate sponsors photo and logo so I can vote for my self-interest!!!

***Let's see where the heck are we? Oh yeah the Cop's... Yeah the Cops... Funny how a knock at your door can change your intention and thoughts! "Bad Boyz... Bad Boyz... What Cha Goona Do!!! What Cha Goona Do When They Come For You... Bad Boyz... Bad Boyz!!!" Just had a cop not a "peace officer" knock on my door and my thoughts went right into defense mode! Now why should this be? As their motto is or is it was? "To serve and protect"! He was offering neither of these services to me and after an introduction, I barley caught, he started asking questions! Well when someone just starts off asking questions and wanting information the first thing I do is ask questions and want some information! Seems these days that they assume that my private life is their business (even have had them stop me walking up to a golf pro shop and ask me what I was doing there??? Golf I think!!! Then IT was OK... Well I could have been lying... ya think... or maybe I was an escaped lunatic... Now that's a real possibility... anyway...). Is that service person you called for "real", or dare because Da NSA FBI'd your DNS so they could eva drop on U like U been ladin? Better check those shiny black shoes!!! Also seems like these days anyone offering me a service, including customer service, is trying to steal another nickel out of my pocket or upselling me that service or some other, that's really not truly a service but another way for them to shake loose my hard earned money from my empty pocket and don't try to speak with a supervisor as the CSR is instructed to shield them from US! Well anyhow... turned out I could help Da Man now standing inside my door as he was looking for someone that no longer lived there or maybe never did as that apartment had been empty a while! Me thinks' IT would probably be a marginal cover story to wander through an apartment complex and see what's going on inside your home! But apparently I have neither right nor reason to know anything except that he wants info from me. My first reaction would have been to shut up and act stupid! Which for me isn't hard to do, the stupid part anyway! Did someone issue them an aggressive stupidity permit when I wasn't looking??? I have found when you stupidly come on aggressively generally aggressive stupidity is mirrored through back at you. But this can be a fun way to preemptively bait your hook when fishing for a little negative reactive action. Well anyway... the men of law enforcement demeanors and motives are questionable these days and they want answers and are willing to give few while answerable to whom! Using trickery rather than applying truth! Maybe we need to bring back Dick Tracey to catch some crooks cause the lawbreaker's seem to be a slippin past Da law officer's while they waste the law abiding's time and resources... This rant is going to take a while so grab a snack and sit back... As Jimi sang "I ain't looking for no trouble now... Ain't looking for no trouble..." Those of service, such as Firemen, EMT's, Dispatchers, as well as the few Police that GET IT... I praise thee. The job these people perform is an awesome one and I respect those that are doing the job right... I just do not seem to meet many servers or feel particularly protected amongst the force of Police!!! When you strong-arm to squeeze money out of me for your benevolence fund, I am not getting a warm

CCXXX

fuzzy benevolent feeling!!! I'd like to thank all the rest... you're the best!!! But for my buddies!!! Here we go...

First off; I ain't your buddy and I ain't your pal till we tip a few back together and you actually are! Secondly; I ain't liken the fact that I am guilty until proven innocent! Thirdly; Rights! Ain't something you just read to me! I was endowed by my creator with certain inalienable rights! Pursuing happiness... I'm pretty sure was one of them!!! Fourthly; The fourth of July celebrates this fact! Fifthly; my sister's birthday is on the fifth! Sixthly; (which is really fifthly) IT is the people like myself, that want to change this world and make IT better, that you better get on your side or your going to have Alien-Nation against you! Unlike the illegal alien nation you should be preventing by deportment and border enforcement! Illegal means the moment you stepped into America you became a law offender and disrespecting US, and all those waiting to legally enter, as US citizens of America anybody illegitimately demeaning our citizenship by illegal action should be considered criminal. Including those openly financially supporting these illegals and yet another Amnesty. If they truly cared for their native land they would ensure that IT was a good and safe place to be known as a child of! I am not a criminal but have been treated like one on several occasions!!! No...Not when, we students, were flippin cop cars over and settin em on fire in Madison, La Crosse, Chicago, or Ohio, while being labeled unpatriotic by the PC's, in order to stop the warmongers... objectionable truth eventually did!!! Some Act called Patriot~~~ renewable ad infinitum ad nauseam adding up too Anti freedom-less Fascism, under the guise of national insecurity!!! Just like the sealed Kennedy assassination files or any other inconvenient documentation, including our constitutional legal process!!! Perpetually I find myself on the wrong side of being right... Flower Power against the war machine! How many lives did we save? Maybe IT was your Dad, Son, Brother, Sister, or Cousin... How many precious lives were lost heedlessly? IT was to late for mine!!! Have they reinforced the empires cities and government buildings under the pretext of national security to keep us safe, or keep us in check? Are they already preparing the internment camps like our brethren Japanese American Citizens endured? How many German American Citizens were imprisoned just because? Selective imprisonment may come to a camp near you just because National Security deems IT to be an instability issue! Wave the flag… flash a photo of a disabled Vet… show grandma with some apple pie and you got patriotism… ~~NOT~~!!! What are we really pledging our allegiance to? False Flag co-opting Capitalism? Da Industrial war machine? Wake up and put your love of country in tune with the love in IT's people by infusing the freedom that is not free! Professing to love your country does not exclude exude anyone else that has a different take on IT, from also loving that same country... unless we live together in oh so different worlds!!! Stand up… don't sit up like a dog trying to please while waiting for a bone!!! If you're looking for a national security threat check into our educational system… I am not a pacifist, as you can read, but either take care of business or don't get into global policing policying… No… I was treated criminally when I was pretty much mindin my own business and not looking for no trouble at all! So because I once fought in the second revolutionary war (entrained thought is radical evolution third revolution) do I deserve to be harassed because you bastards are shoving theoretical square priorities up my round reality hole and the power in your head has a broken dimmer switch! I sense it's a little of both because they still don't like my attitude of freedom and I know many power freaks on superego highs… Fricken up the positive vibe because they live and work in the negative! This new revolution will take place in the hearts and minds IT's just a matter of time~~~ Bring IT to the boardroom, union hall, church, school, or any other meet up space where IT need BE… Then IT will become you!!!

We continue to put laws on the books at such a rate that no one knows what they all are or mean! My last ticket, TWENTY YEARS ago, for a moving violation was for passing leaving an intersection! I never even heard of this!!! Ignorance is no excuse. They have made it almost impossible not to be ignorant of some law! So what this amounts to is, even if you believe your attempting and following all the laws, your going to be breaking some law, somewhere, somehow, even though your intention is to be law abiding!!! This then creates a situation of selective enforcement, as this seems to be what they want to begin with… Governments selectively deciding which laws they enforce, on whom they may choose to dislike, and just incase they feel the need too then always available to intimidate??? More power! More Fear! More BULLCRAP! Keeping the gangs, drugs and violence all packaged together while allowing the gangs to spread the fear and fund their operations selling life depleting drugs * (meth-H-cocaine and now resale of prescribed) on one side, as they (the law) exert fear on the other to apparently lead us to believe we desperately need more police to protect US from the gangs and violence they do little about and actually assist when convenient! The grand old ploy of playing two or three sides against US caste interminably in the middle without recourse! Now before you come to arrest me and take my gun! (Which does me little good when all I can do is bring a knife to a gunfight because of all Dem places I can't carry, in the Supreme work around, Dem state legislate carried!!! I guess only being criminal permits firearm possession in Dem places) Let me assure you I have no ill intent and several attorneys in the family, so if you want a suit let's rock! I prefer peace in the valley (yet I can bring IT (not Da gun) when I need IT) and you CAN go after those that truly need some kind of an authoritarian figure in their life! Like molesters, killers, thieves, rapists, gangbanger's, Internet scammers, Da corporate crooks or politicians!!! Oh I forgot they gave you your job!!! You can't go after them! They're not the easily fined for cash pickings you'd bother going after anyway. You know what I'm saying! Well you could but you don't! But you could! I wish you would!!! How about prioritizing crime and stop going after those who piss you off and start going after those who are pissing on us! "To Serve and Protect" "us" you know the citizens of the U.S.… We the people! You remember! Don't You??? You will be amazed at the response of "We the People" when we the people start seeing you protect and serve we the people! I could go into great length and detail as to the indiscretions perpetrated on me personally by the men and women in blue! That would only serve to make this an even longer diatribe and they all know what I'm expounding about yet they deny away! So why should I return one… or

CCXXXIII

two... or three... or maybe a lot more disservices with another! Let's let bygones be bygones... wait a minute... only I am forgiving... shouldn't this have to be bilateral forgiveness? Seldom is forgiveness utilized by the side perpetrating the act as they feign unconsciousness of IT! Well I guess they need to forgive themselves for what they have done! That would invoke unilateral forgiveness not provoke futility... And Seventhly; I am not a "Perp"!!! I am a 59-year-old law abiding citizen! Eighthly; When will police be held accountable by their department, the courts, or any governmental body. Is this "A Government of Wolves"? We foot Da bill for their lie a bility... let them pay for their plays! SWATING is bararic butt every muni needs to armour up just incase Da invasion comes to Da homeland!!! If they can clean up their act and keep an eye on their internal processes by policing themselves! They will not have to continue to ask for this forgiveness again and again! Come on all you guys and girls out there in blue... I want and try to help and love you... so please reciprocate by going after the criminals that are doing the crime not us U.S. citizens! Go get em! I wish to assist! And so does most everybody else! Just remember we got rights too and I'm assayin to all... If you expect respect you must be respectful!!! Now where the heck was I??? At the ranch??? No!!! Space and Time??? No!!! Well where??? Oh yeah... Gamblin!!! I might be gambling my freedom in this last diatribe? Well I weighed the risk to benefit ratio and came up with the, "What the heck" answer!!! I see on the news today they are making more laws regarding the homeless here. Now they're ticketing and fining them! How do they expect to collect? Oh... they're turning them into WIFI hotspots and calling it job creation! How can every new project create new jobs? Do those numbers include laying off people after they finished the last project to rehire them for another? The begging here has gotten out of control! We ought to offer them a place to live and eat... with requirements! They have learned how to work the system. We need to make IT clear "do not feed the animals"!!! I am of course referring to those who are professional vagrants or choose not to accept help... or only the convenient help they choose. These beggars again accosted me today! They all have some story to guilt you into feeling sorry for them! The injustice they are doing to the truly needy and destitute is a sin and should be repaid with a blunt NO! I now have to try to discern true need from lazy greed!!! Negativity should be approached and dealt with carefully as we do not want to feed the negative energy yet must starve the cancerous cause to death! Speaking of lazy greed are all politics partisan, parochial, and poisonous pretensions, riding a swift boat down the stream of our consciousness or creating an Attack Watch that's almost Orwellian. Wonderin where the stupor PACS are going to take US on a swiftboating cruise this election cycle!!! And why does it seem the deal has already been cut or the plan formed before you get to the table! Who can we trust to clean up the mess that greed has turned our democratic republic into??? I'm searching for possibility opportunity not hand outs under the guise of redistribution. Do you not care enough to share a small part of what you got, raising all of mankind up? I'm asking for ethical capital investment in America. I'm requesting that the door to the club be unblocked. I'm pleading for education and teacher reform. I'm demanding corporations give America back… I'm proposing that if the rhetoric is dropped the truth will not hurt as much as you think…

Please take a second and do a little mind clearing perception shift… Yeah the concept is that you can do this at anytime in any space… So close your eyes, open your mind, and shift a few parsecs (a unit of measure for interstellar space that is equal to 3.26 light-years) just about from here to Alpha Centauri! Several parsecs out the sun would be barely noticeable amongst the cosmos. Anyway I'm pretty sure these law in force men and women are not the center of any universe but I invite them to join mine where the center is everywhere!

Let's see where was I? Gamblin! Yeah the big Gamble! Da immortal gamble… Today there was a funeral over at the Cathedral! I'm pretty sure it wasn't mine! It could have been mine! Nah I don't think it was mine! But it could have been! Are you ready to die? I am! Well not today! I'm ready! Well almost! I got a few things left unfinished! So that's why I hope its not today! Well at least one of the reasons! Fear of having not truly lived, is immeasurably comparatively untold to the content of facing death eased by living bold! I'm ready for death, not really ready to die! Well wait a minute... What if just my body dies! What if my essence just keeps going! Oh! That's the part I'm ready for! Not the body part! The essence part!!! Ok enough with the exclamation marks!!! I do like to over emphasize don't I!!! Well there're ok there!!! But I cannot emphasize enough the wonders I await upon the death of my body and the release of my essence into the cosmos!!! I can almost touch, the beauty, freedom, view, understanding, fulfillment, and the Love that overwhelms my comprehension!!! And I am pretty comprehensive!!! I can wait!!! I'm like a child, waiting with milk & cookies, for the Christmas of my life!!! Well anyway there was a funeral over at the Cathedral today and I hope whoever it was, is experiencing the Love I envision!!! Are you Gamblin or are you ready!!!

Where we been and where are we goin... Oh yeah... I remember... well I did... I gotta go a ways back to remember... The doctor is in... we will now continue to speed our thinking through the P-Brane meta-multiverse!!!

Here's a little formula for THOUGHT:

Thought ≠ Intelligence ≠ Smart ≠ Cleverness ≠ Ingenuity ≠ Aptitude ≠ Shrewdness ≠ Brains ≠ Acumen ≠ Cunning ≠ Talent ≠ Expertise ≠ Adeptness ≠ Skill ≠ Astuteness ≠ Understanding ≠ I.Q. ≠ Wit ≠ Judgment ≠ Wisdom ≠ Sharpness ≠ Discernment ≠ Perspicacity ≠ Shrewdness ≠ Sagacity ≠ Reason ≠ Logical ≠ Rational ≠ Common sense ≠ Coherent ≠ Psyche ≠ Proficiency ≠ Insight ≠ Quickness ≠ Judiciousness ≠ Creativity ≠ Inventiveness ≠ Perception ≠ Humility ≠ Feeling..! THOUGHT... is NOTHING... without LOVE!!!

What's right with you??? Take this and work with IT... IT is all you have... all you have that anybody is really interested in! The rest! What's wrong with you, is the image that we hold in our head that's 99% past illusion now being used for delusion. The baggage... baggage is everywhere and pops up in our lives from different places, as do our issues in this book... this crap is what's wrong with you and is best only pulled out to be, reviewed, inventoried and tossed! You do not need ineffectual inventory in your neural warehouse! Your life needs a spring-cleaning! Do you really believe anybody wants to hear about the same problem you told him or her about two decades, two years, two weeks, two days or especially two minutes ago… You may assert a different problem or say "well you just don't understand"… I am afraid we do understand and the problem is with you living the problem, what's wrong with you, rather than "What is right with you"!!! You and only you have the power to choose whether or not your grateful for what you have where you are, yet maybe not quite completely fulfilled. Are you forever in need and always missing what you think would complete or fulfill you! The old which half, empty or full… I'm pretty sure if you look hard enough you can find something going right with you and this needs to be expanded until you cannot fathom all the blessings abounding around and through you, remain thankful! Be thankful to the point of asking for greater abundance and blessings. There is no ledger so ask always and often. "What is right with you", let me give you a simple example… a person is backing out of a parking space at the same time as you or a few moments after you start… do you swear a blue streak… or just write off the miscue… Well if you wrote off the miscue that's something right with you! Let me give you another example… Your significant other dyes all of your whites pink by accident, stepping up to do the laundry! Do you go south on them! Or temper your response some and show a bit of compassion…if you are the significant other, do you realize if the response, you receive, was tempered by compassion or do you just become defensive? Lots of questions, only one correct response…Compassion… Is IT right with you? Start with common courtesy and then turn that into a trail of positive Karma flowing throughout all unity… fill everyone with blessings and abundance! You can get anything you want if you give others what they seek. Take time to recognize the good things occurring every day as the world turns to seek the sunrise. Failing to do so is why you reiterate your past. People will stop asking what is wrong with so and so may you do the same… My father always intended and thought he was going to meet good people and he did… The universal law of attraction! You are choosing who your dance partner is! Inside all of us are multiple personas and you can dance with the one you choose to bring forth by seeking IT in them and radiating IT's compassion. IT took me a while to figure this out as he was looking for the good in all people, he was finding people as he expected them to be!!! He was looking for what was right with them!!! When I meet you what will be right with you!!! He was also know as the "what chew got in your pocket" man! He always and I mean always had some kind of treat, candy, gum, or his harmonica in his pocket and the only way you can become the "what chew got in your pocket" guy is by always havin something in that there pocket! What chew givin?

Now let's see where should the plot take IT's next turn? I STOPPED SMOKIN AGAIN! Well before I get put into a different plot! What am I doing smoking? I know some of you imagine I been smoking something as I write this! And you are right! I been smoking the worst drug imagined by man! Cigarettes hook... seduce... they're legal Heroin... the dreaded cigarette...Well some of you thought I was smoking something else, I guess you have figured out IT carries through in much of my writing and philosophy! Is that a bad thing? Are you judging again??? Why I say I stopped smoking and not that I quit smoking, is because I have stopped smoking many times before for as long as two and half years and many more times from a day to several months! Cold turkey has me on the run once more... One addiction is easier to quit when you have others to fall back on and into. When you give up that last addiction, because you can't be drinkin without smoking, for a while anyway... unless you count food and water as addictions, although food, especially sweets, can be very addictive... IT is tricky as you have nowhere to look or hide so you get a tad wired and time seems to move rather slowly when your mind stresses towards the addiction... So, like all addictions, I have not quit but hopefully I am ceasing the behavior forever and I have stopped smoking for good! Well IT is for the good!!! I'll keep you posted! Anyway... The plot thickens... and chocolate is tasting great! "And now for something completely different..." In some ways sports, the arts, clubs, hobbies, or any eclectic pursuit, all have over tones of trueΩ religions division... We meet someone and inquire as to their sport, music, art, hobby, or interest of choice as if the answer includes them in our world and beliefs or excludes them as infidels! It is nice to find commonality yet we must diversify our limited thought rather than eradicate any possible concept expansion. As an example "We'll go round in circles" now I am about to piss off half of you in one word and the other half in the other word! NASCAR WHY??? NASCAR promotes a valuable wholesome lifestyle… ~~NOT~~!!! Let's all learn to drive at 200 MPH on someone else's a~~ while advertising drinking, smoking, chewing, amongst other destructive lifestyle habits! After the first lap, admit it, your just waiting for a crash!!! Waiting for the crash!!! I must admit I enjoy the crash but find myself stressed until the driver is out and safe and miss Dale immeasurably, but IT took him to make others safer. This anxiety we interpret as the rush is rear view mirrored and no longer present in our own sedentary lives. The same is true of my beloved football. Please get a life that does not only exude the groupthink NASCAR or NFL or any other exclusionary over indulged groupthink lifestyle interest that leads to going round in ever diminishing circles! I used to be a gear head and could take apart a car and put it back together, prior to needing to be a quantum mechanic to maintain one! I like racing, and almost all sports, most arts and hobbies and try to stay interested. I realize some are more passionate than others, passion is good being a zealot is not! These single-issue experts that echolalia in their repetitious manner have little knowledge about the rest of the universe! I'm sure you could learn to communicate and expand your knowledge if you did not spend your time in that single interest groupthink! Listen up sport fans and any single-issue elitists… Multiple sports do not make for some great knowledgebase, as even though being a child is great, those who participate never had to grow up in the Neverland of the coliseum entertainment escapement, feed the Christians to the lions world, of keeping the people contented and complacent! Allow others to converse with you about genuine relations and stop masking lack of depth of self by sticking to one subject matter, that shows you have a great deal of common knowledge about a single subject, that excludes others that are seeking to know your world or do and are just less familiar with the subject! This extends to many areas of over focus of the locus to the point of exclusion of inclusion based on any hackneyed area of knowledge used to occlude preclude rather than expand minds into new inclusive thought or relations. So get a clue... In my example of my own love of football... I am conscious of the fact that not everyone is as passionate about Da Bears as I, including some of Da Bears! *(Hey Coach... just a concise notion... We got a chip... and we wear IT on our shoulder year round... when you represent dat uniform be prepared to take some Chi town heat for coach speak... the players are playing but the coach's are missin da little things that are makin Da differences in the outcomes! I'm all for serene intensity yet Get tough, Get a line, Get to their QB and protect ours!!! Get the damd play in and Give Da QB optimal optional adjustment Audibility~~~ Dis ain't Da CUBS and we're tired of awaitin!!!) So know I do wear the colors but I try not to overstate my knowledge to suppress theirs, even with other fans, nor do I try to convert them like I'm practicing some trueΩ religion... If we seem to be on the same wave I will ride IT, if not I try to move IT to another space. Just stop going round in the same meaningless circle all the time! I know I'm an a~~h⊗le ... well at least I can admit I'm one! Do not get me wrong again! I am a considerate person, well sorta, I prospectively expend some of my energy on and follow; NASCAR, Baseball, and a multiplicity of interesting to others endeavors, I do not much like, yet care enough to converse at a minimum level with people who live them, so I can find them where they are or at least meeting them halfway, and do not just say screw them nor do I ignore the people who are fan-addicts as I could... That would limit my understanding, connection to, and relations with many wonderful people. I ask if you would do the same for me and begin to discern this quandary? We are perceived by everyone in different ways on different days even at different times of the same day... Put one hat on you're a fan of Mickey Mouse, put another on and you may even be projecting terror... Who are you intentioning and whom is being perceived? Do you change costumes put on some grease paint, a uniform or designer outfit, maybe project a happy, stern, sad, mad, or bad attitude... intentionally or ~~not~~... you are participating in the

CCXL

creation of the perception of you… but this is only half the picture as the 5D HIGH Def receiver of this essence projection (anybody you encounter and some you only sense) is filtering through their previous encounters and experiences with you and all of theirs~~~ Maybe you're the guy who always tells a joke, or maybe you're the gal who mostly laughs as others joke. Maybe you're the one who dramatically emotes or maybe you're the one associated with being cold~~~ I could go on and on, and I do… but I would not want to be associated or assigned the permanent filter disposition imposition of going on and on!!! I think you get this part of this point yet allow me to continue like IT's critical… Yeah this preconceived conception thing is critical to who you are and whom you are thought of! Is the me that IS~~~ being presented, received, and perceived the same as sent; or the same as IT ever was∞ or as IT was once thought of or as you never were or miscued misconstrued you or true view? You cannot sit around obsessing about perception affection but you can be aware of IT and IT's affect on current inflection reception of your intentions, and inquire as to of whom and as whom you are thought as and about but only if it matters to you! Once you've been capped with a hat in someone else's mind you wear that hat until you either manage to change hats in their minds or they are smart enough to allow that we are a hat of a different color and forever changing~~~ If you walk around with a hat of conceit, then when you come with IT full of humility IT may not be perceive received as such… If your hat has been previously mislabeled, poorly received, or improperly satire-gorized, you will still be viewed as once having that attribute or that part in the screen interplay and you cannot change or address this unless you're aware of IT nor can they. Now let's get our heads back in the game… I follow the NFL to release some of my aggravation from care-less agitation. I find myself yelling at the TV "come on bust somebody's head" or break some other part of their anatomy off. All this is emblematic of Rome of ode and psycho symptomatic looming Death Race carousing like soused soccer maniacs, distractively entertaining containing the populace citizenry while they boogie to the detuned fiddle players opus! This is wrong and I am consciously working on IT as I too

CCXLI

have anxiety when a player goes down, as I once did! I include many fans of many sports, the arts, an occasional odd hobby, obscure interest, or obsessive pursuit, as friends, it adds to me, although I'm not sure I'll have any after this book is released, but I would rather you get IT than be my friend without IT, because I Love YOU!!! Which I'm sure most of you do Get IT! See you at the concert, play, or show, chat or game room, sporting event or affair, of choice, Maybe even on Sunday afternoon in the fall, picture in picture or multiple screens... Don't forget your hat~~~ LOL Oh by the way what's with yellow indeterminately interfering official management in the outcome of our sports? Coincidence again??? Not!!! Mans propensity to man-ipulate, intercede, exert his power~~~ OH... one more little thought after thought... How do you invest your time??? Do you spend your time wisely? Are you only supporting others to enable them to live their dream by vicariously expending all your free time following and sustaining their lives, are you disbursing some to actually help others, are you miserly hoarding all your self, or are you wasting most of your time like IT's meaningless? Balance here is crucial as all things in Der time; IT, they, and you... are pulling you inevitably towards your destiny!

70%

Now let me attack!!! I mean describe another great outcrop of mechanical nightmare... The so-called performance products that I can hear from a mile or two away and the low frequency rumbling thump... thump... thump... Hip Hop Bass speaker junk... Must be the same non-regulators that allowed bumpers to match the height of my windshield~~~ Why are select minorities permitted intrusive freedom too superimpose over the highest and greatest utility of the citizenry because there are profits to made? Discount transferring the actual cost to society! I have heard a lot of explanations as to the benefits of loud vehicles and added safety to those that are deaf like me, and no explanation as to why I should have to thump, as well as all the rest of the Horse DUNG at almost the same volume as the vehicles they're attached to! I have a vibe for you that will reverberate through your eternity∞~~~ Then we have the neutron star effect of the Halogen and High Intensity Discharge Xenon headlights that just give me the blues!!! The lobbying going down is almost as intense as the sound is deafening, lights are blinding and life threatening. Why do they continue to allow loudness to be a lifestyle? Money!!! I especially appreciate those small-penised muffler less than fruckers that have to rev up so that you have to look up... This must be the only time anybody, including their mothers, ever paid any attention to them!!! Kinda like the blowers of the plastic sport horns! Everyone seeks validation by others, that they exist and want to be recognized in some way, but tone IT down, as we listen for the whisper harder, longer, and stronger than the sound that is coming so loudly at us from everywhere! So much sound that we can no longer hear the silence! Remember the sound of peace and quiet? I feel sorry for the animals that are bombarded by noise of our making, including sounds such as ELF, low frequency waves transmitted to communicate to our nuclear subs throughout the oceans, earth, and you. Then aberrant non-astral waves sent through our air and us, at rising astronomical rates! They invade our homes and bodies inciting non-communion, thereby deafening any extra soulful communication! Us animals must try to listen through our NOISE, in order to filter out what once was not there, to hear natures sound so clear... The Sea and Earth have a sound and the Sun has a sound... Black holes resonate 57 octaves below our conscious hearing and even all reality may only be a holographic projection from the edge of the event horizon, all the Universe makes sound... this oscillating resonance is part of the vibe we can no longer hear of IT because of the racket that says so loudly look at me... as many insensitively send signals outward that should never be sent let alone received, for they've passed the zero point of no return escape the vibe velocity!!! Or the lights that let you see me but I cannot see the road to where I was going! We no longer can hear that small voice of who we are!!! Actual sounds do not exist outside our brains, even though there are physical vibrations we call sound waves. These sound waves are not transformed into sounds outside or inside our ears, but rather inside our brains and yet close your eyes and listen to the three dimensional sound that resounds in there! The noise we create in our heads is essence deafening! Hear the wee voice of your childhood in prayer, in school, playing with friends, listen to and feel the love that touches you through the wee voice! Prayer can be noisy with our wants and needs. I'm suggesting simple silent selfless intentioning prayer. You must step to the side to be beside IT. Although you perceive existence of a material world external to your brain, light, colours, and sounds do not exist as decoded; only energy exists. There is both light and sound energy that is beyond what we as human's can see or hear. It is easier to listen to the familiar than to hear or view the new. When you are young IT is easy to hear and see, you are open to IT. Even in the quietest moments you may not hear IT, as in that moment you neglect to focus. You may imagine that occasionally the agitation and uncertainty your thinking is betrayal in your mind of your self. Yet this unease means you are alive and internally deliberating possibilities! This wee small voice is always there! You cannot escape IT! You are already hearing IT. You have always heard IT! When you pretend not to hear IT or choose not to listen then your repetitive psychobabble continues. The wee small voice is not your mental monologue schizophrenia that impairs your perception or expression of reality, manifesting as auditory hallucinations, paranoia bizarre delusions or disorganized speech and thinking, that constitutes mind numbing communication. Well For What It's Worth "THEY" want you conflicted constricted... "Paranoia strikes deep... into your heart IT will creep... Well ya better, Stop, children, what's that sound? Everybody Look What's Going Down"~~~ IT instead consists of subtle mindful communion within the unity acceding to the interaction mechanism of the Holographic Resonant sub Planck Zero Point Quantum Entanglement Potentiality Reality! The essential point of universal essence from which all creative potential flows from, to, and throughout Nothing∞ that allows entrained thought to move both backward and forward through time. Thereby allowing us to lay aside our fear's as there will be no unanticipated events only quandaries of acceptance of possibility. I am half deaf so I have an advantage! Truly an advantage, that was likely caused by an a~~h⊗le dropping skids on a concrete floor purposely to make a really loud noise, so everyone in hearing distance would... look at him... hear him! Muffler less frucker like!!! When presented with some hindering impediment that appears to obstruct, you can choose to either enable or disable IT! I am working within the legislative system to disable these muffler less fruckers and I hope to control my impulse to literally toss a monkey wrench into their reality rather than literately!!!

While we're on this detour let's take IT a ways~~~ When you come to a fork in the road take IT. A detour often becomes the new path of life ==<~~~>== The only way we'll know is if we dare to take a few steps after we reach the detour rather than hiding in fear or forever waiting there! If the boogieman's goona get Ya then don't let the fear get you too! Better off going after a new possible rather than what fear presents to us. Play out the possible good scenarios in your imagination not fearing the consequences of failure as you cannot guarantee success but you can guarantee failure especially if you never try! Play to win, like the 63' and 85' Bears, not to just not lose like the 06' or 10' Bears!!! Hear Ye... Hear Ye... What... Huh... You talking to me??? Oh... yeah sorry I wasn't paying attention enough to hear you with my diminished capacity but I sensed your presence... I now focus better than most because I'm not distracted by those that would keep you from your thinking and I have learned to mentally overlay an opposing sine wave to counter whatever is at the cause of the ringing in my ear, either real or imagined. I have once more been able to hear the sound of mental silence although if I even think of the ringing, my mind refocuses and senses the ringing, that may or may not exist there, instantly! I have lost the ability to easily locate sounds in the three-dimensional environment, and also my capacity to pick out and focus on specific sounds in a sea of noise. This is known as the "cocktail party effect" and the masking of noise renders my ears useless and worse I need to block the overwhelming garble of the combined sound of all that must pass through one ear! Yet as I listen to my mind much of this lost or missed input has been replaced by intentional connection of input in IT. This can be dangerous, as I am not hearing what is said or done, I am interpretatively hearing what is intended and sense I am not always on connecting, as some people are offended when you focus on their intentions… yet amazingly accurate most times! The inner and inter communication we are seeking does not come in through your ears it comes by wave to your mind and heart. IT is always present but there must be a quiet spot in our mind for IT to be sensed. I guess you'd call that a handicap… well if you're into handicapping you'd better bet on me as I have an edge you don't! I listen for silence of mind~~~ How can you hear silence if silence is the absence of sound IT would be nothing∞ and we all know there must be something so how can there be silence? There really is always some sound in the universe. Just as you mentally unplug from your body when you move to just mind, you are able to selectively disconnect from your other senses when you shift to Alpha Theta meditation~~~ By releasing your grip on the controls your mind has a chance to tap into the flow, and as IT does your other senses drift away for the moments you stay. Oh… the silence I have been referring to, is the nothing of hearing and in this too may be found Resonant sub Planck Zero Point Quantum Entanglement Potentiality Reality as you set your senses aside! Not the absence of sound but the intentional absence of your own induced mental noise… Just remember that artificially actually avoiding any sense completely, as in being sealed up in your sound proof home cocoon, wearing earplugs to bed, sunglasses in the dark, may induce hypersensitivity to the sense that is muted, just as I once unwittingly blocked IT out and so now enabling a more sensitive connection to IT. This hypersensitivity after muting of the senses is why, the drug addict, alcoholic, psychopath, or on some other wrong path people, experience such extreme sensations when they try to remove the addiction. The normal reality that they had been muting and avoiding seems insufferable because they are now experiencing their senses once more and these signals are received distorted, disambiguated, or magnified, because they have been muted so long and sensing is re-sensitized! I am now addicted to the sense of IT!!!

Some disabilities self impose, some impose on you yet others are imposed on you. Whatever the imposition, you choose to what degree IT imposes on your being. I have not come to terms with why extreme disabilities are imposed on anyone at birth, but there are various environmental, inherited, as well as inherent reasons and causes that are filtering not from God but from man infected dysfunctional mutations in DNA, many of whom would not survive without intervention today! What I really do not like or comprehend are people whom disable themselves and/or their children purposely along with those who may be co dependently disabling others and/or enabling their children to handicap themselves. (Another book)

"And now for something completely different..." Well not completely different... As luck and God would have IT I also had part of my sight taken away about thirty years ago! Now after much research and many doctors I was told that the loss was caused by a parasite! Quite probably from my dog Cosmos... Now how can that be the universe in its complete order? Well God you know has a sense of humor and God must have discerned I was not paying enough attention to what was going on around me so God gave me another advantage by taking part of my sight I now have better insight! I am not disabled... I am not handicapped... I do not have a syndrome... I am not impaired... Although others may deem me to be... I have adapted! My putts are a little trickier and the line drives, when I'm pitchen, are not to be seen~~~' at 59 years I can still stop them with my chest and hopefully not my face! All I ask is that you understand "I'm deaf yet I hear IT!" "I'm blind yet I see."

And now for some eco...ism... Mt Tambora in 1815-1816 exploded to create the year without a summer! Earth can and has spit more debris than man can spew, although we try hard, each year our cars leak the equivalent of the Exxon Valdez into our local waterways and we disgorge everything from heavy metals to carbon dioxide in massive amounts into the envelope we coexist in. Do you take care of your vehicles or are they part of the disposable-planned obsolescence throwaway society you belong to? What are you doing to reduce your waste imprint to not degrade earth more than we already do? Recycle Reuse Repurpose Reduce. Being lied to through embellished partisan factual distortion contortion, (kinda like all issues of Da moment) keeps us from finding and focusing on the actual problems! The Global warming controversy is in fact truth yet manipulated and blown up with everything from being photo shopped too Da hockey stick data skewed like the way we used to soak our sticks in water to bend them! This is another cyclic thing and there actually has been a huge carbon decline over time with an inappropriate large increase in the last 100 years and a minuscule world wide Temperature record rise during the last fifteen years though increasing a few over the last couple of hundred, while the Fifth Estate (the press) has continued to expound the fuzzy lies that have the potential to further stifle our economy, while the rich and powerful divvy up to bargain with carbon discharge credit$, and then charging us for not using them while a burp from a volcano can discharge US all! Efficiency can bring us a one third reduction but we are about to triple world use and EcoAbuse as the third world kicks up their own brand of Dictatorial Warlord Capitalistic Carnage, so the 14 tons of carbon your family's been creatin every year is going to start being multiplied by those who haven't been using any! What's Da weather for Da century gonna be??? Will IT be hot, cold, rain, dry, snow? 950 to 1250 Just about Da Viking Age along came a mini heat wave Medieval Warm Period then just about Da time we get around to settling America Da 1645 to 1710 Maunder Minimum sunspots created the Little Ice Age! There are some nice old sites that have been found in the Alps where *Ötzi the Iceman* lived amongst the high meadows! Although the world was not so overpopulated or living jammed in the flood plain then! Cycling weather changes, burning rainforests, Volcanoes, jet contrails and pollution particulate blocking the sun, ozone depletion from aerosols, or all just carbon industrialization crediting bank accounts adjusting the Economics of climate change mitigation? Actually this pollution is currently deflecting photons but the Venus effect eventually cycles the other way so they stay! The climate changes and nature adapts~~~ so should we cripple our economy to consequently not be able too generate the technology or raise Capital needed to remediate something that may in fact be occurring naturally~~~ What fiscal responsible measures can be taken proactively now with the greatest good and what can we prepare to implement later as we increase our proficiency and technology to do more with less? I do not have this answer, but I'm thinking there are people who know who aren't being heard! Intercede with a bit of Selective D-Growth~~~ More homework for those who are not eco savvy or think they are! We ourselves are made of third generation carbon stardust! Oxygen isotope ratio cycle fluctuates now and then and carbon levels are lower but on a 100-year rise. We need to clean up our act~~~ yet Mother Earth has cycled this way long before we burned the fossils that should no longer fire the fuel of consumption. I am not denying the science but does every issue today have to be over exaggerated, puffed out of proportion, red level alerted, or portrayed as an emergency, to get the attention IT deserves or to implement modifications without Da HYPE modifying Da modification!!! The environment is always cleaner on the other side of self-consuming ignorance! The people that PETA attack have done and do more for conservation as the fisherman and the hunter understand the fragile eco that our expansionism debases while contributing with numerous licensing fees and equipment tax's. When the PETA people find out plants sense... I will not be allowed to cut my grass! Extremism in any form is unconsidered imposition! I believe Clean Air and Water are of primary importance and no living thing should be abused but conserving for further use, does not mean no use at all. We need to lower our particulate Pollution and our trash, as hey… we live here!!! We need to reduce our reliance on oil in general and scrub our coal clean but trade is good and everyone benefits from trade. The oil cartel war game is almost over… Thank God!!! We just haven't finished paying the price at the pump. The crap we add to both the air and water can easily be reduced but not if we focus solely on economic credit fear induction deduction rather than positive personal pollution solution reduction that we all can take credit for! Not just the Oligarch! Hopefully we somehow deduce how to derive energy from carbon as we recycle IT? Be careful how you're green-washed… many products sold as environmentally friendly are not. Our Politburo's policy of self-regulation seems to need an intervention!!! There is now, B certification and new financial legislation that may slowly begin to affect change, as corporations may legally protect themselves some from having to consider only maximized profiteering rather than optimal social conscience Benefits as a business model. My Pee Wee Herman Schwinn keeps my heart beatin and local but I need a bike lane! We been plannin energy conservation my whole life while using more. Sorta reminds me of the conservative agenda that only seems to conserve the power trip of the rich… Consolidate your trips, and do a little peddlin now and then… Plant some trees… an Oak takes a lifetime or two to grow… Get your fingers in the soil. Your great grandchildren will thank you!!! And you may live long enough to meet them! As Albert Einstein wrote, in a letter to his son Feb 5, 1930, "Life is like riding a bicycle. To keep your balance you must keep moving." Oh… and by the by stop the friken breedin… 2X2 should not equal more breedin then we needen!

And now… And now…. And then again for something completely different… (Update) I had a cigarette at the bar Friday night and now I can sit back and understand why I continue to be sucked back in by this demon! 1 cigarette in ten days is getting close to success! Although my writing has been neglected while my physical workout has increased! Cigarettes for a short time give you an altered state of consciousness much the same as liquor, processed foods, sugar, caffeine, cola (the classic that they removed the cocaine from in 1906), denergy drinks, crack, meth-amphetamine, heroin, Mary Jane wanna, and all those little addictions we have, that temporarily take us away from reality and sooth our conscious mind or distract IT momentarily… Some much more addictive than others and some much more insidious than we know! All used to alter our minds that become fixated in no time!!! Now back to the intra-play of the field … The unified field that is… Any who can do… the whatwhenhowwho&why of your interrelation will begin this next communication… Define…

Social Reciprocity (social psychology)

From Wikipedia

In social psychology, reciprocity refers to responding to a positive action with another positive action, and responding to a negative action with another negative one. Positive reciprocal actions differ from altruistic actions as they only follow from other positive actions and they differ from social gift giving in that they are not actions taken with the hope or expectation of future positive responses.

Reciprocal actions are important to social psychology as they can help explain the maintenance of social norms. If a sufficient proportion of the population interprets the breaking of a social norm by another as a hostile action and if these people are willing to take (potentially costly) action to punish the rule-breaker then this can maintain the norm in the absence of formal sanctions. The punishing action may range from negative words to complete social ostracism.

This is an act of demonstrating one's disapproval, at some personal cost, for the violation of widely held norms (e.g., don't free ride). Social reciprocity differs from standard notions of reciprocity because social reciprocators intervene whenever a norm is violated and do not condition intervention on potential future payoffs, revenge, or altruism. Instead social reciprocity is a triggered normative response. I am not foolish enough to put my faith alone in man's altruistic motivation as most people's motives seldom stray far from their self, but I do have reason to believe that most people are social reciprocators and for this reason they will one day reason that IT is in their own self interest to demand normative action to expand our unity in IT!

Social reciprocity works great when our norms are great... I sense though a steady receptivity decline in our social psyche. Initiated so those that would could delude us by trying to include us. Salespeople, boss's and coworkers, family, neighbors, clergy, so-called friends and customer servers, use this norm reform to our disadvantage and they're normatively sticking to you hoping you are codependent to them! Question how norms are being altered to use, question claims of required relation acceptance, and question others' dismal reviews. You can resist being manipulated by these overt covert norm changers. Do you act

CCLI

ethically only up to the official point written in Da HR manual, defined by what's in your barrister's fine line guidebook under lie ability culpability, or do you feel obligated to stay the principled course your heart knows too follow IT unyielding? You know the moral imperative! I can do no other... I guess that's why some call me a dinosaur or tell me I'm abnormal!!! You can also input reformative norms to improve expectations and acceptations with IT. Like Da Honesty cafes but me takes a wait you see attitude as a penny in Da poke ain't a new Mercedes for my vote! Proactive behavioral correction adaptation action with IT is your responsibility! Questioning your acceptance of their reciprocity causes reactance, thus explaining people's anger when they feel threatened in their behavioral freedom with you, so do not be surprised by this. One defense against this manipulation by norms is to think things thoroughly through without fear of social relation consequences. Concentrating on what the thought is projecting or possibly infecting rather than only worryingly reflecting about how many people you are socially reciprocal too. IT is about quality not quantity! Another is to send them a mental note that you see through them and are about to disconnect! Systematic composed thinking while taking a "quick chill" breather to plausibly considerer alternative meanings, conclusions, or if you just construed, is important. The most effective defense is to use norms against norms. The participation of others, as allies, is crucial to successful rebellion but also is how norms are deformed by majority reversion.

Lets see where was I... Oh I was distracted again because some a~~h☹le was too self-absorbed to notice there are people out there, especially himself... that maybe a sociopath or worse a psychopath and needs some direction, encouragement, and subtle persuasion with a gentle lashing over the tip of a tongue or a anecdotal sarcastic correction rather than just assuming (making an a~~ before u and me) that we can do the passive aggressive thing and avoid any appearance of confrontation, even with Toxic² people and thereby continuing to enable through ignoring, the ignorant bastards! I use the terms Toxic² and psychopath to cast a wide net, yet do not conclude delude your self of the peril less fate as the negative feeless set demonstrate Dis trait of superimposing hate on our love state! I have acquaintances whom when shown, exposed, and verified through others, the scientific proof truth of entanglement, they then explain IT away as, being far out there or "that's unbelievable" even though you just provided them the evidence of IT. Thereby verbally retaining their reality and intentionally denying again what IT is! They prefer to remain in their daydream and help the rest of the ignorant bastards to continue stomping on our peace and your tranquility as well as getting away with and thereby enabling normatively a level of a~~h⊗leism never before seen! Now accepted because no one would ever confront them!!! Improve the strength of your coherent thoughts with their disconcert rather than accepting more norm formation in a new standard of ethics! IT's not my job man! I can avoid IT this time and some other poor schmuck can deal with IT rather than me! I can escape again this time... Well they got ya surrounded! Face IT, you're surrounded and IT's your responsibility to jack them back Jack! As a Qigong master does with Qi emissions~~~ Remember the light we all emit! Well when in sync there is a greater coherence and order of brainwaves. In Qi the dominant thought prevails. This is a delicate process, to not detract from the positive vibe while returning their negative BS, marked return to sender... IT can only be done with discernment else more negativity in your flow... adding a little prayer for your peace with theirs... I'm pretty sure that when Christ was confronted by a~~h⊗les in the Temple he tossed a few tables around and let them know that being an a~~h⊗le was unacceptable! Kid's need to join enforces to force Da bully out in Da open for recourse! Force and aggression should be saved for defense only. We must defend ourselves against a~~h⊗les! A~~h⊗les are malevolent forces in our nature, like Virus's are malevolent forces, that we take action to prevent their spreading, infecting and keep them from hurting us. If the A~~H⊗les of the Earth were continuously confronted with some kind of mental imposition that would make being an A~~H⊗le less accepted and harder to manage being, then maybe, just maybe, we could lower the A~~H⊗le factor and they might consider that "this isn't working very well" so just maybe, just maybe, they would be a little less self-absorbed and consider the outcomes and ripples in the Karma that there ripping!!! I'm pretty sure this is called COMPASSION!!! Now if psycho-pathetic A~~H☺les started having compassion well what might be next!!! EMPATHY!!! Since they do not feel anything and are opting out of IT's touch but still in IT, then they must be in need of constant reminders that others do feel and are in touch with IT and so too can they!!! We either live in our cave of fear or they live in theirs... I fear naught, so they better head back to their caves because I do care and am more than willing to prospectively project my thoughts about and around their hardhearted attitude! I'm not talking about proselytizing cave to cave but mind to mind. Empathy is a sense but sensing when you're emphatically being taken for a ride is more difficult. Empathy is universal... IT sees you disquietly equate indifference to distance so open your heart to both the local and nonlocal yokel~~~ Let your essence effervesce! Just remember to keep your defenses up as truly Toxic² people do not follow rules and have no feelings nor do they care about you, this makes them dangerous!!! Also remember there are subliminal, judicious, lucidly coherent thought out ways of getting through to them and IT can be quite fun! A well-placed intention or at least their negative vibe passed back though their quantum reality makes a statement they cannot evade... IT has to be under their radar and done surreptitiously because they actually feed on confrontation and conflict! The only conundrum is that you might think that with all the negative crap and vibes in their lives they would barley notice, if at all, the new incursion to their life but IT is distinctive, memorable, and mind bending! You know this is starting to sound a lot like me!!! No... if you give up the control portion of this thing, use the passion that is left, mix with a little altruism, add a dash of hope, simmer on HIGH, then equally... completely selfless individuals, are rare and unusual too, they choose to live in the soulful light and bring IT wherever they go! "This little light of mine I'm gonna let IT shine".

Light has numerous colours composing the spectrum of pure light that contains them all. ScienceDaily (Sep. 18, 1997) A team of 20 physicists from four institutions has literally made something from nothing, creating particles of matter from ordinary light!!! Alright already... enough with the light and vibe and attenuated being... How does this affect me, my world, or make anything better? Well I'm trying to shed some light where ignorance roams. You may find yourself with the excuse monster stating that this is all beyond my knowledge, capabilities or desires. Well... your not excused... stay at the table and think about IT. See the light that shines within and purify the light you reflect so IT matters! Do not feign incomprehension or profane disbelief by choosing to ignore the darkness, by only shining our light where there already is light and no darkness, our beam shines dimly like a flashlight during the day and is seen as a greyer shade. Do take your intense eternal∞ love and turn that same beam on the darkness of night and IT shines like the Sun! Yet do not overly foreshadow the light of others. If we all chose to share spiritual light to enliven the darkness of others spirits there would be no un-enlightenment! They may not seek enlightenment and that's their choice, but they must stop overlaying their dark shadow onto my hearts delight. Make your light accessible and available, focused and directed, intense yet sublime. Sort of like using an array of reflectors, deflectors and filters on a movie set to enhance and soften harsh reality... The light paradox should be done with love, care, and beware... Love is more than turning the other cheek... Love includes walking a mile in someone else's shoes and loving thy neighbor means being willing to piss him off in order to help him move forward! Including neighborly intention correction! (sidetrip) This brings to mind similar misdirected conflict of neighborly light... Neighbors will shine a light on the whole neighbor hood but will not shine a little light on their own souls or see the light in others! This porch of million candle power torch light that I can't see past to see into and through the darkness to my own yard... because some neighbor either thinks they can light up the entire neighbor hood and believe that Da bad will come out of their shadows or their world vision is as small as the circle of light they are projecting into the wonderful natural light of the country night far beyond their city fright sight! Ever try to see in the dark when someone is shining a light in your eyes? Nothing like tripping over things laying in the shadows... Well use

CCLV

your inner light on those souls hiding in the evil darkness but not on your neighbor's night space! Maybe they think that their overbearing light helps me see but they are only blinding me to Gods light! I only insert this here as I have had several Toxic A$$H⊗les, projecting aimless light over the wonderful little lake I live on, and when approached in a neighborly way, simply stayed with the, ME ignorance way, and would not even adjust something that would affect them little if at all! Maybe someone will read this who is also unknowingly light interfering and make an intensity adjustment! You cannot hide your dim inner light in the eternal∞ radiant light because IT just reflects as another shade of gray to which my eyes must adjust! … Oh by the way if you hear some sh!t coming down outside, you best off slip out the back and view IT from the dark side of the light, rather than stepping out into the light making yourself a wonderful target and seeing nothing outside the ring of light your porch torch is projecting!!! Let's get back to the neighborly way… IT is a fragile thing and there is much risk! Not shining your light too bright into others minds yet shining IT bright as a beacon in the bay of humanity! Let IT shine… Let IT shine… Let IT shine!!! If you would do IT for your own brother or sister who lives in Timbuktu, who you see once every five years and love dearly (you would save or help them right?) and not for your neighbor who you see daily and who's kids play with yours, and maybe even pray and break bread with, because your afraid to tip the apple cart of life!!! Most people today are desperately seeking someone in their lives that actually cares about them enough to tell them like IT is… Help them GET IT!!! I know I am! I'm not talking about being mean, arrogant, egotistical, or critical… I'm talking about taking the time to use your intellect to discern their situation and needs… this particular theory does make the assumption that you are able and willing to use your compassion to discern (listening and watching and sensing and processing) what is going on in their lives and the lives of those around them… This involves active listening, which includes a well-formed open-ended question now and then… Adapting your style of questioning is easier than someone adapting there style of answering… include a bit of humor or a sarcastic retort now and then… listening… listening… listening until your able to pick up on their gifts and trash the garbage to find a wavering brain wave or a treasured thought! Helping them to recycle (Do you?) their garbage into gifts of care and dropping the rest off for disposal (IMAGINE! Everything you use, you will dispose of, in this planned obsolescence society)! Da old UffDa simply seems to make everything more complicated!!! Well once you attune, IT simply is, and all these complications melt away~~~ Right and Wrong return with discernment and correct action second nature. Focus your Qi with care and if others do not respond~~~ remember to include them within solution…

We are moving towards interactive healthcare and remote control surgery as well as Telehealth and Ringadoc, Consultadoc, or Teladoc; which may work just fine and dandy or possibly we will be left more unattended too but either way I'm just wondering if we will still be funding somebody's yachts, beamers, or their kids ivy league vacations??? Well one of these is online MindMentor® future RoboCoach, recommending self solution… Having an interactive session with an artificial intelligence robotic agent is proving successful, one out of two say! By asking, smart questions, MindMentor® addresses the unconscious mental resources from the persons answers. MindMentor® guides you through a process (a series of steps) to help you find solutions within yourself. Psychologists have found that your own solutions are more effective than other people's advice, no matter how well meant (this includes my own). MindMentor® starts this process by asking you "what problem you'd like to work on."

This allows you to accept the answers, as you participated in determining the solution! So remember to invite them to participate or search for your own, as IT leads to successful analysis. Use third party stories instead of telling people how to live their lives. They will figure out how the story applies. Though take care, as IBM's Watson and the machine learning providing the current AI computers, have limitations for the moment but soon to be hard to beat while computing for itself "iRobot" controlled by Da Olio's! The only outcomes will

CCLVII

be the ones they allow!!! Anyway... If those you attempt to help with healing, insist on standing in the middle of the pile and ignoring the stench you better move upwind and be willing to tidy up frequently, as the pile may one day reach you and compiling will supersede you! By ignoring IT and being passive about IT I guarantee that, one day this crap will come home to roost! Maybe not to you but in the flow of things, to your Children's, Children's, Children!!! Or maybe sooner... Take a stand now or prepare to be buried by the pile of MANURE expanding exponentially... This seems a little radical, over a simple a~~h⊗le but they multiply like microbes in a Petri dish and I'm not saying your neighbor, friend, or even you are, I can be one! I try to release or direct this in the appropriate direction that my perception detected reception... We allow barriers to be built and find ourselves confined in prisons of our own making because we are afraid to confront darkness with light!!! Maybe I can get away with this as part of my excuse for being so confrontational and aggravating! I do try to use tact and some diplomacy but the results envisioned by the receiver of the love are not the same as what the sender encoded... I know IT's a broad use of the term love. Who else is going to ever even bother to start to bring them into the light??? If you are having scary thoughts you must review them as just that. They are real thoughts they're just not reality. You must put the thought in IT's rightful place not frightful in your space. Save that anxiety to use like a shot of espresso when you need to pump your life up a notch, not when you're walking down the produce isle or driving into my lane. IT is love if you are trying to enlighten even if you frighten... That's how your mother kept you from sticking a fork in the outlet! Thus the "Telephone Game"! I do not stop sending messages just because the reception is bad... I hope for better reception and clarity of transmission! But you know the resulting thought can be misconstrued when only part of a message gets through! Speaking of a~~h⊗les, please forgive my use of this term. I have heard others refer to me so with endearment, so I hope they are not disappointed when I declare myself a~~h⊗le free! And start to turn the a~~h⊗le tide back against them! With force if needed! For I am not living in fear and I am not afraid to flip over a few tables

CCLVIII

or cop cars in the Tabernacle of life!!! Anyway… Another one distracted me or maybe IT was me?

Now let's see what can I follow that up with? IT better be a little mellower or I risk losing some more readers… Yeah that's what I'm worried about… "NOT!!!" New topic is… "Same as IT ever was ∞" "Well Excuuuse MeeE!" What's your excuse of the day! Too Hot, Too Cold, Too Wet, Too Old? What's keeping you from following your dream? Excuse 276: The dog ate my homework… Or Excuse 399: I don't have time… Or Excuse 4 million two hundred thirty four thousand six hundred and one: I don't remember! "Well Excuuuse MeeE!" for callin out your excuse as BullCRAP! As I said earlier I wrote the book of excuses and keep them right up there on the reference shelf next to the Bible and the Dictionary (thank God for spell check). I try not to refer to the Excuse book anymore (I do refer to the other two) as I pretty much have all, the excuses, memorized and the thoughts contained there in, only interfere with the frequency on which God communicates!!! God is omnipresent and omnipotent! As George Bernard Shaw put it "beware of the man who's God is only in the skies." God is in you and me. Here with and within us! If God is everywhere and all powerful and with as well as within us then we are God! I know this is here say… I mean heresy… or is IT here I say!!! Heaven is here on earth and IT is everywhere in any devised multiverse! Surrender yourself to IT as a drop of water surrenders itself to become one with the almighty sea! The same way we will all one day surrender our last breath to Love in eternity∞. If you really think or feel you don't have the time to meditate, consider the fact that mediators live an average of 12 years longer than non! That should buy you some time!!! Not to even begin to evaluate the enhanced quality of that time!

How many times can you get up each day put on the same underwear, cloths, and excuses that you wore yesterday? You would suppose that even you would fatigue of them eventually as they fatigue you! You can only spin the verbiage so many ways and the excuses soon come out the same! "Same as IT ever was∞" What do you ask others to ignore and suffer because "This is my way"! What do you expect others to do and perform because "My way is the only and best way"! "My way or the highway" not the Good VIBE WAY. Why do you lie to yourself that "IT has to be my way because I'm right"! Or that was what I was taught so that is the why of a thought! How do you know you are right if you do not listen to discern fully and allow others thoughts to enter your process quality control feedback loop? Why is the stupidity you force on others not apparent or clear to you and ever so to those your overtly overbearing! Do you delude yourself that this gives you misplaced power? Do you have a lost sense of control? Do you feel real at all! About others and their quantum thought of you? Do you firmly believe that those that are hearing this Me way, are truly buying the full load of CRAP? Do you believe that when you are done abusing them with your berative logic that they will not narrate this to others! How does this enforcement of your stupidity help your position in society or for that matter inside your own psychology! Do you claim and believe that others are negative or refuse to listen, do not allow you to speak or finish what you are saying because you never finish, are always speaking, never listen, and are always negative… that this gives you the upper hand and goes unnoticed! This is your domain and your defense! We educate our educators and every other smart a$$ to be able to persuade anybody that gives a shit that the bowl of crap they're feeding us is really 100% organic recycled fiber rich nutrient succulent predigested green health food that's good for us, and we not only should acknowledge their superior knowledge but be ecstatic to be informed so, though we really know we're getting a full load of crap we must then suck up and swallow that Shit… hook, line, and sinker!!! Molding your mind thing to bend messaging does not make your meme imitation culturally acceptable but rather like spinning another inhumane bent lament. Why do I need to be persuasively scammed into some reconceived non-truth, supposedly for my own good, simply explained as a problem with my preceptor, that through years of straining training simply cuts through to the bottom line, not always pretty, truth? So basically rather than instructing our youth how to seek and find truth we are teaching them new complex convoluted ways to obscure and construe any old untrue view! Repetitive behavior that is positive needs to replace that

CCLX

which is negative and the only way to do that is to start some kind of positive behavior!!! There will always be a reason AKA an Excuse as to why you cannot start that positive behavior right now!!! Take your pick… you can use my Excuse book if you have misplaced yours, I believe you know exactly where you left them last! If your lucky you set them down long enough to realize that's all you been reading and the dream that you had was right there within your grasp all along, hidin behind that excuses! If I just had… Oh I do have!!! If I could… Oh I can!!! If IT was different… Well IT is!!!

Now lets see whom I can piss off next! I mean what the next topic might be… Well I'm bound to piss off somebody! And as in dealing in generalities that do not belong to all generally. Because I'm actually willin to have an opinion and that in itself should piss off somebody! Probably a lot of somebody's… Well more likely a bunch of nobodies that want me to believe there're somebody's! "Well Excuuuse MeeE!

Next!!! Who am I going to piss off next? You? Or you? Or maybe all you's!!! Why do you's BosNYWash Megalopolisian's take such joy in being impatient impertinent indisputable a~~h⊗les? Maybe because when they compare theirs to ours, they think theirs is bigger!!! No the Apples poisonous… and D.C. Autocratic… I knew there was some A to award in there somewhere… I've seen the D.C. sites when I prayed with the million and would like to see some more… of the sites… and much more proactive prayer! But unless you send all of your biggest a~~h⊗les as emissaries on mission trips to the rest of the country and utilize them locally as greeters from the Chamber I have to assume (there I go assuming again) you's peoples gots tribulation manifestations! I might have to disguise myself as a Native American and hold a Tea party to throw over your vibe… You's knows who you's are and how and why you's are that way and you's might want to address the uppity town edgy neurosis problem amongst you'selve's! Then maybe I won't just have to keep sayin "there goes another BosWash-Megalopolis-a~~h⊗le-alien!!! Perhaps your not as I have perceived? The image projected is successful in negative recollection projection and will take a lot of remedial work to reflect IT affirmatively! Must

CCLXI

be some contagious crap they dumped in the Atlantic, whose residual effect floats restrictively along the East coast from spooky Quantico… around the Chesapeake Bay Beltway… then out past Langley VA. to pissing a ways up the Hudson… with ill effects felt all the way up to Walkers Point Maine. Or… maybe the disease is windborne like Da Kawasaki… Thank God the wind blows from West to East although this puts California only a week away from the main Kawasaki contagion point!!! Is the coincidence that seven of our richest counties surround D.C., or that some of our poorest brothers and sisters live there? I believe the beltway cycles our money to the top believing that what we're gleaning off the bottom of the trickle is their generous gift of philanthropic majesty! This house of cards and mirrors supported by Wall Street and reflected in government is glittering gloom. Lawyers and lobbyists drag huge suitcases filled with mostly ego and maybe a donation or two while you never see a politician carrying those many bills that are being passed! Stop watching tales of the rich and famous and start calculating how they became so on your dime! Step out of the glare of the big city lights and see the wonder of others twinkling galaxies astounding… For America to wake from this current nightmare crap nap of "what can my country do for me" vigilant justice will necessitate constant unbiased persecution solution! We must calmly and thoroughly expeditiously expose those who make and take America's great future as part of their personal potentate treasure state! Will they allow IT? Who's going to shine a light on IT? Who has built up their immunity to the toxicity of this all consuming oligarchy? Who will use their abilities to risk healing our ostensibly never-ending ills? We must try! We need you all!!! Will your life shine brightly light years after your gone? This question for all of us: "to what degree does this mean me?" We should all take lessons from how our neighbors to the North, in Gander Canada, reacted when on 9/11 their population was doubled, with the plane people who no longer could land in their homeland, and responded by giving their homes, food, and caring to strangers from other lands. I pray for those who sacrificed and will never forget them nor ever pardon any of the perpetrators and their kind or allow their deaths

CCLXII

to be used to manipulate my will for freedom! IT was truly synchronic, and more than likely slightly conceived, when Osama's death trumped Trump by choppin off the end of Da has been Celebrity Chumps, conniving derisive divisive ego firing three ring circus TV unreality act, the same week Da Chump was trash talkin birth locale like IT was a swift boat bitizen cruzin past Da Tiny Tower. Election TV is a grand education in abnormal amoral psychology much like realty TV is! May da trash bin laden with da brainless soulless body also dispose of the hateful movement and be emptied of dat misdirected evil negative intention dat was placed in our space by another self-construed untrueΩ religious BS conman, like the one still in his tower! TrueΩ religion can even include the worship of power and cash... No... I'm sure that is trulyΩ religious domain... The Gee odd death spiral bin espoused as change, was regressive suppressive, as only desire for liberty and freedom is bringing change to the Middle East! Some A$$H⊗les don't GET IT till their swimmin with da fishes and spend some eternal∞ time facing their crimes! Nan... Nan... Nana... Nan... Nan... Nana... Hey... Hey... Goodbye!!! I got half a mind too... well actually I got two half' s that can each separately still pretty much function on their own~~~ No not top to bottom, front to back, but left and right that work sorta like a complete back up neural network!!! Well if you can make good decisions with half a mind and function properly why do these halfwit dictates conjugate so much hate??? Next!!!

I know... I know... where I come from is perfect! ~~NOT~~!!! Well at the very least we're civil to others when we're out and about but we're losing that too! You's is not the center of the metro-multiverse and barley part of mine. I know you's have a lot of good you's and I hope to meet all good you's!!! So enough said is enough said... IT's time to do!!!

Next!!! I thought I was next??? Oh well... last again so I got time~~~ When our minds have downtime they can recollect or ponder forward through time, to what was or might be, and become vivid lived reminder or living future mindfulness. What's next... well just clear the registers of your mind, make a little downtime, and consider what could be next... take a moment and perceive

CCLXIII

what you want next...Oh I'm next! That's not what you perceived or wanted... IT is what I'm was typin... writtin... or sayin... Or IT is typin... writtin.. that's all I'm sayin... Next!!!

Well almost next... I was next to last and the last guy (maybe a Megalopolisian), cut the line to save some time, so I guess I'm last! As the story goes the first shall be last and the last shall be first... my last name starts with a letter (U know) at the end of the alphabet so I had an early introduction into being last! Maybe we should mix this up once in a while! I don't mind being last in this world because the here and now is only a short blip in the realm of eternity∞ and then for the rest of eternity∞ I will be first so whatever humility and patience I use here will be like paying IT forward in eternity∞! Eternity∞ what will that be like? Eternity∞ will IT be a while? Eternity∞ I look forward with a knowing smile ☺ Eternity∞ what meaning does IT hold for you? If I start to tell you of my Eternity∞ will IT detract or add to yours? If you want I can go into mine for a moment and pull out what the possibilities could be for both you and for me or I could limit mine and expand yours or I could limit yours and expand mind... I mean mine! You see without your mind... No... I mean you see with your mind... No... I mean with your mind you will come out and see... Without mind there is no Eternity∞ only forever and what would the point of forever be unless something was there to be IT!

Why are the rules always meant for someone else? I mean why does everyone suppose that the rules are meant for someone else and not them? I mean why do we believe that we are exempt from the rules because we're us and not them? Why will people do whatever they believe they can get away with rather than to humbly acknowledge the rights of others and imagine the untruth that no one notices or that IT doesn't matter even if they do? Rules... who needs them? Open up your heart... Rules... they're ridiculous! We start life with cooperate and considerate... then we quickly grow down to what's in IT for me I take. Consideration what's that! There are so many rules why bother? I'm exempt... your exempt... he's exempt... she's exempt... so what's the big deal with all the rules? They aren't meant for me and they aren't meant for you, so who made them and what are they all about if no one must abide by them? Oh yeah order in the chaos! The great debate is unified order VS random chaos! One of the random monkeys typing this is pretty chaotic so some of the thought is considerably esoteric! Like my buddy Imo... the teacher of the 100 Monkey's... my goal is to teach enough of you to GET IT in order to reach the critical mass of an enlightened world!!! The skeptic, in all of us, rebuff any unified science design tryst with negation statistician allegory twist. But there is great order in numbers! I have to state as before there are so many manmade rules you do not know if your breaking one, even if you are trying to stay within them, and I break more than my share when IT comes to PC superposition, but you know when you break those that are natural consideration laws of the universe and your mostly super imposing on purposely. You may deny the fact or ignore without tact and you may dance the dance jack but your not forever absolved in fact! You may remember I named my dog Cosmos and that was because IT means, the universe in its complete order... coherent order rather than chaos... why? God! That part of God in all that is within, that is shared by all, that is here in the now that makes your and my life real. Along with the affirmative reflection of our perspicacity in the way we interact with our being. Now why would we possibly want order in the chaos? Do you feel less anxious, stress, fear, worry, or tension when your world is in order rather than firefighting in the chaos? Most rules are there so that we can live some kind of a life without getting dumped on or dumping on anybody! Do you have one mindset of consideration for all or are we back to situational ethics? Situate your self down and discern what kinda crap your makin! If the rules are for someone else and not you or me... CRAP! On You... and CRAP! On Me! I'm sure you or I will! But when you shift to IT, the discerning empathy precedes far ahead any Earth made rules of law vs. letters of law. This CRAP gets complicated!!! To do good is not equal to being good. To be faithful is not equal to living in faith. To be law abiding is not steadfastly abiding in the laws of universal love. I will have to admit there are some rules that need changing and the powers that be do not like you changing their rules, so if your breaking one of those rules, do so at your own risk of freedom but your free will and your karma will be with the order of IT! Think Gandhi, Martin Luther, Martin Luther King, and Jesus Christ! Think, "jail no bail" as in the freedom riders. You are not they, but components of them are in you as a fraction of each breath we take contains an element of a breath they once made, as the random chaos in the sea of wind has mixed their same molecules with ours. I really do appreciate and am grateful that Jesus died to set me free of sin! So now that I'm free from that, why am I still considered a sinner that's constantly required to repent, by the faith controllers? Matter is neither created nor destroyed, just as universal rules of Love and thoughtfulness are there for a reason and cannot be destroyed and are meant for you and for me, especially you and you and you and I guess well me! So next time your bending or breaking or down right stomping a rule that natural consideration heeds… we are introspecting and your turn is coming! Causal Rule #1: What you do in your mind is what you will be thought of and think as… not the scam you believe no one can see in IT! You must learn to treat yourself well in order to ever have a chance at treating others that way! Golden Rule! Revision* Doing unto others as you would have them do unto you does not cut IT if your beating yourself up and enjoying the pain! Mirroring others neural will reflect their pain and anger as easily as love or compassion. Triggering feelings and un-thought action as reaction. Our ability to thoughtfully discern is what raises us to a humane position rather than the human condition.

Speaking of conditions… "I just dropped in to see what condition your condition was in… Yeah… Yeah… Oh Yeah…" Oh by the way when you go in and look in the mirror, do you do what I do and say, "You're the best looking person on this planet. You love and are loved by everyone" or do you have some negative self-talk or pessimistic view to go along with your image and then carry that with you through out your daily thinking and your life? Just wondering what your image of your image is? Affirmative affirmations of self along with positive self-imaging enhancement of self-estimation, not ego-tripping, reinforces and fortifies what is right with you! Whatever your self-talk, pro or con, your conscious and unconscious mind tries to prove you right and attracts those who are of the same mindset and propels you in the chosen direction. Do not fall into a narcissistic trap! Thinking to greatly of yourself only expands your cortasol not your reality, resulting in merely greatly stressing your opinion of yourself while not actually appreciating the beauty within IT, as to much ego can make you ill! Pin your positive affirmations up next to the mirror. Carry IT on a card with you, reinforcing your image throughout the day! Put the negative through the mind filter shredder destroying them forever. Remind refine redefine redirect to reach the beauty that you know lives within! Again "your only as pretty as you feel inside." (Jefferson Airplane) Love propagates beauty! What's with some studies that state, " only 2% of women think they are beautiful"??? If you give love you are adding beauty, if you receive love you are more beautiful, as you make love you create beautifully. No not just senseless poking love but smoking hot beautiful sensual love. Women's systemic irrational constant body modeling dejection reflection needs mending. You do not need to meet adverting designer imaginings of allure. You create the image you see on the mirror. I have been trying to lose a few pounds for a few decades yet my image of my self is getting more positive each day and is a work in progress. I hear the... No your not... your not right... your not hip or Phat... Your thinking is askew... I'm positive your not!!! I sense much... incoherent envy. Just as the ugly duckling transforms into the lovely swan we may transcend into the beauty of love emerging in IT!

This transaction is one place where the daily energy stealing is performed as one one-ups you to fleece the energy you derive from connection to IT! You are empowered with energy when freely giving IT to others yet disabled when others feel free to take IT from you! Other's can only attain your part of IT if they are left unchecked by your objective observation. I am told that I come across as negative. Now this is a quandary for me as I do not know if I am truly coming across as negative, if I am being perceived as negative, if the person telling me is envisioning and attracting negativity, if I am envisioning and attracting negativity, if I am having a bad day, if I am in a reflective correction mode, if I am truly negative or if again some of my energy was just sapped! That's a lot of "if statements" to process through our perception tree! (For those of you unfamiliar with, "if statements" and computer logic (then… more homework here) as the logic part of our brain makes decisions in much the same way) I guess with my take on the mental state such as IT is, IT would be easy to construe that I am negative on negative being… especially when disguised and surmised as positive PC nun your business "same as IT ever was∞"… a double negative equaling positive truth narrative! No that's not what I said… No that's not what I meant… No your putting words in my mouth… Well… What was IT you were actually conveying when I negated that energy heist??? Many times people hide a bad defense behind a good offense! I often wonder how the decision tree of Da Toxic² is forged into an infinite∞ contentious loop defaulting each time to Da ME and never branching out to further consideration of anything.

We have all sorts of perception filters, lenses, tints, blocks, prejudices, favoritisms, predispositions, preconceptions, insularities, and insecurities that twist, alter, warp, garble, falsify, change, misrepresent, and distort, our perception. Making, this nothing∞ in the Holographic Resonant sub Planck Zero Point Quantum Entanglement Potentiality Reality, tricky to comprehend and taking a little work to get to… nothing∞ (20 minutes twice a day)… You would assume doing nothing∞ (20 minutes twice a day) would be easy! I have worked with people who work harder to do nothing all day than I did doing all sorts of things and their work too. IT allows us to shed all misperceptions, project clearly, and accept others projections openly. Not that you have to accept their conjectures, opinions, beliefs, attitudes, or judgments. This is where caring discernment comes in.   This is clear channel communication! Side note… these Mega communication companies, that old trickle down Ronnie Reagan enabled, like Da unClear chains of homogenized communiqué, are destroying and distorting free communication and plying Congress to gut the FCC!!! The new news paradigm does not invest in anybody to delve more than cursorily deep into any investigative reporting, so now were left with howdy duty rummy dummies tossing softballs for the camera... Anyway... there are numerous ways to adjust, alter, tune, and shift your perception. These range from a simple yawn to days of focused meditation as well as concerted listening, lifting, opening, and shifting miscellaneous filters. You may fold your hands or close your eyes. You may laugh, sing, or beat a drum... You can chant aauum or just hum... So have some fun... refocus or restate, learn to initiate, this step outside to reach within... Breath deep, make the leap... There are many techniques. The trick is to match the technique to the experience and move into the appropriate mode of perception, helping remove deception! Allowing you to make this correction takes some practice and I still miss IT too often. At least I'm trying to perceive IT in multiple ways and processing IT through my perception tree because I'm seeking IT. Unlike those who state "that's the way IT is and always will be∞" when presented with a positive change or alternative to some negative tradition "the same as IT ever was∞" From what I have found IT encourages you to move from the negative into the light! Either my light needs to get brighter or we need more beams. How bright is your light? How's your meditation flowin... let's try a little transformation through meditation... Hum for a few minutes and sense the opening the vibration has made there... try with mind this time to remember someone you have wronged in the past or have ill will towards... now close your eyes and process IT through for a bit.....................

Let's talk SEX... did you follow the meditation or skip ahead because you saw the next topic? Go back if you must and do your transformation meditation! Or is this just another book to cross off your reading list? SEX... You know the birds and the bees! Nah let's talk SEX! "I ain't looking for no trouble N.O.W." I probably should leave this subject alone or at least to some EXPERT!!! Well you know me by N.O.W. I go places no man dares tread and IT is cold here outside your heart, so here goes SEX... I ask your pardon in advance, if your not living some part of the following. Congratulations!!! I owe you one... maybe two... If not then hold on tight and read IT with the love I am missing... not the sexual love, which I miss too, but Agape love. Here boy's is where

CCLXIX

woman have won on the intuIT genetics game and will always continue to as men have much to learn from woman yet ego over IT as we are programmed to defend… Women have the sixth sense in their genes… Many men use only tactile sense and are taught to suppress intangible feelings as weakness when children, yet expected to know what is going on inside women's mystifying minds while sorting through painful feelings that were long ago buried deep within as a form of mental protection. When and why did man dethrone the mythic goddesses? Those men and the ones that continue to proliferate the man state need to dispose of that penile mental hate. Women you should be pissed when the Ad boys always show a man buying a woman some expensive trinket and never a woman buying a man well… anything! Although they're not afraid to depict men as completely incompetent and superfluous! You want equal? Start with the image projected in Media. You know like "Sex in the ch!tty" or "Dispirited unreeled Jersey Housewives" or the Karpdashians. They do show men being inept, thick, uncaring, and portrayed as unfeeling or even heartless, constantly! What's with that message you're moving into the quantum mind… like really? They do show women man-ipulating and being drama queens, like really! I am trying to figure out if men are that inept and stupid how can they afford all those expensive gifts? Oh… the glass ceiling, that you believe in order to break through, you must become some bitch! Well that just occludes the view of you so when, some man not caught up in his own $h!t, looks around for someone to help right the ship he looks right past you to some other that isn't adding to his problems. Again I generalize (sorry). Men like to make decisions and exercise their injudicious feelings of ego independence formed in the misguided status ordering hierarchy that is based upon one-upmanship! So when you ask him "What do you think" and are looking for interactive interdependent consensus building foreplay he thinks you just asked him to make a decision and he's more than glad to oblige to reward his independent ego mechanism which you classify as chauvinistic. We're put together differently like the yin and the wang just as all people are, but we used to need each other to accomplish our life's mission even though those missions do not exactly match. IT's good to see women coming forward if they are being sexually harassed, as IT should be, but if this is viewed to be used as a threat to the boys position @ the table... Well... If there ain't no girl around, she can't take me and mine down! Show me your intelligent and kind, and I will bend over backwards to help you succeed. You're being hosed still on Title 9 by sexual harassment on campus (so too are little boys?)... as well as by the instructors and institutions that continue to be proven to give more of their attention to males and this continues into mans workplace and shouldn't. School appears to be a place where separation by sex is not equal but better, as the form of education that appears to be most successful. Single sex institutions provide better education but put off social amalgamation assimilation... Trade offs??? Be tough, be aggressive, be all that you can be just don't be a bitch to me! Barbara Walters when asked if she needed to be any number of things, including a bitch, to succeed, she said she was not a bitch, and even though I occasionally thought she could be, I would have to agree, that overall, she is not. This goes to show that you do not need to be one to succeed. Life is not some soapy drama and Queen for a Day here and there is OK. But when even little girl's dolls and now even themselves have to be bitchin lookin or have that ho some look with padded bikinis that are stylized idolized for 7 year olds, I just have to ask... WHY??? Get your daughter a Madam Curie doll and start to explain who she was and how she got to who she became or maybe Florence Nightengale, Susan B. Anthony, Jane Adam's, Rosa Parks, there are many better role models than hook a man thin sheik barb Da Brat!

Men being a~~h⊗les comes naturally but not exemplified as an endearing trait on the road to success! This natural trait of being to near the prostate we must prostrate. Men you must closely discern that, as the male, you must first serve women in order to lead. IT is through this service that your dreams will be realized! My Viking ancestors are often portrayed as barbarians yet the Viking women had a vote and were considered equals... So who was more uncivilized the Vikings... or the good old boys @ the Vatican, Mosque, Temple, and those that are missing in action in their women and children's lives? Men do act like the moonstruck Bonobo's we evolved from, but there is a titanic difference between horny lovers, and third world dick-stators hiding between the lines of some so-called holy book, fighting Chimp like wars, to protect their dominance over the harem. Women deserve respect! Let's get INTIMATE for a moment~~~ First we need to recognize this means different things to men and women!!! Men do not want to have to hold a discussion, which they equate to asking permission, every time they need to take a crap. They get enough of that crap elsewhere! They would like to have some small part of their life where they are allowed to be king of their domain. Where as; women are striving for inclusive consensus and Da need to feel. Clearly there's conflict built in. Men have a hard time finding and dealing with their own feelings let alone trying to decipher yours~~~ Ladies you must reach the middle ground as the swampy bog is all around. Gentlemen you must learn to feel and share with care, those issues that drive you deep down inside~~~ Back to their gift… women have developed this IT sense over the millennia as a form of protection for themselves, their children, their families, and each other! Did you ever wonder how your mother knew you were doing something wrong or you were lying a bit? They have developed this gift that we all have to use, to protect, care for, and love those around them! Ladies and I mean that with all respect, you have used your gift wisely until N.O.W., I do not know what the frick all this liberation did to your love and kindness but I have only felt small bits and pieces of IT in the last 30 years!!! I used to walk down the street, in the stores, and especially in the parks in the spring sensing the love you were sending and N.O.W. nothing, not a good nothing either!!! "Give me your heart♫♫ make it real♫♫ else forget about IT". If anything I have changed for the better as well as having compassion for the deficiencies in women's treatment by society, industry, and trueΩ religion in the past and through to this day! I gave women more respect for a long while until I got tired of the rejection! I still respect those few that respect me. But which came first the chicken or the egg, maybe they're both possible first causes, so I will give you my respect unless you chose to lose IT.

What is with the fact that I must steal you from someone else as you hold on to the current Mr. Wrong while looking for Mr. Right (does not exist), you get what you intention! Relations often end the way they begin and many are predestined breakdowns based upon imitation creation. I refuse to become part of that caveman satire. I told you earlier I am not much of a salesman, so I am not going to try to sell you that line of crap that you seem to want to hear or convince you the relationship your currently in is not as good as one with me. I can love you for what's in your heart and mind if you clear the mindfield surrounding IT! I am not sure why you no longer share your gifts with man? IT could be this is your edge and you want to retain IT... Oh that's where the Sex comes in... No you don't share that either anymore... Sex has become a commodity, an exchange based economy, a balance of trade agreement! If my mind serves me well, which IT surprisingly still does, well fairly well, prior to and during the era of free love... most women were not bitches... I know my repeated use of this term is going to engender anger! Try to remember I deal in the Agape truth!!! Men have a longstanding list of love deficiencies as the image is sculpted to remove feeling as equated with weakness. Men if you do not begin to show and share those feelings you need a nagavator to get to, you will never find IT. Men and women can sometimes be a little bitchy a day or two here and there, as I'm a little bitchy too now and then! Sex has probably always been a tool yet so is a stool to a lion-tamer... although not used to beat the lion over the head with! Strip clubs proliferate... Designers shape the models they designate as sexy and inject, operate, and decorate fake visions of image into our self-review! Obsessing and distressing over bodies rather than caressing and impressing within minds! The same liberation that freed you is now enslaving you... There was always some infighting because of the socio-economico-classico-lookinggoodo-whosdatingwho fixation, not this "Bad Girl" object being, where the bigger the bitch the better the bitch!!!

N.O.W. oh yeah N.O.W. that's what happened N.O.W.... Are you actually happier N.O.W.? If so I don't see IT... This is another complicated issue. I sense N.O.W. is not like living in the now, as the stress and expectations have not been good for your gift! The negative attitudes I currently perceive we're either suppressed before or created for a different edge... I am what all the women say they are looking for according to what I read and have heard, from women, on the dating sites, in magazines, and on TV shows... I try hard to be caring, truthful, compassionate, loyal, honest, open, active, semi-attractive, and straight (maybe that's the problem), I am a willing listener and I will call... can I get a response let alone a date? Ok I admit I am no longer a, 21 year old, bad boy liar that will f Ya and forget Ya! I guess I'm, far to real to deal... with and unwilling to put you ahead of enlightenment! I do not buy into the co-dependent paradigm as it is controlling drama. Lifting others up in love is non-controlling karma. Why you lovin and huggin those guys that are walking around with a woman three feet behind them in servitude! Or the rich old a~~h⊗le... Is that servitude or prostatude? They're still a~~h⊗les! I do not want to cast the first stone as I am not without fault but I didn't start this rock concert and I am casting a perceived thought in this direction of negative reflection. Men perceive they need sex, women perceive they need relationship. Women need sex as well but can manage the desire and relate with other women who are managing their men while men need relationships but relate better with other men because they can talk about the sex they are either imagining, getting, or ~~not~~. I could simply trade in my truths, beliefs, and virtues for SEX! I could just lay out some line the ladies want to hear, just pour them another beer, just use them and confuse them, just let them believe I've got some cash, just use a little something from my stash, just keep them thinkin I'm listenin, just do a little a~~kissin! This all would be simple to implement as so many do! I'm afraid though looking in my mirror would be different! So I do come equipped with a hand crank and I'd like to keep my other virtues in my life's bank! If this is your defense system, this bitch thing, for all the a$$h⊗les out there, you better fine tune your discernment because the vertical and especially the horizontal is out of synchronicity... Your defense appears to be an attractor beam. I know guys that are using IT as a cover, in church, metaphysical groups, AA, Meetup's, and use anything and everything to make you... even though they don't Get IT and are there to get something else. They got the lingo, read the books, act the act, play the vibe, and many of you seek this jive... Cut off these a~~h⊗les, learn to discern, applying love where imperative and IT will be yours once more! SEX is great, women are wonderful, Intimacy can be really free as we can be lovingly kind, and we can all serve as equals. If I discern this correctly, women N.O.W. not only want to be equal they want equality with all the services and benefits they once enjoyed as ladies in waiting! I'm pretty sure that plus that equals superiority!!! Well ladies you can either be an equal women or a lady in waiting but you are never going to be both... guys listen up... As you will find that instead of love we often will just be using the other and when there is no give only take there is no incentive or satisfaction in which to partake so IT all becomes fake!

80%

SEX is great but we must get past SEX and back to Love! SEX is gratifying but Love is truly hedonistic, as the more we love the more love we get and the more love we get the more love we can give! We must learn to serve each other asking nothing more! Discerning control, manipulation, ego, and the Me... Both entities must be free! Ladies... Expect more, accept more, but work on solutions not problems. And "Daddies don't let your children grow up to be bitches" and keep your hands off them. Mainly the Daddy realsizes this in his daughters, as he makes them so special that no man can ever reach the level of expectation expected! This is also where they learn man-ipulation, reinforced by their mothers man-edging! My daughters, I hope, are not bitches as I have taken much care and time to help create two of the strongest Princess Warriors who take no crap and give a lot, not crap but compassion, they have managed to retain their caring femininity and yet stand strong with IT! As Jimmy B sings "Only Time Will Tell if I am right or if I'm wrong♫♫... There's a message in this song". I wouldn't be bringin any crap their way because if one don't get cha than the other will! Oh yeah this started out as a compliment to women, see how twisted I can get!!! I love women they just don't seem to love me anymore, except my family, and this makes me sad ☹ as love is what I'm about and what IT is about... Can you remember when SEX was about feeling, sharing, and touching the love and not a commodity to use, trade or get paid for? Well maybe IT always was and I was dreamin! I'm always dreamin... This restricts a part of IT to me and I miss IT... Being single hardly makes you odd man (or woman) out anymore! I'm pretty odd and I do feel out, as my love continues inside of me for eternity∞ Work on the image, you are projecting, in your head. So the image in the mirror reflects the smile of love and the image of care. Then you will regain your rightful place on the goddess throne!!! I look forward to feelin your lovin warm heart touch me once more as I walk in the streets, in the stores, and especially in the parks in the spring rather than this heartless cruel frozen wind I've been sadly sensing during this 30 year war! Peace! That's all... I've had enough... I can't take anymore... this guy spends all of his time writin about his bitches... "Get back... Get back... Get back to where we once belonged!" Ladies... I can only perceive from my male perspective and experience... I apologize for my harshness as I do endeavor to transcend the female point of view. Yet ironically in discussions with some women they seem to be of the same mind as I, to the Bitch supposition. Close your eyes and take a short walk in your mental park in the spring... You do have one?

The next topic up for discussion is equally controversial and involves similarly broken relations and normative reformation... I am talking about Gays though I would rather not! First off why do I need to know anything about your sex life to begin with? Not my business and I really don't want to know and I promise not to tell you about mine! Gay is just another label separately defining your diversity that you demand of me to tolerate. Amazing to me how some modify how they talk, dress, act, and even revise their thought process to fit the model, as they become Nuevo in the "natural" gay way. I am an accepting type of guy, but I take exception when confronted by accretion of assertion of media hype and insertion of disinformation into my Quantum life. Your life is your own to do with as you please as long as IT does not step upon others rights so please don't come into mine and expound on your right to... Display in the street... Infiltrate my beliefs... Permeate my life's perception gate... I do not parade around shaking my penis and stating I'm a heterosexual or that I am anything other than a fellow human being. Go ahead and live as you choose you don't need my or anyone else's permission except your own cognition. Protest as you need but once you succeed please leave my perception screen. I believe in your equality but this superposition is not equal just demanding and demeaning. I do not want to be bombarded by your choice!!! Should I demonstrate and castigate others over my right to excrete in the street because it is a natural human function. Marriage is a manmade religious sanctified acknowledgement of God joining a man and women in a spiritual union, while a partnership, is brought together by pen and law. Where government got involved in marriage... I can only guess that a tax or fee was involved! Not a thing is stopping you from creating a Gay trueΩ religion and getting married there!!! So you can believe whatever you expound!!! I wish you the best. You have surreptitiously infiltrated and infuriated many houses of the holy leaving a karma trail of disharmony behind thee. You got my vote to get you equal protection of that partnership under the law. Do not demand that others sanctify your choice... I am what you label your average homophobe, yet IT's more like heterogeneous indictments of your self-styled selective social consensus truths. In certain societies: fratricide, cannibalize, incest, mutilation, bestiality, molestation and other societal deviation or perversions are OK in a normative way... just not mine! You possibly got lost in Da wrong multiverse, where your choices may not only be tolerated but be Da norm, the problem is you're living in this one where we already got enough abnormal reformative and not enough informed norm! I know... who's the keeper of the norm??? Well IT is. Just ask IT if what you are doing is righteous and you will be answered... But make sure your willing to hear Da truth. Maybe I got this one wrong??? I'm more than willing to admit that as a possibility and may have to answer to IT in the future but are you as open to the possibility I just might be correct? I will not take our time to digress into every sexual deviant like cult, as people seem to be quite creative in

CCLXXVII

this area. I also will not endeavor into every twisted turned behavioral modification movement, there are way too many, and at this time not very relatively relating. As I believe all people are in need of my love but they cannot seem to become unstuck to the infinite∞ tape loop playing with their lives as excuses for their actions! I know... I'm just not being tolerant... well I guess your right. Seems we can try to justify any behavior in which we choose to participate by classifying anyone who disagrees as "intolerant" of that act! So watch for my new act coming to a theater near you soon... IT will be starring me as a normal intolerant human being... Boy that should sure sell some tickets... OH... $hit... Charley already did that... No... He missed the normal part of that act!

How bout a little diatribe on TV shows, News, and now Sports! They can be a great way to waste a couple of hours~~~~~ Remember when reality TV was called the "NEWS" and soap opera's were the artificial reality that are now portrayed by scripter's in Reality TV, where supposedly real people act dramatizing worse thus normalizing outlandishness from bizzarro world! People emulate this life deeming tragedy sold as entertainment comedy and regarded as life's actuality! Separating the boob tube from your minds view is like swapping back edutainment attainment for the current infotainment impediment! Pretty soon there will be no real news as none of the current models supports investigative reporting... Then we have the "Reality" of over dramatization and the crappie ways they portray treating each other along with breaking every societal rule that can be imagined, lowering our expectations for our own relationships and helping to rationalize poor behavior that is not as bad as theirs! More normative ethics! The carnal carnival like sideshows are internalized as we associate our lives with theirs... These preplanned programmable platitudes of plot make our wonderful lives seem contrite and ordinary in comparison! Go ahead and watch if you must (I must admit I do, selectively) I also make sure I separate them from my reality! Infotainment is idioizing individual intelligence. We search for Confirmation bias...as we look for confirmation of what we want to or already know, rather than information about what actually is… that which we may actually discern something from. We all need to escape reality now and then but this move to the edge of the outer limits is mostly composed of dribble drabble scribble scrabble lets hope they don't change the channel before the next commercial babble. Advert-teasers now jumble grammar, overtly dubbing, and focusing in on selective brain activities to sell us whatever, while attenuating the sound compression to embed an impression. And while we're on this wave do you not think… I mean do you not think that the powers at be, do not know that through their control of the airwaves they are controlling our brainwaves! You know either flat lining our waves at the same time or having us all ride the dumb fricker wave into the future? Mass control by Holographic Resonance using sub Planck Zero Point Quantum Entanglement Potentiality Reality Physics… now… can you imagine that might be possible? Did those programs that the government ran for all those years just fizzle out and go nowhere or have you been reprogrammed? I am a conspiracy theorist, because there is conspiracy to make the almighty dollar and somebody's is always trying to control or have power…(Check out: Bilderberg Conferences; Trilateral Commission; Council on Foreign Relations: and the Ride of the Rich, Rancheros Visitadores, as well as the ever famous Bohemian Club) They compose the shadow government that orchestrates all… no matter who we the people vote for or elect!!! Just as in the French revolution the third estate "US" do not really need the 3% who live in the estates. I know that this is real and so does our government! Conspiracies exist and some are more apparent than others! Enslave US economically… then control of our everyday wave~~~ TV mind wave entanglement meld!!! One day to possibly become much like the brainwave manipulating Riddler did in Batman Forever~~~ Five or six companies control most of the content we are assailed through. More and more of our waking consciousness are spent following the negative manipulation of perception by media overkill and dramatization spiraling downward. We must pull out of this spin… They add a little heart constricting fear, assimilate in a lot of multimedia BullCRAP, augment and reintegrate actuality, while diluting the brain pool, re-mastering history as they attenuate

CCLXXIX

our Reality and alter our living truth… Wonder how many dollars are expended inhumanly evaluating human mind commercial time tolerance? Watch Da hyper-news and everything is huffed & puffed beyond reality, from weather to sports, from markets to traffic~~~ Media excites your fears, like some Martian radio broadcast from Grover's Mill, NJ!!! Then eases your dis-satisfactions as you compare your crappy existence~~~ to those getting whacked, rolled, and robbed or Da big bad wolf is after... I'm glad I didn't get eaten today!!! I must have IT pretty good~~~ I keep a waiting for the announcer to break in and announce this is just all a bad scene of da matrix dream~~~ We're all vibing along on their wave~~~ Think digital… Think 2009… Think little boxes… Think little digital boxes in or on every TV that our government subsidized! Used to be, our minds would all interact with live events in real time, you could feel the rush syncing. Now in delayed virtual reality we glaze at live events historically without rush or resonance within the orbs. Nah there's no conspiracy… If you believe this is impossible, ponder about what Microwaves were, that became infrared Radar Ranges, that became Microwaves again, and what microwaves were before discovery, so we could pay dearly for the first micro Burnt Wienie Sandwich? Why do, we the people, have to pay so dearly for technology invented on, we the people's, dime? The smoke and mirrors did not start here… early Christians in Alexandria were manipulated by primitive hydraulic and thermodynamic black magic used by the priests, this was preceded by the ancient Greeks and that was probably preceded by cave clerics! I'm pretty sure all this was impossible too… just as the Papacy chose to keep people in the darkness of ignorance for centuries our leaders are keeping Holographic Resonant sub Planck Zero Point Quantum Entanglement Potentiality Reality Physics to themselves! How they managed to keep nothing∞ from us is their secret. This is **The** true **Secret** and we need to GET IT's secret out! There are many other so called esoteric secrets, fraternal orders, and in trueΩ religion specifically, obscure forms of beliefs and practices, illusively distracting, deluding, and dividing… all claiming to be societies with secrets… exampling Kabbalah any inkling what their secret is? The real secret is to GET IT out in the light of day because hiding secrets in the dark recesses of your mind is unhealthy~~~

In the ancient belief of Kabbalah, the mystical tradition of Judaism, they believe the world was created through the use of language. Another words IT was spoken into existence. Kabbalah practioners and many Jews, consider the book of Zohar to contain mystical truths about their relationship to God. In the Zohar " In the beginning God created"… is really interpreted in Hebrew to " In the beginning God was created"! Meaning, In the beginning infinity∞ created God! The concept of the Bible being explained in metaphors is also expounded upon. This is not new but probably true! Including the concept that Adam cast out God from the garden and not God whom expelled Adam! The original sin was hiding IT rather than admitting IT and taking responsibility~~~ and this curse of hide and deny perpetually haunts every aspect of all of our everyday lives! We are still in the garden and IT is about regaining our discernment of God. I do concur with the concept that we cast God from our lives and that we have never left the Garden! Shekinah is the balance of the feminine side of God that has been depicted strictly as male throughout Western history and is a much clearer fairly balanced depiction. In Kabbalah the Goddess reemerges. Adams wife, the woman (Lilith) in Genesis 1, is like the modern day woman whom grew tired of her spouse. She is not the woman (Eve) in Genesis 2. They also see God and Evil as dependent on people. You can rescue yourself from the exile by deconstructing your normal ego conscience and thus you can open humane consciousness. You also have the good old Talmud crew of the dim~Illuminati, or the un-Freemasonry, Da Rosy cursians, Skull & cross-Bones, human evil empowers the cosmic evil. Secret encrypted trueΩ religion is just another example of elitism, they bring some good notions to the table then put their own special twist of forbidden secrets and who will control this knowledge and the world… Sound familiar! The Hasidic Jews are a branch but modify the technique to find God in this world. They, like so many others of self-import, also believe the world only exists because God needed somebody to relate to. Meaning that God has a need for love and relationships. Well IT does… but not to satisfy some human like desire or need but to share all the extra love contained there! And rather than a belief in the big bang expansion they propose that God withdrew in all directions creating the void, an empty spot within God, of nothingness in which to create. Well this fits my nothing∞ theory so I guess they kinda GET IT but come to another self-centered conclusion! Then we have the basic philosophy of Zen that IT is the negation of all concepts and things so that everything is "no-thing". In Zen, reality is neither thesis nor antithesis. Zen philosophy believes reality must be understood as neither/nor. The nature of reality that corresponds to this principle is called emptiness. Everything is no-thing because everything has emptiness. Enlightenment is the realization that one's individual self is the dreamlike manifestation of emptiness, and once this is realized, one can follow the middle path, reject asceticism, and partake in the splendor of everything just as it is. Like space… within the emptiness there exists something and that something is the Quantum Jitters of paired virtual particles in the vacuum, one positive and one negative… A little Yin and Yang in the nothing∞ There are a lot of good beliefs here as there are in most trueΩ religions. Yet you… discern which ones compose your reality and not allow any trueΩ religion to dictate self-edifying dogma to you! We, as one with God are God! God is not out there somewhere… God is everywhere and can be found anytime anywhere. You may find my thinking a bit warped but so is spacetime, the Universe, and almost everything is a little warped so try to stay ahead of the curve in IT. We are the people we been waiting for! IT is the profound revelation we have been waiting for! So whether you follow Kabbalah, Hinduism, Buddha, Mohammed, Christ, Confucius, Scientology, Taoism, Zen, Naturalism, or Mickey Mouse! We are all mystical beings!!! "Mystic" is a term meaning "one who is initiated into the mysteries." In general, mysticism involves the union between the self and the ultimate principle of reality. Not the gang or cult-like tight "belonging-feeling", of the mystical "Dis" Orders. But the free to be, mystical union with IT, typically involves the blending of one's personality with the nature of God or ultimate reality to the point where there is no distinction and self-identity is put aside. Esoteric or exoteric as this is, the

CCLXXXII

only mysterious thing about this is why so few people are willing and able to do nothing∞ (20 minutes twice a day). This harmonious attitude of thanksgiving is a fulfilling feast of beatific gratitude. Scarcely few are seeking the view so come now and join the freed unbeing of sacredity. Meditation is basically the sustained contemplation of Gods quintessence idealized thanksgiving prayer inspirit of focused thought reflection or maybe just contemplation of relaxation for a bit. Pretty complicated nothing∞ or sublime simplicity! Meditation composes the mind with practiced abstraction from sensory experience. Uncomplicated nothing∞... The aspiration of meditation is to be aligned with the true nature of reality, whatever one's beliefs may be. Hence, meditation is not necessarily associated with mysticism nor any religion, as is often thought to be the case. IT's results will result in faith in IT! IT is free and you are not dictated to, so go ahead and use IT. Speak IT or just mentally repeat IT, gently and prolonged **aum** (Aaa...uoo...mmmmmm, like a hum), a Sanskrit term meaning "assent." A long used vibrational symbol that stands for the whole of reality.

Unlike the 'Dis Orders... along with all the power and money concentrated in the top 1% or the "Pyramid with the All-Seeing-Eye" on our dollar bill and the symbolism on the Great Seal??? Must be coincidence... Oh that's right I already wrote that coincidence is not coincidental IT's synchronic? So these symbols and how they became representative of our world and what they mean would have to have some rationale that's relational? A pile of cash nor the stuff you stash does not measure achievement and success. Success and achievement are measured internally by reference through IT and your desire for connection to IT, as this can be taken with and utilized when you get to IT! Success is achieving your intended reality. Money and power are their trueΩ religion! The Bible addresses the topic of money more than any other issue, more than 2,000 passages discuss money and emphasizes the importance of giving, interpreted as primarily to the church. You can be generous in lots of ways. Money should bring people into the kinship, helping those that don't have. A key teaching in Islam about money and finances is the idea of moderation, the idea of balance, of maintaining a good livelihood for yourself but at the same time not being exuberant. Reflected of course in the Mullahs, Emirs, Sultans, and military ministry leaders. I'm sure the top 1% wants us to join them at the top! Not only do they not want us they don't want you… a staggering 19% think and say they are in the top 1% where 250% of all real income growth has occurred since 1979… I guess even the want to bee's, want to move on up from the top 20s to in Da 1%, egos cannot accept their serf ism!!! The walls they install are there to stop the other people, not you! Lets see… 10 of us are at a Banquet and desert is being served… A pie is cut into 10 pieces… one chump says 9 pieces are mine and you nine can fight over the other piece!!! That's where we're at in the zero sum game!!! Capitalist's can use their Capital to destruct as well as construct. Capital can create value or devalue the intrinsic value of the infrastructure and the means of production when pillaged and plundered of IT's worth. This is where Christian Right Capitalistic Military Complex has taken us!!! Christ said "give to Caesar what belongs to him" " my Tabernacle will be a place of prayer" tossing out the thieves like I toss this thought at those who are stealing our Democratic Republic under any guise; whether; Free Marketers, Right, Religion, Judicial, Military, Left, Fascist, Dictatorial, Financier, or just complacently passive??? The inequality and disenfranchisement that is generated under these disguises perpetuates the hate and anger amongst, those that claim IT for themselves, those that are trying to GET IT, and those that have decided they will never be able to have IT. The first mistake in this argument is that someone has to give up a piece of their pie to give to someone else... well I got news for them... all that pie you got ain't all yours to begin with! Chances are if you're worried about losing some of your pie in an equitable divide you already got more than your share!!! The pie that divides us can be offered up to be shared by all, as IT provides enough for all, yet some chimps assert that they own IT while some have figured out how to claim a larger slice and you should go make your own even though they control the access to all the ingredients too! The anger from this conflict begets hate that displaces our love state!!! Oh well… roll another one~~~

CCLXXXIV

Here's another entangled attenuation for you... The electricity that flows through every space in your life can be manipulated to affect your consciousness!!! On the electromagnetic frequency appliances are giving off confusing waves that interfere with both coherent thought and health. Walk through your house with an AM radio and see how much EMF there is! Every electronic product out there gives off some form of this and according to the games theory the Federal Communications Commission sells the licenses that they then monitor the use of all of them. Some of which are the same frequencies that our brains may communicate on and that IT communicates on! This is not some psycho statement I'm just examining the possibilities given the data available. The Government can use this 60 cycles per second to generate anxiety and fear the research is there! Think about the pest deterrent that can be plugged into any electric system. Are they? They have manipulated Photons to create 3D invisibility! Politicos run on change and then change zilch from zero equating too same as it ever was∞ Lie to our face in the A.M. and we will forget IT by the evening news cycle! What change in the wave is next that even they and their families are not exempt from? Mind mitigation capacitating or encompassing conspirator theorizing! I'm not sure that this cannot mess my vibe up as well, even knowing about their ability to mess with IT and their ability or inability to do IT properly! IT's a powerful tool if used lovingly! IT is a powerful weapon if used un-discretionally! IT's also a powerful intended thought especially if coherently thought as one! People use Biofeedback machines and IT every day to make informed decisions. But, whoever is doing the translations controls the interpretations! Like the inter-pitters of Scientology.

I really, really, really... love the people and the land this country is made of! Yet I suppose I should discern a little on public opinion surveys in general and politics in specific, even though I would rather have an endoscope stuck up my... well you know! Anyway here goes nothing and I mean it literally here! Why do I mention both public opinion surveys and politics together? Will take a little survey to find out! What comes into your brain when a topic of political comparative presents itself or is purposely offered to feed the monster? What is presented to us through political solution? What actual alternatives, that we would like to see and know should be implemented, are offered rather than all these broken policies lobbied to institution? "There is no political solution" as IT requires a mind frame game change! This is where the public opinion surveys play roles in decisions that we expect our politicians to make, for our benefit, without constant consideration towards reelection. Excuse #2: I have no other choice... Is a lie of your choice!!! We're only offered pre-selective alternatives that merely continue broken paradigms, never allowing inclusion of solution through re-Constitution. (Can you imagine what these A$$H⊗les would do if given a chance to frick US up the A$$ by rewriting the only piece of paper that stands between our enslavement and our current level of freedom? Thank God, God was in the hearts of the men that composed IT.) You do not give a whining uninformed child everything it wants by survey! This system of, he said she said Da poll numbers said, insertion of bad tradeoffs into bills, deal muckraking, in-discretionary funds, post reemployment, continual vote pursuit, earmarks deflected to nearby project developments, and machine patronage needs to be thrown out with the other dirt we call our democratic political system. I'm pretty sure Rome had a similar glitch! Will there be future descendents too look back one day in awe of how we advanced so far, as they speculate in wonder of our even greater decline??? If so maybe they'll, by chance, find a copy of GET IT and discern some of IT's truth, I hope for them the best in fact! There is no such thing as a Free Market economy... There is opportunity for Free Enterprise as working for free seems to be the new archetype, all transactions, including bartering, are regulated by law. The real question is if the regulations are fair and enforced or selectively un-enforced and determinably unfair? The only way enterprise pays off is if you can finagle your way through tax law, or bankruptcy debt relief! This shift from collective hunter-gatherers to the competitive everyone for him or herself economics, has left us alienated from the rest of humanity! "Keep your hands off of my stash". We have traded anxiety of scarcity for anxiety of abundance. If Pure Capitalism worked there would be no need for conscience fair market regulation. **Pure Capitalism**: An Economic system operating unfettered by any limiting factors, such as government control or interference. Through inference, government performs little except those functions that cannot be performed by other entities... Yet without regulation the Mega industrialists would have enslaved their consumers and destroyed our environment by now! Oh... they have!!! What we need is a reorder to that of fair and limited limiting judicial regulation to remediate the take that's been taken! If you are a consumable resource you better have a good hiding place or we're going to find you and use you until we use you up! As our resources become limited and we are restricted, we will conflict over scarcity that once was security. The components of our Capitalism, if tempered by a little conscious people's conscience Democracy, is doable and sustainable, yet the proponents of the Capitalism we're living exploits all resources until they are thoroughly devoured, including human resources! Data collection and invasion of privacy through intelligence pretexting, biometrics, profiling, genetic bias, psychological testing, and credit discrimination are fueling big brother. Why should the poor pay more for financial services or be denied them because their credit score is based on their paying cash for everything because they can't get credit! Watson's next generation siblings, of Big Blue, will soon be keeping an ever-closer AI on you! There will soon be a required black tracking box in every car just as we now carry a locator phone! We have a constitutional right to privacy... but that only is a right to privacy from government intrusion, while Uncle Sam intrudes everywhere... Anybody else, from your employer to your child's school, that wants to intrude into your private life may do so and does, as they are seldom caught or prosecuted, like IT's their right to know! We are defrauded into adopting the negative intrusive parts of communism without gain of the socially beneficial aspects... thus continuing Edwardian upstairs downstairs economic and social stratification referred to as Capitalism. I am not a communist nor do I wish to be enslaved; so we need to constantly and consistently filter a larger portion of the pie to include and enable all... as Da power, authority, and wealth, is being unremittingly concentrated in an ever diminishing percentage of the populace. Your wealth is your self and wealth should serve humanity, and not the other way around. I would probably label myself a Democratic Libertarian Fair Market Social Conscience Capitalist, if I were into labeling... what a conundrum, as I believe we should remain Free while using our Capital for Societies highest and best good rather than the Oligarchies whims and the Richs fancy! Free economy embodies kickstarter participation and microlending reinvestment... We are supposedly a Democratic Republic not a Capitalistic Theocracy! The marketing of conspicuous consumption, to promote a different it in the Roaring Twenties, found a nook and took advantage of gotta have it me'ism. The marketers turned our Democratic Republic into consumption junction what's your compulsion! Resulting in the today way of, what I got is who I am, who you are to me, and who I am to you! America is already a shadowy shell of what IT once was or could be, will it fade into oblivion? We are living on the national debt that our children's children will pay for with diminishing life. What's the exit strategy from this economic tragedy? I'd gladly pay you tomorrow for a hamburger today! Everything marked down 50% off all the time... 50% off what???

How long until no one wants to buy our T-Bill debt? "The end of the world as we know IT". You would think @ %36 interest along with late fees, the credit card companies, that allow you to borrow your way to bankruptcy (Oh they eliminated the peoples benefit side of that option!) so you can start the cycle once again with a clean slate, would be nicer to those that make them rich, as they love the fact; that you know and don't mind feeling the leaches sucking your life's blood from your financial soul and since you always live in negative cash flow you won't mind too much if the government spends a trillion here or there that does not exist! The rich receive wonderful treatment at reduced rates. The poor pay more juice and are treated like $h!t... Remind me again what was the definition of usury... or maybe explain why we stopped arresting loan sharks and started giving them cushy jobs with a Wall Street address? Our country and our selves are living on Payday loans... Federal debt influences our foreign policy leaving those we should be helping and protecting at the mercy of those we owe that are heaping us monetarily, feeding our credit addiction, enabling our spending what we don't have and our children never will! Our foreign aid is being siphoned off to fund the supreme corrupt speakers and seekers of current election fraud much like our domestic situation. There is no such thing as National Security, as the CIA is tied to criminals that implement our governments, so called foreign policy, and the FBI is spying on you…The WEB is woven with these spider web crawling tracking JARS of cookies and aggregated data Googlebot's that filter using super computers. Will Silicon Valley return to "Valley of the Heart's Delight"? Government convoluted overt policies similarly have included webs and filtered outright lies, knowledge of and/or direct participation in the events leading to the start of every war we say we we're sucked into (most wars are an excuse for ethnic cleansing). Just where were we in Cambodia, Bosnia, Rwanda, as these people were butchered rather than going and finding some already suppressed people to butcher in the interest of ourselves? These wonderful inhumane endeavors that, Eisenhower warned US of and knew well, are brought to US by the military industrial complex that quite simply is exploitation Return On Investment death puppet manipulation. Do you enjoy being lied to and then finding out, some but still not all of the actual truth years later, that the evidence used to justify and modify our perception of their intervention was an invention. We are protecting, funding, enabling, and encouraging these criminals and now half of the countries in the world report to or are controlled by criminal elements! Now were handing out code, like StuxNet, that can be turned around on our infrastructure to enable our own machines to take US down!!! Did the CIA create this web or is it an effect or did they in effect create the cause? Politicians are staying one step ahead of the campaign reforms they enact. Surveying the political scene reminds me of watching old cartoons that were well thought out and drawn yet absurd in their believability. Have you ever met someone that has a problem? I mean a real problem? Well our government has a real problem… And we are the someone with that problem… And we are the someone we have been waiting for to make a change… Our government has lost the trust of the people as well as our image and trust throughout the world, and is creating fear in the hearts of those whom would guard, support, secure, protect, and defend IT! "Get up… Stand up" "Turn…Turn… Turn…I swear it's not to late"… The government is considered to be a bureaucratic monster that will only get worse and not better… Local governments simply reflect national predisposition only at the micro scale. When politicians throw out the terms: Accountable, Fair, Right, Transparent, or Choice, then the subject matter does not matter as everyone just starts bobbling their heads in agreement while the politicos fiddle their song of askew attune and dance a jig around us subjects with little regard for truth or consequence! They limit our choice to only their desires so as to never get to the heart of any of our issues allowing us too chose only what form of crap we must swallow, Fairness becomes only a grey area shaded by their ability to take advantage of differing perceived realities with us only fairing slightly better than enslavement, The shakedown $h!t life draining economics following Da Oligarchies housing bubble will never be accounted for in terms of human strife and plights. How this shady wrong affects our eternity∞ is immeasurable~~~ Just another economic adjustment in the deliberate take all Capitalist$ model! The better than thou borrowers bought the bubble by takin the free bacon in a Pavlovian satiation schema that fed them an unearned got to have more reward now and forget about IT latter pooping point! Right, as I stated earlier, is mainly in the eye of the beholder, which they constantly redefine in innumerous ways to vary the chance of defining true righteousness and insures our right to remain silent. Accountability is turned back on US because we are not holding ourselves accountable for implementing the checks and balances needed! Ballot Referendum throw up, used to block true popular change by limitation and confusion too overt get the party vote out dilusion! So passively we thereby facilitate their capacitance not to be held responsible! Just for affect they throw in the term "balanced perspective" so as to unbalance any rational proposition along with some ridiculous irrational opposing views… while benchmarks, waypoints, and stretch goals, are seldom checked against what's best of class for the human race! Participate in this race today... tomorrow... and make everyday the best! This FOAF social network 2.0 will either be a bunch more whining self interested moaners and flash mobs or we can hold everybody Accountable... We need to stop passing the buck and insist with our buck$ on implementation of a simple open process of measurable metrics obliging answerability... this should apply to Mega Corporation as well or maybe we need our own not so little social network meet up in Liberation Square... Could IT be another serendipitous coincidence that this little meetup is already virally going global... 800,000 told BOA where to stick their account fee while 800,000 others sent Netflix a return to sender message... No... no ones lookin... let's stickem with that fee now!!! Gotta keep up Da good work vigilantly... Actually quite surprised the toleration and restraint being shown. But then again the polls show the people are supporting IT! But remember they like to let you think you're being heard, making Da difference, Winning your point, and then the critical mass is diffused and broken back into self-interest diversions settling down to "The same as IT ever was..." Should have finished and published Da Book sooner... Just like we should have finished what we started in Da 60's~~~ OH procrastination!!! Da revolution will not be televised... who will enforce a US protective no fly zone? Oh Da FAA will to suppress Da Press!!! Take your business to those who care and you'll find out how much they do! Now... back to the current rant... How do we go back and indict the son if a B's that are retired on the pensions from the government units they controlled while underfunding, sacking, and stealing, from those same pensions leaving our children to foot the bill! And while we're here how about the Classless action litigation leaving victims without recompense enumeration or settlement by consent decree without declaration nor admission of real guilt should never be! When I hear on the news that Japanese auto part makers are being fined millions upon millions of dollars for price fixing and gouging US, my mind wonders back once again to who may get that fine money??? Probably not you or me who overpaid for those parts somewhere along the line already! I also hear about but never receive any part of the high fines and settlements that are levied all the time for infringin illegally in some fringe of my life... maybe you're gettin your share but I ain't never seen my share... ever! On the flip side if you spill hot coffee on your lap or trip over your own stupidity you should admit your own ineptitude rather than continue the indignation by suing unjustly because no one issued you a warning label when you were born! No one wants to, admit, acknowledge, own up to, or take any responsibility as if somehow gremlins are provoking all our actions. We spend way more money and time training marketeer's how to turn a sow's ear into a silk purse than we do to prepare and educate those who are spending what's in IT! Our governments cut deals to grant currency to their spendthrift patrons, while inactions are the only rewards for those who were truly screwed by the knowing misdeeds of the hidden identity Directors of the Bored! Everything that is criminal should have a consequence and should not just have a price tag attached, as the price of wrongdoing now is a line item cost of doing fuzzy math busine$$. Exemption of government and corporate officials, from many of the same rules we must abide by, must end! Congressional perks, benefits, patronage, and law immunity are only exceeded by Corporate greed bonuses, stock options, and legal speak thieves, leaving US to foot the bill or do the time... sometimes for their crimes!!! There are not many much worse inequalities yet there are some, such as when countries refuse humanitarian aid and thousands die, the leaders should be tried in the World Court for genocide, many others are endemic. Decline is a choice... I know I offer a very idealistic view on general generational problems allaying few direct solutions but the knowledge is there to disentangle this mess. US as a people need to begin to act in our common honest denominator interest of outcome resolution revolution! IT is a dynamic thought of potentially possible, rather than self-interest derisive parochial. Innovative outcomes that I'm purveying, hoping, and praying may become our new reality! We need to define our aspirations in order to induce processes that result in an altered paradigm. IT's that ideal that made America what IT once was and can be again! ! What you see on the tube is just a magic show for you and me. If you knew what they do, we would be revolted by the view. I mentioned "We the people" earlier. Well "We the people" better start getting up off our a~~es and into some faces so that when we are presented with two faces, there is somebody in both of them and they get off theirs! They're more concerned with keeping their JOB than doin IT! There is much taking and little given! Given that taking is habitual, consider giving in equal measure multilaterally. Discoursing bipartisanship is lip service disservice partisan same old course for our ship of state. We need to take names and kick some A$$ to restructure objectless formless nameless THEM into an US in God we can begin to trust!!! I remind you again~~~ IT is done without some trueΩ religion, biased poly peoples party, or overt revolution… IT's just you, I, and Da every body in unity with IT~~~ naming, facing, and kicking, our way to Da day of the way IT could BE!!! We have the power to individually be the difference this world is in dire need of. So take IT wherever you are and BE what IT needs~~~

Oh boy… I'm on a roll today… Get out the Sunday soapbox as I begin this sermon!!! During the last street revolution we we're looking for understanding and peace, we smoked a little tea at our party, our tolerance had run out, and so the Suits became intolerant of us. The current TEA party has many grand ideas but is obscured by the smoke of the Suits at that same as IT ever was∞ party! No one appears ready to pay for today or yesterday, so how do we embark on the mission to pay IT forward! If you're always saving IT for tomorrow all you have done is wasted IT yesterday! What's an UffDa know about busyness??? Well back in Da early seventies some of that econ slipped into my mind while I nodded off in class~~~ actually a great way to learn... as your mind is alphaing along~~~ and like most things once the concept is understood over time you kinda develop that interest and interesting the monkeys in their busyness are. The Suits have financed their ego driven lifestyles on the backs of US while banking the profits and disinvesting in US and now proclaim US is costing way too much, proclaiming big US is getting in the way of big business. Are these the same businesses that outsourced our way of life? Take your thumb off the scale and readjust your purpose too add positively to the credit side of the balance sheet of life! Is the party of NO (Nothing Owed) planning to use our

CCXCIII

children as armed forced bodyguards, since inequality continues to grow exponentially and a less peaceful revolution, than we projected, is inevitably held. Will they continue to hide behind the Wall on their Street! We thought we won nonviolently… well maybe some bricks and mortar were tossed about but nothing like the bullets from the Guards M16's… I embrace the Constitution that TEA has symbolized in many ways… but watch out for whose pulling what strings in the carnival game these barkers exclaim to reclaim! "Come inside the shows about to start… guaranteed to blow your head apart!!!" (ELP) Mix a little constitutionality with some good ole boy top profit distributing then spin in a variety of meaningless oratorical recorded rhetoric shaken a finger not stirring the mind while adding subterfuge with a hint at un-American or terrorism and you basically boil the $hit down to the same tainted TEA we been drinkin. We need a new dictionary to translate their lexicon of fiscal conservancy that still does not benefit you or me! Ya come up with a good idea like TEA or OWS and the next thing you know the cause is hijacked by someone with their own agenda!!! The best form of revolution is Gandhi like Satyagraha… the peaceful nonviolent civil disobedience of the arcane laws constraining the masses! As Gandhi said, in listing the four phases of peaceful civil disobedience: "First they ignore us, then they ridicule us, then they attack us, then we win!!!" One suggested "redistributive fair market solution" if you want actual Democratic Capitalism: set a flat tax and apply a one-time reassessment 50/50 luxury surcharge social remediation equalization factor and "redistribute" IT… You cannot just start fairly flatly taxin from here without an equalization factorial, as the past's monetarily fat cattin would still not be remuneratively remedied and Da poor would again still be proportionally unjustifiably taxed overtly burdensomely as they have less disposable money left over after tax's and bills to begin to be a Capitalist and inflation caused by new demand would strip out most of the equalization! But the field would be leveled and a new game could begin. While we're here lets drop a zero off the end of all money and prices… a nickel raise might mean something again! How much skin you got in Da game affects how committed you are to IT's outcome… "Redistribute", that 12 letter word associated with ism's, then we can begin the true Democratic Fair Market Republic that was hijacked by the elite Plutonian's from the beginning, by rules and laws that their accountants and lawyers loop-holed and skewed favorably their way, while being aided and abetted by their governments failed enactment or non-enforcement of a variety of other statutes and decrees that would have leveled the playing field~~~ "Redistribute" only back charges the privileged few who benefited while driving Us into the ground through special pecuniary planning, monetary policing, insider trading;" lawmakers who direct money to institutions with ties to their relatives and appropriations for work in close proximity to commercial and residential real estate owned by the lawmakers or relatives", legal tax amending and war profiteering... the STOCK Act does not permanently ban pork-barrel spending or the practice of lawmakers earmarking near their properties! (Plan Aye) 50% of every thing you own will go into the pot and 50% inheritance tax is reinstituted. 50% of that pot is then divided equally by all "American born citizens" of legal age... as "redistributed" return to you as a time reparation payment of 25% over the course of 5 years to lesson the exchange pain... a 25% credit towards your future flat tax's, so even the rich get something in return, and only the top 5% would likely get a bill for the reconciliation but this way the filthy rich still got a lot of skin in Da game but are still filthy rich... learning to live on a 100 or so million dollars might help them comprehend the value of a dollar to the less than fortunate multitudes! The other 50% of the pot goes to heal this county, create real jobs, and put a down payment on our future!!! This includes the cash stashed in Da islands and the Alp$... Maybe a Buffett like person could oversee the metrics of Da re-allotment, as US would lose 50% in Demon cratic evaporation. I know this sounds un-American but that is only because they've been painting the idyllic American economic equality depiction in the gray matter of your mind. Open the books on the internet, fairly compensate "merit" based government workers participation, incentivizing "provable" cost containment, institute "demonstrated" best practices, rewarding and protecting whistle blowers, punitively punish noncompliance and negligence whether intentional or just consequential. We all want everything on our what's the best way list but there is a lot of garbage we all haul along... Take the very best from column A list and the very best from column B list repeat for C D E lists... and get rid of the rest... I'm sure there are much greater minds than mine that could be put to task on a fair solution, but IT seems they already are, and sum of the greater minds are a part of the current problem not the solution! Can our children afford to survive another generation of investment divesting bankers? Corporations will no longer be considered individuals and their income and assets must be connected to someone's taxpayer ID... This stuperoir SUPER PAC way of funding deceitful negative ads sponsored and subsidized by a candidates buddies while retaining deniability even when outright lie ability is incivility abused! Do you know that all you need is a cover letter declaring your intent to be a Super PAC to be one (like Cobert)? If you got Da money you can pervert truth and never answer for the crime! We should replace this judicial indiscretion with judicial inspection of all political pacs and who's in u end owing! The "Redistribution" may need some tweaking so Da Plutocrat's don't kid nap our kids and Da Blutocrat's don't debase their future!!! IT'S really that simple... Watch them run like Rats R US when you try that, or watch them lick their chops at a chance to get a hold of all that money that they can connive to steal! That is why IT will never happen without a re Constitution in our idealism, reframing reality, and reformation in spirit, for that in doing so those that have all the chips @ the Texas Holdem table would have to let you back in their game! Are they growing profits or are they investing in all our futures through education and delivery of "desirable" job development, not just Mickey D'ing type job numbers abound, creating indentured minimums and deleting living wage principles? Might have to deprogram and retrain a bunch of people that currently serve Da Plutocrats needs and desires! Yeah... this will all happen, and social equality will become the model??? What's all this got to do with Da vibe??? Well until US get back our country you and me ain't free to truly be!!! We can be... butt only truly be totally in tune in my wildest dreams!!! Let's work on IT!

Well my patience is tolerated out again. I will not tolerate any term, including tolerance, to be used as a reason that forces acceptance of negative untrue A$ $h⊗lism. People intolerably use words they do not mean nor understand to stand behind their living lies! This includes the term diversity, which really means myopic division multiplicity based upon differences rather than the similarities. I can and have tolerated much in the name of God, and I AM done having my being restrained and retrained because others are living the inane! The use of diversity acceptance as the reason I should accept and tolerate others: such as third world customs and castes, so-called traditions and acceptance conditions, esoteric religions or terror convictions, economic stratocracy or oligarch omni potentate enabling, and any actions that include female subjugation, mutilation, sexual deviation, education manipulation, dress code regulation, or ignorance propagation, and just general exploitation of any kind, because I'm such a tolerant diverse kinda guy, is unreasonable and quite inexcusable to me. I am a diverse gumbo of genetic nationality as we all are, given recent DNA findings, yet brought up in the ethnic customs of Scandahovian-way. I do not hold this superb tradition as a superior condition or required state for relation. My thinking is so diverse on relations that I base IT on truth tolerance rather than the forced manipulative totalitarian relativist view that both tolerance and intolerance are equally valid and rather than flip-flop to accede, I abide in my right of objective disagreement in conviction of intolerable traditions! I treat everyone equally as they come to me… Everyone starts out with the benefit of no doubt and we can then take IT wherever we precede! I try, like IT, to be predisposed to the positive but am not afraid to call on IT to persuade any negative projection with reflection back to origin! So what and who am I to be labeled as? I'm sure there have been some interesting labels applied to some of my unfathomable possibilities! I have encountered some people that are so diverse I was not sure they were of this earth! Just as equality does not grant impunity, diversity does not equal righteousness. Tolerance should not measure the amount of crap I need to take. Profiling of A$ $h⊗le traits and tendencies does not automatically permute to prejudice, IT does though keep past, present, and future intentions part of my reception protection perception. I can only make a difference or change where I am. I choose to not allow negative backassward thinking to change my world to their indifferent thinking thus intolerance becomes change management! Like Da manual taking of my right to parade in Chi town, under the guise of time for change... like this bull lessening of my Rights is an upgrade in my best interest! There is a big difference between compassion and totalitarian toleration! One is to sympathize with. The other is to suffer for! If rational rather than bemused reasons are present then forward-enlightened bilateral understanding may progress but the argument that I must be tolerant of irrational behaviors propagated through norm usurpment! Well... now warrantless searches and indefinite incarceration without providing cause are on the fascist government agenda! I sympathize much yet suffer too much as IT is... You may ask how this relates compassionate or empathetic Agape love??? And you would be raising a legitimate query... Just as I am done having my being abused by people taking advantage of my tolerance I am just as done with those manipulatively advantageously working my compassion with enmity not empathy. If they are legit and even when their not but seeking IT, they get the full Agape love treatment... But if they're knowingly purposely seeking to damage my Love vibe well~~~#~~~ then they reserve what I send in return! I realize that this creates conflict but I'd rather have the conflict out where I can see IT and do something with IT rather than to continue fighting this manipulative unresolved conflict within. Many do not want to acknowledge or begin to deal with the conflict within, let alone take IT to the streets! My next tome may entangle normative tolerance enhancement enchantment world diversity disorder or maybe IT is already in here!

Maybe with a little luck the Amazing Grace that brought us to this point will reemerge and this country and its inhabitants will be known throughout the ages for IT's compassion not failed aggression. I choose not to be subjugated by the Baron Tycoon tighta$$ titans who Captain our industry barren of economic equality! "God Bless America my home sweet home!" I want my great-great-

great grandchildren to proudly sing this song! I am 4th generation American. My More Grandma came into this country with my Grandmother under one arm and her sewing machine under the other... ready to become American! I may emigrate back to Norway, a more social society, if this country continues to lower itself down to the level of oligarchies and dictatorships and the average A$$H⊗le or maybe I could save some money by committing some crime, that ought to be easy, and just have ICE deport me back to Da homeland... then just sneak back next spring traversing the soft ICE. If you are new to this country add to IT as you have chosen US as your life's place. Now that your ready to ship me off maybe you can understand that leaving would be a whole lot easier than staying and being the change. I have lived my life staying and changing rather than fleeing, hiding, or faking. I have encountered and observed many that turn, avoid, escape or even actively participate in the problem rather than meeting the challenge! We've learned to work the system, we've learned how to work each other, we need to forget that and relearn how to work together and once again love each other. I know your thinking, what's this self-anointed critic of Da everything doing writing about everyone lovin everybody! But love ain't just some big "Love In" with a huggin and a kissin make up story, love involves caring... I mean truly caring enough about what is going down in the everywhere everything kinda unified way, to correct our course of actions that results from our unaware inaction! This involves breakin a few eggs to make Da break last~~~ We must be resolute in our demand that this country be returned to its rightful place in history... Not by rewriting history but by changing today so that tomorrow's history will reflect the country we so love! This may only be accomplished one infinitesimal step at a time but we need to start now to avoid the fate of ancient Rome! When my daughters were 10 or 12, I took them to the movie theater. I went to purchase the tickets and the manager questioned the appropriateness of bringing my daughters to an R rated movie at their age... I told him that I knew what I was going to see and that I wanted my daughters to know and have IT etched in their minds... he looked at me kind of odd and proceeded to sell me the tickets... The movie was "Saving Private Ryan" and I wanted them to know that our country and their Grandfather fought tyranny and many died for our liberty along with the freedom to worship IT... And that this may happen again... Not this replay of Vietnam in the Gulf. No! Here on our turf... How many of you are preparing the next generation of Warriors or Princess Warriors to stand for IT's truth! Where are the bodies and the coffins from Bush's war??? Is your son or daughter just looking to follow or acquire a posse of WanaBee's... We're gonna need everybody when the crap comes down! Here's another couple of survey questions. Do you think the towers were the end or the beginning of what's in store? Have we made the country safer? Have we created more terrorists? Is our country stronger? Did we saddle another generation with more debt, and the guilt of PTSS, poorly acknowledged or funded Vet's? What was gained and what was lost? These Polly's are anal, why do we retain them? VOTE! VOTE often!!! Use your vote the way it has been tactically abused on you. If all else fails use your vote to screw up their statisticians costing them some of their almighty dollars used buying our vote!!! Funny how election night software glitches are the new hanging chad!

I am going to take a little speculative side trip... I have pulled wire as an electrician, I have built circuit boards and tested computers, I have studied basic physics and astrophysics, I know enough to know, I am a kindergarten electronics buff! But please jump into the energy field I am about to generate. I again use WIKI as my citation. I am basically proposing that all energy is spooky and similarities exist within the macro and the micro. Consider the Aurora, the interaction of energy between the Sun and Earth's magnetic field and the Aura, the interaction of energy between our minds, bodies, and our space, maybe even into space~~~ through the Shumman sprite lightning resonance field vibrating the earths atmosphere at the same frequency our minds Alpha waves pulse. The actual science linking these phenomena is being measured now... IT is illustrating coherent interactive thought! Even if only a fractal part of what I espouse on the unified energy fields of, light electric body mind spirit, is spot on, the way we mess with crap and the way crap is messing

CCC

with IT might have something to do with the state of the mess of crap we're in! As a scientist I must be clear... I have seen Aurora's and been to Aurora, IL. I have also sensed Aura yet cannot describe IT completely but the interaction evidences Aura's existence. By coincidence or not NASA has a mission that is called Aura, part of the A-Train. http://aura.gsfc.nasa.gov/ NASA's Aura researches the composition, chemistry and make up of the Earth's atmosphere as well as the ozone, air quality and climate. Utilizing assorted frequency images to monitor the health of our planet. While a project at Carnegie Mellon University, Project Aura strives to provide distracted users of computers with an invisible halo of computing and information services that persists regardless of location... the cloud that is gathering will not reflect the halo if not amended to intend IT. Aura's goal is to provide each user with a "personal information aura" that spans wearable, handheld, desktop and infrastructure computers. Neither of these things are, what I'm trying to speculate or stipulate.

Now we pause for another Update... Updates... What's up with all the fricken updates? Well I realized it was time to update my computer and I broke down and bought a useful 17" laptop with Vista™... Oops... Never easy to make transitions from what you know to the unknown, especially when you have to pay for IT with more than cash. How's that you may ask? Or you may not... but when you throw a product out on the street that is only half of what you advertise with thousands of known errors and is incomplete but is sold as the latest and greatest, your name must be Mr. Bill. Sell an OS code you don't even own yet to big blue and the rest is fabled story, like a dime novel that we paid big time for! With a few tweaks and upgrades it is a useable machine, once the crapware is removed and the first service pack is in place but the updates flow like a leaky faucet... trying to fix what their hackers put in and put out with little introspection, incessantly coding to attend to the under attended ciphering other hackers tend too! Dribs and drabs fixing what's bad... You need to be a computer physicist to have any idea what is happening out of view behind the Vista™... They have dumbed down the file system to the point I have to change permissions to even see them. I have to admit that there are some pretty pictures inside of pictures, yet see no real upgrade to the interface or info-relate! In 30 years this is the best we could do? Wonder what we could do if we could open source the duopolies of MicroApple and GoogooFace! Just another step in the product life cycle to sell US along the way to maximized profitability while skipping ahead to advancements waiting their turn on the shelf could truly re-enable US! Yet we will all be living in the cloud soon~~~ How long will this peuter last in this disposable economy is anyone's guess. The mother was recalled, the bios flashed again and again, and not enough RAM to see the Aero Vista™!!! I was not fly on their FB wall during the planned obsolescence economic lifecycle stage of that project! Vista's™ lifecycle was a short but embarrassing time and Microsoft is ultimately trying to quell the embarrassment of the poor Vista™ debacle (much like the new Millennium™) by making a b"**old**" move with Windows 7™ to win back customer loyalty and generate positive spin to get back market share for its most lucrative product, that I am stuck repairing again and again. Me thinks' Mister Bill should have used some of that cash he stashed to give me a usable product that does not waste great amounts my time because he saved some and depletes my positive energy rather than polishing his image as a philanthropist with my money that was the monopolist ransom to compete by compute with the suits. The ghosts of Christmas must have visited Mr. Bill as he stares into the neuron mirroring even as MS still monopolizes the operating of the system while I watch the hourglass spin! 7, which is probably Vista™ completed properly, was "coincidentally" ready for Christmas 2009 and marketed as the simplest and easiest Windows™ ever? I'm pretty sure that's why I bought Vista™!?#* Will Windows™ 8 again late, short on features, and requiring us to learn how to do the same old thing a different way metrolly, 9 another dime, or 20/20™ mine; help me see simply more clearly in Da cloud? Move along little doggies move along... I am just again considering the knowledge imparted through the net... Dittering Twittering is inputting overwhelming output... of throughput of IT... but this interconnectivity, analyzing every word communicated to the point that even the CDC is able to diagnose Da diseased, as well as the spider bots have interesting permutations of possibilities in our consciousness; if we can just shift through the Data social debata I got no life outasidea collective useless info overload... There is an enormous amount of incorrect or bad information as well as custom distortion of the poorly reported, and dramatic followings of demented view-pointers in cyberspace camouflaging good data that you must strain to find. Be mindful where you point that Browser IT may be loaded and the first of the search may not lead you to what you are researching, so look some more... Be careful what you allow through your malware truth filter! Pops and Pirates can be killed with ALT/F4 but probably not PIPA. Can you perceive that maybe Micro-Apple has been directed by the government to put a backdoor into your peuter, smart phone, and GPS??? While the Government requires ISP's to keep track of your tracks~~~ If you think News Corps hacking is invasive... FOX guarding the hen house and buying the boobies... just think what the possibilities are with super computers and NSA, FBI, or CIA, playing the hack in game!!! Not sure how loss of privacy became the default state but my Big Brother says he knows! Do you think FB, Twitter, or any social communication that is deemed unsociable during any kind of an uprising will not find IT's signal disrupted or the plug pulled! Probably generating the paperwork to nail my a$$ with sedition charges right now... or at least going through my garbage looking for counter revolutionizing conspiracy, which is a lot like reading my book...LOL... IT is not seditious for each of us to independently be free to choose to live in truth and apply our positive vibe to retune the machine~~~ Individuality infers taking responsible actions of being free, not idly awaiting that freedom to arise or be granted! Liberate your self as true revolutionary change comes from within! Do what's right, not just convenient or egocentric! IT is not conspiracy to choose to live within the positive unifying force~~~ In America... YET...   Ask yourself how your thoughts and actions will alter all futures? You must set down your device for a moment to follow your thoughts down the many paths your actions flow to begin to know what outcomes you've conceived! "Device etiquette" ~~not~~ my problem! Most do not ponder the affects of their actions very deeply, thus the rest of us have much more to consider in our efforts to overcome toxic apathy and wonton selfishness! First we are "humans" of planet Earth, which takes all precedence over any local colloquial nationality or religious vehemence! As fellow humans of Earth we should be living and loving rather than hitting and shoving one another, as IT is in our mutually shared interest for all to succeed! Except many tolerate sublimation of mutual welfare by the so-called human condition (selfish ness) that undermines the unity... By interacting with pure humanistic thought we can overcome the inane insane! We quickly find faults but obvious similarities go unrecognized... We search furiously for errors rather than practice simple compassion... We divide as if differentiation somehow equaled liberation... Our independence does not negate our interdependence just as being part of the unity does not negate our own unique essence!!! Do not wait for the human condition to change, make a point of being human without conditions. Lots of stuff going on already... Duh... derailed again... follow along... back to the track... try to follow that!!! That is the mindspacetime light track. Ahh... bandwidth... yeah... but the full spectrum of IT's connected possibilities possibly... Life is energy. Energy is everywhere. Why would the different collections of energy fields be separate entities rather than union fusion from the one energy source??? You know the routine... Define...

Aurora Defined WIKI

Auroras (Polar Lights; or aurorae) are natural coloured light displays, which are usually observed in the night sky, particularly in the polar zones. It often appears as a greenish glow (or sometimes a faint red), as if the Sun were rising from an unusual direction. Auroras are produced by the collision of charged particles from Earth's magnetosphere flowing from the earth's core that is like the field of a bar magnet. The Earth's "magnet" is wound deep in the core. Earth's magnetosphere is the space region dominated by its magnetic field. It forms an obstacle in the path of the solar wind, causing it to be diverted around it. Most Aurora's originate from the Sun and arrive at the vicinity of Earth in the solar wind and accelerates the reconnection of magnetic fields accelerating the particles towards Earth. When the solar wind is perturbed, it easily transfers energy and material into the magnetosphere. The electrons and ions in the magnetosphere that are thus energized move along the magnetic field lines to the polar regions of the atmosphere colliding along the way with gas atoms, causing the atoms to give off light. The Earth's field is compressed on the dayside, where the solar wind flows over it. It is also stretched into a long tail like the wake of a ship, which is called the magnetotail, and points away from the Sun. Satellites show electrons to be guided by magnetic field lines, spiraling around them while moving towards Earth. The collisions in the atmosphere electronically excite atoms and molecules in the upper atmosphere. The excitation energy can be lost by light emission or collisions. By a strange twist of physics, the magnetic disturbance on the ground due to the main current almost cancels out, so most of the observed effect of auroras is due to a secondary current, the auroral electrojet. The convergence of magnetic field lines near Earth creates a "mirror effect" which turns back most of the down-flowing electrons (where currents flow upwards), inhibiting current-carrying capacity. While this mechanism is probably the main source of the familiar auroral arcs, formations conspicuous from the ground. Some O+ ions ("conics") also seem accelerated in different ways by plasma processes associated with the aurora. These ions are accelerated by plasma waves, in directions mainly perpendicular to the field lines. They therefore start at their own "mirror points" and can travel only upwards. As they do so, the "mirror effect" transforms their directions of motion, from perpendicular to the line to lying on a cone around it, which gradually narrows down. Aurora appeared mainly in the "auroral zone", a ring-shaped region with a radius of approximately 2500 km around Earth's magnetic pole, not its geographic pole. It was hardly ever seen near that pole itself. The instantaneous distribution of auroras ("auroral oval", Yasha/Jakob Feldstein 1963) is slightly different, centered about 3-5 degrees nightward of the magnetic pole, so that auroral arcs reach furthest towards the equator around midnight. The aurora can be seen best at this time. Geomagnetic storms that ignite auroras actually happen more often during the months around the equinoxes. It is not well understood why geomagnetic storms are tied to Earth's seasons while polar activity is not. But it is known that during spring and autumn, the interplanetary magnetic field and that of Earth link up. In addition, the aurora and associated currents produce a strong radio emissions. The ultimate energy source of the aurora is the solar wind flowing past the Earth. Scientists have found that an energy source for auroras are giant "Magnetic Ropes" or the energy which comes from a stream of charged particles from the Sun "flowing like a current through twisted bundles of magnetic fields connecting the earth's upper atmosphere to the sun". Birkeland current carrying plasma flows trail millions of miles through space. The energy is then abruptly released in the form of a shimmering display of lights.

Auroral events of historical significance

The auroras, which occurred as a result of the "great geomagnetic storm" on both August 28, 1859 and September 2, 1859, are thought to be perhaps the most spectacular ever witnessed throughout recent recorded history. The latter, which occurred on September 2, 1859, as a result of the exceptionally intense Carrington-Hodgson white light solar flare on September 1, 1859, produced aurora so widespread and extraordinarily brilliant that they were seen and reported in published scientific measurements, ship's logs and newspapers throughout the United States, Europe, Japan and Australia. It was said in the New York Times that, "ordinary print could be read by the light [of the aurora]". The aurora is thought to have been produced by one of the most intense coronal mass ejections in history, very near the maximum intensity that the Sun is thought to be capable of producing. It is also notable for the fact that it is the first time where the phenomena of auroral activity and electricity were unambiguously linked. This insight was made possible not only due to scientific magnetometer measurements of the era but also as a result of a significant portion of the 125,000 miles of telegraph lines then in service being significantly disrupted for many hours throughout the storm. Some telegraph lines however, seem to have been of the appropriate length and orientation, which allowed a current (geomagnetically induced current) to be induced in them (due to Earth's severely fluctuating magnetosphere) and actually used for communication. The following conversation occurred between two operators of the American Telegraph Line between Boston and Portland, Maine, on the night of September 2, 1859 and reported in

The Boston Traveler:

Boston operator (to Portland operator): "Please cut off your battery [power source] entirely for fifteen minutes."

Portland operator: "Will do so. It is now disconnected."

Boston: "Mine is disconnected, and we are working with the auroral current. How do you receive my writing?"

Portland: "Better than with our batteries on. Current comes and goes gradually."

Boston: "My current is very strong at times, and we can work better without the batteries, as the aurora seems to neutralize and augment our batteries alternately, making current too strong at times for our relay magnets. Suppose we work without batteries while we are affected by this trouble."

Portland: "Very well. Shall I go ahead with business?"

Boston: "Yes. Go ahead."

The conversation was carried on for around two hours using no battery power at all and working solely with the current induced by the aurora, and it was said that this was the first time on record that more than a word or two was transmitted in such manner.

<u>Please allow me this short side trip into Norse folklore.</u>

The first Old Norse account of norðurljós is found in the Norwegian chronicle Konungs Skuggsjá from AD 1230. The chronicler has heard about this phenomenon from compatriots returning from Greenland, and he gives three possible explanations: that the ocean was surrounded by vast fires, that the Sun flares could reach around the world to its night side, or that glaciers could store energy so that they eventually became fluorescent.

An old Scandinavian name for northern lights translates as "herring flash". It was believed that northern lights were the reflections cast by large swarms of herring onto the sky.

Another Scandinavian source refers to "the fires that surround the North and South edges of the world". This has been suggested as evidence that the Norse ventured as far as Antarctica, although this is insufficient to form a conclusion.

Aura Defined WIKI

Aura in parapsychology, spirituality and New Age belief; an aura is a subtle field of luminous multicoloured radiation surrounding a person or object as a cocoon or halo. An aura may be held to represent or be composed of soul vibrations or charkas, and may reflect the moods or thoughts of the person it surrounds. This supernatural energy field or life force hypothetically permeates all things. Aura is considered both an energy field and a reflection of inner self.

Where does our consciousness reflect? This is a part of our Nature. "Ultraviolet, Infrared, and X-ray... Beauty to find in so many ways!" Everything in the Universe has a vibration, aura, and carry's a resonance, our thoughts and consciousness are electronic waves with frequency vibrations. Our hearts beat differently based on the solar winds. There is more agitation in our minds and bodies because of IT's interaction with the ever changing magnetosphere. When IT is active we are more ordered. The stars burst with gamma rays abounding. We burst with Gamma waves astounding. Science believes that the large and the small will one day be unified in theory. My theory is IT already is! Most progress in science began on the periphery of experience, where anomalies lurk! Does your intention end up being your coherent projection or is your invention of intentionality pretendin a contention? An Aura is an electro-photonic vibration of a light form, in an excited state, that contains information. A fourth Al… I mean a half an Al… this time… Yeah…. Fritz-Albert Popp discovered that, we and all living things, emit light and termed IT biophoton energy, a physical interaction with the, Holographic Resonant sub Planck Zero Point Quantum Entanglement Potentiality Reality. People, animals, and plants use light, an energy biophoton, to both communicate within and without. How this affects Vegans is yet to be determined but being Veganish is a good thing, as health wise 75% of our health costs can be linked to obesity, and eco wise… the raising of meat for protein is exhausting our planet. Cleve Backster, of CIA counterintelligence and of lie detector renown, discovered alleged meta-communication in plants using a conscious intention to burn a leaf and was amazed to see a reaction indication. The plant seemed to learn that he was truly not intending to burn it and the response appeared to subside! This thought has been flashed in here because the name of the light or the form of light or the substance is not the matter, IT is the proof in the setting of the pudding, that there is such an energy lightwave… Aura is our spiritual signature. The saying "you have a dark cloud over you" is reflective of the Aura and a dark one is an ominous halo to carry around. Halos are depicted throughout art history by different non-local* cultures. They can even be found in prehistoric cave paintings.

Aura is partly composed from EM (electromagnetic) radiation, ranging from microwave, to infrared (IR) through UV light. The low frequency microwave and IR part of the spectrum (body heat) seems to be related to DNA, metabolism, and circulation. The high frequency, UV part, is a result of our conscious activity such as thinking, creativity, intentions, sense of humor and emotions. The high frequency UV may be seen with naked eyes.

An aura can help you sense another's being, if the Holographic Resonant sub Planck Zero Point Quantum Entanglement Potentiality Reality Aura does not sync with what this person is saying, you effectively can sense a lie anytime and every time, if you are discerning. IT is part of the ultimate lie detector. You cannot fake the Holographic Resonant sub Planck Zero Point Quantum

Entanglement Potentiality Reality Aura. YET??? I always was curious as to whether or not I could beat Backster's machine, I think I could as this only measured elementary conductance, which is controllable not IT's whole vibe? IT shows our true Nature and intentions. When people realize their incoherent thought is on display so anyone may see IT, they will begin to examine their behaviors like pictures they have put on exhibition. IT should be part of any reality check when shifting consciousness. IT will become part of your personal defense system and is a necessary check of another's intention and trustworthiness! When you receive this vibe IT tunes out all pretenders. Like the rest of IT, we have been taught since we were children that IT does not exist but we have faith and believe in IT anyway, but we have been trained not to sense IT! The brain itself supplies much of the visual perception and thus filters in or out supplementary information based on perceptions and beliefs. Some may learn to fake IT and like with body language, professional professors will teach how to alter and hide IT! Making IT almost impossible to Get IT! You will have to keep sharpening and shaping your discernment to stay with IT.

All right... hold on tight... if you have not studied physics before, do not throw the book at the wall!!! Again... This is all understandable at a seventh grade level so put on your smarter than a current seventh grader hat and drop your doubt off with the rest of your baggage because the flight into Holographic Resonant sub Planck Zero Point Quantum Entanglement Potentiality Reality is about to leave the spaceport!

*Non-localized phenomena and Quantum Entanglement

*Imported reference work on quantum physics, numerous citations, by numerous scientific studies, IONS info, PEARS research, and multiple Authors describing and defining similar assumptions, hypothesis, and conclusions. Based on <u>Albert Einstein</u>'s quantum theory duality nature of particles and waveforms. **Important homework!** Interconnectivity at the non-local quantum level is now measured in very clear ways, you can purchase a Random Event Generator for a few hundred dollars that is used to measure some of the effects of our consciousness on others and our own consciousness. IT was my intention to put this towards the end of the book as I know it is heavy and as you read you gain momentum. So if you made IT to this Zero point in the nothing∞ you will be starting to Get IT... Then it is my intention to invite you to reread Get IT with more discerning intention! ☺

90%

Nonlocality From Wikipedia

In physics, nonlocality is a direct influence of one object on another, distant object, in violation of principle of locality. In classical physics, nonlocality in the form of action at a distance appeared in corpuscular theories and later disappeared in field theories. Action at a distance is incompatible with relativity. In quantum physics nonlocality re-appeared in the form of entanglement. Physical reality of entanglement has been demonstrated experimentally, leading to its application in quantum cryptography and quantum computing. Entanglement is compatible with relativity; however, it prompts some of the more philosophically oriented discussions concerning quantum theory.

*"Quantum entanglement", a phrase first coined by Erwin Schr"odinger, describes a condition of the separated parts of the same quantum system in which each of the parts can only be described by referencing the state of other part. This is one of the most counterintuitive aspects of quantum mechanics, because classically one would expect system parts out of speed-of-light contact to be completely independent. Thus, entanglement represents a kind of quantum connectedness in which measurements on one isolated part of an entangled quantum system have non-classical consequences for the outcome of measurements performed on the other (possibly very distant) part of the same system. This quantum connectedness that enforces the measurement correlation and state-matching in entangled quantum systems has come to be called quantum nonlocality.

Albert Einstein and his coworkers Boris Podolsky and Nathan Rosen in their famous EPR paradox paper2* first highlighted nonlocality*. They argued that the nonlocal connectedness of quantum systems **requires a faster-than-light connection** that appears to be in conflict with special relativity. Despite this objection, quantum nonlocality has been demonstrated in many quantum systems. In the physics community it is now generally acknowledged to be implicit in the quantum formalism as applied to entangled systems.

*Spin Zero

In 1935, Einstein, Podolsky and Rosen published a thought experiment with which they hoped to expose the inadequacies of the Copenhagen interpretation of quantum mechanics in relation to the lack of determinism at the microscopic scale that it described. In particular, they hoped to demonstrate that the probabilistic nature of the results of measurements on particles could be described through the means of some 'hidden' variables that predetermine the result of a measurement, but to which an observer does not have access.

In physical terms, this experiment can be represented as a spin-zero particle decaying into two spin-half particles such that there is no interaction between the two particles after decay. Since spin is a conserved quantity, measurements of spin on the two particles must anti-correlate.

To Einstein, Podolsky and Rosen, the implied effect, needed to be transmitted at superluminal speeds and in doing so, violating the laws of special relativity. Their position was that this suggested the presence of hidden variables that predetermined the value of the measurement at the time the particles were entangled, which would restore determinism to physics.

Quantum Holography

Second sight and remote viewing are terms used to explain charlatans' supposed psychic ability to see hidden objects in terms of pseudoscientific gibberish.

Quantum holography, on the other hand, is a method firmly grounded in modern physics that permits the imaging of hidden objects with entangled photons. Of the quantum entanglement phenomena that Einstein described as **"spooky action at a distance,"** quantum holography may be the spookiest to date. Researchers at Boston University's Quantum Imaging Laboratory (Bahaa Saleh) propose to create holographic images of objects concealed in a spherical chamber. Ideally, a small opening in the chamber wall permits light to enter, but lets no light out. The photons in a beam of light directed through the hole, scatter from the enclosed object, and ultimately strike the inner wall of the chamber. According to the scheme, the inside of chamber would be designed to detect the time when a photon hits the wall but not where it hits. Classically, there is no way to generate an image of an object with this sort of configuration. Quantum mechanically, however, it's possible to build a hologram of the hidden object provided that the photons in the illuminating beam are entangled with photons in another beam.

Each photon in an entangled pair has properties (such as momentum or polarization) that are unknown until a measurement is performed on one photon or the other. When a property of one of the photons is measured, corresponding information about its entangled mate is instantly determined.

That may seem spooky enough, although in quantum holography, things get spookier still. Holograms are typically constructed with interfering beams of light, which provides more information about a subject than simple illumination can. The additional information helps build a three dimensional image of a three dimensional object.

In quantum holography, the researchers measure the simultaneous arrivals of an illuminating photon that is sent into the chamber and a companion photon in the other entangled beam. This measurement tells the researchers about the interference of various possible paths that the single photon inside the chamber could travel. And it's the interference of the possible paths that encodes the holographic image of the hidden object. Very spooky indeed.

When Einstein used the word "**spooky**" he was referring to the sub-atomic phenomena whereby the building blocks of our material reality exist both as particles and waveforms at the same time. This makes it possible for a particle to be present everywhere simultaneously throughout the universe. This is known as **superposition** (The sum of all possibilities).

What is "spooky" about superposition is that it only occurs when it is not being observed or measured. Once a measurement of this phenomenon is attempted, the superposition of the particle being measured in its all-pervading waveform collapses into a single particle with space-time dimensions. Superposition will even collapse in *anticipation* of a measuring device detecting it *after* a measurable event takes place. **This gives superposition an omniscient quality in addition to being omnipresent.** Einstein characterized this non-local* aspect of quantum measurement as "spooky action at a distance".

Superposition also contains all of the possibilities within which the particle can interact with all other particles. It is, therefore, in a state of infinite∞ quantum potentiality. The waveform of this state is said to be in perfect coherence as there is nothing there to create an interference pattern. It is the measurement that interferes with this state of coherence and acts like a filter, which allows only one of the infinite∞ alternative possibilities of the particle's position to materialize. Without measurement the particle aspect slips back to the quantum state. Therefore, the particles that make up our "reality" require constant measurement in order to maintain their physicalness.

This superposition is unlike the superior position that the Illuminati claim yet nevertheless they probably control all research and benefit of. This is the illuminating spooky waveform of enlightenment not unlike their super conspiratorial secret.

Vascular restriction when remembering those people and events that we hold negatively or when we are around those we have not forgiven, along with the tension that is unresolved in our minds and hearts affects our health! Electric effluence and garbage in the greenhouse dissolves our health and affects our heart of mind. Ion's in our environment are depleted by pollution and thereby fatiguing our life. Recognizing and reorganizing the depletion of coherence of the ionic brings rejuvenation and restoration, very iconoclastic.

Quantum Homeopathy

At the cellular level it is the cell that acts as the measuring device that collapses or de-coheres the quantum field into a particle reality. Experiments in what is known as the "inverse Zeno effect", show that a series of measuring devices can collapse a quantum superposition so that the particle will be detected by the first measuring device and will then take a "quantum leap" to appear at the next measuring device. A series of measuring devices will act to capture the particle and drag it along the measured path. In the same way, enzymes possess this unique ability of being able to capture and transfer electrons and protons along a path to various protein molecules in order to activate each protein's specific function.

There are several other quantum-measuring devices within the living cell. DNA, RNA, ribosomes, and mitochondria are all proton, electron and photon level apparatuses. The motion and placement of electrons and protons within DNA initiate gene expression. Single protons are battered across membranes to power the molecular turbine engines of mitochondrial respiration.

The cell is the bridge between the quantum world of unlimited possibilities and what we experience as reality. It is the cell's ability to choose or measure the quantum world that separates inert matter from living matter. A chair or a rock represents the measurement states of particles with no possibility of slipping back to the quantum level. A living system is able to go back and forth between the classical reality state and the quantum state.

Disease can therefore be seen as the result of the cell's distorted quantum perspective. Electrons become misplaced in protein molecules and metabolic processes become derailed as a result. Changes in cellular metabolism can set off a whole cascade of mutations. Because the cell's monitoring of the quantum field is constant we must move in and out of superposition trillions of times per second. Each time we go into the quantum state we freeze particles in the reality state based on what or how we are taking the measurement. We can set up our measuring device on the upper end of the coherence continuum or the lower non-coherent end. **In either case, our measurement device (focus of consciousness) will cause a collapse of the quantum superposition and will act as a filter between all of the infinite∞ possibilities.**

This maybe explains how schizophrenics can move in and out of different personalities with completely different states of physical health from one instant to another. It also helps explain how chickens deprived of calcium intake can produce eggs with complete shells containing healthy levels of calcium. Calcium after all is only a molecule made up of protons and electrons. In the quantum world of infinite∞ possibilities there is no difference between a calcium electron and any other electron. The chickens know (**intend**) that their eggs are made of calcium so they produce calcium rich eggs, from their bones, whether or not they have adequate supplies of dietary calcium.

Quantum Mental Entanglement

Our minds are also quantum-measuring devices. Our thoughts produce electromagnetic waves that have the ability to induce electrical impulses in neurons. This is how our thoughts or consciousness translates into nerve impulses that put us into action. This conscious electromagnetic field (CEM-field) is transferred throughout the body by the oscillations carried through the cerebral spinal fluid and the interconnected crystalline structure that makes up the body holographic. Our cells respond and entrain to our CEM-field by adjusting their quantum-measuring apparatuses to select that which conforms to our conscious or sub-conscious expectations.

Yogis that have reached enlightened states of consciousness are also able to tap into the quantum world. What is an altered state of consciousness but the merging with the state of infinite∞ possibilities?

Holographic Repatterning is a quantum tool. It allows us to break the pattern of our cellular consciousness that repeatedly reaches into the quantum realm only to continuously bring back the same old low energy state in our relationships or physical health. The Holographic Repatterning modalities change the vibration of information frequencies at the cellular level. Once the intention has shifted our cellular quantum-measuring apparatus will manifest new and exciting realities from the quantum world of infinite∞ possibilities. Transferring energy, momentum, etc, while observing all of the laws of energy conservation. This Quantum Repatterning is where miracle transfiguration resides! God's infinity∞ transcending divinity through the heart of humanity forever reflecting IT's love!

Researchers are moving ahead boldly. As exampled: For three months in 2002, Kevin Warwick, a cybernetics professor at the University of Reading in England, lived with electrodes implanted in his arm. In one test, he wired them to an Internet-connected PC and then temporarily attached electrodes to his wife's arm as well. Warwick described this experiment in a 2006 interview with ITWales.com: "When she moved her hand three times, I felt in my brain three pulses, and my brain recognized that my wife was communicating with me. It was the world's first purely electronic communication from brain to brain, and therefore the basis for thought communication."

Quantum teleportation is, a quantum state transmitted completely by sending not only the information bits, but e-bits, or entanglement bits. This entangled information has proven to have a manipulability nature. The Holographic

CCCXVII

resonance retains all we have been and all we have interacted with as well as that which exists and is eternally∞ part of our reality interconnected at the quantum level. This causal weave of interconnections I believe is the essence of God. Belief is relative but this connectivity is absolute! Physicists are the Alchemists at the forefront of integration of matter and spirit... Many are currently trying to disprove Gods existence. Yet they are piecing together our new reality that many already believe! The nature of reality, our being-ness! Not the, anything can mean anything reality. Not the, way you want IT to be reality, but a, defined consensual reality everyone is invited to participate in defining collectively not allowing just any one to make up their own reality as the defined reality. The whole is much greater than the collective parts. Just the concept of being is incredible, but the perception~~~ that through emergence into a unity of all we are part of the most power full force in the universe~~~ IT is awe-inspiring! Which by the way if you do the goesintas... trillions divided by millions still leave billions of possible places for other life forms to coexist!

God is a circle whose center is everywhere and is to be found in the nothing∞! Synergy with IT avails the most powerful techniques for humanizing reality.

Maybe we ought to meditate on that circle for a moment or two, as things caught by gravity continue to circle the dominant object until either reaching escape velocity or retrograding to be sucked in to destruction. Are you accelerating or is your orbit degrading?

Meditation

Controversies concerning the brain, mind, and consciousness have existed since man cognitively debated about the nature of the mind vs. body relationship without resolution. Scientist's postulate the mind is in the brain and that consciousness is the result of electrochemical activity. On the contrary there is no neuropsychological research that conclusively shows that the extended levels of mind such as, intuition, insight, creativity, imagination, understanding, thought, reasoning, intent, decision making, knowing, will, spirit, or soul are located in brain tissue or exclusive to humankind. I again postulate that: The brain is the organic biologic interactive apparatus that serves the mind and multiplexes with others and all including the Cosmic mind~~~ The sum of all thought~~~ More and more scientists are expressing doubts about the neurologists' brain-mind model because it fails to answer so many questions about our ordinary experiences, as well as evading our mystical and spiritual ones. The scientific evidence supporting the phenomenon of remote viewing alone is sufficient to show that mind-consciousness is not a local phenomenon. A resolution to the controversies surrounding the infinite∞ mind and consciousness problem in general involves a shift to include extra rational ways of knowing and cannot be comprehended by biological brain studies by themselves. The human mind continues to function even under anesthesia. Brain waves are nearly absent while the mind is just as active as in the waking state. The only difference is in the content of the conscious experience. Evidence suggests that reduced cortical arousal while maintaining conscious awareness is possible. These states are variously referred to as meditative, trance, altered, hypnotic, and twilight-learning states. Broadly defined, the various forms of altered states rest on the maintenance of conscious awareness in a physiologically reduced state. Recent physiological studies indicate that maintaining awareness with reduced cortical arousal is indeed possible in individuals as a natural ability or as an acquired skill thus enhancing the "self sense" by activating what neuroscientists call the "default mode network" in the brain.

Mind-consciousness appears to be a field phenomenon, which interfaces with the body and the neurological structures of the brain. One cannot accurately measure this field directly with current instrumentation. On the other hand, the electrical potentials of brain waves can be measured and easily quantified. Contemporary science likes things that can be measured and quantified. If you can't measure IT you can't test IT, then IT does not exist! The problem here lies in analysis of the observations. EEG patterns measured on the cortex are the result of electro-neurological activity of the brain. But the brain's electro-neurological activity is not mindful consciousness. EEG measurements then are only an indirect means of assessing consciousness interfacing with the neurological structures of the brain. Rudimental interpretations of certain EEG patterns have been historically associated with specific states of consciousness, as I previously stated. It is however reasonable to assume that if a specific wave pattern emerges it is probably accompanied by a particular defined slice of that state of consciousness. IT seems we are capable of extraordinary intelligent cognitive juggling moving amongst experienced perceptual influences and conceptual ideas, instinctively firing neurons based upon genetics, environment, experience, and even apparently inspiration along with processing IT through our reason rational filter then taking under due consideration~~~ our emotional state and our will! Some of us must be pretty quick thinkers... others... not so much! Wonder if some either never made it out of Da cave or if they're just on their way back?

Back to juggling cognitively what I'm striving to state... Meditation is recognized as a component of almost all religions, as IT has been used to communicate with God and been practiced for time eternal∞. Meditative disciplines encompass a wide range of spiritual and/or psychophysical practices, which can emphasize development of either a high degree of mental concentration, or the apparent converse, mental quiescence where all effort to meditate is the denial of meditation. Meditation can be highly focused or the ending of self-thought. There you will find a different dimension, which is beyond time and space. IT can be achieved through peace and tranquility or an active dynamic exercise or dance. IT's practical meditation procedure requires no effort, except nothing∞ (20 min twice a day), no out of the ordinary concentration, no special skills, and no change of lifestyle. We are not accustomed to non-analysis of the thoughts being triggered in our brains although IT's a natural process of deep rest that puts you in contact with your inner pool of positive creativity, energy and intelligence, and adds IT's support to all you do and enriches life day by day. Quantum Meditation encompasses full time awareness and observation of your interactivity with the quantum meta-multiverse and you are in control of your actions in IT while maintaining a positive state of mind. The possibilities are endless∞. There is not one specific meditation experience. IT is not rote rehearsal performed for some achievement. This is where you need to learn to use a technique appropriate to the situation. You may have thoughts or experience nothing∞ These thoughts can help reduce anxiety and release stress. The Nothing∞ helps you relax, Focus or concentrate minimally, just slip into IT… keeping your attention softly. Put your self aside. Do not force your mind clear, or chase away thoughts as you reduce your physical and mental tension, quietness and self-calm will come. Settle your mind and body to experience this unique state of restful alertness. Be aware of the streams that run through your nervous system. Because really your nervous system is a bioelectrical construct that relies on the transfer of information amongst the various plexuses we have in our body. Sense and release your body, do you remember how to relax… seek out the tension in your body and then consciously breath in a deep breath and then tighten all your body… release the muscles and the breath… sense your bodies release … let those senses go… As your mind becomes more silent, your body becomes deeply relaxed. At the most settled state of awareness, your mind transcends all mental commotion to experience the simplest form of aware consciousness. When thoughts appear, go with the flow or let them go... when distracted or consciously aware of thinking, return to your breathing, mantra, or prayer… If your attention wanders, slowly return to the object, sensation or movement you're focusing on. You can use an image to bring yourself back to your focus if you'd like. Each meditation will be somewhat different. Something important is transcending each time you meditate. If it appears as though nothing∞ is happening, the meditation transcends positive changes on planes both within and without thus reframing perceptions and events, focusing attention on the process while disregarding its purpose or final outcome. We are accustomed to putting forth effort and then there is a measurable result. IT is neither effort or measurable yet you will sense the renewal sensation. IT is simply unbeing with mindful presence in the now! Maybe remotely in the past or the future, but mainly where, who, and how you are in the now. Not the remindful past of what we are not now! The past that needs healing, pleasantly experienced once again, or learned from. The future will be and the only way you can influence IT is to image IT and act now! No... do not jump up from your meditation to chase some forgotten thought, unless you left the stove on... IT will still be there when you arise. Before long you will begin noticing the changes apparent in your life and in your world. A healing awakening is occurring, you may sense some negativity, process this to be free of these restrictive negative energies. Negativity is persistent so recognize the recurrence to avoid the influence. Advancement of conscience is the moral virtue of purpose brought about through self disciplined directed use of your freewill! The Chaos that contains evil negativity is in the nature of the physics of having the freedom of choice amongst all possibilities in the entro-peeing cosmos. As consciousness becomes more coherent IT begins to resonate with greater moral purpose and usurps negative possibility! You may consciously or unconsciously conjure up excuses not to meditate. This is mostly your voice of change management. Since time and space are relative, start today... IT is New Years Day everyday since no one really knows what day this all started on anyway. Seems to me Gods calendar would have started at a solstice just to keep things simple. Feel and listen to the wee small voice that urges growth and make that positive change. You will gain the ability to meditate while walking or doing simple repetitive tasks. You don't even have to believe that it works! IT will if practiced. Do not doubt whether, your practicing IT correctly or IT's meeting your expectations, as this is the cycle you are trying to step from. You must know where you are in order to journey forward. Acquiescence does not dictate. IT expands intended choice. Stay with IT... The more you stick with IT the more positive IT becomes. The less anxious you are about the meditation, the easier and better it gets and the less fear, anxiety, expectation, stress, you carry into each subsequent meditation and IT Gets stronger. Meditation is self-regulation of attention according to focus. Some meditations focus on mindfulness, maintaining an open focus shifting freely from one perception to another while you stay in reality or your self-being. No thought, image or sensation is considered an intrusion. You with a nothing∞ attitude continue in the here and now returning consistently to be present, avoiding analysis or self desire regarding the inner awareness, and increasing acceptance and reduction of secondary thought processes. IT's amazing as you develop deliberate objective meditation and IT will enhance your focal spirit with practice. Holding your attention on a particular object or a repetitive prayer while diminishing distractions, bringing the mind back to concentrate on the chosen thing. Experiment, and you'll likely find out what types of meditation work best for you. Adapt meditation to your needs at the moment. Use IT to feel better, care more, increase or decrease, just about anything. But if you're attempting to use IT to increase negativity IT's vibe beats yours, as IT has a propensity towards positive. One day your vibe will, will be striped and laid bare, as your negativity bounces aimlessly about the dark mete-multiverse rather than becoming the purposeful everlasting light of universal love. Remember, there's no right way or wrong way to meditate. What matters is that meditation helps you be coherent, self-tuned, clear, in joy, as well as confident of your present state while promoting healthful body, providing stress reduction and calmer better feeling overall. This is not selfish; this is a positive effect of willfully being with IT. I flows to IT, IT flows through you and I, you and I become they, they are part of everything. This flow that we blind our senses to that holds the power of life! No trueΩ Religion, No Dogma, No Division, No No... well... you know! Or do you??? As our senses limit input to what we deem we need... There is so much more and other life sources are able to explore and perceive IT! Our refining filter process has screened IT out at the homeland security checkpoint, denying our passage through trial by error and thus adaptation to this stimuli that is viewed as distracting~~~ but in missing IT, IT is lost on IT's way to the door of our perception thus actually detracting from IT!

PSI

Robert G. Jahn and Brenda J. Dunne of the Princeton Engineering Anomalies Research (PEAR) have spent their lives meticulously researching PSI. I do not wish to cite them with only this part of their studies as I have so much enjoyed their work in my reading but theirs is the only study I could find that responds accurately to the negative intention correlation.

The following is a synopsis taken from PEARS Change the Rules. VI. The Down Side:

The PEAR operator pool contained a small fraction of participants that tended to produce results opposite to their pre-stated intentions, to a statistically impressive degree. This propensity to "psi-missing"… may also derive from the inclination of some operators to invest more of themselves in the resonance of the interaction than in fulfilling a particular intention, with the result that for them a deviation from chance in either direction of achievement constitutes a "successful" result."

On a broader cultural level, persistent negative correlations bring to mind personalities… for whom life is an endless stream of aggravations and failures to cope, and who are doomed to wander about unhappily and ineffectually… If we stay trapped within our present causal logic, we are forced to engage the dilemma of whether it is their negative personalities that cause, or at least attract, the depressing events, or whether it is the incessant stream of those events that deforms their personalities. But in the correlation approach, we need simply acknowledge the consistency and synchronicity of the negative mental and physical expressions.

"One can of course add the storied "gremlin" effects of the Second World War; our personal "Murphy's Law" experiences of automobiles, household appliances, and computers failing at the most inconvenient moments; the capacity of certain people to repeatedly disable their own watches, clocks, and other programmed utilities… And of course the bizarre assortment of reported poltergeist phenomena that appear to correlate with repressed emotional stress in certain adolescent agents may be the strongest indicators of the negative capacities of the unconscious mind*.

To pursue these inverted manifestations of consciousness-correlated physical phenomena (CCPP), one should probably distinguish among those effects that appear spontaneously, possibly correlated with some form of psychopathology; those that arise from inadvertent or naive misapplications of the psychical strategies (cf. for example Larry Dossey's treatise "Be Careful What You Pray For"*); and those that are deliberately malicious invocations of esoteric techniques. We have neither the experience nor the understanding to attempt to clarify this issue further here, other than to note that the same array of subjective correlates found in the positive events appears to be involved at all negative levels, as well, i.e., intentionality, whether conscious or unconscious; prevailing uncertainty, complexity, or disorder; characteristic attitudes; and generous involvement of the unconscious mind in the interactions. It would be comforting to contend that the remaining major correlate, i.e., resonance or coherence, would by its nature exercise a beneficial constraint on the process, but unfortunately we are all too familiar with organizations and individuals whose religious or political zeal engender intense sacrificial commitment and unity of purpose to their malevolent agendas..."

Their paper continues on to explain other troubling implications posed by this knowledge or lack thereof. Please access their work to better comprehend the gift they have given.

Thank you Robert and Brenda for all the years of research. I was fortunate to meet one of your staff in Tampa, from Psyleron. As tribute I include the poem you cited by James Russell Lowell entitled "The Present Crisis*."

"New occasions teach new duties; Time makes ancient good uncouth;
They must upward still, and onward, who would keep abreast of truth.
Lo before us gleam her campfires! We ourselves must Pilgrims be,
Launch our Mayflower, and steer boldly through the desperate winter sea,

Nor attempt the Future's portal with the Past's blood-rusted key."

Anyway… back to the thought… what was I thinking??? I guess a little mental injection of energy into our orbit through meditation will help in either case to improve our pace…

I said we would get back to purpose and quiver of life and remember remembering. Well… I hope you find IT and use those tools in your quiver to consciously add to IT rather than detract from IT. As long as your still searching for purpose IT will be there to find and each discovery will add a new tool to your quiver to be used for the eternal∞ purpose.

Hey… Hey… do you remember… Oh yeah… I kinda do… But is my memory construed, is my thought lost, has my brain been altered, where the heck did that thought come from??? Well even though our minds function similar to computers our memory banks are dynamic, organic and interactive and we sometimes misplace the pathway or the circuit to the stored information. Possibly your mind did not move the info to long-term storage when clearing the crud. Memories are the building blocks of who we are. Yet may be lost or destroyed thereby losing part of self. This can be self-selective, due to injury, environment, and diet, even hereditary, there are many causes for these losses. Yet IT seems to provide restoration on occasion of thought that was lost. Triggers very as synapse grow weary yet going into your old allows other thoughts to unfold. The information appears to be stored but you have not visited with it lately. Seems like it becomes hard to tell if the memory is just what you replay as IT or the actual coherence you once were immersed in? Truth is in the fine detail. Are you reminiscing an embellishment or bringing the Heliographic Resonant reality to the forefront of your attention? Re-immerse your self as you sense or are trying to sense a memory and poke around in the corners of that thought. Seemingly when done intentionally with discernment it is hard to tell the memory from the original experience. Finding these memories are like finding a gem. You have to be looking in the right place at the right time. Occasionally you find a dark lump of coal, so burn it, even the coal has purpose. You have those trivial things you remember at two in the mournin and you have those important things you keep at the forefront of your thought that need to be put away when you meditate so you can get past them to your memory. There are many ways and methods suggested to remember most anything and the majority are very useful but to process that info into your permanent knowledge base I have found that a memory clearing meditation or a good REM cycle is needed. Ever cram on an all niter and then come up blank on fill in the _____? Well you probably did not process what you were memorizing. When you Get IT inside your head, IT works with you to find the info your searching for. IT is the energy of thought. If you are blocking IT IT will still never block you. You put up the obstacles to coherent thought, You create the incoherent mumbo jumbo, You delude the probability of possibilities. Come on... open up that can of worms... climb on in... and just remember...

Have you tired of my repetition? Does my lingo grow old? Have I indulged myself? Is there any relevance? What the heck was that about? I want to kick I want to shout! Well I guess I got you thinking... that was my intent now what's yours? I have more by using less, I bet that's hard for you to process. I'm laughing as I write this. Not about you and not about me, I'm laughing at the fact that I did not know... I did not know I was going to write this or any other book! IT has been an unbelievably insightful process and I learned more than I can convey to you. I was indulgent, in that IT increased in me. I was repetitive as my mantra. My lingo is old! I hope IT was relevant! I am insane in an inane sort of way. I hope I made you kick and shout when you began to process what IT is about! Intend to contend a new paradigm, as a fine day here without IT pales in comparison to any day in IT.

This is IT... the Alpha and Omega∞ As we reach the end of GET IT may we begin to GET IT! I hope the "Journey to the center of your mind" is a pleasant one! Thanks for the chance to dance this parlance to enhance our chant... recant, decamp, revamp, the "I can't". I hope I have not been too obnoxious or odious in describing some of what needs to be addressed by those who are willing to discern IT. If we gather enough momentum and begin to create a new reality with sufficient positive thought, like children without discipline, these self-indulgent and ego-tripping toxic² bastards will come seeking IT! For they will be ferreted out, hopefully then seeing, possibly seeking, maybe even sensing, a new paradigm like paradise and will begin to search desperately in their lives for IT! IT is everywhere, nowhere, and now here always, IT in our garden called earth, IT amongst the people that inhabit the garden, for we are the people we have been waiting for IT. The garden has some weeds that need tending to, in order for us to enjoy the harvest of our God given reality. The weeding needs to start before we can no longer find our fruit! We lead by humble example and servant actions not by pronouncement or cliché. Have you ever met someone that has a problem? I mean a real problem? Well now there's something you can do about IT! Change your perspective and use your sub-conscious mind to interact with theirs, to both; send them the message that's appropriate, not hurtful or spiteful but knowing, because their sub-conscious is used to filter blocking lots of crap and their reaction to our reaction is the action cycle itself. Use your mind to send a more caring and complete synchronic coherent thought, formed so that IT may have a chance to get past their thick persona. Just as a particle, quantum tunnels, through the seemingly impervious we may peek behind their mask and into their essence as well as strip off our own perception of "The Problem" to remediate most solutions. We cannot continue to remonstrate rather than demonstrate just how much love we are willing to use on those that are abusing us! Be precautious that IT not "ME" discerns the problems you see! Have you ever met someone that has a problem? I mean a real problem?? Now you can improve life on Earth as IT is here that you will find Heaven... by taking the time to reach into these minds and yours, become one with IT, and use this to get down, up, or multi-dimensionally to their level... and move around in yours, Another words... find them where they are... not only where you are or where you imagine they are... did you get that??? Find them where they are... Most people don't like you looking into their souls; they don't even want to look at their own!!! Find you where you are... not the idealized location your mind advertises as you but the true you locus of focus that realizes how far you've come or gone to get there! You deserve you! You may have to look out to see in and as you see in lookout… IT's an amazing dangerous place! Taking time for your self, in a selfless way, is not selfish. As opposed to self-denial I propose self-development as the key to eternity∞ What other reason can you think of as reason why we are reasoned thinkers other than to develop that thought? Start with one minute if IT's all you can spare? You can really spare more if you care… Time spent in IT exposes you to hurt, trouble, trial and tribulation… as well as the love of others, ease of relief, release of life, regenerative reformation and other rewards are infinite∞ Feel again, Give again, Touch again, Love again, Live again! On occasion you need to lose people where they are at, as they are so Toxic² that they are dangerous! Use this discretion sparingly, always remembering the love you make is equal to the love you take and IT's all been meant for you my friend… So why not change the world a little bit in this space and time! First your perception then your reality! Then our perception of your reality, and then our reality.:! Now IT's up to you! Yeah U… What ya gonna do? We are capable of changing all, surmounting any deficiency, and accomplishing everything stated here. So why do we live in hate, not admit our mistakes, and just move IT forward? Do you really think that begging Gods forgiveness for your transgressions through some religion is goona get the job done let alone save you? Start with nothing (20 min twice a day) and become entangled with the flow then turn IT into something! No more BSn the BSr!

99%

My life story continues evolving. I hope to age like a fine wine… enhancing my flavor each day then ultimately being released to transmute complex nuanced joy~~~ I'm looking prospectively toward spoiling… I mean teaching, playing and praying with my Grandchildren~~~ In Da interim I am POP POP to all kids!!! I highly anticipate being with Da family on Holiday~~~ and daily

hangin in Da hood, kickin some tunes, and laughin with Da neighbors...
sometimes after Da punch line~~~ cause UffDa doesn't always GET IT~~~

If you have read to here... you have been changed~~~ I hope I did not waste
our mindspacetime~~~ May the change be positive and strong in you! Hope
you have a Yogasm!

Time to grab another cup of java and think of other ways to help to GET IT
done!
With All My Love; Da UffDa!!!
Namaste ~~~ And so GET IT, is written... Amen

Appendix

[1]Binaural & Sound

One of the first things we sense is sound in our mother's womb, and since time immemorial human beings have been using sound waveforms to enhance altered states of consciousness. Brainwave entrainment through sound has many historical and social manifestations. Natural occurring sound was enhanced early on through, chanting, drum circles, and staring at fire as our ancestors partook in the phenomenon. They passed down an advanced intuitive knowledge of how the frequency tuning of the bowls, bells, drums, flutes, chants etc. created vibrational interference patterns whose pulsation modulation rates influenced brain function and states of consciousness.

Limbic Sound

The Limbic System is a pivotal part of the nervous system that converts thought, senses, and emotion into information. Where our consciousness interacts and the body and mind-spirit connection has its validity. Connection with the primal sound and raptor instinct has been available ever since we started our existence as humans. Sensed emotions provoked by both environmental sound and vocal communication invoke our emotional state. Particularly mood fluctuations or anxiety can increase overall arousal and enable us to detect potential threats in our environment. This is a normal protective mechanism. These emotional changes can also increase the apparent loudness and irritation of sounds to which we are already sensitive. These primordial sounds consist of deeply recognizable sounds to the subconscious mind, both nature sounds and physical organism sounds. These sounds can have a profound beneficial impact when disguised in such a way that the conscious mind does not recognize them. Sometimes people become hypersensitive to various stimuli, be it vision, touch, heat, smell, taste or pain, sensitivity may increase greatly the perceived intensity creating an association of fear or dislike with the appearance of the sound or sense whenever it occurs. Your attention and focus then becomes filled with that sound or sense so that interference with concentration occurs. These habituated responses act like survival reflexes and have to carry a message of unpleasant emotion, in order to ensure that a response occurs. They also stimulate the autonomic nervous system to prepare us for 'flight or fight' triggering other body responses. Listening to sound environments of disguised primordial sounds, a state of entrainment occurs in which a heightened openness of the mind transpires. Many of the sounds of sonic nature fall into similar patterns only different in the range of time, octave, or itineration. The similarities of NASA recordings sent back from space sound hauntingly similar to nature that has been electronically disguised. Quantum physics demonstrates that as matter is reduced further you have a universal energy matrix of relationships of vibration patterns rather than smaller particles. In actuality there is nothing solid in the multidimensional universe at all. Consciousness itself is a vibration pattern.

Binaural Sound

Binaural literally means "having or relating to two ears." Binaural hearing, along with frequency cues, lets humans and other animals determine direction of origin of sounds. Binaural beats or binaural tones are apparent sounds perceived in the brain independent of physical stimuli. Heinrich Wilhelm Dove discovered this effect in 1839. Eventually giving rise to a new field of science called psychoacoustics in which physical and psychological responses are formed using electronically disguised and manipulated nature sounds as well as other frequency vibrations. The human ability to "hear" binaural beats appears to be the result of evolutionary adaptation. The frequencies at which binaural beats can be detected change depending upon the size of the species' cranium. Under natural circumstances a detected phase difference would provide directional information. Resonant entrainment of oscillating systems is a well-understood principle within the physical sciences. If a tuning fork is struck and then brought into the vicinity of another similar tuning fork, the second tuning fork will begin to oscillate. The first is said to have entrained the second or caused it to resonate. The physics of entrainment apply to bio-systems as well. Electromagnetic brain waves change frequencies based on neural activity within the brain, altering the brain's electromagnetic environment through induction, or through resonant entrainment techniques using binaural beats that involve different neurological pathways than ordinary auditory processing. Thereby allowing postulation that the non-local correlation between neuropsychological events, expressed as a deviation from statistical independence across these events in distributed neuronal groups and areas, which produce the brainwaves. Lower level brain frequency, associated with deep sleep and meditation are not audible to humans. The brain produces this phenomenon resulting in low-frequency pulsations in the loudness of a perceived sound and processes this anomalous information differently when two tones at slightly different frequencies are presented separately, one to each of a subject's ears, using stereo headphones. A beating tone will be perceived, as if the two tones mixed naturally, out of the brain. The frequency of the tones must be below about 1,000 hertz for the beating to be heard. The difference between the two frequencies must be below about 30 Hz for the effect to occur; otherwise the two tones will be heard separately and no beat will be perceived. When the perceptual integration of the two signals takes place, the sensation of a third beat frequency occurs. The two different input frequencies mesh in and out of phase resulting in an amplitude-modulated standing wave, a binaural beat, being perceptively heard. Brain function is thus enhanced through the increase of cross communication between the left and right hemispheres of the brain as well as order. Binaural rhythms can rapidly entrain motor responses into stable steady synchronization states below and above conscious perception thresholds. Brainwaves synchronize with the frequency following response is a naturally occurring phenomenon where the human brain has a tendency to change its dominant EEG frequency towards the frequency of the dominant external stimuli applied to it. When the perceived beat frequency corresponds to the delta, theta, alpha, beta, or gamma range of brainwave rhythms, the brainwaves

CCCXXXIII

entrain to or move towards the beat frequency. For example, if a 255 Hz carrier frequency wave is played into one ear and a 265 Hz one into the other, the brain produces a pulse by combining the two tones and the brain is entrained towards the beat frequency of 10 Hz, in the alpha range. Another words Alpha is entrained through sound or another brain wave state may be entrained as desired! Some are oscillating infernally stuck and unable to move in any discernable direction!

Uses of audio with embedded binaural beats that are mixed with music or various pink or background sound are diverse. Musicians know these beats as tremolo. In more subtle ways the entrainment of brainwaves is used to produce relaxation and other health benefits. Increased endorphin levels have been attributed to the use of binaural beat audio technology. Some of the effects and benefits are lucid dreams, altered states of consciousness, deep relaxation, sense of euphoria, increased intuition, enhanced awareness, emergent creativity, accelerated learning, psychic abilities, elimination of insomnia and the symptoms of stress, as well as positive affirmations and visualizations. Today there is a multitude of binaural psycho acoustical media available and is used extensively by the medical community in healing!

Ambient

In atmospheric sound transmission or noise pollution, ambient noise level is the sound pressure level at a given location, normally specified as a reference level to study a new intrusive sound source. Ambient noise level is sometimes called background noise level, reference sound level or room noise level ambient noise levels may be measured to provide a reference point for analyzing an intrusive sound to a given environment.

White Noise

White noise contains all frequencies and can be used to disorient individuals prior to interrogation as well as being used as part of sensory deprivation techniques. White noise machines are sold as privacy enhancers and sleep aids and to mask tinnitus. White noise CDs, when used with headphones, can aid concentration by blocking out irritating or distracting noises in a person's environment. White noise is used as the basis of some random number generators.

Noise Canceling

Sound is a pressure wave, which consists of a compression phase and a rarefaction phase. A noise-cancellation speaker emits a sound wave with the same amplitude and the opposite polarity in anti-phase to the original sound. The waves combine to form a new wave, in a process called interference, and effectively cancel each other out, an effect, which is called phase cancellation. Depending on the circumstances and the method used, the resulting sound~wave may be so faint as to be inaudible to human ears.

Sound masking

Sound masking is the addition of natural or artificial sound of a different frequency (more commonly though less-accurately known as "white noise" or "pink noise") into an environment to "mask" or cover-up unwanted sound by using Auditory masking. This is in contrast to the technique of Active noise control. Sound masking reduces or eliminates awareness of pre-existing sounds in a given area and can make a work environment more comfortable, while creating speech privacy so workers can be more productive. Sound masking can also be used in the out-of-doors to restore a more natural ambient environment.

Sound masking can be explained by analogy with light. Imagine a dark room where someone is turning a flashlight on and off. The light is very obvious and distracting. Now imagine that the room lights are turned on. The flashlight is still being turned on and off, but is no longer noticeable because it has been "masked". Sound masking is a similar process of covering a distracting sound with a more soothing or less intrusive sound.

Low frequency, broad banded sounds (like water running) will mask higher frequency sounds, which are softer at the listener's ear (a conversational tone from across the room). For a single frequency masking tone, Broadband white noise tends to mask all frequencies, and is approximately linear in that masking. By linear you mean that if you raise the white noise by 10 dB, you have to raise everything else 10 dB to hear it.

Dynamic range compression

DRC (often seen in DVD player settings), audio level compression, volume compression, compression, or limiting, is a process that manipulates the dynamic range of an audio signal. Compression is used during sound recording, live sound reinforcement, and broadcasting to alter the perceived volume of audio. Most television commercials are compressed heavily (typically to a dynamic range of no more than 3dB) in order to achieve near-maximum perceived loudness while staying within permissible limits. This is the explanation for the chronic problem that TV viewers and listeners have noticed for years. Compression algorithms have been engineered specifically to accomplish the task of maximizing audio level in the digital stream. Hard limiting or hard clipping can result, affecting the tone and timbre of the music in a way that one critic describes as "dogsh!t". The effort to increase loudness has been referred to as the "loudness wars".

Quantum Vision and Hearing

Close one eye and you still perceive 3D rather than mono even though your eye only has one degree of truly clear resolution. The optic nerve receives the particle light waveform reflected and acts as an Imax 3D projection screen connected directly to your brain, filling in the blanks and blurry portions then adding the missing portions to create the perception you model as reality.

The same with hearing… block one ear and you still hear spatially. You hear sound where it is out there! You block what noise you deem unneeded and are able to frequency hone on seemed needed. You sense with your eyes and ears the teaming energy brought interpolating through them rather than in your brain inside there. We thus implore much more past modeling on present reality than we imagine or do we??? Imagine imaging imagination! Or hearing only what we want! Only we control the horizontal and the vertical~~~

Quantum Entanglement

²TOXIC

There are many kinds of Toxic people but many fit into some sub category of "**The Psychopath**" The state of mind itself has been acknowledged for centuries, described with many different nomenclatures, such as "madness without delirium" and "moral insanity" then in the late 1800s it was given a psychoanalytic label, "psychopath" and its synonym, "sociopath". A classification of people that feel neither guilt nor sorrow and are remorseless as they are unable to form real emotional bonds or the touch of compassionate love! Because they have little or no conscience, they're natural predators! Many Hundreds of thousands of psychopaths live and work and prey not pray, among us. Your boss, your girlfriend, your mother, your neighbor, your best friend, could be a "sub-clinical" psychopath, someone who leaves a path of destruction and pain without a single pang of conscience and utter lack of consciousness of yours. They also have very short tempers, huge egos, and a craving for exhilaration... a treacherous combination! Psychopaths love chaos and hate rules, so they're at ease in the fast-moving modern corporation. They're con artists and charismatic to the point of manipulating people! They are attracted to positions of power and everyone has been suckered by a psychopath. Psychopaths' brains work differently from ours, especially when processing emotion and language. The Psychopath is someone who doesn't understand what's going on emotionally and has no compassion rational, but does understand that something significant is happening! **Unlike schizophrenics, psychopaths aren't loners** Psychopaths' brains are in deep-seated ways dissimilar from ours, getting them to be like us is almost impossible, that would involve feeling. It's a matter of different wiring not faulty wiring. This different wiring cannot be rewired to IT. As they do not feel, sense, nor seek IT. No one has yet found the way to do so. That part of their brains were trimmed off long ago and they do not respond to punishment or the reward behavior model, yet we are politically incorrect should we attempt to declare someone to be beyond rehabilitation, as is their case. Don't worry about what ²toxic people think of you. As they deflect IT without intention, not allowing thought through IT to IT about IT and never giving IT a second's thought! Whether or not they choose to acknowledge IT is unknown? (Return 1)(Return 2)

What Psychopath Means... It is not quite what you may think

PSYCHOPATHS AMONG US

Contrary to popular belief, the Hippocratic Oath is not required by most modern medical schools.

[3] *Hippocratic Oath*—Modern Version

I swear to fulfill, to the best of my ability and judgment, this covenant:

I will respect the hard-won scientific gains of those physicians in whose steps I walk, and gladly share such knowledge as is mine with those who are to follow.

I will apply, for the benefit of the sick; all measures [that] are required, avoiding those twin traps of over treatment and therapeutic nihilism.

I will remember that there is art to medicine as well as science, and that warmth, sympathy, and understanding may outweigh the surgeon's knife or the chemist's drug.

I will not be ashamed to say "I know not," nor will I fail to call in my colleagues when the skills of another are needed for a patient's recovery.

I will respect the privacy of my patients, for their problems are not disclosed to me that the world may know. Most especially must I tread with care in matters of life and death. If it is given me to save a life, all thanks. But it may also be within my power to take a life; this awesome responsibility must be faced with great humbleness and awareness of my own frailty. Above all, I must not play at God.

I will remember that I do not treat a fever chart, a cancerous growth, but a sick human being, whose illness may affect the person's family and economic stability. My responsibility includes these related problems, if I am to care adequately for the sick.

I will prevent disease whenever I can, for prevention is preferable to cure.

I will remember that I remain a member of society, with special obligations to all my fellow human beings, those sound of mind and body as well as the infirm.

If I do not violate this oath, may I enjoy life and art, respected while I live and remembered with affection thereafter. May I always act so as to preserve the finest traditions of my calling and may I long experience the joy of healing those who seek my help. (Please <u>return</u> to IT)

A den dum

*Forgive my not distractively chaptering so that you could easily return to where you left off.

*Forgive me my vanity to assume the responsibility of my presumed unity inflection perfection.

*Forgive me as I know not how my ignorant thinking is stinking so I think I'll think some more.

*Aaa~~~uuuuuu~~~~mmmm

Did you look for the hidden track... secret message... invisible writing... or maybe just enjoyed reading your way through GET IT??? Well IT's a good thing because there is no way to hide IT!

^Additional free information is available everywhere so go out and inform yourself to reform your self!!!

A lengthy list of some additional readin ([Return])

© Margins of Reality By: Robert G. Jahn, Brenda J. Dunne
© Science of the Subjective By: Robert G. Jahn, Brenda J. Dunne
© Transpersonal Research Methods for the Social Sciences
    By: William Braud, Rosemarie Anderson
© Distant Mental Influence By: William Braud
© Mind-Matter Interaction: A Review of Historical Reports, Theory and Research
    By: Pamela Rae Heath
© The book of NOTHING: Vacuums, Voids, and the Latest Ideas about the Origins of
    the Universe, 2000 By: John D. Barrow
© Entangled Minds By: Dean Radin
© The Conscious Universe By: Dean Radin
© Understanding Reality- Wu Chen Pi'an By: Chang Po-tuan
© Project Mind- The Conscious Conquest of Man & Matter Through Accelerated
    Thought By: T.Kun.
© Measuring the Immeasurable: The Scientific Case for Spirituality: A Compilation
© Autobiography of a Yogi- By: Paramahansa Yogananda
© Channels To A New Reality The 5th Dimension By: Shiela Petersen
© Essential Reiki: A Complete Guide to an Ancient Healing Art By: Diane Stein
© Illusions: The Adventures of a Reluctant Messiah By: Richard Bach
© Incognito: The Secret Lives of Brains By: David Eagleman
© Sum By: David Eagleman
© The Four Agreements By: Don Miguel Ruiz
© Ptaah Tapes An Act Of Faith By: Jani King
© Between Death and Life By: Dolores Cannon
© Fring-ology: How I Tried to Explain Away The Unexplainable And Couldn't
    By: Steve Volk
© Time, Space, and Knowledge By: Tarthang Tulku, Rinpoche
© Mt. Shasta Ascended Master Teachings By: Nola Van Valer
© Sacred Contracts: Awakening Your Divine Potential By: Caroline Myss
© Good Faeries Bad Faeries By: Brian Froud
© Jacob The Baker By: BenShea
© Forgiveness And Beyond By: Marlene Oaks
© The Crystal Bible By: Judy Hall
© The Holy Bible By:

© What the Bleep Do We Know!?: Discovering the Endless Possibilities for Altering
    Your Everyday Reality By: William
© The Tibetan Book of Living & Dying By: Sogyal Rinpoche
© You Were Born Rich By: Bob Proctor
© Darkness Visible By: William Styron
© Foucalt's Pendulum By: Umberto Eco
© Spiritual Regeneration By: Torkom Saraydarian
© The Secret By: Rhonda Byrne
© The Alchemist By: Paul Cohelo
© The Prophet By: Kahlil Gibran
© Spirit Guides By: Iris Bellehayes
© Initiation By: Elizabeth Haich
© Stillness Speaks By: Eckhart Tolle
© Spiritual Growth By: Duane and Sonya Roman
© Artful Work By: Dick Richards
© Entering the Castle: An Inner Path to God and Your Soul By: Caroline Myss
© Earth's Birth Changes By: St. Germain
© Opening to Channel: How to Connect with Your Guide
    By: Sanaya Roman and Duane Packer
© Ami, The Child From The Stars By: Enrique Barrios
© HowMuch Did You Love? What Did You Learn?By: Alex Jones
© The Secret Doctrine By: H.P. Blavatsky
© Mutant Message Down Under By: Marlo Morgan
© A New Earth: Awakening to Your Life's Purpose By: Eckhart Tolle
© Path of Empowerment: New Pleiadian Wisdom for a World in Chaos
    By: Barbara Marcinial
© The Third Eye By: Tuesday Lobsang Rampa
© When Things Fall Apart: Heart Advice for Difficult Times By: Pema Chodron
© Feel the Fear… and Do It Anyway By: Susan Jeffers
© A Guide for the Advanced Soul: A Book of Insight By: Susan Hayward
© NewTeachings for an Awakened Humanity: The Christ By: Virginia Essene
© Power vs. Force: The Hidden Determinants of Human Behavior By: David R. Hawkins
© Bridge Across Forever By: Richard Bach
© Srimad Bhagavad Gita By: Swami Tapasyananda
© Conversations with God: An Uncommon Dialogue (Books 1, 2 & 3)
    By: Neale Donald Walsch
© You Can Heal Your Life By: Louise Hay
© The Reconnection: Heal Others, Heal Yourself By: Dr. Eric Pearl
© Angel Therapy: Healing Messages for Every Area of Your Life By: Doreen Virtue
© Manifesting Your Heart's Desire By: Fred Fenfler & Todd Varnum
© Remember, Be Here Now By: Ram Dass
© Siddhartha By: Herman Hesse

© Kryon Books I through III

© Love is in the Earth: A Kaleidoscope of Crystals By: Melody

© A Course In Miracles By: Helen Schucman

© The Body is the Barometer of the Soul, So Be Your Own Doctor By: Annette Noontil

© You'll See It When You Believe It By: Dr. Wayne Dyer

© Ask & It Is Given By: Esther and Jerry Hicks

© Living with Joy: Keys to Personal Power and Spiritual Transformation
   By: Sanaya Roman

© Vision By: Ken Carey

© Creating Money: Keys to Abundance By: Sanaya Roman and Duane Packer

© The Last Lecture

© Hands of Light - A Guide to Healing Through the Human Energy Field
   By: Barbara Ann Brennan

© Serpent of Light: Beyond 2012 By: Drunvalo Melchizedek

© What is Lightbody? By: Tashira Tachi-ren and Archangel Ariel

© Many Lives, Many Masters- The TRUE Story By: Dr. Brian Weiss

© The Divine Matrix: Bridging Time, Space, Miracles, and Belief By: Gregg Braden

© The Hidden Messages in Water By: Masaru Emoto and David A. Thayne

© The Third Millennium By: Ken Carey

© The Meditative Mind By: Daniel Goleman

© Science Of Mind By: Ernest Holmes

© The Passionate Mind By: Joel Kramer

© The Seat of the Soul By: Gary Zukav

© The Way of the Wizard: Twenty Spiritual Lessons for Creating the Life You Want
   By: Deepak Chopra

© The Book of Stones: Who They Are & What They Teach
   By: Robert Simmons and Naisha Ahsian

© The Art of Spiritual Healing By: Joel S. Goldsmith

© The Pathwork of Self-Transformation By: Eva Pierrakos

© The Power of Radical Forgiveness By: Colin Tipping

© The Nature Of Personal Reality By: Jane Roberts

© The Power of Now: A Guide to Spiritual Enlightenment By: Eckhart Tolle

© The Science of Mind:

© The Voice of Knowledge: A Practical Guide to Inner Peace
   By: Don Miguel Ruiz and Janet Mills

© The Book of Knowledge: The Keys of Enoch By: J. J. Hurtak Ph.D.

© Anna, Grandmother of Jesus By: Claire Heartsong

© The Power of Intention By: Dr. Wayne W. Dyer

© The Power of Infinite Love & Gratitude: An Evolutionary Journey to Awakening Your
   Spirit By: Dr. Darren

© The Art Of Happiness - A Handbook For Living
   By: His Holiness The Dalai Lama and Howard

© The Teachings of Don Juan: A Yaqui Way of Knowledge By: Carlos Castaneda

© Electric Koolaid Acid Test By: Tom Wolfe

© The Mists of Avalon By: Marion Zimmer Bradley

© The Law of Attraction: The Basics of the Teachings of Abraham
   By: Esther and Jerry Hicks

© Awakening To Point Zero: The Collective Initiation By: Gregg Braden

© The Amazing Power of Deliberate Intent: Living the Art of Allowing
   By: Esther and Jerry Hicks

© The Astonishing Power of Emotions By: Esther and Jerry Hicks

© The Celestine Prophecy By: James Redfield

© FLIGHT: A Quantum Fiction Novel By: Vanna Bonta

© Illuminata: A Return to Prayer By: Marianne Williamson

© One By: Richard Bach

© Anastasia - The Ringing Cedars of Russia Series By: Vladimir Megre

© Sastun By: Rosita Alvarez

© Running From Safety By: Richard Bach

© Jonathan Livingston Seagull By: Richard Bach and Russell Munson

© The Ancient Secret of the Flower of Life: Volume1 By: Drunvalo
Melchizedek

© Your Sacred Self: Making the Decision to Be Free By: Wayne W. Dyer

© Journey of Souls: Case Studies of Life Between Lives By: Michael Newton

© Animal-Speak: The Spiritual & Magical Powers of Creatures Great & Small
   By: Ted Andrews

© Life and Teaching of the Masters of the Far East By: Baird T. Spalding

© Life in the World Unseen   By: Anthony Borgia

© Anatomy of the Spirit By: Caroline Myss

© Guardians Of The Spirit Energy By: Anthony Michael

© Alternate Realities: The search for the full human being By: Lawrence Le
Shan

© The Field: The Quest for the Secret Force of the Universe By: Lynn
McTaggart

© Way of the Peaceful Warrior: A Book That Changes Lives By: Dan Millman

© Way of the Mystic By: Betty Bethards

© Power Of The Mind And Consciousness By: V. Van Dam

© Light Emerging: The Journey of Personal Healing By: Barbara Brennan

© Bringers of the Dawn: Teachings from the Pleiadians
   By: Barbara Marciniak and Tera Thomas

© Return of the Bird Tribes By: Ken Carey

© Healing with the Angels By: Doreen Virtue Ph.D

© 2150 By: Thea Alexander

© Change Your Thoughts Change Your Life: Living the Wisdom of the Tao
   By: Dr. Wayne W. Dwyer

© Personal Power Through Awareness By: Sanaya Roman

© Ageless Body, Timeless Mind: The Quantum Alternative to Growing Old
   By: Deepak Chopra

© 7 Laws to Spiritual Success By: Deepak Chopra
© Whatever happened to Divine Grace: By: Ramon Stevens
© The Omega Transmissions By: Nancy Parker
© Dweller On Two Planet By: Phylos
© The Holographic Universe By: Michael Talbot
© Trust Your Vibes: Secret Tools for Six-Sensory Living By: Sonia Choquette
© The Magician's Way: What It Really Takes to Find Your Treasure
   By: William Whitecloud
© The Lightworker's Way: Awakening Your Spiritual Power to Know and Heal
   By: Doreen Virtue
© God Talks with Arjuna: The Bhagavad Gita By: Paramahansa Yogananda
©Three Majic Words By: U.S. Andersen
© The Life You Were Born To Live: A Guide To Finding Your Life Purpose
   By: Dan Millman
© Excuse Me, Your Life Is Waiting: The Astonishing Power of Feelings
   By: Lynn Grabhorn
© ET 101
©

(Return)

The following hung above our family's door throughout my life!!!

By: DEAN ALFANGE
I DO NOT CHOOSE TO BE A COMMON MAN
IT is my right to be uncommon… if I can.
I seek opportunity… not security. I do not wish to be kept citizen, humbled and
dulled by having the state look after me. I want to take the calculated risk; to
dream and to build, to fail and succeed. I refuse to barter incentive for dole. I
prefer the challenges of life to the guaranteed existence; the thrill of fulfillment
to the stale calm state of utopia. I will not trade freedom for beneficence nor my
dignity for a handout. I will never cower before any master nor bend to any
threat. IT is my heritage to stand erect, proud and unafraid; to think and act for
myself; enjoy the benefits of my creations and to face the world boldly and say,
this I have done. All this is what IT means to be an American.

110%